WOMEN, WELFARE AND LOCAL POLITICS 1880–1920
'We might be trusted'
STEVEN KING

sussex
ACADEMIC
PRESS

BRIGHTON • PORTLAND

The right of Steven King to be identified as Author of this work has been asserted in accordance with the Copyright, Designs and Patents Act 1988.

2 4 6 8 10 9 7 5 3 1

First published 2006 in Great Britain by
SUSSEX ACADEMIC PRESS
PO Box 2950
Brighton BN2 5SP

and in the United States of America by
SUSSEX ACADEMIC PRESS
920 NE 58th Ave   Suite 300
Portland, Oregon 97213–3786

British Library Cataloguing in Publication Data
A CIP catalogue record for this book is available from the British Library.

Library of Congress Cataloging-in-Publication Data
King, Steven, 1966–
Women, welfare and local politics, 1880-1920 : 'we might be
    trusted' / Steven King.
    p. cm.
Includes bibliographical references and index.
ISBN 1-84519-087-4 (h/b : alk. paper)
    1. Women in politics--England--Bolton (Greater
Manchester)—History. 2. Poor laws—England—Bolton
(Greater Manchester)—History. 3. Public welfare—England—
Bolton (Greater Manchester)—History. 4. Pressure
groups—England—Bolton (Greater Manchester)—History.
5. Women—Suffrage—England—Bolton (Greater
Manchester)—History. I. Title.

HQ1236.5.G7K56 2006
362.5'0942—dc22

                                            2005024380

Typeset and designed by G&G Editorial, Brighton & Eastbourne
Printed by The Cromwell Press, Trowbridge, Wiltshire
This book is printed on acid-free paper.

Contents

Maps, Tables and Figures

Maps

Tables

Figures

Acknowledgements

This book has been embarrassingly long in the making. I first discovered Mary Haslam, the woman whose career lies at the heart of this work, in 1994. Her working diary and associated personal and family records caught my imagination, prompting me to think about changing my historical period and engaging with literatures that I had not previously given the consideration they deserved. Thought and action, however, are two different things and it has taken over a decade to bring the project to fruition. My debts of gratitude have grown correspondingly. Catherine Robertson transcribed Mary Haslam's diary, a thankless task given Haslam's awful writing. She also transcribed travel diaries, letters and associated material, and I am very grateful to Catherine for her efforts on the project. My good friend Margaret Hanly has also transcribed material, as well as providing breakfast, dinner and tea during my long trips to the Bolton Record Office. In turn, the archival staff at Bolton were splendid. I owe them a profound debt for their diligence, good humour and hard work; if ever there was an advert for the value of local government spending, this is it.

I am very grateful to the archivist at Bolton Record Office for granting me permission to reproduce the sources (ZHA 17/2, ZHA 17/16, ZHA 17/17) presented in Part II. Much of the reading and writing for the resulting book was done during two visiting professorships. The first, in 1998 at the University of Trier, was organized by my friend, co-author and fierce critic, Professor Dr Dietrich Ebeling. The second, in 2005 at the EHESS in Paris, was organized by Professors Paul-André Rosental and Laura Lee Downs. To all three I am profoundly grateful. Back at Oxford Brookes University, Carol Beadle, Elizabeth Hurren and John Stewart have been consistent supporters of the project through all of its (and my) ups and downs. They read drafts, offered perceptive criticism and provided red wine, good humour and places for me to escape and write. The book would not have been completed without them. Many of those to whom I would have most liked to present a copy of this book have passed away during its making. I will not make the same mistake again. Finally, Willow has been with me through this right from the start, and it is to her that I dedicate this book.

SK, Crowfield, 2005

PART I

Rethinking Women, Welfare and Local Politics

CHAPTER ONE

The New Poor Law, Female Agency and Feminism

In January 1922, the town of Bolton mourned the death of its most active and influential female campaigner, Mary Haslam. While much attention was focused on the way in which she had driven the local suffrage movement and campaigned tirelessly for the citizenship of women, the warmest praise was reserved for her work in the administration of the New Poor Law. The *Bolton Chronicle* noted that

> she found herself chiefly engaged in pioneer work, hewing out paths, clearing away obstacles and leading the way along untrodden routes . . . It was undoubtedly Mrs Haslam's influence which, working through the group of women members of the Board of Guardians [from 1895], raised the efficiency and humanized the spirit of local Poor Law work. And with the experience thus gained she and they went on to wider aims of emancipation, and the training and use of women in public service of all kinds, as well as in the everyday responsibilities of citizenship.[1]

A wealthy middle-class woman in her own right, Mary Haslam had clearly used her status, philanthropic experiences and campaigning skills to drive a highly effective local women's movement. We will encounter her and other female activists again later, in a case study of the Lancashire town of Bolton.

In the meantime, Mary Haslam's glowing obituary functions as an historical prism, shedding light on the three interlocking themes of this volume: the character of the late Victorian and early Edwardian poor law; the role of women in influencing poor law practice and changing the experiences of the poor; and the development of the women's movement from the late nineteenth century. These issues have, of course, generated very considerable debate, and the rest of this chapter is dedicated to exploring and unpicking the historiographical literature.

The chapter first turns to the development of the New Poor Law from its inception in 1834 until the First World War, though with a particular focus on the late Victorian and early Edwardian period. We will see that empirical studies of the later decades of the New Poor Law are rare and that generalizations on the period have become commonplace. At the heart of such generalization is the idea that the New Poor Law sank into stagnation and decay from the 1880s. We will explore this notion, point to the vibrancy and rapid change in poor law practice that can often be seen at local level, and suggest that the time is right for a reconsideration of the character of the late Victorian and early Edwardian poor law. The chapter then turns to trace the development of female involvement with the New Poor Law, looking at the ways in which historians have thought about the motivations, experiences and achievements of women, like Mary Haslam, who stood for election as poor law guardians from the 1880s onwards.[2] Such women are often seen to have faced overt or direct hostility from male guardians and workhouse staff. While many commentators have acknowledged their contribution to improving the lot of the indoor poor, most suggest that female guardians were marginal players in policy terms. We will take issue with such views, suggesting that despite the early work of Hollis and the ubiquity of ad hoc references to women and welfare in much of the secondary literature, the role of women in instigating, managing or facilitating welfare reform is an issue that remains substantially under-researched. Systematic local studies, it will be argued, provide an opportunity to rethink notions of marginality and to take a more positive view of female agency in local and municipal politics.[3] Finally the chapter builds on these perspectives and engages with the burgeoning literature on the development of later nineteenth-century "feminism" and "feminist campaigning". After clarifying the terminology, we will trace the development of feminism from the 1860s and the relationship between feminism and poor law work in the individual and collective feminist journey. Much of the historiographical literature sees welfare and welfare reform as just one (and often a minor) issue taken up by some of the small group of women whose lives and experiences have come to represent the emergence of a national, self-conscious, feminist movement in the later nineteenth century. We will argue, on the contrary, that at the local level feminism and welfare reform may have been inextricably intertwined, a key practical, political and experiential staging post in the journey from philanthropy to suffrage and citizenship.

Perceptions of the Victorian and Edwardian Poor Law

The 1834 Poor Law Amendment Act replaced the English and Welsh Old Poor Law of 1601, with the so-called New Poor Law. Welfare historians disagree on the extent to which this reform had popular support. However, Eastwood's commentary on rural England, that "The battle against poverty and the merciless expense of the poor rates had gone on too long for parishes to offer anything serious by way of self-defence" to reform in 1834, could equally be applied to many industrial and urban districts. Indeed, it probably reflects the attitude of officials in the majority of the 16,000 units of welfare administration in England and Wales by 1834.[4] The subsequent legislation sought to move the focus of poor relief away from small administrative units (parishes and towns) towards much bigger poor law unions containing dozens of places and many thousands of people. It also sought to make the workhouse and indoor relief the centrepiece of English and Welsh welfare, to impose more disciplined, centrally directed, and professional administrative structures, and to place poor law strategy into the hands of an elected board of guardians. Historians disagree on what yardsticks we should use to judge the success or failure of the New Poor Law.[5] They also disagree on what, if anything, about welfare personnel or the experiences of paupers actually changed in the immediate aftermath of 1834.[6] After all, it was not until the 1840s that the New Poor Law was fully in place in the north of England.[7] Moreover, this was a system that had a centralization ethos but little central power to curb regional variations of practice. It was also a system founded on the premise that the rural able-bodied poor must be discouraged, and had few answers to the problems of under- or unemployment in urban and industrial areas.[8] These debates on the transition to the New Poor Law are well documented and do not need to be revisited here.[9] Two important aspects of the current state of our knowledge on the poor law once it was established do, however, require further consideration if we are to understand its character and to ground the experiences and achievements of women such as Mary Haslam: the small number of published empirical studies and the fact that historiographical and empirical analysis of the New Poor Law is very uneven on a chronological basis.

The relatively limited empirical base for generalizations about the New Poor Law is intriguing. Recent scholarship on the detailed records of New Poor Law unions has started to build upon the agendas set in much older regional surveys from commentators such as Digby, broader national surveys such as that of Crowther, and statistical overviews from

Williams.[10] Hollen Lees has developed her work on London. She explores the issue of how much changed after 1834, using the example of Atcham union to show the harsh human impact of poor law reform in places where the first flush of enthusiasm for the New Poor Law carried on into the 1840s and 1850s.[11] Hurren has a later focus, revisiting the planning, execution and impact of the "campaign against outdoor relief" instituted by the Local Government Board (hereafter LGB) in the 1870s. Focusing on Brixworth union in Northamptonshire, she argues that while the exact confluence of circumstances here may have been extreme, the multi-layered policy approaches that underpinned the crusade, not least a trade in pauper cadavers, were widely diffused. In Brixworth, the poor law became the focus of competing ideological frameworks, with aristocrats and ratepayers forcing harsh welfare regimes onto the labouring poor, who noisily asserted their rights, combined, protested and ultimately exercised their votes after the extension of the franchise in the 1890s.[12] Robert Dryburgh has revisited the long and painful birth of the New Poor Law in Lancashire, using the example of Bolton union. Setting poor law practice in the context of the wider economy of makeshifts, he exposes the corruption, political posturing, neglect of the poor and harsh attitudes that often went hand-in-hand with resistance to centralized inspection and control.[13]

These are valuable perspectives. Yet in total (and even if we include older studies of unions in Lancashire, Bedfordshire, the northeast and Norfolk,[14] or analysis of particular client groups such as the aged or sick[15]), the number of detailed *empirical* studies of the scope, character and day-to-day operation of the New Poor Law between 1834 and 1914, remains small. Within this broad framework, we might also point to the uneven chronological focus of empirical analysis. Thus, in 1978 Pat Thane called attention to the relative empirical neglect of the period between 1880 and the Liberal welfare reforms of 1906.[16] Almost three decades later, this lacunae remains. Stapleton's insightful analysis of intergenerational poverty finishes in 1850.[17] Ashforth's detailed analysis of policy in Bradford union finishes in 1871, while Driver's review of workhouse building under the New Poor Law ends in 1884, and Martin's wide-ranging discussion of the nature of local poor law administration is curtailed in 1865.[18] Harris lumps the period 1871–1914 together in his consideration of the crusade against outdoor relief.[19] In general much more detailed local work has been directed towards the first fifty years of the New Poor Law than towards the two decades thereafter. Indeed Finlayson's review of the key turning points in the history of the New Poor Law cites the periods 1830–50 (foundation and implementation), 1874–80 (the crusade against outdoor relief) and 1906–11 (the Liberal welfare reforms), leaving the period between 1880 and 1906 in historiographical limbo.[20] A renewed interest in pensions, the Liberal welfare reforms and the postwar sentiment of the poor law merely emphasizes the neglect of the period 1880–1906.[21]

We should note, however, that the lack of empirical work has not prevented generalization on the later nineteenth-century poor law, though historians conflict as to how the period should be represented. Thus, some see later nineteenth-century developments as a positive staging post to new forms of welfare organization. Wood, for instance, labels the years 1865–95 as "the coming of age of the poor law", while the post-1895 period attracts the label "the doubts of middle age".[22] Rose talks of the 1880s and 1890s as an era of new departures, a period when the true potential of the New Poor Law was tested, after the 1860s and early 1870s had forced the poor law to undergo a "searching re-examination".[23] Evans sees a direct overlap and link between the New Poor Law, the Liberal welfare reforms and the rise of collective security, suggesting that the period 1895–1914 saw "The birth pangs of welfarism".[24] De Shweinitz agrees, labelling the period 1880–1909 "a new ferment" in "England's road to social security".[25] Other commentators are more negative. Finlayson, for instance, argues that "there is nothing especially remarkable about the later decades of the century and, equally, it is possible to exaggerate their significance in social terms". Moreover, he suggests, "The most that the new state that emerged before 1914 can be called is a 'social service state' which laid down certain minimal, non-pauperizing standards for certain sections of the population seen to be at risk".[26] Fraser likewise plays down the achievements of the late Victorian period, suggesting that while there were advances in the treatment of the sick poor and pauper children, "these minimal but universal provisions did not become the foundations of a more splendid edifice, but became ruins alongside which a welfare state was constructed" because of the "unacceptable social price demanded by the [late Victorian] poor law".[27] Moreover, while Crowther sees the later Victorian workhouse as an "embryonic social service", the post-1880 period was also one in which the ambit of the poor law was constrained and its basic relevance questioned.[28]

Recently Hollen Lees has marshaled the whole of the period 1860–1948 under the heading "Residualism reevaluated and rejected". She suggests that during the late nineteenth and early twentieth centuries an 1834 poor law designed mainly for dealing with able-bodied men in rural areas came under pressure. Growing urban poverty,[29] the conclusion of social investigators that much poverty was involuntary, the increasing effectiveness of pressure groups, and the progressive removal of certain types of pauper from the workhouse, compromised the basic foundations of a law that had implicitly blamed poverty on those who were in need of assistance. The New Poor Law in many ways contained the seeds of its own destruction and the result, she argues, was that the post-1870 poor law was neither progressive nor oppressive but simply slipping into stagnation and decline.[30] Vincent concurs, arguing that "by 1914 the most striking consequence of the welfare legislation was not how much but how little had changed . . . the poor were destined to remain guests at the table of an increasingly prosperous society" and not much of interest happened inside the poor law after the faltering of the crusade against outdoor relief.[31]

This pessimistic generalization on stagnation, decay and irrelevance as key features of the character and role of the late nineteenth and early twentieth century poor law informs much of the rest of this book, and is a useful backdrop to the case study of Bolton with which we engage in subsequent chapters. At this stage, however, it is important to understand the evidential basis for such pessimism through a brief review of the development of poor law practice and structures. Thus, most commentators acknowledge that poor drafting of the 1834 legislation, administrative inadequacies, uncertain political support and a flawed ideology left little scope for the rigorous enforcement of the policies enacted in 1834.[32] Initial success in controlling expenditure levels soon gave way to renewed rises. Deviation from the principles of 1834, particularly over contentious policies such as the recognition and treatment of sickness, was marked from an early date.[33] Constant political sniping and endless discussion in political circles, pamphlets and newspapers, compromised the authority of poor law administrators at all levels.[34] Moreover, the central administration proved unable to effectively tackle intra- and inter-regional diversity on matters such as outdoor relief and the size and function of workhouses. The fact that the correspondence files of most unions are full of repeated central exhortations on issues such as economy, workhouse segregation and the circumstances in which out-relief might be given, is stark testimony to the fact that local practice was, and was seen to be, diverging markedly from national guidelines. The vast majority of all of those on poor relief continued to be relieved outside the workhouse, and while there was an upsurge of capital expenditure on buildings, such as workhouses and infirmaries, major regional differences in the commitment to workhouse building were pronounced. In effect, this inability to control local practice meant that many "national" developments in poor law policy were little more than a codification of prevailing local practices and sentiment.

Karel Williams warns that we must judge the New Poor Law against appropriate yardsticks, noting that the authors of the 1834 legislation were not really concerned with the deserving poor or with enforcing national uniformity and so should not be judged by their achievements or lack of them in these areas.[35] Yet, it is hard not to concur with Rose that by 1860 the New Poor Law had reached a critical point.[36] Indeed, there are many good reasons to regard the 1860s as an era which offered the potential for fundamental change. The 1865 Union Chargeability Act, which finally carried into force the inevitable financial logic of the 1834 Act and made unions rather than parishes the basis of revenue-raising, was just one of a series of measures in the 1860s, revising union finance, borrowing, and pauper settlement, that removed impediments to the efficient operation of the New Poor Law.[37] This was also the decade when the Poor Law Board became a permanent Department of State (the LGB), removing self-doubt in the minds of poor law administrators at both local and national level.

The potential for fundamental change was not, however, ultimately realized. In 1869 the Goschen Minute[38] called for a new partnership between formally organized and directed charity and the state in order to enforce key principles of the 1834 Act. This Minute, the formation of the Charity Organization Society, and the advent of the LGB with its agenda of cutting outdoor relief expenditure, are usually seen as the touchstones for the 1870s and early 1880s crusade against outdoor relief.[39] Spending did indeed fall after 1869, though whether this reflected the development of a widespread crusade mentality, or simply improved economic conditions, is a matter of debate.[40] Certainly some of the biggest urban unions took the exhortations to cut outdoor relief very seriously indeed, with both Manchester and Liverpool held up as models in the 1870s. The "Manchester Rules" governing the granting of relief were circulated as an urban exemplar in 1872. In most other places, however, the effect was more short-lived,[41] and considerable differences between even adjacent unions on key issues such as the relative proportions of indoor and outdoor paupers soon re-emerged. By the 1880s regional differences in union expenditure per capita could be as much as 10s., and the fact that the provisions of the Goschen Minute were restated no less than five times between 1869 and 1884, suggests that the New Poor Law continued to drift in ideological, political and policy terms after the first flush of enthusiasm for reform subsided in the 1870s.[42] For Finlayson, the later nineteenth-century poor law "offered a scene of considerable diversity and confusion".[43]

In effect, then, the New Poor Law had missed its chance and it is here that we should locate the foundations of the pessimistic view outlined earlier.[44] In the 1880s, many commentators suggest, social investigations went some way to exploding the illusion of individual responsibility for poverty, chipping away at the ideological base of the New Poor Law and providing the bedrock for a popular position on welfare which was to accept much wider state intervention after 1900.[45] The idea of state pensions and insurance schemes was given a wide airing in the later nineteenth century, part of an international exploration of alternative ways to organize national welfare schemes.[46] Pressure groups such as New Unions, the Fabians and the Social Democratic Federation raised the profile of those afflicted by the essential uncertainty that continued to characterize the life-cycles of many otherwise perfectly respectable labouring people, even at the end of the nineteenth century and against a backdrop of rising living standards.[47] The slumming craze in London and its counterparts in social work and the Settlement Movement may also have raised poverty in the consciousness of elites on the national stage, as might the work of the health visitor movement.[48] Certainly, commissions of enquiry consistently urged the removal of certain types of pauper from the workhouse system altogether or called for their more benevolent treatment within institutions, a moral case that had already been won at local level in many places before this date.[49]

By the 1890s, when the LGB was trying to engineer the liberalization of poor law practice, most notably by physically breaking up workhouses to make specialist units, there is a broad historiographical consensus that the initiative on welfare had been lost.[50] The 1894 Local Government Act "failed to lead to any dramatic changes in poor law policy",[51] though it did bring women like Mary Haslam into the administration of the poor law. Consequently, reform sentiment flourished and cottage home movements, sanitary and infirmary inspectors, workhouse visiting societies, institutions for the disabled and the orphaned and the medical establishment wrested away some of the moral and actual powers of the guardians. This presaged a much wider dilution of their remit after 1900, as legislation on pensions, unemployment and children bypassed existing welfare structures.[52] Of course, considerable regional diversity remained. Kidd reminds us that "there was no entirely consistent or uniform national poor law" but "an organized diversity of practice with considerable leeway for local discretion".[53] Nonetheless, the key point is that a poor law which in basic conception had been an instrument to discipline the rural ablebodied, was ill-equipped to cope with this late nineteenth-century reality.[54] Fraser suggests that, "Though potentially a welfare organ with wide social purpose, it could never naturally develop in this way because its growth was always inhibited by its own history and traditions".[55] Given this backdrop, it is little wonder that the period 1880–1906 can be seen as a closed station on the railway track of welfare development, and that many commentators, as we saw earlier, characterize the late Victorian and early Edwardian period as one of stagnation and decay, where the powers and rationale of the New Poor Law were stripped away.

Yet, while these pessimistic generalizations no doubt have some foundation, three broad observations suggest the need for thinking again. *First*, as we have already seen, our understanding of the character and role of the later decades of the New Poor Law is based upon a very limited number of empirical studies; even Crowther's magisterial study covers only selected unions in London, Nottinghamshire and Kent. An extended empirical study of the poor law in Bolton, presented in CHAPTERS TWO, THREE, FIVE and SIX, suggests that images of stagnation and decay in poor law practice might not stand up to wider empirical challenge. *Secondly*, a cursory glance at the mountain of later nineteenth-century poor law statistics suggests that there were really quite rapid and radical changes in the relative positions of different regions on, amongst others, issues such as workhouse building, levels of outdoor relief and the propensity to place children into cottage homes. To take just one small example that is important for this study, Lancashire moved from near the bottom of national league tables of capital expenditure on the fabric of the poor law before 1860, to the very top of that league table after 1865. This changing position must have resulted in modifications to the built environment of the workhouse, the experience of the indoor poor, and the attitude of the outdoor poor to institutional provision. It must certainly reflect significant changes in the sentiments of Lancashire guardians.[56] In deciding how to characterize the New Poor Law, these changing relative positions are significant and require further exploration. Moreover, we might add that even within regions there were astonishing changes in the relative position of individual unions when it came to workhouse provision, child education, levels of outdoor relief, staffing levels, and dietaries.[57] While it is true that the late Victorian period saw no major legislative changes to the poor law, it would be very wrong indeed to portray the period as one marked simply by stagnation or decline. *Thirdly*, neglect of the poor law in the period after 1880 conveniently, and wrongly, marginalizes the impact of women, who became involved with welfare as workhouse visitors, sanitary reformers, philanthropists and ultimately as poor law guardians once the nature of the local franchise had changed in the latter part of the nineteenth century. By implication, women's growing involvement in the poor law has been seen to coincide with mundanity, failure, stagnation and the slow dismantling of the poor law system by a male state.

The inferential link may not be a deliberate or conscious one. After all, very few welfare historians have written anything at all about women and the British welfare system prior to the Welfare State.[58] Those that have, tend to talk about women simply as beneficiaries of, or workers in, the welfare system, or about the influence of maternalist thinking on male policy-makers.[59] Nor have gender historians sought to compensate for this neglect by undertaking detailed analysis of the day-to-day work of women poor law activists. As we shall see below, there has been a tendency to see poor law activity as part (often a small part) of the development of a feminist movement, and to subtly relegate it to a position behind campaigns over suffrage, contagious diseases, social purity and women's property.[60] Such a rendering is strange given the prominence that women themselves gave to poor law work, something recognized in the obituary with which we started this book. In fact, as we shall see, extended discussion of the activities and achievements of female poor law guardians in Bolton provides no support whatever for a link between women's local government work and poor law stagnation and decay. A brief consideration of historiographical perceptions of the relationship between women and welfare work thus forms the second core theme of this chapter and the wider book.

Women and Welfare: Historiographical Perspectives

Few women were involved in the formulation of poor law policy or the dispensation of welfare under the Old Poor Law.[61] Women were very much subject to welfare policy rather than shaping it, arguably a position they have retained in many subsequent welfare developments in Britain and Europe.[62] That position did not improve during the first decades of the New Poor Law, though, as CHAPTER TWO suggests, women's *philanthropic* work on welfare issues was flowering at this time. By the 1860s, however, four developments were to stimulate a more vigorous and direct engagement of middle-class women with the poor law in particular and public service in general.[63]

First, the degree of public knowledge about workhouse conditions increased markedly. While negative commentary on workhouses by newspapers and the central authorities was sometimes politically or administratively motivated, many local surveys also called attention to the poor conditions of indoor paupers.[64] The impact of workhouse scandals and critical local reports was to place the state of the poor, and particularly women and children, firmly on the philanthropic, civic and local political agenda for middle-class women.[65] *Secondly*, by the mid-Victorian period the concerns of such women were increasingly channelled into action by formal organization – Louisa Twining formed the Workhouse Visiting Society (WVS) in 1858 as a means of bringing women's influence to bear on the moral, physical and spiritual lives of the indoor poor, with a particular focus on children, the sick and "the ignorant and depraved".[66] It arguably represents the foundation stone for a variety of other poor law reform and "women in the poor law" campaigning organisations, including the Workhouse Nursing Association, Women's Local Government Society and Women Guardians Society.[67] The fact that the WVS was formed should not, of course, surprise us. As CHAPTERS TWO and THREE show, by the 1850s middle-class women were involved in a variety of philanthropic, moral and political campaigns, so that the transfer of their attention to workhouse conditions might be regarded as natural.[68] This said, the really important thing about the WVS is that it provided a bridge between philanthropic work and engagement with the public and political sphere of organized welfare policy for a wide range of ordinary middle-class women who were not already active campaigners. Moreover, in a women's movement subtly fractured by political leanings and attitudes towards charity organization, sexuality, and the domestic sphere,[69] workhouse visiting provided an invaluable local focus for unified female effort. It matters less that workhouse visiting committees were often in place under sufferance, that they had to play a delicate game and that such committees may have been welcomed by male guardians as a spoiling tactic to try and avoid the election of women guardians,[70] than that they were conceived and brought into existence in the first place.[71] By the time the WVS folded in 1865, "it left behind a habit of workhouse visiting which spread into the provinces", though a habit that was only formally embraced by the LGB in 1893.[72] More importantly, workhouse visiting had created "an informal interest group among them [middle-class women] which exercised significant political and social pressure on the direction and administration of official policies towards the poor".[73] Such themes will be explored in more depth in CHAPTER THREE.

Meanwhile, the extension and formalization of philanthropy was a *third* significant driving force prompting female middle-class engagement with poverty and local welfare structures. The nature of, and motivations for, philanthropic endeavour are considered at length in CHAPTER THREE. It will suggest that there was a significant expansion of nineteenth-century philanthropic activity, and that a significant core of that expansion involved women as organizers, fundraisers, case workers or administrators. While for some philanthropy was simply "a socially acceptable way for married women and their daughters to engage in purposeful work",[74] some commentators have suggested that "Visiting the poor . . . gave women a taste of power outside their own homes".[75] Prominent female philanthropists began to look towards formal participation in local government, framing their aspiration in terms of rights, or more often obligations, as citizens and, at least by the latter part of the nineteenth century, the essentially female characteristics and morals that they could bring to the role of a "citizen" as an unselfish act for the wider good.[76] For Nym Marshall, "emphasis upon duties over rights provided an appropriately self-sacrificing language within which women could lay claims to citizenship" and a wider role in formal welfare provision.[77] On a related note, a *fourth* influence encouraging wider middle-class female involvement with the poor law was the emergence of an organized feminist movement, a theme that we take up below.

As these four stimuli began to coalesce in the 1850s and 1860s, so changes to the nature of local democracy began to extend female opportunities.[78] Single female householders regained the municipal vote in 1869, and by the 1880s they might form up to 25 per cent of the municipal electorate in some places. By 1900, the one million plus female voters at local level represented, according to Harris "a female Trojan Horse within a still overwhelmingly masculine national constitution".[79] Equally significant, however, were attempts to have women enter the formal world of local administration, politics and policymaking through election to office. This was no easy task, since prior to the 1890s candidates who lived outside London had to hold property in their own right and with a rateable value of at least £15 per annum. The first female guardian elected under such rules was Martha Merrington in 1875. Thereafter progress was either slow or rapid depending upon the yardsticks by which one judges achievement. There were fifty "lonely and isolated"[80] female guardians in 1885 and 136 by 1892, with a particular concentration around London and other urban centres. They formed a tiny percentage of the total number of guardians, but their presence probably represented a supreme feat of organization, networking and electioneering by the increasing number of formal women's organizations working to increase the presence and functionality of women in local government.

However, it was the 1893 decision to reduce the property qualification for candidature to £5 and the subsequent 1894 decision to abolish it altogether, that allowed substantial numbers of middle-class women to stand for election in their own right. Whilst the number of women elected never approached that of men, their numbers did increase rapidly in the 1890s. By 1895 there were 802 female guardians in England, with 86 in London and further 70 in Lancashire, and this figure had risen to 1,655 by 1910.[81] Key organizations, such as the Women's Local Government Society and the Women Guardians Society, offered support to localities in finding candidates, getting them elected and keeping female guardians in place.[82] This notwithstanding, historians are under no illusions as to the problems that women encountered in getting elected, establishing a presence on the board of guardians and making a difference to the lives of the poor. These themes are taken up in subsequent chapters, but a brief review is also needed here.

Thus, a major issue for women seeking a formal role in local government was the dual problem of how to break out of the Victorian cultural straitjacket of a woman's natural place, the private and domestic sphere, and at the same time claim a space in the male public sphere. While some historians have questioned the value of the notion and language of separate spheres for an understanding of the position of nineteenth-century women,[83] there is *no doubt* that many nineteenth-century female activists both used this language and felt the weight of expectation and obstruction that ingrained perceptions of a woman's place and code of behaviour imposed. The rationale of many such women was to extend the boundaries of the domestic, familial and parental, claiming for instance that involvement with women, children and the sick under the poor law was a necessary and natural extension of their domestic roles, rather than trying to subvert the notion of separate spheres.[84] Thus, commentators such as Digby or Koven have characterized women involved, or seeking involvement, in poor law administration as caught in the borderland between public and private roles, using the language of the domestic and maternal to extend their influence over real lives.[85] They faced explicit and large-scale hostility when their language and actions took them too blatantly out of this borderland and we find women characterizing themselves as a moral vanguard,[86] drawing upon historical and current notions of citizenship,[87] appropriating images of slavery and pointing to natural law in an effort to extend the grey area between public and private. Even where such boundaries were not transgressed, however, implicit and small-scale hostility appears to have been the norm and female guardians apparently had to tread a precarious line between hostile colleagues, an ungrateful pauper host and the competing demands of class, politics, domestic life and local government office.

Hostility really started at election times. Rubinstein feels, for instance, that women "sometimes faced strong opposition on grounds of their sex" and "were often unwilling to face the expense involved".[88] Hollis is more optimistic, noting that women campaigned as vigorously and in the same way as men, and she suggests that "most towns had a wealth of leisured women formidably well-qualified for public office, born into powerful, political families, trained in voluntary work, feminist, cultivated, self-possessed, and competent" who could have stood for elected office.

Nonetheless, finding candidates willing to undertake the time-consuming, occasionally conflictual and always public process of getting elected was often hard.[89] Once elected much of the historiography suggests that female guardians faced a tough time. Acknowledging that some unions were very proud of their female guardians and that their hard work might win over both the electorate and male colleagues, Hollis nonetheless suggests that,

> It took considerable courage to endure the snubs, smuttiness and cold shoulder treatment women met on many boards . . . For the most part, women won grudging acceptance – it was seldom more than that – which they achieved by tact, persistence, silence and hard work.[90]

Autobiographical accounts, letters, and articles suggest that female guardians routinely faced the suspicion of those who wanted to keep local poor rates down, and there were persistent complaints about the costs of the amendments to workhouse regimes and other "domestic" matters over which women appear to have gained some provenance. Ingrained prejudice and hostility meant that men were unwilling and unable to value the contribution of female guardians seriously and women had to contend with the "almost reflex hostility of many guardians and most local poor law officials to women joining their boards".[91] Hollis provides a litany of newspaper reporting and articles in periodicals and journals from female guardians about their treatment, suggesting that "women counseled each other to take great care, to sit quiet, and not contribute until they were well established" and that "women were never allowed to forget that they were interlopers; and that they had to maintain standards and justify their position in ways that no man would ask of men".[92]

In the face of such hostility, women were apparently directed to "female" tasks, such as modifying the scope and experience of the "misconceived and misbegotten" workhouse,[93] and excluded from the "real" business of unions, notably decisions on changing the physical fabric of the poor law, staffing, finances or outdoor relief policy.[94] The most active female guardians potentially placed severe pressure on the boundary between male and female areas of responsibility. However, historians differ on the extent of their broad achievements. Crowther, for instance, contends that "women guardians initiated no striking new policies", while Lewis suggests "it is not my intention to claim that their work had a significant effect in terms of improving the welfare outcomes for the poor women and children who were their chief concern".[95] Hollis believes that many of the early female guardians were staunch supporters of the ideology of 1834 and temperance supporters to boot, alienating paupers, institutional staff and male guardians alike, and placing strict limits on what could be achieved. More widely, Rubinstein concludes that "The novelty of being an elected woman, her minority status, and the inhibitions of education and socialization mean that it was often difficult to institute policies of aggressive reform", though there was progress on humanizing the workhouse.[96]

Levine offers a more positive interpretation, arguing that women were at the forefront of pioneering new ideas and practices (some of which were subsequently adopted by the LGB), as well as forcing through considerable improvement in day-to-day institutional lives. This, she suggests, was "an impressive showing in so short a period of time, more particularly since legislation could do little to counter the prejudice they continued to endure". Summers concurs and questions the extent to which female guardians were conservative and backward looking supporters of the 1834 reforms.[97] Jones goes further, suggesting that there were enough female guardians to "influence local provision and policies. They could network effectively, and offer a distinctive contribution to the public, although still local, world".[98] Harris is equally positive, noting that "A supra-class public service approach to local politics was further strengthened by the admission of women".[99] Nonetheless, while the best female guardians were overhauling their workhouses, Hollis suggests that ultimately "The scale of their [women guardians] failure is to be seen . . . when elderly people shun hospitals that were former workhouse infirmaries".[100] It is in this sense, then, that poor law stagnation and decay and an extended role for women in poor law administration can be seen to coincide. The late Victorian and early Edwardian poor law drifted, and women activists were too few in number, hampered by the need to tread carefully in the public sphere, and too ineffective as guardians to make any significant inroads into the direction of poor law policy and thus prevent the drift.

Despite the force of these conclusions, we should perhaps be wary. The working lives of most ordinary women guardians have remained as obscure as the generalizations on the nature of their work have been frequent. Much of our perception of hostility towards, marginalization, and relative failure, of female guardians is based upon the experiences of just a handful of prominent activists on the national stage who have become important symbols for historians. The Countess of Warwick, Rosalind, Countess of Carlisle,[101] Mary Carpenter, Louisa Twining ("the originator of workhouse reform"[102]), Emmeline Pankhurst,[103] Eva Muller, Charlotte Despard, Hannah Mitchell, Sophia Lonsdale, Mrs Lyttleton, Hannah Lees, Brodie Hall, Selina Cooper, Florence Davenport Hill, Margaret Collett, Harriet M'Ilquham, and Augusta Spottiswoode are part of the list.[104] In turn, their *generalized* experiences with the New Poor Law found expression in articles for journals such as *The Westminster Review*, in books and pamphlets, speeches, newspapers, correspondence, and in their autobiographical writings, dominating our understanding of the relationship between women and welfare activism. Yet, some of this evidence is at best slim, with Emmeline Pankhurst's ghost written book of 1914, for instance, devoting fewer than ten pages to her work as a guardian.[105] The negative poor law experiences of these women is to some extent reinforced by the ordinary female guardians who contributed to poor law conferences and journals, sources that lie of the heart of Hollis's survey of the subject area. All too often we hear of their problems and all too infrequently do we get to learn about their day-to-day successes. Overall, we know surprisingly little about the lives, strategies, experiences, negotiation tactics and local achievements of almost all of the 1,000 or so women who were serving as poor law guardians in the last years of the nineteenth century.[106] Privileging the perspectives of the most prominent women also disproportionately highlights the experiences of those who spent least time engaged with the poor law. While the average woman guardian in Lancashire served for just under nine years between 1894 and 1914, the equivalent figure amongst the most prominent feminists on the national stage would be less than five years.[107] It is thus not simply that our knowledge of ordinary women guardians is limited, but that the literature has concentrated on the women who moved on rather than remained engaged with poor law activism. Yet, as Hollis notes, to be a woman involved in poor law administration "required *staying power*, hard work, firmness, training, and selfless personal service".[108]

Moreover, we should be wary of talking in any simple way about female failure in the board room. Levine reminds us that we must judge what happened against what was possible rather than what was desirable. We must, in other words, use appropriate yardsticks. Hence, while women's supposed lack of experience in public speaking, electoral processes, committee meetings and fighting entrenched male power has certainly been overdone,[109] it inevitably took time to establish oneself in a new public role. Against this backdrop it is a mistake to simply contrast the language, experiences, strategies and achievements of female guardians with those of men. More pertinent comparisons might be made between the language, experiences, strategies and achievements of women and other new groups who entered the poor law forum in the 1890s, such as smaller tradesmen or working-class men, or between higher middle-class women and their higher middle-class male peers.[110] Nor should we forget that both women and men often found themselves limited by central policy direction and the embedded nature of some local practices that required more than a new broom to sweep away. They also shared the competing demands of class, politics, domestic life and local government office, albeit they often dealt with the tensions generated in very different ways. The need for appropriate *local* yardsticks is something that seems to have bypassed much of the secondary literature on female guardians.

Yet, reconstructing the nature of women's experience in, and contribution to, poor law administration; gaining an understanding of the significance of that work to their wider roles as campaigners and philanthropists; and embedding their achievements in an understanding of what was possible, is a difficult task. It involves synthesizing detailed local information from a wide range of sources. However, as we have already seen, just as welfare historians have largely neglected local records for the 1880s and beyond, so gender historians have also tended to eschew such detailed, union-based, local work. This does not reflect a lack of sources. Indeed, in **Part II** of this volume, "Born to Intellectual Freedom? The Record of Mary Haslam, Bolton Activist", we reproduce a variety of documents that can help us to reconstruct the personal and professional life of Mary Haslam, the Bolton activist with whose obituary we started this chapter.[111] Rather, a failure to engage with detailed empirical work reflects the way in which some historians have approached the writing of feminist history, with an overemphasis on national figures and movements. This lack of engagement is unfortunate because not only does it reinforce perceptions of poor law stagnation and decay and downplay the individual and collective achievements of local female guardians, but it also leads to misapprehensions of the place of poor law work in the individual and collective feminist journey of provincial women. It is to the broad theme of feminism, then, that we now turn.

Feminism and the Poor Law

By the 1850s and 1860s we can begin to talk confidently at the national level about the emergence of a group of women with a considerable history of campaigning work, the sort of woman, indeed, with whose obituary we opened this chapter. It would be wrong to assume, however, that the transition from campaigning reformer to self-conscious "feminist" was either easy or automatic. The issue of timing is intricately tied up with complex questions of how contemporaries defined terms such as "woman", "feminist" and "suffragist", and how we as historians have and should define them.[112] There is not the space here to review these questions in depth, and nor, given the current state of our knowledge on motivations and experiences of individual women – increasingly good for the national figures in the feminist movement but persistently poor for their local and regional sisters[113] – would we be likely to reach any satisfactory conclusion. The issue of what made a nineteenth-century feminist remains contested and hence the foundations of the mid-Victorian feminist movement have been traced variously to: the political rhetoric of chartist women,[114] the emergence of the Langham Place group in 1850s, the coalition of radical-liberal men and members of the female social reform movement around the 1867 Reform Act,[115] the failure of numerous back-bench bills on suffrage, or success against the Contagious Diseases Act. If, however, we take feminism to mean a conscious appreciation of the structural nature of women's oppression and the need to confront such oppression with collective woman-centred solutions at the national level (the definition applied throughout this book), then we see the tentative emergence of a national feminist movement in the 1850s.[116]

Subsequently Victorian feminists became involved as individuals and organized groups in an increasing number of discrete and overlapping campaigns.[117] The list of post-1850 successes is considerable. Women gained position and strategic possibilities in education, welfare organization and delivery, and factory inspection, as well as securing legal advances in their own status or the removal of legal disabilities. Kanner and others have traced a short and unproblematic jump from this sort of activity to suffrage campaigning, and indeed there is important evidence that prominent mid-Victorian feminists soon came to voice the need for the vote as a means of both achieving more rapid change and undermining the essential tools of male oppression that generated the need to campaign in the first place.[118] Whether the leap was as easy and natural for all prominent women, and more importantly whether the same was true for women at a local and regional level, is a theme to which we return in CHAPTER SEVEN.[119]

Unsurprisingly, it is possible to see weakness in the diversity of campaigns, and to query whether there was a unified and self-conscious feminist movement before the suffrage campaigns of the twentieth century. Engagement with such perspectives has been surprisingly understated – the undoubted tendency for feminists to get involved in lots of single issue campaigns has been explained away as either a failure of historians to see the overlapping personnel and ideologies involved in diverse campaigns, or a reflection of the multi-layered nature of male authority and hence female oppression. A better response, and one particularly pertinent to this book, might be that the very need to offer explanation of diversity reflects the continued focus in the historiographical literature on individual national figures and small groups, when a series of systematic local and regional studies would demonstrate all too well the existence, vibrancy and width of integrated feminist thought and action at the grass-roots level.[120] Again, we return to this issue in CHAPTER SEVEN. However we view diversity, it is clear that the feminist movement of the later nine-teenth century was a rapidly evolving and remarkably complex entity. Theoretically hemmed in by notions of separate spheres,[121] a restricted view of citizenship, multiple and overlapping fields of the public and the private,[122] repressive notions of female respectability and sexuality,[123] and turmoil in conceptions of the national and local state,[124] feminists had to develop a coherent ideology, a linguistic register, an identity, and a stable organizational structure.

The literature on feminist responses to such challenges after the 1850s is now considerable. In ideological terms, it is clear that different groups of feminists (and even the same feminists over time) borrowed ideological focus from religion, liberalism, constitutionalism, moralism, philosophy and the theory and practice of empire, and were well-capable of the inter-pretation, reinterpretation and reinvention of such ideological structures. Banks identifies three ideological "faces" of feminism – evangelical, enlightenment, and socialist[125] – and to these we might add the ideology of radical feminism,[126] citizenship and localism. The linguistic register of the feminist movement was equally flexible, drawing variously on the rhetoric of religion, science and law at the same time as it drew on the language of constitutionalism and citizenship. Campaigning successes also allowed subtle development of feminist rhetoric, celebrating female moral superiority and demonstrating their positive capacities, rather than simply focusing on their disabilities and oppression. Certainly by the 1890s we can detect a linguistic register that is rooted in shared experi-ences and a shared analysis of the causes and consequences (if not its remedy) of female oppression. In organizational terms too, feminism was an evolving phenomenon. The majority of its organizations were short-lived but alongside such fluidity we find long-term campaigns over sex and status within marriage, or the rights of women to exert control over their own property and the local public purse. As Mary Haslam's obit-uary suggested, at local level these sorts of organizations could result in a continuous and multi-level engagement of women with public life.

Making sense of the evolving language, experiences and structures of feminism is clearly difficult. Not surprisingly, some commentators have sought watersheds for the development of feminism and feminist activity. The 1883 Corrupt and Illegal Practices Act brought women's lack of enfranchisement into sharp relief. As we will see in CHAPTER FOUR, under the terms of this act middle-class women increasingly found themselves campaigning for male candidates but they were themselves unable to cast a vote when an ever wider (and increasingly socially inferior) network of men, could.[127] For some women this act was certainly a wake-up call, and more widely Hall has argued persuasively that the whole decade of the 1880s was a watershed for feminist campaigning, analysis and discourse.[128] John and Eustance likewise see feminism caught up with a wider "disintegration of the mid-Victorian state and civil society" after 1880, while the National Society for Women's Suffrage clearly identified the 1880s as a period of transition between concerted effort and diffused effort in suffrage terms.[129] Not all commentators agree. In line with Rubinstein's appeal, the 1890s have been restyled as a period that laid some of the linguistic, ideological and strategic foundations of the early twentieth-century suffrage movement.[130] That said the 1890s were not just about suffrage. At one end of the decade substantial numbers of female guardians were elected for the first time, while women consolidated their position as social workers, health workers and municipal citizens. At the other end of the decade there was a "certain loss of momentum and confidence in local government growth", which, alongside tentative steps to major social reform, served to free up the energies of many local feminist groups.[131] Moreover, from the 1890s, it became readily apparent that feminists in England were part of a functional international movement.[132] Suffrage, however, was the issue that would not die, hardest fought because it was the area that men least wanted to concede, and some have suggested that the watershed for feminism lies in the franchise campaigns of the early twentieth century, rather than the 1880s and 1890s. The details of suffrage campaigning is considered in CHAPTER SEVEN, but for now what matters is the sheer size and growth of the suffrage movement as a whole, which by 1914 easily numbered several hundred thousand. If we were to add in the discrete membership of other new or ongoing feminist campaigns from 1900, then it must have been clear to contemporaries that there had been a step change in the critical mass and reach of the feminist movement. Equally, increased levels of activity were allied with a diversification of tactics and a more substantial national and local media presence, so that the range of public spheres within which feminists were seen to be involved must have expanded considerably in the public imagination.

Of course, none of this should make us think that the feminist movement was in any sense unified. While it is increasingly clear that on the national stage feminists became part of an identifiable group linked by friendship, shared values, location and upbringing, the movement as a whole was riven with explicit and implicit tensions. These issues are explored in CHAPTER SEVEN, where we attempt to shift the focus from the national to the local feminist movement. Meanwhile, and despite the excellent work of Levine, Caine and others, it is clear that the interconnections between different feminist campaigns also require further inves-tigation. In particular, the relationship between feminism, the individual feminist journey and women's work in local government, one of the central foci of this book, is somewhat ambiguous. From exhortations in the *English Woman's Journal* in the late-1850s for women to develop local workhouse visiting committees, through the formation in 1869 of Josephine Butler's Ladies National Association for the Repeal of the Contagious Diseases Act, and to articles in the *Westminster Review* urging women to stand as councillors in the early 1900s, it is clear that a national feminist leadership was active in trying to stimulate engagement with local government. Whether such activity was framed in terms of middle-class women applying their domestic skills to the task of municipal house-keeping, or whether it was informed by a more fundamental feminist critique of the nature of male power and female oppression, the point is that feminist engagement with local government provided a focus for practical work at the local level in the later Victorian period. Indeed, one commentator argued in 1896 that "the more women can be interested in the local government of their parishes and towns, the fitter they will be for taking part in the government of their country when the time comes for them to do so".[133] This explicit link between local government, national governance and suffrage is an important one, and we will return to it in CHAPTER SEVEN.

When we turn to the individual feminist journey, however, the connec-tions between participation in local government, the development of feminist ideals, and wider feminist campaigning, are apparently looser. It is now well established that women who were elected to the position of guardian invariably had prior and contiguous involvement in local and national philanthropic work, either as donors or social reformers. Moreover, in their work as guardians they had to work in an official capacity with a wide range of local philanthropic ventures in most towns.[134] For some women, poor law and philanthropic work, including visiting, social work and campaigns on housing and morals, was enough to fulfill their personal or spiritual needs, allowing them to extend the domestic into the public sphere using the language of social motherhood, moral and religious duty, and citizenship. Whether such women could claim to be feminists is unclear, though some would argue that even those who confined themselves to philanthropic and social campaigning can be seen as such.[135] Some women for whom such work was not an end in itself probably also confined their activity to philanthropic and local govern-ment ventures because of practical difficulties. Full engagement in these areas demanded considerable commitments of time and monetary resources, and Lewis's analysis of five prominent activists suggests that they faced a constant tension between their public and philanthropic work and their domestic and familial roles.[136] Such tensions might emerge even where, as was often the case, women activists could boast supportive familial, friendship, political and domestic networks or had supportive husbands.[137] However we explain the situation, there is clear ambiguity on the relationship between the poor law work and the individual feminist journey of such activists.

For other women, engagement with local government represented just one, and sometimes a very brief, stage in their development as feminists.[138] They participated successively and contiguously in a range of overlapping campaigns which could boast a shared feminist membership.[139] These campaigns might be on moral or social issues (slavery or factory reform, for instance) or they might be woman-centered, for instance in their concern with women and divorce, property or contagious diseases.[140] Indeed much of the effort of historians in the recent past has been devoted to constructing a rich tapestry of the lives of the prominent, largely London-based, middling and aristocratic women who experienced this sort of feminist journey in the later nineteenth century. Thus, Harrison has provided detailed biographies of Millicent Fawcett, Emmeline Pankhurst, Teresa Billington Greig, Nancy Astor and Eleanor Rathbone, seeking to "rescue neglected talent from the enormous condescension of contemporaries".[141] Others have shared this biographical approach. Rogers has sought to rejuvenate the career of Jospehine Butler and to rethink the social purity movement as a feminist rejection of the male constitutional framework and established Liberal political traditions.[142] Parker has reconstructed the lives of, amongst others, Francis Power Cobbe; whilst Rendall has investigated the "critically supportive" relationship between Barbara Leigh Smith Bodichon and Bessie Rayner Parkes.[143] Caine and Levine have also conducted large-scale detailed studies of the major feminist activists on the national stage.[144] These studies confirm that engagement with local government could be undertaken by very experienced women and informed by a subtle feminist critique of women's role in local, regional and national society and politics. Yet, engagement was often brief and for many of these women local government work was simply the briefest of stepping stones. At best, as with Emmeline Pankhurst, it provided grounding in electioneering, leadership, committee work, network building and fund raising, rather than underpinning a longer and wider feminist journey.[145] At worst, it was an irritating experience, to be dispensed with as soon as possible.

Moreover, it is also clear that some feminists and female activists had no experience at all with local government work. Biographical studies of the thirty or so women whose experiences do most to inform our understanding of female campaigning reveal that the majority had no connection with the New Poor Law. The renewed suffrage campaign of the early twentieth century emphasized this disjuncture.[146] While common perceptions of militant suffragism as a fractured, confrontational, fragile and relatively small wing of suffrage activity have recently been subject to reinterpretation,[147] one of its unintended consequences was to give renewed energy to local branches of the non-militant suffrage organization. By 1910, for instance, the National Union of Women's Suffrage Societies had more than 400 affiliate branches and an active membership of over 50,000. Many of the middle-class women who rallied to the cause had no direct experience of local government work (thought they were often supporters of the organizations such as the Women's Local Government Association). In so far as they were interested in issues other than suffrage, they wished to conduct their public activity through broadly based movements offering a more general critique of gender, economic, social and political relations, such as Women Citizen's Associations.[148] It is important to realize that feminism, women's campaigning activity and suffrage were always separate issues, and that while suffrage has come to dominate historians perceptions of the feminist agenda for the early twentieth century it has done so at the cost of an appreciation of the continuing vibrancy of local feminist philanthropic, campaigning and local government networks. Nonetheless, the fact that many feminist campaigners, particularly in the early twentieth century, did not appear to engage with any aspect of local government work is clear.

To recap, then, while nineteenth-century commentators urged women to engage with local government because it was their duty, it provided training for national governance and it was part of the feminist journey, when we turn our attention to the majority of individual middle-class feminists on the *national stage*, local government work generally and poor law work in particular, is either temporal or absent altogether. This is puzzling. As we saw at the start of this chapter, the poor law work of Mary Haslam was at the very centre of her public activity. Moreover, those who pioneered the working-class women's movement often seem to have had a more vigorous engagement, becoming involved in local government and poor law work at the earliest opportunity.[149] This apparent disjuncture may well arise out of the tendency in the secondary literature to focus on the lives of the most prominent feminists, or to concentrate on discrete sources such as articles in feminist journals. Against this backdrop the problems and failures of female poor law guardians are privileged above success and achievement, and individual feminist journeys with particular staging posts become the norm. Yet, as we have seen, almost nothing is known about the 1,000 or more female guardians who had been elected by the end of the 1890s, and even less about the relationship between their personal and feminist journey and their work with the poor. At various points in this book we will implicitly and (in CHAPTER SEVEN) explicitly, explore this issue and the wider feminist context of local activism.

Conclusion

The rest of this volume, then, takes up these complementary themes of local poor law practice after 1880, the role and achievements of female welfare activists and the feminist credentials of those who became involved with the poor law. Focusing on late Victorian and early Edwardian Bolton,[150] its underlying impetus is the idea that observations of stagnation and decline in the poor law, ineffectiveness on the part of female guardians and a limited role for welfare activities in the wider feminist movement are misleading. Such characterizations, the book argues, reflect the lack of detailed and contextualised local analysis to underpin the wider historiographical debates. The case study of Bolton will reveal that female engagement with the poor law and the wider philanthropic sphere could be at the centre of the development of local feminist movements. While the suffrage campaign brought many new converts to the feminist cause, at local level it was women – middle and working-class by the 1890s – firmly grounded in engagement with the New Poor Law who drove the feminist and suffrage movements, holding both together through the lean times of the 1890s and early 1900s. These women were self-confident, well networked and shrewd political operators in the sphere of the board of guardians. Their tactics headed off male hostility and their firm responses where such hostility did manifest itself resulted in the female guardians of Bolton making a substantial contribution to a radical turnaround in local poor law policy and practice. They were not silent, marginalized and underachieving, but noisy, central and core members of a local reform movement. The obituary with which we opened this chapter stands as explicit testimony to these ideas and as a reminder of the need for more local studies of this sort.

This book is split into two parts. **Part I** explores the nature of poverty, philanthropy, the poor law, female engagement with the public sphere, feminism and suffrage in Bolton, attempting to rethink issues of women, welfare and local politics. The chapters here draw together extensive source material on nineteenth-century Bolton, so often ignored for the later nineteenth century, including the voluminous records of the board of guardians, union correspondence, the records of philanthropic ventures, newspaper reporting, surveys, obituaries, biographies, autobiographies, letters and diaries. CHAPTER TWO addresses the issues of poverty and poor relief. It locates Bolton in its national and regional context and shows that poverty in the late Victorian and early Edwardian period was severe. A detailed analysis of union expenditure records suggests that the response to such poverty was vigorous and that, in Bolton at least, there is little cause to characterize the poor law as subject to stagnation and decay. CHAPTER THREE investigates the scale and nature of philanthropy and public service in Lancashire and then Bolton, suggesting that a small core of male and female philanthropists drove a tide of late nineteenth-century philanthropy that stood alongside the activities of the poor law. Such giving both benefited the poor and gave women donors in particular a way into public and political activism, campaigning on social and moral issues and debates over local citizenship. CHAPTER FOUR demonstrates how women activists in Bolton built upon their engagement with the philanthropic, political and campaigning spheres to fight elections to the board of guardians in the 1890s and beyond. It suggests that such women were skilled political operators and developed a smooth electoral machine that could not be mirrored by men. CHAPTER FIVE traces the way in which elected female guardians negotiated influence and power on the Bolton board. It suggests that the administrative and policy decisions taken at board level were the outcome of a complex, multi-layered, set of power relations, only one level of which was the struggle between men and women. The chapter will trace how female guardians used such fractures to gain wide influence in the union, becoming involved in all of the areas – finance, out-relief, building policy – that the historiography sees them marginalized from on the national stage. CHAPTER SIX traces the impact of the work of female activists on poor people in Bolton, arguing that they had a fundamental impact on the lives of the indoor and outdoor poor. Finally, CHAPTER SEVEN considers how, with imperfect or ambiguous sources, we can reconstruct and characterize the local dynamics of feminism. Suggesting a framework for local analysis, it traces the emergence and development of the Bolton feminist movement and locates the work of women with the poor law as a central platform in the individual and collective feminist journey.

Throughout the book, the life of one particular feminist and poor law guardian will be used as an historical prism on the nature of public life, feminism, suffrage, philanthropy, women's citizenship and poor law reform. Mary Haslam, with whose obituary we opened this chapter, has bequeathed to us a rich diversity of records that can be synthesised and contextualised. Not least of these sources is a working diary of her time as a member of the workhouse visiting committee and then as a poor law guardian, providing a unique insight into the day-to-day work, ideology, strategy and thoughts of a tenacious female guardian. **Part II**, "Born to Intellectual Freedom? The Records of Mary Haslam, Bolton Activist", reproduces annotated versions of this and other sources, including her travel diaries, autobiographical notes and a suffrage pamphlet. These sources give her a voice of her own on issues where male rhetoric has dominated for so long, and can be used to trace an individual feminist and political journey in ways that are impossible for other local activists. Of course, there is a danger in this that I will be focusing, as with so much of the rest of the literature, on "unusual women and unusual activities" and on women who "were exceptional, either by virtue of personal ability, ambition or circumstance".[151] Even if this were true, the career and successes of Mary Haslam are a useful counterbalance to much of the negative literature on female guardians. The point about this book, however, is that the detailed analysis of local sources needed to establish representativeness or otherwise has not been done.[152] We return to the question of representativeness again in CHAPTER FIVE, but in the mean-time, a cursory survey for the purposes of this book has suggested at least twelve other Lancashire feminists for whom similar studies could be conducted.[153] Undertaking such studies would do more than simply adding to a list of individual feminist activists. It would allow us to give substance to Caine's view that prominent Victorian activists offered a "model of female excellence which combined accepted ideas about women's morality, chastity, and nurturance with an assertion of their intelligence, their independence, and their personal strength", through which they laid very effective claims to the rights and duties of local citi-zenship.[154] In the meantime, Mary Haslam's personal, political and feminist journey can offer a window onto the lives of many other local women activists in the late Victorian and early Edwardian period.

CHAPTER TWO

Poverty and Poor Relief in Lancashire and Bolton

The Context of Poverty

As the previous chapter suggested, the nineteenth century saw the experience and concept of poverty brought to the very forefront of public consciousness. Social surveys, investigative journalism, regional and national statistical societies, novels, published diaries and a plethora of philanthropic initiatives that put middle-class people into the homes and districts of the working-class, gave poverty and its causes an immediacy that had not been present before.[1] This chapter takes up the theme and explores the dynamics of poverty in Lancashire as a whole, and Bolton in particular. It suggests that grinding poverty remained a common experience in the late Victorian and early Edwardian era and, in the context of Bolton, traces the nature of official responses to that poverty through the poor law. Engaging directly with the idea that the New Poor Law in this period experienced stagnation and decay, we will see that the case for pessimism is not as strong as it appears from the national perspective.

As a starting point, we should recognize that the size of the poverty problem in Lancashire, England's most important industrial and urbanized county, is often understated throughout the New Poor Law period. After 50 years of proto-industrialization, urbanization, factory development, transport change and rising per capita wealth, the county as a whole could boast relatively low percentages of the population on poor relief at the time of the advent of the New Poor Law in 1834.[2] However, quoting such figures gives a misleading impression of the scale and intensity of poverty in Lancashire around this time. If we turn our attention to the adequacy or otherwise of the relief given, and the number of people who were poor but not relieved by the poor law, the matter takes a different hue. On balance the pensions (regular monetary relief payments) offered by Lancashire poor law authorities in the three decades before 1834 were the lowest in the country.[3] Midwinter claims that such allowances improved under the New Poor Law, suggesting that by 1844 the average pension in Lancashire had risen to 4s. 7d.[4] Yet, how to read such figures is a complex question given uncertainty over the number of people such payments were supposed to support, and continuing intra-regional variation in the scale of provision. Thus, within Bolton union, Bolton township set its pensions in 1842 at 2s. per week, but the more rural parishes in the union were still paying just 1s. 6d. Burnley union paid out an average of just 1s. 6d. per person for those on its pension list in 1840. Even in the early decades of the New Poor Law, therefore, the parsimony of some Lancashire communities is notable.[5] While, as we will see below, the real value of outdoor allowances rose after 1850, there is no evidence that paupers ever received enough from the poor law to guarantee even basic subsistence at individual and family level.

Nor should we forget, in thinking about the scale and intensity of poverty in Lancashire, that many who were poor did not apply for or get poor relief. Recent analyses of pauper letters have begun to suggest that paupers were more willing and able to engage with and manipulate the poor law system than welfare historians have ever allowed.[6] Nonetheless, there is convincing Lancashire evidence that individuals and families did all they could to prolong the time between the onset of need and the destitution that might drive them to the poor law, by exploiting aspects of the diverse economy of makeshifts in the county. One contemporary commentator, Cooke Taylor, noted of Bolton people that

> nowhere have I seen misery which so agonized my very soul as that which I have witnessed in the manufacturing districts of Lancashire. And why? Because the extreme of wretchedness was there, and there only, combined with a high tone of moral dignity, a marked sense of propriety, a decency, cleanliness, an order . . . I visited several families of the distressed operatives in Bolton, accompanied by a Gentleman well acquainted with the locality . . . The invariable account given in every place was "no work" and, as a consequence, "no food, no furniture and no clothing . . . [7]

Doing without, credit, pawning and selling goods and borrowing from family and neighbours were familiar, if fragile, coping strategies that might mean the difference between independence and an application to the poor law. To leave his audience in no doubt of what the latter would have meant, Cooke Taylor noted of one Bolton couple "They may have been talked into a hatred of the New Poor Law, but from their souls they loathed pauperism, as being odious to that sturdy pride of independence which no race of mankind ever possessed in such superabundance as the men of Lancashire."[8] Whether this perspective is true or not, there is evidence that many of those who overcame their moral scruples and thought that they were entitled to relief were turned down, both under the Old Poor Law and the New. By the early 1820s up to 50 per cent of those who applied for relief were turned down immediately or had their cases delayed for review, and this figure had not improved much by the 1840s.[9] Even in 1870, before the onset of the crusade against outdoor relief, Haslingden union was turning down 62 per cent of all of those who applied for relief.[10] In short, there was very considerable and grinding background poverty which went unrecognized by the welfare system. Indeed, by 1842, according to Cooke Taylor, "The fact is, that the mass of the population is on the very brink of sheer destitution, and that thousands are absolutely starving".[11] Similar observations could have been made about 1862 and 1905, both depression years in Lancashire.

These may seem odd conclusions, notwithstanding the well-known evidence of slum dwelling in some Lancashire towns.[12] After all, individual wage rates for both men and women in Lancashire were high throughout the nineteenth century.[13] Indeed, the family wage economy for Lancashire people engaged in some occupations may have been the strongest in the country.[14] Such perspectives are, however, misleading for five reasons. *First*, the Lancashire economy was a complex economic organism. By the mid-nineteenth century it combined areas of highly commercialised and very backward agriculture; vibrant urban–industrial production of textiles with bleaching and textile production in the remote and bleak Rossendale valley; highly mechanized textile production and vibrant new industries such as engineering with structural decline in hand-loom weaving and other trades;[15] and, at the level of individual towns, high paying jobs for the healthy at certain parts of the life-cycle with a vast array of poorly paid urban casual trades.[16] Wealth, then, was not spread out evenly across the life-cycles of Lancashire people, across those in all trades or across the rural and urban landscape. *Secondly*, while Lancashire did not have the endemic low wages that we see in nineteenth-century southern England,[17] it did have to cope with substantial wage instability and sharp fluctuations in the purchasing power of money wages because of unstable food prices, the seasonality of work,[18] and periodic trade fluctuations. The latter could throw whole districts and towns out of work, overwhelming charitable and poor law resources combined and creating intense poverty.[19] Indeed, there were fundamental trade slumps in 1837, 1841–2, 1847–8, 1854, 1862, 1866–69, 1874, 1879, 1886, 1889, 1892–95, 1903–5 and 1909, generating mass unemployment of the sort observed by Cooke Taylor.[20] Headline figures of high wages thus tell us little about the variability of the purchasing power of those wages, and mask wage and income instability.[21]

The *third* problem with an optimistic view of the ability of the Lancashire economy to avoid or combat poverty is that industrial disputes could generate very considerable short-term hardship. This was true of southern England too (as Hurren, for instance, shows[22]), but nowhere were strikes, lockouts, wage reductions and disputes over perquisites and fines as frequent and intense as in Lancashire. Huberman suggests that by the late nineteenth century Lancashire employers had to give more thought to industrial relations, human capital and worker turnover, but many flashpoints remained, including the role of women workers, piece rates, rules on deductions, blacklisting and de-skilling.[23] *Fourthly*, while the demography of Lancashire has never been adequately explored, there is some evidence that ill-health was a particular problem for workers in Lancashire communities.[24] It is quite true that workers in textile factories received higher wages than their counterparts in the ribbon weaving industry, southern agriculture or London dockyards, but the average value of those wages over a year or life-course may have been much lower because of sickness. *Finally*, and *fifth*, it is important to remember that while the Lancashire economy of the early nineteenth century may have been booming, by the later nineteenth century domestic and international competition in textiles, engineering, chemicals and bleaching, brewing and agriculture had begun to eat into the health of this urban–industrial economy.[25]

There are good reasons, then, to think that poverty in nineteenth-century Lancashire may have been severe. Of course, it is difficult to calculate the proportion of the Lancashire population in poverty at any point in time, not least because, with the advent of poverty lines which incorporated absolute as well as relative indicators, defining what "poverty" was at any given point becomes more nuanced in the later nineteenth century.[26] This said, the evidence of endemic poverty in Lancashire towns and rural areas between the 1830s and 1910s is strong. For the period 1836–41 William Neild found that almost one-third of working-class families in Manchester could barely make expenditure and income balance, producing very low living standards.[27] Household budgets for Warrington also show that many families ran a weekly deficit on even the most moderate of expenditure.[28] Margaret Simey observed that in the 1840s, "Poverty was more desperate, housing more squalid, social distinctions more cruel, the state of public health more shocking in Liverpool than elsewhere".[29] By the 1850s "Every tide floated in a new importation of Irish misery, and the snow was loosened from our doors by hordes of bare-footed beggars".[30] Foster's work on Oldham shows that even in the relatively prosperous year of 1849, 15 per cent of *families* were in absolute poverty.[31] Social surveys in Manchester consistently revealed 20 per cent or more of the population in absolute poverty in the 1860s and 1870s, more if one accounts for the Irish and other cellar dwellers likely to have avoided the survey process.[32] In Bolton, as we have seen, a trade slump decimated the economy in 1842. It was also hit heavily (though less than communities that relied on the coarse cotton trade) in the cotton famine of 1861–63. Newspaper summaries reveal that 16.5 per cent of families were on relief in February 1863, and to this number we might add many thousands more struggling to avoid a relief application.[33]

Retaining our Bolton focus, Bowley's 1914 survey encompassed 3650 Bolton *households* from a population of 180,851. He concluded that "Bolton was a town of small families" and that while "the proportion of incomes over £2 weekly was greater in Bolton than in any of the other [Warrington, Northampton and Reading] towns" still "7.8% of the working class households containing 8% of the persons of the working class, were found to be below the New Standard" set by Rowntree's poverty line.[34] This point in time measurement is illuminating, but it is also misleading. A consideration of numbers on poor relief, in receipt of charity, using charitable institutions and in receipt of extraordinary doles for the period 1860–1914, suggests that few in Bolton could avoid poverty at some point in the life-cycle, and that contact with the poor law was highly likely.[35] Such statistics are given a very human face in the diary of Alice Foley of Bolton, who, reflecting on her late nineteenth and early twentieth-century childhood, noted that her life was "an odd corner of strife and poverty" and that "we lived frugally and austerely. I recall that we had no cups and saucers. Our diet was mainly milk, porridge, pota-toes and butties of bread and treacle with a little meat at weekends". Of her sister, Alice noted "She had suffered much privation in infancy and early childhood, had borne the brunt of dire poverty", and when Alice went to work "For the majority, especially those with ageing parents to maintain, there was constantly the ache of fear at recurrent periods of short-time working and unemployment".[36] Foley's experiences chime with the comments of another nineteenth-century commentator, Allen Clarke, who suggested that in Bolton "there was much intermittent, half-ridden, but severe poverty which had particularly sad implications for wives and female children who were expected to bear the brunt of the privations".[37] Poverty was, then, an ever-present spectre in nineteenth-century Lancashire and in the next section we focus our attention on the evolution of formal welfare policies in response to these sorts of experi-ences.

The Lancashire Poor Law Context [38]

CHAPTER ONE noted that the majority of empirical work on the New Poor Law has been conducted for the first four decades after 1834. Lancashire is no exception to this rule, though one might observe the relative dearth of detailed published studies on the county for the *whole* New Poor Law period. The perspectives that we do have seem to paint a relatively clear general picture. Contemporaries keenly appreciated the difficulties likely to be encountered in implementing the New Poor Law in Lancashire.[39] Large populations, high population density, the problem of industrial unemployment, a limited pauper problem in "normal" times, the presence of some major aristocratic landholders, and long-entrenched belief in autonomous local government, prompted some communities to claim that they were "different" and ought to be excluded from the rules of 1834. Indeed, the sense of Lancashire outrage over the New Poor Law can be seen in the letters of Richard Hodgkinson, estate steward to Lord Lilford in southwest Lancashire, who noted indignantly of a circular received from the government that,

> I have now to observe that Culcheth and Lowton are parts of the parish of Winwick, why they are put into Leigh Union we have no means of knowing. It is the general wish and has been the general expectation that Leigh parish wd form a board of itself . . . How 8 townships extending over a space of ground nearly 8 miles in diameter and containing a population of more than 24,000 souls can be brought in one short fortnight to act consistently upon any uniform plan, I am at a loss to know.[40]

More widely, many poor law officials clearly concurred with Midwinter that "the Old Poor Law in Lancashire was a more vivid advertisement of what the Poor Law Commissioners planned to do, than of the faults they so sternly denounced".[41]

It is unsurprising, therefore, that historians have identified Lancashire as one of the most vigorous foci of resistance to the Poor Law Commission.[42] The initial process of unionization did not go smoothly, though it is important to acknowledge that there was no consistent and uniform reaction to the process.[43] Areas such as Leigh or Southport, which co-operated with the unionization process, posed logistical problems of dividing up large parishes and aristocratic estates into convenient unions. Other areas capitulated only after wringing significant concessions from Sir Alfred Power, the assistant poor law commissioner with a brief for Lancashire. Some communities resisted vigorously and persistently,

Map 2.1   Lancashire New Poor Law Unions

becoming skilled in harnessing popular disquiet about centralization to support a policy of prevarication and inaction. Indeed, Lancashire dominates the list of parishes reorganized late in the national process. Blackburn Union was not formed until January 1838, Clitheroe until January 1839 and Bury until 1840. Rochdale was not unionized until 1845, and the activities of the Anti-Poor Law League in this area have been well documented.[44] Indeed, it was not until the late 1840s that 466 parishes were finally formed into the twenty-nine unions identified in map 2.1.[45] Even then, union structure tended to be volatile.

Meanwhile, if unionization was slow, it was also unsatisfactory in the sense that many unions had an impetus to instability and inaction built into their very fabric. Midwinter suggests that the decision over which communities to force into unions was "haphazard", and that "quite incompatible communities" were brought together. Thus, in unions like Bolton, a large town dominated the rural parishes and townships unionized with it, creating animosity over the perceived cross-subsidy of urban poverty. In other unions such as Ormskirk, the lack of a powerful urban centre generated rivalry between equals. Union populations varied between 11,000 in Garstang to over 80,000 in Bolton, while the number of parishes in unions varied between twenty-nine in Preston and four in Salford. More generally, because the New Poor Law conveyed inadequate powers to both the central authorities and unions, boards of guardians were "dependent upon the townships for personnel, facilities and rates". In other counties this may not have mattered, but in a county like Lancashire where community independence was highly valued, boards "were then a talking shop in which deadlock and animosity could breed".[46]

While exogenous factors contributed to this slow and unsatisfactory process – the personalities of assistant commissioners, wider debates about the nature and function of local government and its relationship to central authorities, the fact that in many areas the rating system had been overwhelmed by urbanization, and the politicization of local government of all sorts[47] – we should be clear that late unionization very clearly reflects a culture of resistance. In many respects, then, unionization in Lancashire was simply the start of more serious problems for the central authorities. Once created, Lancashire unions elected some of the most grudging and obstructive poor law guardians, who were those least likely to respond favourably, or at all, to central initiatives. Moreover, the ability of auditors to surcharge guardians for disallowed expenditure,[48] circulars and orders from the Commission, and unannounced inspections of union facilities, were a considerable irritation to poorly motivated guardians. In the early phase of the New Poor Law they reacted by refusing to appoint paid staff, make adequate returns, respond to letters and reports, raise adequate yearly income, or to assert the authority of the union over the townships. Thus, Oldham had no union-controlled outdoor relief until 1847.[49]

It was on the issue of workhouse building that Lancashire unions did most, according to the historiographical literature, to frustrate the early logic of the New Poor Law. As in other matters, Blackburn Union proved the most accommodating. At formation it had five workhouses but closed four of them over two years, with the workhouse in Blackburn serving the union.[50] Other places were less willing to reorganize their provision. Rochdale kept all seven of its workhouses in operation until the mid-1850s, while Bury used its seven workhouses to institute a system of pauper classification based upon different workhouses (as incidentally envisaged in the report of 1834) and did not build a union workhouse until the 1880s.[51] Haslingden union had two workhouses at its formation and kept them until 1870, while Preston fought tenaciously with the central authorities to retain its right to determine the best constellation of workhouse provision, in a dispute that stretched over a decade.[52] More generally, "During the early years of the Poor Law Commission northern unions were far busier closing old workhouses than opening new ones."[53] Lancashire, then, was a thorn in the side of the central authorities.

Even where they were built, the earliest of the new workhouses were often inadequate. Ashton workhouse, for instance, had a capacity of 145 to serve a population of almost 100,000. Though the Haslingden guardians agreed to build a new workhouse in 1863, they did not get around to purchasing a site until 1866, and the workhouse itself was not built until 1870. When it opened, the workhouse had a capacity of just 450, less than 5 per cent of the union population.[54] By the time many unions acted (post-1860) to build the large general workhouses envisaged by the New Poor Law, the tide of national sentiment was already beginning to turn in favour of distributed sites for different categories of pauper.[55] Unsurprisingly given this sort of building programme and its underlying culture of resistance, Lancashire unions maintained only small numbers of paupers via indoor relief, both absolutely and compared to other regions. Midwinter concludes that the guardians "inherited a dual system of poorhouse relief and residential doles, and in general the net result of their work was to perpetuate this dualism". In 1839 Lancashire had 18,195 outdoor paupers, the highest in the country. By 1843, this number had risen to 80,000, with a further 8,000 indoor paupers, only 2000 of whom were deemed able-bodied.[56] Returning prosperity brought a rise in the ratio of indoor to outdoor paupers (to 1:7) by 1846, but between 1846 and 1865 this ratio dropped once more to almost 1:10 and remained very low throughout the later nineteenth century.[57]

Against the backdrop of the tortuous birth of the New Poor Law, much of the historiographical comment on the early decades of its operation in Lancashire has been highly critical. Roberts argues that workhouse conditions in many Lancashire unions were appalling suggesting that, "In part, of course, they neglected their workhouses because they did not believe in them, but they also neglected them because they were indifferent towards the poor."[58] Midwinter has claimed that, "all in all, the more Lancashire's poor law changed, the more it stayed the same. On examination, the gap between the pre-1834 and the post-1834 poor relief services closes considerably, and, in the mundane passage of everyday poor law affairs, it is difficult to visualise any startling changes of officers, paupers or ratepayers."[59] Crowther notes that unions such as Todmorden made no attempt to classify, clean or ensure adequate diet for the indoor poor.[60] Rhodes Boyson is also scathing of the early history of the Lancashire New Poor Law, pointing to poor attendance from guardians, the election of penny-pinching small ratepayers, dishonesty in the award of contracts, resistance to the implementation of standard dietaries,[61] and the appointment of unreliable officers.[62] However, he saves his most penetrating criticism for the relief process itself, noting that decision-making remained firmly located at local level, even as the basis of finance for the poor law moved slowly from parish to union between the 1840s and 1860s. Lancashire unions were the first to re-introduce the consideration of out-relief applications at township and district level in sectional relief committees. In Rochdale, decisions on relief applications were taken by a locally elected committee outside the scope of poor law administration, while in Bolton and Blackburn such applications were reviewed by a small committee of guardians sitting with co-opted local employers. Such local decision making, Boyson claims, allowed unions to mask the scale of the poverty problem, give inadequate indoor and outdoor relief, and prevent paupers from exercising their rights to appeal.[63] Poor relief per head of union population in Lancashire was just 3s. 6d. between 1834 and 1865.[64]

There are, however, two problems with this generally negative view of the early decades of the New Poor Law in Lancashire. *First*, the reality of poor law practice and sentiment was more complicated than even the exhaustive study of Boyson has indicated. We saw earlier that outdoor relief levels were set at an average of just 2–4s. during the 1840s and 1850s, certainly not enough to guarantee subsistence and probably an indicator of substantial background poverty. Yet, we should remember that the Old Poor Law in Lancashire had paid out *irregular* and small amounts to a limited number of people. The New Poor Law paid out *regular* (if still small) amounts to a larger body of people.[65] Moreover, we should be clear that these allowances rose steadily in some areas, that they were usually given irrespective of other income from charitable sources and that allowances were given for individuals rather than families, so that family income from poor relief in the 1840s could have been above income levels for the same family under the Old Poor Law. Nor should we forget that variation in allowances was far more dramatic between parishes within unions than between Lancashire unions themselves. Bolton is a classic case in point, with the sectional relief registers suggesting that levels of outdoor relief could vary by more than 150 per cent across the union in the 1850s.[66] Moreover, while it is certainly true that conditions in many workhouses were poor, Boyson reminds us that most Lancashire unions continued to pay allowances in aid of wages until at least the 1850s, a pragmatic solution to address structural decay in core industries, and in flagrant breach of the central authorities.[67] The same unions consistently defied the Commission in its attempts to ban payment of rents, buying of tools and expenditure on food and clothing. Most also resisted the application of any consistent labour test to outdoor relief.[68] None of this detracts from the accuracy of the characterization of the Lancashire New Poor Law as "harsh", but such observations do show that the picture is more nuanced than has thus far been allowed.

The second problem is that the negative picture of Lancashire senti-ment and practice and a concentration on the culture of resistance, allied with an almost total lack of published empirical research on the Lancashire poor law after 1850, has perhaps obscured some of the dynamic and thoughtful practice that manifested itself in some unions in the later decades of the New Poor Law. We have simply assumed that resistance to the central authorities and questionable treatment of the poor continued. In fact, from the 1850s and 1860s, the weakening of some of the key pressures on welfare and governance in Lancashire towns – population growth, rapid urbanization and structural decline – created the framework for guardians to look again at how they coped with desti-tution.[69] In terms of the poor law fabric, Driver reminds us that Lancashire unions accounted for 25 per cent of all authorized expenditure on poor law hospitals between 1865 and 1871, and one-third of all expenditure on new workhouse facilities and extensions between 1854 and 1870. After the crusade against outdoor relief faltered in the 1880s, Lancashire unions once again accounted for almost one-third of all authorized capital expenditure.[70] This was a measure of just how far behind the south and midlands the Lancashire unions had fallen in terms of spending on fabric, but the opportunity to build and extend from this low base allowed the inclusion of latest thinking on design. It also provided for the evolution, or indeed wholesale change, of previous poor law practice.

Thus, while unions such as Preston and Todmorden appear to have had a particularly (and consistently) poor record on most aspects of welfare, others were cited for best practice in the 1880s and 1890s, including Oldham union which had been famous for its neglect of indoor paupers between 1840 and 1870.[71] Not all of these commendations should perhaps be regarded as positive. Clitheroe union was commended for its relentless pursuit of the relatives of poor people in order to obtain contributions to relief costs during the crusade against outdoor relief in the 1870s. Manchester, Preston, Oldham and Liverpool also made huge strides in, and were commended for, slashing out-relief in the 1870s. Manchester introduced a set of rules on eligibility for relief – the Manchester rules – that were to be recommended as a national standard. Moreover, as late as 1897 Manchester union was introducing the Tame Street Able-Bodied Test Workhouse to try and dissuade people from making relief applications. This experiment was to last ten years, placing massive demands on charitable income in the city, even as the central authorities were favouring more humanitarian treatment of the poor.[72] However, most Lancashire unions failed to adopt the worst aspects of the crusade for any length of time,[73] and the reports of inspectors and the correspondence of unions engenders a pervasive feeling of dynamism about the Lancashire poor law in the later nineteenth century.[74] The District and Sectional Relief Committees that so disturbed Boyson continued throughout the later New Poor Law period, but by the 1880s they had in most unions ceased to be instruments of oppression and rate-saving, and become instead flexible policy bodies attuned to the needs of the local poor.

There were also other indicators of change and flexibility. While less than fifty unions at national level had instigated any sort of quarantine for patients with tuberculosis in 1900, most of the urban unions in Lancashire had at least a segregation ward, if not an entirely separate building by the 1890s. In addition, Lancashire unions invested heavily in cottage homes, and were amongst the first areas to discuss and adopt the case paper system, whereby detailed records on the poor and the impact of different relief measures were kept and monitored. Chorlton and Liverpool workhouses were employing trained medical staff and instituting separate wards for midwifery as early as the 1860s.[75] More widely, the culture of depositions of Lancashire guardians visiting the institutions of other unions to try and establish best practice was well established in the 1880s.

By the later nineteenth century, then, it was the rural unions of the south, east and midlands which were to be perceived as the main drag on efficient and humane welfare delivery, taking over from Lancashire in this respect.[76] For Lancashire at least, there is no sense in which we should be thinking about the stagnation and decay of the New Poor Law. Within this framework, it was the east Lancashire poor law unions in particular that moved, often silently and unnoticed, from amongst the most backward to amongst the most progressive of administration units. Nowhere are the complexities of the implementation, practice and experience of the New Poor Law in Lancashire illustrated so clearly as in Bolton, and it is to this location that we now turn.

Bolton Union

Bolton as a town was deeply enmeshed in the Lancashire cotton spinning and finishing industries and acted as a commercial centre for many outlying industrial areas. Large fine spinning, bleaching and engineering firms dominated the local economy, marking Bolton out in an area otherwise dominated by coarse spinning enterprises. In the 1840s and 1850s, textiles accounted for over 40 per cent of male employment, and workshops, mining, metalworking and building a further 42 per cent.[77] The later nineteenth century was to see growth in retail, service and professional occupations, but by the 1890s Bolton was still a town dominated by textile and metal production and associated industries. The other communities in Bolton union had a more rural complexion, but even in these places industry, mining and merchanting might absorb the energies of a considerable proportion of the working population. Notwithstanding Walton's observation of the "distinctively bottom-heavy social structure of the cotton towns",[78] both the town of Bolton and the outlying parishes of the union could boast a prosperous middle-class, albeit one hopelessly divided along political and religious lines up to 1850. By the later nineteenth century such differences had been repaired and Liberal and Tory elites were substantially intermarried, creating a powerful civic leadership.[79] This was also an increasingly wealthy and, as we will see in the next chapter, philanthropic, elite.

Yet, if the middle class were prosperous, the same cannot be said of working people in the town and its out-parishes, as we have already seen. While Hannah Mitchell talked of Bolton in the early 1890s as "an essentially decent hard-working northern town", the rest of her autobiography paints a picture of exploitation and sweat shop work.[80] Alice Foley noted that "For me the deadening monotony of machine minding was remedied only by the harsh necessity of earning a living".[81] Walton suggests that "Bolton, with its specialization in fine spinning and its extensive engineering works, stood at the top of the Lancashire wages league".[82] Yet in 1891 the *Bolton Chronicle* ran a series of articles on poverty "In darkest Bolton", calling attention to the poor state of housing, health and family economy amongst Bolton cotton operatives, and noted the "social misery and the moral and spiritual darkness of the slums".[83] Almost ten years later the same newspaper revisited the issue of poverty, noting that sickness because of poor housing and living conditions often laid the main breadwinner low and that "The anxiety of the medical attendant in these cases is often extreme. He sees the suffering, knows only too well what conditions are necessary to alleviate it, but in very many cases he is almost helpless".[84] The particular impact of such conditions upon women is perhaps testified by the emergence of Sarah Reddish, Cissy Foley, Alice Collinge and other Bolton women at the forefront of important organizations such as The Women's Co-operative Guild in the 1890s and early 1900s.[85] In short, Bolton and its hinterland had a complex economy and the board of guardians faced a vociferous and active constituency of both ratepayers and the poor by the later nineteenth century.[86] Against this backdrop, an understanding of the formation of the union and nature of poor law practice can help us to gain a more nuanced picture of the character of the late Victorian and early Edwardian poor law and the particular achievements of female guardians from the 1890s.

Resistance to unionization was less severe in Bolton than in other parts of Lancashire, not least because there were so many other competing pressures after the 1835 enabling act to establish municipal authorities. As Taylor reminds us, the middle class in Bolton, the potential seat of opposition to the New Poor Law, were hopelessly split between the Anglican Tories on the one hand and the Radical/Liberal manufacturing and tradesmen elite, at heart a nonconformist group, on the other. By the 1830s and 1840s, the Radical/Liberal axis was trying to seize control of local government and repeal, or limit the powers, of the traditional offices (such as vestries and churchwardens etc.) held by the Tories. Energies that might otherwise have gone into opposition to the New Poor Law were thus dissipated in local political contests and disputes.[87]

The first meeting of the Bolton board of guardians was on 9 February 1837. The union had a population of 82,000 people spread over twenty-six parishes (map 2.2), split between the town itself and suburban and rural areas. One township (Lostock) failed to accept either the letter or the spirit of the 1834 act, implementing a voluntary rate and consistently failing to meet their obligations to the common fund.[88] This notwithstanding, the guardian's minute book of 25 March 1837 noted that,

Townships not in Bolton Union

+ Workhouses

Note: Little Hulton & Westhouhton Workhouses closed by Board of Guardians in 1837–8.
Great Bolton (Fletcher Street) & Turton Workhouses closed in 1861.
Fishpool Union Workhouse in Farnworth built 1860–1.

Map 2.2   Bolton Poor Law Union

"Administration of the poor law has been well and sufficiently conducted with as much attention to economy as a due regard to the necessities of the poor permitted".[89] In practice this meant opposition to central tenets of the New Poor Law, such as compulsory entry to the workhouse, new workhouses and the strict segregation of indoor paupers. At its inception Bolton had four workhouses, in Great Bolton (capacity 253), Turton (capacity 100), Halliwell (capacity 100), and Westhoughton (capacity 100). By 1841, there were just 209 inmates in all of these workhouses – 39 old and sick, 13 children under the age of five, 39 children aged between five and nine, and 118 able-bodied people, including the mothers of illegitimate children. In a retrospective of 1930, the Public Assistance Department noted that three of the four workhouses fell into disuse, leaving only the Great Bolton workhouse to serve the needs of the union.[90] The capacity of even the four workhouses was tiny compared to the number of outdoor paupers, which in 1841 totalled 8,890, rising to 9,285 by 1847.

The condition of the Bolton indoor poor under these circumstances is difficult to pin down. Guardians resisted any attempt to impose a published dietary. The chairman of the board claimed in December 1842 that "those in the workhouse are better fed than many of the ratepayers outside it".[91] Not until 1852 did they introduce a dietary acceptable to the Poor Law Board, and even then frequent changes and local manipulation meant that the diets of those in the workhouse bore little resemblance to the formal dietaries. By 1856, the guardians were explicitly directing workhouse staff to ignore published guidelines, whilst maintaining that the standard, quantity and variety of food on offer in the workhouse was better than for many working people outside it.[92] Hygiene and disease in the workhouse attracted much negative central government and local commentary. An investigation of pauper deaths in January 1843 revealed that the Great Bolton workhouse was overcrowded, with little segregation by age or sex. Diseases such as scarlet fever were rife and there was little by way of oversight by paid union staff. The situation was no better in 1848, when a team of inspectors arrived to investigate deaths in the Bolton workhouse and condemned conditions there.[93] On the positive side, however, Bolton had an open workhouse, with inmates free to come and go and even to sell excess food that they had not consumed. Moreover, the guardians invested in steam heating and piped water in 1845. The latter was a considerable feather in the cap of the guardians given that well over one half of all dwellings in the town of Bolton itself had no piped water at the same date.

Conditions for the outdoor poor in the early decades of the New Poor Law are equally difficult to pin down. The guardians resisted directions and suggestions from the central authority about the salaries of medical officers and the size of their medical districts. Boyson points out that by 1847, all of the Bolton medical districts were more than double the maximum size permitted by central government.[94] Not until 1853 did the guardians comply with central requests on the number, remuneration or duties of medical officers, and even in 1858 they were seeking to save money on salaries and extra costs by ordering the relieving officer to send cases of sickness to the Bolton dispensary. More widely, Dryburgh argues persuasively that there was a marked tightening in the scope and scale of outdoor relief between the 1840s and 1860s and that the proportion of poor law resources spent on outdoor relief tumbled correspondingly.[95] On the opposite side of the coin, Bolton continued to give paupers a choice of medical practitioner (regular and irregular) until the 1850s.[96] Meanwhile, if per capita rates of outdoor relief remained relatively low (2s. 11d. in 1850), allowances often came with supplements not available to paupers in other unions. Thus, Bolton continued to pay rents in defiance of the Commission, regularly spending between £500 and £1,000 per annum between 1840 and 1855. The guardians also continued to provide allowances in aid of wages.[97]

If there is doubt about how to characterize poor law policy in the early decades of the New Poor Law, it is rather clearer that there were significant changes of sentiment, policy and practice after 1860, and particularly after 1880. Thus, at the end of a 1909 guardian's meeting to discuss the majority and minority reports of the Poor Law Commission,[98]

> Mr Knott showed how progressive Bolton had always been by quoting from a local paper of 1865, when an attempt was made to put out workhouse children into homes that were respectable, and today the guardians were considering the taking of children away from the workhouse . . . They were already sending all except the very little ones to public schools, without any special garb; trying to treat the sick in an efficient manner; classifying the old people into three or four sections, and adopting the Case Paper system, so that so far as the poor Law Commission went Bolton was doing what it was proposed some other authority should do.[99]

Such positive commentary echoes earlier newspaper coverage of the activities of the guardians. On 5 June 1890, for instance, the *Bolton Chronicle* noted the publication of a Lancashire relief "league table", suggesting that "the figures showed that the Guardians of the Bolton union were neither too lavish nor too screwish in the administration of relief and that they occupied a very honourable position in this respect".[100] A consideration of the detailed records of the union gives some backing to these positive views, and should cause us to question once more the idea that the later New Poor Law should be characterized as stagnant and decaying.

In terms of the basic fabric of the poor law, the union had built the Fishpool workhouse to replace the older workhouse stock by 1861. The cost was between £25,000–£35,580 depending upon how one calculates what was and was not "workhouse" expenditure. On 29 September 1861, the *Bolton Chronicle* congratulated the guardians on a building with spaces for nine hundred paupers, running water (hot and cold) and hot air central heating that had "superior workmanship and [was] satisfactory in every minor detail as any workhouse in the United Kingdom".[101] As in other Lancashire unions, late building allowed the design of workhouses along the most modern lines. While Bolton did not go to the excesses demonstrated in other major urban unions,[102] its workhouse promised much, with sufficient rooms to allow the detailed classification of the sick by sex and complaint, and provision of double rooms for old people and mothers and infants. Large windows and extractor fans guaranteed good ventilation and all washrooms were fitted with individual cubicles rather than communal facilities. This was a substantial investment, and it marked the start of an expenditure programme on the poor law fabric that was to mount to £100,076 between 1871 and 1910. Authorized borrowing ranged from two loans of £10,000 (one for buying land near the workhouse in 1894 and the other for extension and refurbishment of the infirmary) and one for £11,568 (as a contribution towards the costs of a nursing home), to loans of £468 and £800 (for more inside toilets and furniture for the infirmary). Most of the loans were taken out over twenty to thirty years at interest rates between 3 and 4 per cent, and sources of funding included savings banks from across the country, local firms and the Bolton Corporation.[103]

The overall list of buildings and improvements is considerable. Three new wings were added to the workhouse in 1864, two of them for the infirm to allow further classification of diseases, and a fever hospital was erected in 1872. A large infirmary was built in 1894 and then supplemented by an isolation block for twenty patients with a veranda, patio and beds that could be easily shifted into the fresh air. A casual ward was added in 1876 to cope with the 5,000 casuals per year, and this facility was extended and refurbished in 1897. In 1875 the workhouse was altered to create a reading room and between 1879 (when the board borrowed £6,500 to start its programme) and 1882, fourteen cottage homes and three school rooms were built. By the early 1890s, Bolton had more cottage homes than any other union in the northwest.[104] A new nurse's home was constructed in 1901 and between the early 1880s and late 1900s the *Bolton Chronicle* was carrying between four and ten articles per year on the changing fabric of the poor law. Such articles often had a particular focus on the sick poor, and in terms of the fabric of the later New Poor Law this was entirely justified. By the 1880s the union insisted on classification of the sick poor and had built a fever hospital. In 1894, the guardians borrowed a further £2,800 to create an isolation block separate to the infirmary, agreeing also to send smallpox and typhus cases to the infectious diseases hospital in Farnworth and to isolate tuberculosis patients on a separate site. They had also been amongst the first unions in the country to set aside a separate midwifery ward, created in 1863 and refurbished in 1870. Workhouse provision, the separate infectious hospital and a subscription to the Bolton Royal Infirmary that allowed guardians to send 100 patients a year, ensured a dense network of medical services in the area by the mid-1890s. Thus Bolton union was amongst the most progressive in the country in terms of its treatment of the sick. It is unsurprising, therefore, to find the *Bolton Chronicle* carrying an article on the fabric of the poor law in January 1891 in which it noted approvingly "Here they were at the end of 20 years with substantial buildings, sufficient to deal with present and future needs, without having their operation restricted by a heavy burden of debt".[105]

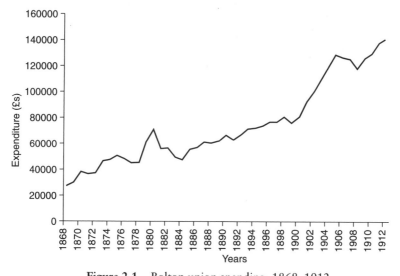

Figure 2.1 Bolton union spending, 1868–1912

Source: BRO GBO 14/2-10, Guardian Financial Statements, 1867–1912.

If we turn our attention from loans to the trajectory of aggregate spending, it is also possible to see the later Victorian and early Edwardian period as one of progress. Spending in Bolton union increased substantially from the later 1860s, checked only temporarily by the crusade against outdoor relief in the later 1870s and early 1880s. Figure 2.1 traces the course of union spending in totem for the period 1868–1912, and we can see expenditure doubled between 1868 and the early 1890s, rising substantially above the national average. The 83 per cent rise in expenditure between 1895 and 1907 was also well above the national average and suggests that central initiatives to lighten the image of the poor law through more specialist and sensitive treatment were taken very seriously in a union which had in any case substantially increased spending since the 1850s.[106]

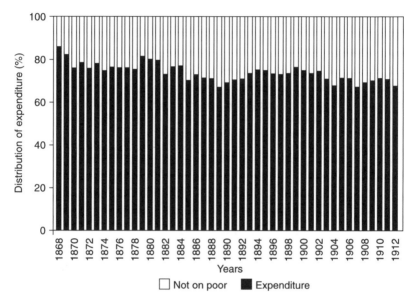

Figure 2.2   Distribution of Bolton union poor law spending

Source: BRO GBO 14/2-10, Guardian Financial Statements, 1867–1912.

Aggregate spending is not, of course, a reliable guide to the treatment of the poor. As elsewhere, only a proportion of the yield of the poor rate was actually spent on the poor, and figure 2.2 suggests that while 84 per cent of all rate expenditure was on poor relief in 1868, by 1912 this figure had fallen to well under 70 per cent. These figures include costs such as the salaries of officials, workhouse furniture and interest on loans as expenditure on the poor. Excluding them would generate a very steep fall indeed in the proportion of rate expenditure devoted to the poor, sinking to under half by 1910. Indeed, in March 1894 it was noted that, "The Chairman [of the Bolton guardians] . . . had often been taunted by ratepayers with the disparity between what was expended on relief of the poor and the amount collected as poor rates".[107]

The need to concentrate just on resources expended for the relief of poverty is clear, and so doing generates illuminating perspectives. Figure 2.3 suggests that a relatively constant one-fifth to one-quarter of expenditure was deployed to fund the workhouse, broadly in line with the national averages calculated by Williams. The proportion of resources devoted to outdoor relief fell from a substantial 45 per cent in 1868 to under 25 per cent by 1912. Again, this is in line with the average figures calculated by Williams, though in Bolton at least, and as we shall see later and in CHAPTER SIX, such decline masks a significant absolute uprating of allowances in the early twentieth century. Staff costs absorbed around 10 per cent of poor law resources, in marked contrast to some metropolitan unions where much more substantial figures were common, and well below the national averages calculated by Williams. Fluctuations in the "other" category moved in tandem with changes to the fabric of poor law institutions, since the biggest single item here was the provision of furniture for workhouse extensions and new buildings, followed closely by the costs of providing firewood and coals. However, it is the cost of providing for pauper lunatics that dominates this graph. Absorbing less than 20 per cent of resources in 1868 (already well above the national average), the expenditure on pauper lunatics rose in absolute and relative terms throughout the later nineteenth and early twentieth centuries. By 1910, the 29 per cent of resources spent on lunatics in Bolton dwarfs the 16.2 per cent national figure calculated by Williams.[108] While the real burden of such individuals may have been partly offset by a grant in aid, it is notable that the guardians constantly debated the pauper lunatic problem in the 1890s and 1900s.[109] Bolton, then, was in many ways an archetypal semi-urban northern union, spending substantial amounts on buildings and equipment, relatively little on staffing and a dwindling proportion of relief on the indoor and outdoor poor collectively.

Such conclusions can, however, understate the nature and degree of change in attitudes towards paupers and their care in the later nineteenth century. Thus the declining proportion of resources spent directly on the poor was in part a reflection of the spectacular increase in the share of resources spent on lunatics. Moreover, the significance of these observations can only be gauged if we tally spending proportions and amounts against the number of recipients. This is not easy. The problems associated with discerning the numbers of distinct paupers in receipt of indoor and outdoor relief (as opposed to the number of times people in the union received relief during a year) are well known. Workhouse admission and discharge books often failed to distinguish between those who came to the workhouse and stayed, those who came and left, and those who came, left and went back again.[110] Out-relief books constructed by sectional relief committees pose exactly the same problems. It is thus unsurprising to find Thane suggesting that the total number of people admitted to the workhouse, excluding tramps, ought to be adjusted downwards by 20 per cent to take account of problems of nominal identification and thus approximate to the real numbers relieved.[111]

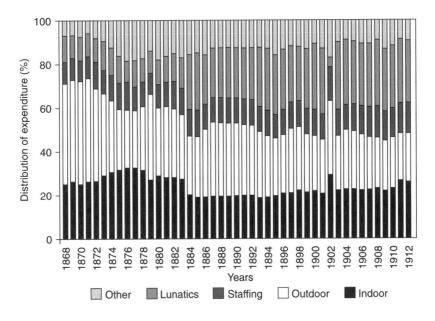

Figure 2.3   Detailed distribution of Bolton poor law expenditure, 1868–1912

Source: BRO GBO 14/2-10, Guardian Financial Statements, 1867–1912.

The sources on numbers of recipients in Bolton are very detailed indeed. Out-relief registers appear to have been conscientiously updated, and they make a consistent distinction between new and existing recipients. It is thus comparatively easy to count the number of distinct people relieved during the course of any year. On the face of it, workhouse admission and discharge registers should be equally easy to use since they appear to record truncated payment histories where a pauper resident at the start of a year then left the workhouse. However, an initial analysis of workhouse admission and discharge episodes between 1890 and 1900 conducted in the early stages of research for this project suggested that the clerks never resumed a payment history if someone moved out of the workhouse and then came back again, in effect creating two payment histories not one.[112] Thus, for the purposes of this study, the workhouse admission and discharge registers for Bolton in the period 1868–1912 were entered into a database and then subject to crude nominal record linkage on the basis of surname, forename, age and status. The exercise reveals that official statistics on the indoor poor for this period overstated numbers by almost 24 per cent.[113]

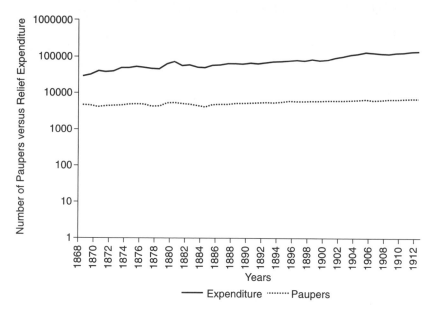

Figure 2.4   Number of paupers versus expenditure in Bolton union, 1868–1912

Source: BRO GBO 14/2-10, Guardian Financial Statements, 1867–1912; BRO GBO 23, Summary of Relief Returns; BRO GBO 9, Bolton Union Workhouse Admission and Discharge Books; BRO GBO 8, Sectional Relief Registers.

Figure 2.4 plots, on a logarithmic scale, the number of distinct paupers relieved indoors and outdoors by Bolton union against relief spending directly on the poor, and we can see that, as in the national figures constructed by Williams, spending increases substantially outstripped the changing size of the pauper population. Consequently, as figure 2.5 demonstrates, per capita poor law costs rose consistently from the later 1880s notwithstanding the proportionate changes identified in figure 2.3.[114] On 29 February 1888 the *Bolton Chronicle* noted with respect to a regional survey of out-relief expenditure that "this union stood in a much better position as regarded the relief question than it had been supposed to be. It had been believed that the Bolton union was the most pauperised place in Lancashire, but it was now found that we occupied a midway position with 1:47 paupers and an average cost of [out] relief of 1/9".[115] This figure was broadly in line with the national average. Thereafter, mean outdoor relief increased consistently, reaching almost 4s. by 1908/9. On the face of it, then, Bolton union had much to recommend it in terms of its generosity of treatment compared to others in Lancashire and similar urban unions up and down the country.[116]

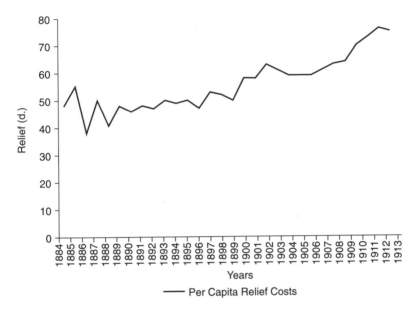

Figure 2.5   Relief expenditure per capita in Bolton union

Source: BRO GBO 24/1-2, Statement of Costs Per Capita, 1884–1914.

Bolton union was apparently less progressive in terms of its expenditure on staffing, which lagged behind the national average. The guardians, as we saw above, had been reluctant from the earliest days of the New Poor Law to co-operate with central authorities on the number, duties and remuneration of medical staff. The union was also a laggard when it came to phasing out the practice of paupers nursing each other in the workhouse, something to which we return in CHAPTER SIX. Indeed, the fact that a fairly constant 10 per cent of income was spent on staffing might be taken as an indication that the Bolton union was inadequately staffed and that staff were inadequately paid.[117] Such perspectives are misleading. There were very wide disparities in the number of paid staff per capita even amongst unions with a good overall reputation. Some, such as Bolton saw modest but sustained absolute increases in the scale of their expenditure on salaried staff (from £2,382 in 1868 to £6,565 in 1900), while others, such as Lancaster or Garstang, financed both relative and absolute increases in staffing costs. Other unions with substantial absolute and relative staffing costs (Chorlton, Manchester or Preston, for instance) had poor reputations.[118] In any case, a pessimistic interpretation of the nature of staffing in Bolton union does not really stand up to a detailed investigation of the personnel files. Bolton appointed its first professional midwife in 1869, well ahead of most other unions. By 1900, the union had three professional midwives, and the Ladies Charity for the Relief of Poor Lying in Women used the facilities of the workhouse for their charity work. In 1885 there were seven teachers in the union, substantially above the average for Lancashire as a whole. A cook and storekeeper were appointed in 1887, a laundress in 1894 and a resident engineer in 1896. By the later 1890s the number of paid staff had increased substantially, and, amongst nurses at least, staff qualifications and experience had also improved.[119] Indeed, there is little support in Bolton for Crowther's conclusion that "neither the central authority nor the guardians really tried to improve the calibre of staff".[120] The failure of the proportion of resources spent on staffing to rise reflects both rapid absolute and relative spending increases elsewhere, particularly on pauper lunatics, and the fact that salaries in Bolton remained relatively low compared to those that could be obtained in other unions in Lancashire.[121] There is also, of course, another way of looking at staffing quality. Thus, as staff became more professional from the 1880s the number of complaints from paupers themselves about staffing and staff activities fell, so that by the later 1890s the Bolton newspapers were reporting less than one complaint or investigation per year. Nor did the staff conflict with guardians as they did in other unions. In February 1894, for instance, the Chairman of the Board, John Haslam, gave a dinner for 20 union officers to thank them for their efforts and their kindly disposition to the guardians and "to cement the close feeling of friendship which undoubtedly exists between them".[122]

Conclusion

There is little doubt that poverty in nineteenth- and early twentieth-century Lancashire was severe. The same can be said for Bolton itself. Whilst Bowley found greater levels of need in towns such as Reading, industrial decline, overseas competition and trade fluctuations bequeathed endemic life-cycle and inter-generational poverty to Bolton. There are no hard and fast measures, but a consideration of all of the evidence available suggests that upwards of 25 per cent of the population were poor at any time and that the majority of working-class people would expect to come into contact with the poor law. The Bolton newspapers, as we have seen, were alive to the scale of poverty and associated issues such as poor health and slum housing. Like their counterparts elsewhere in the county, middle-class people in Bolton rethought their duties as citizens and organized to fight such poverty with philanthropy. This is the subject of the next chapter. For now, it is important to recognize that just as they highlighted the problem of poverty, the Bolton newspapers were also avid commentators on the day-to-day activities of the poor law as one of the buttresses against pauperism. There were scandals of course. In 1889, a guardian had been accused of having sexual relations with an inmate and a nurse, an allegation which, while never proved, obtained wide publicity both locally and countywide.[123] Yet, much of the hostility to guardians and their policies that can be observed in other provincial newspapers, is missing in Bolton. Certainly from the mid-1880s newspaper commentary was overwhelmingly favourable. Indeed, in October 1901 the *Bolton Chronicle* reported approvingly that during a recent poor law conference, "Bolton union came out well compared with other Lancashire unions and Sir J. T. Hibbert, the President of the conference, spoke of them as a progressive Board."[124] We see little support here or in other newspaper coverage for the idea of Midwinter that "The abiding feeling evoked by a study such as this is a sad awareness of the miseries of Lancashire folk throughout all the dreary years considered, and of the chilly appraisal of misfortune by those more prosperous and in authority."[125]

There was good reason for favourable commentary. We have seen that the late Victorian and early Edwardian period in Bolton witnessed very significant additions to the fabric and personnel of the poor law, changes in allowances and important changes of practice where the indoor poor were concerned. It is not appropriate, then, to talk of stagnation and decay in the poor law. To some extent these local experiences were part of a county-wide transition whereby vigorous resistance to unionization, workhouse building and inspection, gave way to a more sensitive appreciation of the needs of the poor and the obligations of localities and their ratepayers. While there was no consistent Lancashire picture, the majority of unions did move from being backward and awkward to progressive and constructive in the latter part of the nineteenth century. However, it would be wrong to understate the local flavour and impetus of these changes. Lancashire towns had very different population trajectories, resources for philanthropic effort, religious composition, traditions of public activity and service, rate bases and spatial architecture, all of which could influence attitudes towards the poor at different points in time. The transition of Bolton from reactionary, backward and spendthrift union to pace-setter in the later nineteenth century is an excellent case in point. Here, factors such as moderating population growth, the recovery of the rate base after the depression of 1842 and the Cotton Famine of 1861–63, the mobilization of local religious networks and local social surveys, melded with a longstanding and rich tradition of philanthropic work and local social action by Bolton elites to create a situation in which radical change in poor law practice was possible and desirable. From the 1870s, a new impetus was thrown into the melting pot in the form of coalitions of prominent local women who sought to extend their philanthropic and public roles into the area of social welfare. In the following chapter, there-fore, we take up the second of our core themes and consider the nature of philanthropy and public action in Bolton, with a particular focus on the emerging role of nineteenth-century Bolton women.

CHAPTER THREE

Preparing the Ground? Philanthropy, Public Service and Activism

The previous chapter traced significant levels of poverty in Bolton and began to reconstruct the nature of official responses to the problem via the poor law. Particularly in the later Victorian and early Edwardian period, we have seen that the New Poor Law became a dynamic institution, and that Bolton moved from poor law backwater to regional, and in some cases national, leader. However, reform of the poor law was only one of the potential responses to the poverty problem, and this chapter focuses on a second avenue, that of philanthropy. Initially reviewing the national and regional philanthropic context, it will move on to consider the nature and scale of philanthropic activity in Bolton. In particular, the latter parts of the chapter will concentrate on the philanthropic and campaigning activism of Bolton women, reconstructing organizational and personal histories. It will argue both that women's philanthropic activity was significant in its own right and, beginning to take up the second of our core themes, that philanthropy provided a bridge to more formal female involvement in public life, citizenship and poor law administration in the later nineteenth century.

Philanthropy: National and Regional Context

Historians of welfare and philanthropy agree that the nineteenth century saw not only an expansion in the scale of giving, but also a change in its nature. Kidd thus traces the decline of giving in the form of endowed charities at death and the rise of donations to individuals, organized charities and charitable institutions within the lifetime of the giver. Victorian men and women gave to a blinding array of charitable causes, aimed variously at immediate relief of crisis, provision of food, moral and sanitary reform, medical institutions, education, housing, and children.[1] Donors might be motivated by genuine humanitarian concern about the material and moral state of the poor, concerns over the physical separation of rich and poor, evangelism, an increasing appreciation of the nature of risk in Victorian society[2], fear of crime, or civic pride. Indeed, "the motives for charitable activity were as diverse and plentiful as the charities themselves".[3]

There is also agreement in the historiography that from the 1840s and 1850s we see growing concern about the impact of un-coordinated giving on the morals of the poor. While it is not the purpose of this chapter to trace these debates, their outcome – the idea that donors, when deciding what to give and to whom, ought to be discriminating, to have personal contact with the poor, and to foster self-help and moral reform – is significant. By 1869 there was an impetus to the organization and co-ordination of charitable activity through local branches of the Charity Organization Society (COS). Historiographical perceptions of the purpose, practices and achievements of the COS are complex and have been well covered by other authors.[4] Whether the COS represents a profound countrywide and concerted middle-class attempt to use charity to take the frugal and deserving out of the ambit of the poor law and engineer their social, moral and physical reform, or whether the COS was a patchy and generally ineffective attempt at social control by elements of a divided middle class, is open to interpretation. What is clear is that, however briefly, the COS and its principle of organized giving had an important influence on many localities.

Yet, if we find some agreement and clarity in the historiography, we also find disagreement and haziness. There is, for instance, no national, or reliable regional, picture of the scale of resources devoted to philanthropy. Lack of comprehensive national returns, the personal and unrecorded nature of much charity, poor survival of records for charities convened to meet specific crises and the patchy survival of the records of endowed charities, hamper even rough approximations of the volume and trajectory of private charity. The idea that the scale of charitable resources applied to poverty in London in the early nineteenth century outweighed that of the poor law, and that even as poor relief and the underlying poverty problem grew, charity remained a major plank in the nineteenth-century economy of makeshifts, is a commonplace of the literature.[5] Similar observations might be made about Manchester and Bristol, where ad hoc collections combined with endowed and subscription charities amounted to perhaps two thirds of the money raised by the poor rate by the mid-nineteenth century.[6] Whether such charity was sustained and its scale was duplicated in rural areas, other provincial towns, industrial cities and town hinterlands is a question to which we have no reliable answers.[7]

Nor is there agreement on the exact trajectory of philanthropic giving and expenditure. Kidd suggests that a stream of charities was founded from the 1860s, but claims that by 1894 "the great age of Victorian philanthropy was past".[8] Ashton, on the other hand, suggests that the 1830s–1850s represents the most important period of philanthropy, at least in the great cities.[9] Harris agrees with Fraser that there was a "vast outpouring of philanthropic activity in the middle years of the nineteenth century", and he links charitable giving to "the loss of religious faith and the search for a new secular morality".[10] Finlayson characterizes the whole nineteenth century as the period during which charity came to a "luxuriant bloom",[11] while Gorsky, focusing on the formation dates of Bristol charities rather than their resources, offers a more precise chronology. The early nineteenth century and the 1870s witnessed an upsurge in the philanthropic imperative, while the middle decades of the nineteenth century and the 1880s witnessed a decline in such endeavour.[12] Prochaska, meanwhile, reminds us that the scale and trajectory of philanthropic activity had distinct regional characteristics, and varied considerably according to life-cycle, gender and established traditions of giving, making a truly representative national trajectory hard to locate.[13]

If we take up Prochaska's challenge and investigate the volume and trajectory of philanthropy at regional level, however, the results are sometimes equally unsatisfactory. The example of Lancashire is instructive. There are good reasons to expect a nineteenth-century upsurge in philanthropy in the county. Heavy urbanization, rising numbers of the middling-classes and rising per capita wealth amongst them, a vocal and effective network of women activists and philanthropists,[14] a strong newspaper culture, a complex religious patchwork and a notable civic pride movement, created an ideal demand and supply framework. Extensive working-class self-help networks in Lancashire also eased the ideological problems sometimes associated with philanthropy.[15] In this sense, it is unsurprising that Lancashire has sometimes been seen as a cornerstone of the nineteenth-century expansion of philanthropic resources and volunterism.[16] A brief study of the county might, then, help to flesh out the bare bones of national generalizations on the nature of nineteenth-century philanthropic effort.

The *Charity Returns* of 1803 suggest that endowed charities in Lancashire could claim a notional capitalization of well over £300,000. As Shapley and others have suggested, however, Lancashire communities also had a contemporaneous philanthropic movement involving ongoing charitable donations at individual level, collections for specific purposes and the creation of voluntary institutions. The resources generated by such philanthropic effort in the early nineteenth century were substantial.[17] Yet, for the rest of the nineteenth century, the volume and trajectory of philanthropic resources is unclear. Studies of Manchester, Liverpool, Blackburn, Wigan and Tottington trace a collective 564 charitable initiatives for the period 1820–1890, with the majority coalescing around the mid and late nineteenth century, once the political standoffs of municipalization had been laid to rest.[18] The scale of resources involved in these initiatives could be considerable. Thus, the Quaker Eckroyd family collected almost £12,000 for their work with the sick and destitute in Tottington between 1822–39. A charity committee in Blackburn collected £4,000 for the relief of poverty during the harsh winter of 1846; a survey of charitable resources in the Leigh, Southport and Croston Poor Law Unions in 1874 suggests a nominal income equivalent to 63 per cent of expenditure on indoor and outdoor paupers in these places.[19] In Manchester, a survey of 10,500 people who gave money to charity in 1884 "found that 8,200 (78 per cent) subscribed to only one society; 1,065 gave to two; whilst a minority of 420 (4 per cent) supported more than five".[20] These ad hoc observations are significant, suggesting as they do a sustained nineteenth-century philanthropic imperative, though one that did not really accelerate until the 1840s and 1850s. A more precise quantitative survey of regional philanthropy is, however, impossible without a systematic consideration of the family, estate and poor law collections of all of Lancashire's 466 parish and township administrations.

In the meantime, local studies can take us slightly further forward, as we can see by dwelling briefly on the experiences of one of the best documented of Lancashire towns, Manchester.[21] The range of charitable initiatives in the town was literally breathtaking. District visiting associations, a lying-in hospital, a house of recovery, a Dorcas Society, the mission movement, night shelters, feeding stations, clothing societies, the Education Aid Society, societies for protecting vulnerable women and children, and general and specialist voluntary hospitals, interacted with much older endowed charities, private charity and some 140 ad hoc collections between 1840 and 1880, to create a culture of giving.[22] From the 1860s "there ensued a stream of newly founded charitable societies for the poor, many of which provided institutions for the reform as well as the relief of particular categories of destitution".[23] Some of these charities were of fundamental importance. The Manchester and Salford Ladies Sanitary Reform Association of 1862 may, according to Kidd, "justifiably claim the credit for health visiting",[24] while the Manchester Eye Hospital was one of the foremost specialist institutions in the country. More local studies of the sort offered by Gorsky, Shapley and Kidd are clearly vital if we are to pin down the scale and trajectory of philanthropy on the national scale. Such studies are also important if we want to establish the meaning and character of philanthropic effort, and it is to this theme that we now turn.

Thinking About Philanthropic Activity

We have already hinted that the motives of donors were complex and varied. Though this is not the place to take up these broad and important themes, what is clear is that for many, giving to charity and undertaking voluntary philanthropic work reinforced social, religious and political authority and generated and exemplified public spirit, civic pride and citizenship.[25] Often, philanthropy was more than passive, and philanthropic and campaigning activities were conducted in tandem. Commentators such as Prochaska, Kidd and Harris thus trace a rising tide of voluntary public action, with donors, campaigners and volunteers working directly to modify the moral, housing, physical and economic conditions of the poor at the same time as they engaged with slavery, the corn-laws, factory exploitation and prostitution.[26]

Within this wider framework, there is overwhelming evidence that nineteenth-century philanthropy was an outlet for the talents of middle-class women. While, it is important to acknowledge the deep historical roots of women's philanthropic work,[27] the blossoming of philanthropy after 1834 provided new opportunities for women as givers, fundraisers, distributors, instruments and recorders of philanthropic endeavour.[28] Yet, how to characterize and locate such female activity is by no means easy. This is not least because of the continuing shortage of studies of the overlapping, complementary and contradictory campaigning, local government and philanthropic activities of individual women, and the absence of material detailing their thoughts on such work.[29] Consequently, many important questions remain inadequately addressed. What was the function of philanthropic activity for women? Did women donors and volunteers play a valuable and leading role or did they lag behind the efforts of men? Did activists seek and make philanthropic careers in the same way as some men? Was philanthropy a stepping-stone to other areas of political and social campaigning?

These themes resonate with the issues raised in CHAPTER ONE and require further exploration here. However, the historiographical literature provides complex and sometimes contradictory perspectives on such matters. Let us turn first to the function of female philanthropic activity. The idea that middle-class women faced multiple overlapping constraints on their actions and ability to advance in public life is a commonplace of the literature on nineteenth-century women. Models of order, private domesticity, cleanliness and motherhood dominated much of the contemporary literature and they have a powerful hold on our understanding of middle-class female action. To develop one of our themes from CHAPTER ONE, the idea that philanthropic activity provided a mechanism by which women could use the language of the domestic, moral and maternal to break the rigid divisions between the spheres of men and women and enter public life has underpinned much of our understanding of women's public philanthropic activity.[30] Thus, Davidoff argues that, "the organized charity of the latter part of the nineteenth century was an attempt somehow to reproduce the organic community . . . For this alone women might leave their homes, their place".[31] Lewis, in her study of the lives and experiences of five feminist activists, notes that women saw the solution to social problems "in the family and . . . social work performed voluntarily by middle-class women who thereby fulfilled their citizenship obligations". However, such interests had to be reconciled "with an equally strong commitment to domestic duties and late-Victorian ideas about female propriety", and because "The boundary between male and female spheres had to be respected", though "they were not agreed on exactly where it lay".[32] Vicinus argues that 'It was from the narrow base of women's special duties and obligations that women in the nineteenth century came to expand their fields of action and their personal horizons'.[33] Other commentators have offered a more nuanced interpretation of the relationship between philanthropy and the public, private and domestic spheres. Many of the women who became involved in philanthropic work, they note, had a long *family history* of charitable endeavour and campaigning.[34] Moreover, the most prominent women, as well as many of those for whom we only have the briefest of biographical details, had by the later nineteenth century done considerable amounts of both philanthropic *and* campaigning work. This makes it much more difficult for us to see a concrete dividing line between public and private.[35] Philanthropy, then, was much more than a simple vehicle for pushing back the limiting boundaries on female action.

More complexities emerge if we consider whether, once in the public sphere, women played a *leading or lagging* role in philanthropic work. We saw in CHAPTER ONE that many of the women who became involved with the poor law are seen to have achieved little. For some historians, the achievements of women in the philanthropic sphere are equally limited. Kidd, for instance, suggests that "women played an auxiliary role in the running of most charities, forming ladies committees and concentrating on fund raising and home visiting", only taking the lead when dealing with groups like children, where their mothering and domestic qualities gave them special competence.[36] Prochaska, on the other hand, notes that as well as being major charitable donors in their own right, women activists (voluntary and paid) underpinned the nineteenth-century visiting movement and played a prominent role in philanthropic work linked to questions of sanitation and hygiene.[37]

The lack of clarity on this issue leads on to a further matter about which we have contradictory answers, namely the place of philanthropic work in the *personal development* of the women who undertook it. For Kidd, only where: "personality and intellect challenged the conventional stereotype", as for instance in the case of Louisa Twining, were women able to "carve out philanthropic careers".[38] Recent work on feminist biography both confirms and challenges such a view. On the one hand it has focused almost exclusively on the philanthropic careers of women such as Octavia Hill, reinforcing the idea that a woman needed to challenge the female stereotype if they desired a philanthropic career. On the other hand, feminist biography has suggested that relatively few women wanted an all-encompassing philanthropic role.[39] Some were happy to work on ad hoc philanthropic projects that fell well short of a career, while other women found philanthropic activity that was divorced from wider issues in the public and private arenas frustrating and limiting.[40] Indeed, for many women philanthropic work served the dual role of being valuable in its own right and constituting a *stepping stone* for wider engagement with the public sphere. Hence Davidoff argues that "by the end of the century", if not before, "experience in philanthropy was leading to career opportunities for women in other areas of public life".[41] Such sentiments echo Finlayson, who suggests that women's "involvement in philanthropy – while often combined to a somewhat subordinate and 'domestic' role, reflecting their political position – could afford experience which might be carried over into public and political activity."[42] Jones likewise concludes that, "Every step . . . into the local public world of policy making and policy implementation was ideologically and organically linked to the previous one".[43] These aspects of philanthropic work are addressed further below in the specific local context of Bolton.

In the meantime, we should not forget that almost all women philanthropists and activists for whom we have detailed biographical information were supporters of many overlapping causes at exactly the same point in time and over their lifetimes. The women who campaigned around issues of marriage in the early and mid-nineteenth century were usually active philanthropists and were those, according to Levine, who "argued so vigorously in favour of women's suffrage, local government and the variety of campaigns which feminists opened up" in the later nineteenth century.[44] Female philanthropists might take part in campaigning forums shared with men – for instance on the issue of slavery, local politics or sanitary reform – or forums dominated by, but rarely exclusive to, women. Here we might include campaigns on the Divorce Act in the 1850s, the rights of married women over property in the 1880s, the Contagious Diseases Act, or suffrage.[45] And while Hannam reminds us that there was no inevitable link between philanthropic and campaigning work and political action, both sorts of activity provided the experience, skills and confidence for women to contemplate wider political activity at the individual level.[46] In this sense, we might argue that female philanthropists were not simply in training for a wider public role, but part of a self-conscious women's movement with feminism and a feminist critique of male power at its core. As CHAPTER ONE suggested, we can engage in debate over what a nineteenth-century feminist was. We might also question when the cumulative experiences of individual women meld together to form a self-conscious regional or national feminist movement – Hall, for instance, suggests that the 1880s marks a major turning socioeconomic, cultural, political and feminist turning point, something that we do not see in the work of Levine.[47] Nonetheless, individual women did seem to think about their overlapping philanthropic, campaigning and political activities in terms of a feminist journey (see CHAPTER SEVEN), and it is only by looking at these issues in the local context that we can understand and contextualize the role, motivations and achievements of women philanthropists and local government activists. To this end we turn our attention once again to Bolton.

Philanthropy in Bolton

The elites of Bolton had a long history of providing endowments and ad hoc charity. A collection to provide food and allowances was made in 1691, and almost all of the hard winters of the 1690s prompted collections.[48] Endowed charities for Bolton and some of the parishes that were eventually to compose Bolton union yielded a notional income of £1,200 in 1723, exceeding by some distance the amount spent on formal poor relief.[49] By the early nineteenth century, however, the situation had deteriorated. Endowed charities had an income of £2000 plus but even if we also factor in the ad hoc collections and other charitable giving that can be traced between 1800 and 1810, the ability of formalized charity to supplement rapidly rising poor law resources had dwindled significantly.[50]

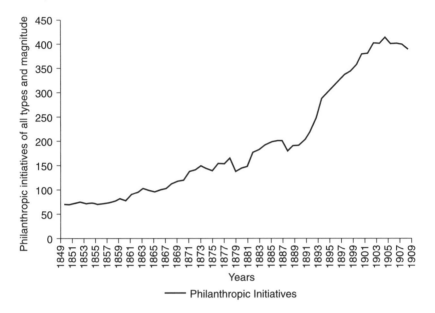

Figure 3.1 The number of philanthropic initiatives in Bolton, 1849–1909

Source: See text.

Figures 3.1, 3.2 and 3.3 take up the nineteenth-century story, detailing the number of traceable charitable initiatives, their value and their type between the late 1840s and early 1900s. These figures should be interpreted with caution, for though they arise out of an exhaustive combing of family letters, diaries, newspaper reporting, charity and poor law records and begging letters for Bolton and surrounding parishes, they probably miss some organized and formalized charity and very much that was individual and personal. Nonetheless, they are revealing and provide support for Hollen Lees who argues that urban areas had "greater assets to throw into the struggle against destitution".[51] Figures 3.1 and 3.2 suggest that it was not until the end of middle-class battles over municipalization in the 1850s that the number and value of charitable initiatives rose significantly.[52] Once the movement was underway, however, the results were profound, and the resources devoted to philanthropic causes by the late nineteenth century were a significant

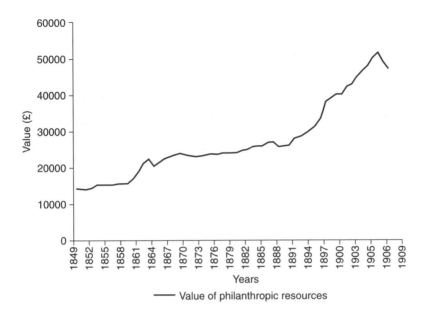

Figure 3.2 The value of philanthropic initiatives in Bolton, 1849–1909
Source: See text.

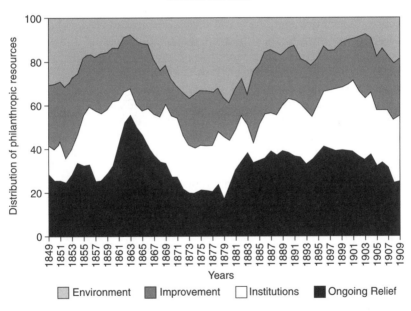

Figure 3.3 The distribution and classification of philanthropic effort

Source: See text. *Note*: This is a distribution of the number of philanthropic initiatives rather than value and arises out of a combing of all extant sources throwing light on philanthropy for Bolton union.

complement to formal poor relief. There were 110 registered charitable trusts in Bolton in 1900, rising to 234 if we also include other parishes in the union, and the scale of income from these and ad hoc collections and regular charitable giving may have constituted some 50 per cent of the yield of the annual poor rate. Contemporaries were certainly aware of the importance of the philanthropic effort. An illuminated address from the Bolton Board of Guardians to Dr and Mrs Samuel Taylor Chadwick, presented in gratitude for a gift of £17,000 to build dwellings for the poor in January 1868 talked of the "tide of charity" from Bolton citizens.[53]

These observations are not surprising. If we take three prominent Bolton families for which records survive over all or part of the period 1845–1900, we see large-scale engagement with philanthropy. Thus, between 1845 and his death in 1868, Robert Heywood gave the equivalent of £1,200 per year to charitable causes broadly defined, including land for a recreation ground and public park, and over £8,000 to the local infirmary. His son, John Heywood, gave a site for the foundation of a new public baths in 1902 and donated over £500 per year of his recurrent income to philanthropic purposes.[54] Stephen Blair, Bolton's first Conservative mayor, bequeathed £30,000 at his death in 1870 "for the erection and endowment of a convalescent hospital, the Blair's hospital". In the previous thirty years he had donated £23,000 to local philanthropic ventures.[55] The Ainsworth family was similarly generous, donating £3,000 to the Infirmary between 1860 and 1872, and founding a Night Refuge for the homeless in 1874.[56]

As in other places, those who contributed to philanthropic endeavours did so across the spectrum of potential beneficiaries. Figure 3.3 codifies the plethora of charitable initiatives under four broad heads.[57] *First*, there were charity funds devoted to the immediate or ongoing relief of poverty. Prominent male members of the middle-class formed the Bolton Fund for Relief of the Poor in July 1840 and this became the Poor Protection Society in 1850, relieving 120–150 families per year at a cost of £2200 in 1840–41. In 1891, the Society was dealing with 773 applicants (3092 persons), "this society was *the* charitable organization of the town", and by the early twentieth century women were prominent as both donors to, and committee members of, the Society.[58] On a smaller scale, but no less important, some £260 per year was being raised by the Bolton Society for Preventing Destitution in the 1870s, offering loans, grants, tools and food to people who might otherwise have to turn to the poor law. This Society was re-formed in the early twentieth century as the Bolton Distress Committee, setting up labour exchanges, emigration schemes and public work initiatives. Three prominent female philanthropists and activists,

Mary Haslam, Martha Moran and Sarah Reddish, were on the organizing committee.[59] Other initiatives were less formal: a charity dinner to celebrate the Queen's birthday in May 1839 raised £450 for food kitchens and cash doles;[60] three collections to offer support in cash and kind to unemployed textile workers in the 1842 depression raised almost £6,000, and that figure more than quadrupled at the time of the 1862 cotton famine.[61]

Secondly, charitable funds were directed to the establishment or maintenance of institutions. Robert Heywood had been one of the founders of the Bolton dispensary and infirmary and was one of its leading contributors, officeholders and fundraisers between the 1820s and 1850s. While women never served on the infirmary committee, they became increasingly important as subscribers and providers of gifts in kind as the nineteenth century wore on. They became even more important in terms of benefactions, occasionally outstripping the sums contributed by male philanthropists.[62] There was, then, a real appetite for investment in institutions. From 1868, the Thomasson family paid for the building and endowment of a school for the blind and deaf and a remedial speech training centre, as well as a series of nursery schools for the children of working mothers.[63] In 1913, a subscription had raised £15,000 for a new nursing home at the infirmary, while John Haslam used £30,000 from the sale of his firm in 1920 to refurbish the nursing home and provide better training facilities for nursing staff. His gift followed on from that of his sister-in-law, Mary Haslam, with whose obituary we started this book, who in 1908 had given a house and grounds to the town for the treatment of tuberculosis patients and met the full costs of equipping and running the institution.[64]

Thirdly, much philanthropic activity was devoted to the moral, physical or spiritual improvement of the poor. Robert Heywood had subscribed to the Mechanics Institute in 1826 (though only on the basis that it offered classes for women), was on its committee, a trustee from 1833 and a president in 1852. When the Institute needed new accommodation in 1857, Heywood led a subscription committee that raised £5,300.[65] The members of the Bank Street Chapel founded a reading room in 1856 specifically designed for working and poor people, while John Hick built fountains in the market square in 1860.[66] In January 1868, Dr and Mrs Chadwick made a joint donation of £17,000 to fund a series of model dwellings and an orphanage.[67] Mrs Greg, a female poor law guardian, paid for the building of two summer houses for workhouse inmates with tuberculosis in 1897, and between 1888 and 1902 there were 211 individual charitable initiatives launched to improve the moral, physical or spiritual lot of workhouse inmates, orphans and disabled children. Female philanthropists were particularly active organisers of, and contributors to, organizations such as the Poor Children's Toy Fund, the Hospital Work Society, the Nightingale Fund, and the Bolton District Nursing Association.[68]

Finally, those who formed the philanthropic core of Bolton seem to have been keen to contribute to initiatives that improved the long-term environment for the poor. Robert Heywood gave land for the Heywood recreation ground in 1866 and paid for the construction of tennis courts.[69] Charles Darbishire donated a two-acre plot of land in central Bolton for the foundation of a playground in November 1868. Samuel Taylor Chadwick donated £5,000 to the building of a museum in 1870. John Thomasson donated £1,000 to equip it and buy exhibits, following up this action with the donation of the Mere Hall estate to act as the core of a library, art gallery and swimming complex. By 1899 William Lever had offered his estate to the town as a museum and park.[70] Female philanthropists such as Margaret Greg, Martha Bridson and Mary Thompson all gave housing stock to act as a halfway house between the workhouse and the wider community.

In terms of the range of beneficiaries, then, Bolton looks much like other north-western towns such as Manchester, but the relative importance of different beneficiary groups diverges from that seen elsewhere. Thus, while substantial amounts (and substantial numbers of charitable initiatives) were focused on medical care for the sick poor and broadly defined educational purposes – so called preventive charity – cash distributions at times of crisis, expenditure on initiatives to help the able-bodied outdoor poor and initiatives to improve the lives of the indoor poor – subventive charity – were often more important, particularly towards the end of the period considered here.[71] Bolton was thus a complex philanthropic microcosm. Whatever the motivations of individual donors, table 3.1, quantifying the overlapping charitable interests of Bolton union philanthropists, suggests that there really was a philanthropic spirit in the town, though one based around perhaps no more than 350 individuals and family groupings. The majority of those who contributed to one cause during the period 1873–1910 contributed to at least one other, and a very significant 19 per cent of traceable donors contributed to five or more causes at the same time. An even more significant 41 per cent of those who donated did so to at least five causes over their traceable life-cycle.[72] Such observations do, of course, raise the question of how we should characterize and locate philanthropic endeavour on the part of this core of Bolton men and women, and it is to this question that we now turn.

Table 3.1 The concentration of philanthropic effort in Bolton, 1873–1910

Number of donors	Philanthropic causes	Percentage of donors
138	1 cause only	38
65	2 causes	18
55	3 causes	15
40	4 causes	11
70	5 causes	19

Source: Based upon a comprehensive analysis of all surviving subscription lists, diaries, newspaper records and official reports for Bolton union between 1873 and 1910. All figures rounded up. Total sample size 368.

Activism and Public Service in Bolton

Initially, it is important to acknowledge that in Bolton, as elsewhere in the country, philanthropic giving was inextricably tied up with social activism and public service. Certainly by the 1860s we see in Bolton the rise of the triumvirate of philanthropic voluntarism, public service and civic pride which were, albeit slowly, creating the notion of a Bolton citizenship.[73] Biographies of the male elite in the town provide ample evidence of this. William Haslam, prominent cotton manufacturer, was a town councillor, an elected member of the Bolton School Board from 1879, poor law guardian and trustee of the Hulton Charity. His brothers, Joseph and John, were both town councillors, as well as trustees of the Bolton Institute for the Blind and members of the management board of the Queen Street Mission. John P. Haslam, William's uncle, was a justice of the peace, poor law guardian and president of the Bolton Home Visiting Society.[74] Robert Heywood was founder member of the Bolton Fund for Relief of the Poor, the Widows Fund, and Mechanics Institute, a trustee of Great Bolton, the Hulton Charity, Bolton British School, justice of the peace, and twice mayor of Bolton.[75] At his death in 1868, the *Bolton Chronicle* celebrated his devotion to public service and concluded that, "to give a detailed biography of such a life would be to write the local history of our time".[76]

Other names will be familiar from the foregoing discussion: the philanthropic and public service ethos of William Lever and John Thomasson, for instance, were recognized in November 1902 when they were given the Freedom of the Borough of Bolton. While the public service of such men was not entirely altruistic – enduring political divisions in Bolton were played out in conflicts over control of bodies such as the Mechanics Institute, for instance – by the later nineteenth century the major philanthropic families were united by interests of business, kinship, religion or friendship.[77] The men of these families played, and continued to play in the later nineteenth century, a leading political and public service role. They had philanthropic careers, campaigned on multiple social and moral issues, and were engaged in the building of civic pride and concepts of citizenship.

It would be wrong, however, to confine our discussion of philanthropy, public service and citizenship only, or perhaps even mainly, to men. Middle-class women in Bolton were not limited to the passive philanthropic giving that we saw in the last section (pp. 66–8), though they did give substantially. Rather, from the end of the eighteenth century they had begun to develop traditions of, and competencies in, active philanthropy. Maria Ainsworth, for instance, was on the organizing committee of the 1798 charity collection to "relieve the suffering of the poor of Bolton in the late trade depression", and five local women were amongst the sixteen volunteers who located poor families and distributed aid in cash and kind.[78] The Bolton Royal Infirmary was, as we have seen, heavily dependent upon women who were active in church societies, schools, political associations and, later, as female poor law guardians, for fundraising, subscriptions and benefactions. As elsewhere, female volunteers were at the heart of the home visiting movement in Bolton.[79] Women also provided the administrative support for charitable initiatives such as the Unitarian Charity Drive of 1851.[80]

In turn, active philanthropy melded subtly into campaigning and public service. The most prominent female philanthropists formed the Bolton Ladies Workhouse Visiting Committee (BLWVC) in 1893, and five women were elected to stand as poor law guardians in the year 1895/96. Some of these women, as well as many older female philanthropists who did not get involved in public service, were also active campaigners on social, moral and political issues. The Ladies Charity for the Relief of Poor Lying-In Women, for instance, had been founded in 1798. By 1838 it was obtaining subscriptions from women across the socio-political spectrum, and campaigning for the improvement of maternity services.[81] Hannah Ormrod was a trustee of the Bolton Society for the Abolition of Slavery and was a signatory to three petitions to parliament by the Society.[82] Elizabeth Harwood was vice-president of the Bolton Evangelical Revival Committee; Mary Haslam, Martha Moran and Sarah Reddish were committee members for the Bolton Distress Committee between 1905 and 1912; Emmeline Hoskins was president of the Bolton Adult Deaf and Dumb Society; Margaret Mothersole was secretary to the Bolton Poor

Protection Society.[83] Most of these women had been involved in the campaign against prostitution in Bolton, and many of them would go on to have involvement in the highly active women's suffrage movement in the town during the first decade of the twentieth century.[84] These sorts of activities have, of course, also been identified in broad-brush surveys of other places, but they do suggest a rich culture of female activism and public service by women in Bolton.

However, a listing of this sort gives only the very briefest hint of the complex dynamics and meaning of women's philanthropic, campaigning and public service activities, and the place of such activities in their personal development. Four aspects of the underlying picture are worth exploring further.[85] *First*, the activities of Bolton women must be understood against the backdrop of rich family traditions and networks of philanthropy, activism and public service. When they gave to philanthropic causes, they usually did so in conjunction with other male and female members of the extended family. The same is true of other towns, but what is also noticeable about Bolton is the frequency with which certain men appeared as founding patrons, chairmen and major movers in Bolton philanthropic ventures and, in turn, the frequency with which women who were major public campaigners and activists came from the same families. George Barlow was one of the founders of the Bolton dispensary, a councillor and justice of the peace. His wife had been a prominent campaigner against slavery, had written addresses against the corn laws and was a founder of the Queen Street Mission and Children's Aid Society.[86] William and John Haslam were major philanthropic figures in late nineteenth-century Bolton, as we saw above, while Mary Haslam was organizer of the BLWVC, a poor law guardian and suffrage campaigner. Dr Mothersole was a trustee of Bolton Infirmary, the Mechanics Institute and president of the Bolton Improvement Trust. His wife was a poor law guardian, secretary to the Blind Welfare Association, and suffrage campaigner.[87] Other examples abound, but in broad terms it is clear that all of the most prominent female activists in Bolton came out of a rich family tradition of philanthropy and public service. Of course, much of the recent feminist literature has also traced an overlap between the philanthropic, campaigning and public service interests of men and women drawn from long-established family networks of this kind, but in Bolton we see the inter-relationships played out particularly strongly.[88]

Secondly, it is clear that women founded or ran, rather than simply administered and contributed to, campaigning, philanthropic and volunterist organizations in Bolton. They played a leading, rather than a lagging role. Some of their ventures, the Ladies Sewing School or the Toy Fund, for instance, were modest and ad hoc affairs.[89] Others were much more substantial and important. The Ladies Charity for Poor Lying-In Women, encountered earlier, was founded by the wives and daughters of the Bolling, Blair and Ainsworth families with the aim of being "not only the means of temporal and transitory relief, but also of permanent good, of moral and religious advantage both to rich and poor". Whether we regard this sort of ideology positively or negatively, this was a charity organized and run by women (the constitution specified a committee of ten, six of them women) and also financed by them. In 1837, for instance, 54 women contributed £54 to the funds of the charity.[90] The Queen Street Mission was similarly dominated by women philanthropists and campaigners. The executive committee of twelve "are prominent members of the various branches of the Christian Church", with the balance in favour of women trustees throughout the life of the Mission. Helping over 1,000 children per year with education, clothing or emigration, most of the volunteers and all of the paid inspectors were women.[91] Meanwhile, women were also elected as trustees to the Bolton Improvement Trust, which aimed to improve housing standards in the town. Mary Haslam, Margaret Greg, Hannah Barlow and Ellen Reid were all elected between 1880 and 1893. This group of women were in turn to form their own campaigning orga-nizations, including the Bolton Women's Local Government Association (BWLGA), The Association for the Return of Women Poor Law Guardians (ARWPLG), the Bolton Women's Suffrage Association (BWSA), The Bolton Sanitary Society, the Bolton Women Ratepayers Association, and the Women Citizens Association (WCA), as well as women's political organizations within the local Liberal and Conservative parties. Whether such multiple overlapping membership indicates a self-conscious feminist movement is a question to which we return in CHAPTER SEVEN, but for now it is clear that philanthropy and philanthropic activism really was just one part of a complex personal journey. While other surveys have highlighted a proliferation of societies and associations in the later nineteenth century, only when faced with a micro-study such as this can we really grasp what such a proliferation must have meant for the substantial public prominence of the core group of women involved.

Meanwhile, a *third* underlying observation is that Bolton women and men usually campaigned together on the same issues. To some extent this is an inevitable consequence of the centrality of philanthropy and campaigning based upon family connections. Indeed, many of the men from these philanthropic activist networks were also prevailed upon to become the nominal heads of women's voluntary, charitable and campaigning organizations. Thus, the BWLGA was founded in 1897. Its vice-president's included John Heywood and George Harwood MP, respectively brother and uncle to Mary Haslam, the founder of the BWLGA. The general committee, responsible for campaigning, election management and fundraising, included both John and J. P. Haslam, in-laws to Mary Haslam.[92] Unrelated women and men also campaigned together on a variety of issues, including slavery,[93] temperance and the exploitation of children and animals. It is in the later nineteenth century, however, that the composition of campaigning organizations becomes most intriguing. Thus, the Infant Life Protection Society was formed by Thomas Barlow in 1889, and its director was his wife Jane. The committee consisted of the prominent female philanthropists and Liberal women activists Margaret Greg, Susannah Swan and Mary Haslam, alongside Dr Mothersole (whose wife was to become a prominent suffrage campaigner) and the Conservatives John Scowcroft, William Bolling and Henry Ashworth. Organized to campaign for better housing and nutrition standards and the reform of local sanitation, the committee brought together men and women who, on issues such as suffrage or the place of women in local government, would otherwise be implacably opposed. The Bolton Committee for the Reclamation of Unfortunate Women also brought campaigning and philanthropic women and men together. Founded in January 1867, "the town clerk apologised for the absence of Mr William Haslam, who he said thoroughly approved of the object of the meeting and would willingly contribute to any fund which it might be thought desirable to raise". Despite his absence, the Haslam family, women and men, were well represented. So were the Heywood, Dakin, Hulton and Scowcroft families. An advertisement for subscriptions was placed in April 1867 and it was noted that "Mrs Dakin and Mrs Shearon are already going amongst these women".[94]

The issues of women and local government or suffrage brought women and men most closely together in campaigning terms. The ARWPLG was perhaps the most effective campaigning organization in nineteenth and twentieth-century Bolton. It was a forum for women who were active campaigners, those who played a more passive philanthropic role, and those with little experience of either sphere. It also brought together middle and working-class activists. Alongside them, both in terms of general membership and inclusion in the organizing committee, we find men such as William and John Haslam who had been active campaigners and philanthropists in their own right and were proven supporters of women's activism. However, its founder, Mary Haslam, spread the membership and organisation net wide, drawing in Conservative and Liberal clergy, justices of the peace, prominent local manufacturers and, most importantly of all members of the local lower middling sort and Conservative manufacturing interests.

CHAPTER FOUR traces the involvement of this sort of membership in the successful campaign to elect female poor law guardians in the 1890s, and the great skill of Mary Haslam and the other female activists who underpinned the ARWLPG was to keep this constituency on board. On 5 April 1907, the ARWPLG received a motion to amend its rationale "for the return of women on all public bodies for which they are or shall be eligible and be known as the Women's Local Government Association". On 8 July the annual meeting determined that "the time had come when the association should identify itself with the claim of women to serve on public bodies in general".[95] The ARWPLG continued to be a jointly male and female campaigning group even after this resolution. Meanwhile, some of those involved with the ARWPLG were also members of the BWSA, founded by Mary and Mildred Haslam. Like the ARWPLG, this organization brought together male and female poor law guardians, male and female philanthropists and men and women of widely divergent political persuasions to mount a sustained local campaign for the recognition of the citizenship of women through political emancipation.[96] The overlap was by no means complete, however, since some men and women who supported local government involvement were anti-suffrage. This theme is taken up in CHAPTER SEVEN.

It would be easy to move from these observations to an assumption that there was a linear organic progression from philanthropic work through to public service. However, a *final* observation is that there was a distinct trajectory to the volume of women's philanthropic activism and public service. There was a significant upswing in the number of initiatives and the size of the philanthropic or campaigning cohorts after 1880. This remains true even if we control for the working-class women who joined the local government movement and dominated organisations such as the Bolton Women's Co-operative Guild (WCG) from the later 1890s.[97] Moreover, within this trajectory there was a distinct change from philanthropic to campaigning work from the mid-1880s, with the BLWVC, considered further below, a key crossover point between the two forms of public involvement. On the face of it, philanthropic participation was impressive. In total the number of people involved in traceable philanthropic and campaigning activities in Bolton from 1860 to 1914 numbers at least 1300. As elsewhere, however, and for men and women, activism, public service and philanthropy in the town was driven by a small core of people with multiple and overlapping activities. Amongst men this core included Liberals and Conservatives, manufacturers and tradesmen, nonconformists and Anglicans, and amounted to no more than 250 people for the whole period 1860–1914. While philanthropic donations and activities were relatively widespread amongst middle-class women in

Bolton, as we have seen, those who combined such causes with campaigning and public service were smaller in number. Indeed, for the period 1860 to 1914 less than 100 individuals drove the women's movement in the town. Inevitably, this meant that activists were engaged in many more overlapping activities than their male counterparts, a theme to which we return in CHAPTER SEVEN. It would be easy to argue that these women could undertake such public involvement by virtue of the fact that they were able to draw upon family wealth and did not have businesses to manage. Indeed, such views have become a commonplace of the literature.[98] For Bolton this perspectives is misleading, not least because many of the most prominent male activists in Bolton had either sold their businesses or installed managers or partners to give them more time for philanthropic work and civic duties. In Bolton there was a quantitative and qualitative difference between the levels of engagement of male and female activists, and one based upon female choice rather than male-enabled opportunity. The truth of this claim is nowhere demonstrated better than in the foreword to the *Survey of the Bolton Women Citizens Association*. This noted, "When an inquirer asked a public man 'What does the Bolton Women Citizens Association do?' he received the candid and remarkably truthful reply 'They meddle in everything'".[99] In this sense, we probably need to know much more about some of the female activists in Bolton, an issue to which we now turn.

Bolton Women Activists: Some Brief Personal Histories[100]

The most important activist in Bolton, judged by the scale of her philanthropic activity, the numbers of campaigns and charities that she was involved with or, in retrospect, the opinion of local newspapers, was Mary Haslam, with whose obituary we began this book. She had been born into the Heywood family, the middle of three children, on 11 August 1851. Brief autobiographical notes, written on the occasion of her sixtieth birthday (and reproduced in CHAPTER EIGHT) remind us that her grounding in activism, philanthropy and public service began early.[101] Thus "My feeling towards my brother John was chiefly one of intellectual interest as he grew up and we had in common a large amount of public interest, so sympathy of tastes formed the bond between us." This is hardly surprising, for "My father was constantly at meetings of either the Town Council or some other public body on which he served", and

My father used to read aloud to my mother every morning the newspaper, the news and leading articles, and if we children stayed in the room, strict silence had to be observed. This was also the case when friends visited our parents and I think this blending together of young and old, and the former hearing the grown ups conversation, lead to a taste in public questions, and an interest in the latter which developed in later years.

However, as a girl it was the arrival of the Bolton philanthropic, civic and political elite at her father's door that made a real impact on her future life. Haslam notes that "my father's public position made his house the centre of much of the life and thought of the Town and there was constantly a guest staying the night, or a small party to meet someone". We shall see that many of the family contacts made at this point were to underpin Mary Haslam's strategy in extending her influence in public life during the later nineteenth century.

But this was also a lonely life, no doubt prompting the self-reliance, resourcefulness and stamina that we see demonstrated later in her public activities "I had few friends, and those of my parents who visited us, seem elderly as I look back. My father was more grandfather than father to me, as he married late in life, and my sweet mother seems to have obliterated nursery out of consideration for him".[102] School in her early teens brought more formative influences. Haslam went to school in Bolton along with girls from other members of the Bolton elite, such as Margaret Greg and Hannah Barlow, almost all of whom were later to become active in public life, campaigning and philanthropic work. However, it was her teacher who was to have a real formative influence:

> Miss Carbritt, who kept the school, was a large minded, large hearted woman . . . 'A law to yourself' was one of her favourite phrases . . . Our minds became open, and the habit of judging anything on its own merits strengthened our powers of reasoning and observation . . . Whatever I have done later in public work, or in the principles which underlie it, I owe to her who was the inspiration of my youth.

Importantly, though, she adds "(leaving aside the more direct influence of the [married and girlhood] home.)" Her father appears particularly influential. After his death when she was 17, Haslam notes "for years I could not listen to the begging tale of any old man, willingly finding pennies to give him, just because it was age and reminded me of my father." [103] Subsequently, her schooling resumed, but this time in London and without sympathetic teachers. At Hampstead School, however, she learnt the useful skill of subverting accepted rules, a theme to which we will return in later chapters and "Consequently the evening before I left I was taken into Mrs Lalois private room and told that I should regret all my life the way I had set myself in opposition to all they had tried to do for me". The obituary with which we began CHAPTER ONE suggests otherwise!

Mary Heywood married Robert Haslam the year after she left school, aged 19. While early marriage was relatively common in Bolton and for female activists more generally,[104] the key point about this marriage was that it linked together two of the most wealthy, philanthropic, engaged and radical Unitarian families in Bolton, both with rich traditions of public service.[105] During the period between her marriage and the mid-1880s, Haslam was active in all sorts of philanthropic and campaigning work. However, it was the death of her six-year-old daughter, Muriel, in 1878, rather than any public service, citizenship or feminist agenda that sparked her initial thrust into public life. After a long period of mourning for her daughter, Haslam notes that she was determined that "nothing sad or wrong should go into her memory, and so I would do what I could to help to reduce the sum total of sorrow in the world. This was the key to the different bits of public work that afterwards became of so much interest in my life."[106] Those public works had a profound impact and explain much of the increase in activism, philanthropic work and campaigning in later nineteenth-century Bolton.

By the time Mary Haslam wrote more notes on the occasion of her sixty-sixth birthday in 1917, her one remaining daughter (Mildred) was dead, "My husband too and I am very lonely. I miss the faithful companion of 45 years, always kind in unmeasured degree to me and to all others, always putting himself in the background and encouraging me to lead and do what I wanted. As I look back I see now how impatient I was and how little tolerant. I was keen and active and wanted to do so much".[107] It is at this point that we see the first seeds of self-doubt emerge:

> My children are one and all most sweet and dear, and I am very conscious of what they are to me, but I don't want to live to be a burden and a constant thought to them. And I don't feel ready to be put on one side yet, but I want to find and go on with some of the things I have cared about so long – but – it just is all so difficult that I doubt and wonder.

Go on she did, however, and the biographer of her father noted that she "gave a lifetime of public service, particularly as the first woman guardian in Bolton, and at the time of her death it had been proposed that she should be made a freeman of the borough".[108] At the time she wrote in 1917, Mary Haslam had guided the suffrage and women's local government movement, come to dominate the board of guardians and proved herself one of the most active and successful philanthropists in the north-west.

We know less about the detailed lives, motivations and backgrounds of the other middle and working-class women who became active in phil-anthropy, campaigning and public service in the late Victorian and early Edwardian period. Unsurprisingly, Mildred Haslam followed her mother. Before her premature death, she had served as the honorary secretary of the BWSA and was acknowledged in their report of 1910 as "so much the moving spirit of our organisation". She was also secretary to the Bolton Mother and Child Welfare Association.[109] Other women were also promi-nent players. Margaret Barnes was the daughter of a Conservative mining family, donor or organizer to 47 traceable local charitable initiatives, served seventeen years as a poor law guardian and three terms as chair of the board, was second president of the WCA, founder of the Junior WCA, and was awarded an OBE.[110] While her motives for becoming involved in philanthropic and public service activities are unclear, Barnes was a staunch supporter of suffrage agitation and had clear feminist credentials by the early twentieth century. Richenda Ashworth came from the parish of Turton. Married into the prominent Quaker and manufacturing Ashworth family, her religious beliefs pushed Ashworth heavily into the philanthropic sphere and at the time of her death in 1898 she "was promi-nently identified with many local charitable causes, but was perhaps best known as one of the most active Lady Guardians on the Bolton Board". She was secretary for the National Home Reading Union, committee member of the Lancashire Needlework Guild, a member of the manage-ment committee of the Blair Hospital, Trustee of the Popplewell Charity and committee member of the Bolton Ladies Lying-in Charity.[111]

Alice Collinge was a working-class poet and suffrage campaigner who "made many political speeches in Bolton, sometimes helped by the dignity of a platform, but more often with only the doubtful aid of an orange box". Of Scottish origin, she trained as a teacher near Bolton, "But I hasten to pay my tribute to Bolton, for my real education began there. Coming into contact with the virile Labour church, social proclivities which had been lying dormant, wakened and the Socialism of that day claimed me". Then "the suffrage movement proved an outlet for other social activities, and for the time being, I surrendered almost everything to further the Cause". She was active in the Women's Textile Society and campaigned on suffrage and local government issues with prominent middle-class feminists, such as Mary and Mildred Haslam, Annie Barlow and Jane Scowcroft. Driven by the desire for wider political and social reform, she suggests at the end of her brief autobiographical notes "What days those were, standing in the market places lit up by pitch torches, and braving all kinds of weather. How we all entered heart and soul into the fray . . . I would not have missed those days for all the gold in Golconda".[112] Sarah Reddish, meanwhile, left school at eleven years old to work in the mid-Victorian Bolton cotton mills. Part of a generation of young women "dissatisfied with their work and its humiliating pay and conditions" she became a working-class radical suffragist, committee member of The Lancashire and Cheshire Women Textile and Other Workers Representation Committee, contributor to the *Labour Gazette*, member and organiser of the Women's Trade Union League, and president of the WCG in 1897. Rooted in a socialist-feminist critique of social, gender and class relations, Reddish became a Bolton guardian in 1905, and a member of the Bolton School Board, ARWPLG, BWLGA, WCA, and BWSA. She was also on the Bolton Distress Committee between 1905 and 1912, establishing a permanent labour exchange in the town in 1908 and driving a census of the unemployed in April 1909.[113]

We could go on with these thumbnail sketches of prominent female activists in the town. Broadly, we have done enough to suggest that Bolton possessed a small core of women whose philanthropic, public service and campaigning activities were considerable by any local standards. However, these observations tell us little about the collective and conscious identity of such women, and thus about the function and proper characterization of philanthropic and public service work. In political and religious terms, there was little cohesiveness. The Haslam's were Liberal Unitarians, the Greg's were Anglican Conservatives, while Mary Ann Howard came from a Methodist and apolitical background. Richenda Ashworth was a Quaker, while Alice Collinge seems to have had no active religious belief. Nor was there a unity of experience in terms of philanthropy, public service and campaigning activism. While Hannah Bolling in the 1840s and 1850s and Mary Haslam from the 1880s participated in almost all campaigns and philanthropic ventures and were active in public service, the rest of the core group of Bolton women made more directed, if still substantial, contributions to public life. Thus 17 women had either stood for, or been elected to, the board of guardians by 1902, but of these only 14 were also active in the suffrage movement, and only nine had any wider active political role in the locality. The group were certainly unified by family connections. Richenda Ashworth and Margaret Waddington were related by marriage; Marian Orrell and Alice Caldwell were sisters, while Mary Ann Howard was a cousin to the Haslam family. However, evidence for the friendship networks amongst women activists that have become a commonplace of the feminist literature is ambiguous.[114] On the positive side, when Richenda Ashworth was drowned on holiday in 1898, the female guardians sent a note to her husband mourning the loss of a friend as well as a colleague and respected guardian.[115] Moreover, Mary Haslam opened up her house to parties in order to sway people who might influence policy on issues of social welfare or suffrage, organizing such events with fellow female activists.[116] There was also an annual social calendar that brought women together in both private and public capacities. Garden parties, parades, fairs, official openings, meetings of boards of trustees and, by no means least, the social events consequent upon their work in the poor law system, must have brought groups of women activists together as often as once per week in some months, irrespective of their private activities and networks.

This said, I have been able to find little evidence, either in personal records or newspaper coverage, that these women formed a solid group of friends. As well as being divided upon religious, political, kinship and residential lines (many women activists came from communities outside Bolton itself), the women were also split in terms of socio-economic status. Mary Heywood was the daughter of a major cotton manufacturer, while her husband William Haslam was also prominent in the textile trades and a major economic force in the town. She was wealthy in her own right and by virtue of the activities of her husband and family. Hananh Bolling was likewise of a high social and economic standing. Other women were the wives and daughters of doctors, tradesmen, lawyers, minor bleachers, small merchants and even shopkeepers, and had little economic independence. How far we should regard such divisions as a fracture in the core group of women is uncertain. Artisanal, professional and retail classes in Bolton had, since the early nineteenth century disputes with the Tories over control of the instruments of local government, allied themselves with Liberal manufacturers and merchants, so it should be no surprise to see women of the same classes sharing a campaigning, philanthropic and public service platform. Moreover, the rise of female working-class activists also seems to have been accommodated remarkably easily in this core group. While working-class women constituted the majority of those on the committee of the WCG, Mrs Mothersall, Mrs Howarth and Mrs Hargreaves, also members of the committee, were middle-class poor law guardians or had stood for elected office in this capacity.[117] The signals about the group cohesiveness of Bolton women activists, philanthropists and public servants are thus mixed.

The same problems emerge when we shift our attention to the question of whether the group were in an ideological sense, self-conscious. Different groups of women had very different stances when it came to the purpose and conduct of philanthropy, public service and campaigning. The women of the Conservative Bolling family founded and were mainly involved in philanthropic and public service work that involved moral reform and visiting. Mrs Mothersole, from a Liberal background, was also active in this sort of work. Mary Haslam, Richenda Ashworth and Marianne Orrell contributed to such causes but concentrated their campaigning energies on efforts to influence policy makers. The latter group were frustrated by their lack of local power and tried to use philanthropic work as a launchpad for wider political and local government roles. However, the women who formed the Conservative Primrose League refused to support such a departure, though they campaigned with Haslam and others for Infant Life Protection. That said, Hannah Barlow, from a staunchly Conservative and Anglican background, was an active member of the group of women seeking election to poor law guardianship and a campaigner for women's suffrage. Some of those who supported the BLWVC refused to be involved in the campaign for the election of women guardians, but some of them were active in the suffrage movement ten years later. Mary Haslam, the most active of Bolton women, was not a member of the campaign for the reform of married women's property laws. The motivations of the core group of women for public and philanthropic involvement were also apparently diverse. Mary Haslam got involved, as we have seen, to lift her depression after the death of her daughter. Margaret Greg became involved in public work because of her commitment to philanthropic work, while Richenda Ashworth appears to have had a religious motivation. Mrs Mothersole became involved because of the work of her husband as a mill doctor. Sarah Reddish and Alice Collinge, the most prominent of the working-class radicals of the 1890s, clearly had a feminist agenda and motivation, as well as one tempered by class. We return to these issues in CHAPTER SEVEN.

The Bolton women's and philanthropic movements were thus multilayered, organic and in some ways fractured. While the most nuanced of the recent literature has made the same point, more studies of the sort conducted here are clearly needed to explore and interpret these nuances.[118] For now, our brief biographies of Bolton activists have begun to suggest that philanthropy, public service, campaigning activism and perhaps feminism were forcefully brought together in Bolton from the 1880s. The formation of the BLWVC both exemplified and facilitated this overlap, and it is to this organization that we turn finally.

Women and Welfare: The BLWVC

Visiting institutions was a key element of the nineteenth-century philanthropic strategy for both men and women.[119] Bolton guardians had established the first (all male) workhouse visiting society in 1842 but its membership and commitment waned over time. This left a significant gap in the market for public service by women, especially in light of the fact that the WVS had, as we saw in CHAPTER ONE, been established in 1858 as an organisation aiming to institute a "voluntary system of visiting, especially by ladies, under the sanction of the guardians and chaplains", to improve the moral, educational and physical condition of indoor paupers.[120]

Bolton women took up this invitation, under the leadership of Mary Haslam, with the formation of the active and influential BLWVC in 1893. The initial complement of volunteers included women drawn from the Greg, Ashworth, Haslam, Scowcroft and Barlow families, all of them experienced campaigners, philanthropists and public servants. Mary Haslam is particularly important in this context because she kept a detailed working diary during her time as an organizer of the BLWVC and her subsequent work as a poor law guardian, the only diary of its kind known to exist.[121] However, her experiences do much more than simply add another personality to the small collection of women reformers who are so familiar to us. Rather, the story of her involvement in workhouse visiting, the guardian elections of 1894/95, and her subsequent activity on the union board allows us to question broad generalizations about the effectiveness of women in local government, stagnation and decay in the late nineteenth-century poor law, and the role of poor law work in the individual and collective feminist journey, the themes that frame this book.[122]

As a starting point, it is important to understand that while women organizing visiting committees in other areas appear to have encountered considerable and persistent hostility from guardians – in Sussex, unions imposed a "prescribed list of subjects on which they had to report to the guardians"[123] – women seeking to use the BLWVC to make a transition from philanthropic work to public service seem to have encountered remarkably little opposition. A motion to establish the BLWVC was put before the board on 8 February 1893 with the names of nine women activists appended. Hannah Barlow, who we encountered earlier, had agreed to "act if the regulations were not too narrow", testimony to the active engagement of female philanthropists and campaigners with this scheme. The BLWVC was formally established on 22 March 1893, reporting to the workhouse sub-committee. Its establishment was openly welcomed by the newspapers and even by many male guardians.[124] The early history of the committee can be traced through newspapers and the minutes of the board of guardians, and these suggest that while the BLWVC and the guardians clashed when the visitors were seen to have overrun their remit and begun commenting on salaries, in general the two bodies worked well together. Indeed, the visiting committee was given control over boarding out of children by April 1894 and was solely responsible for responding to government initiatives in this area.[125] During the most active phase of the organization in the run up to the 1894/95 elections to the board of guardians, the working diary of Mary Haslam provides a key insight into the role, achievements and strategies of women in the development of policy in Bolton union.[126] It suggests, as we shall see in later chapters, that the work of female workhouse visitors and their subsequent work on the board of guardians must be regarded as a seamless and self-reinforcing web.[127]

The diary shows that some of the work of the BLWVC was recognizably "domestic housekeeping" of the sort explored in much of the historiographical literature. For instance, the committee was active in brightening the specialist units of the workhouse, such as the maternity wards, in regularly re-designating room usage to prevent boredom, putting up pictures, and in questioning and changing the dress codes of children and the old. Less familiar in the current literature is the way in which these women sold reform to the male guardians and to workhouse staff on more fundamental care issues. In July 1894, for instance, the BLWVC *recommend* to the guardians that they provide dedicated birthing rooms, as well as convalescent beds for recuperating mothers. The expenditure was accepted and the work completed by 15 August. With a paid midwife already in place, this concern with the issue of maternity placed Bolton at the forefront of more enlightened practice at the national level, as we saw in CHAPTER TWO.[128] Other important interventions should also be noted. In September 1893 the committee put forward a plan for the classification of mental patients in the absence of adequate county asylums. This plan was accepted without debate. In November 1893 the BLWVC *suggested* a new policy whereby the task mistress was authorized to reward those who volunteered to give their time and work in the laundry, suggesting the allocation of £5–£7 worth of stores for this purpose. By January 1894 the women of the BLWVC had got the guardians to agree to the establishment of further isolation wards in the hospital, segregating consumptives from the rest of the sick. This created a system which, two years later, was to be commended by the inspectors from the LGB. Later in the same year, they introduced a scheme whereby young women leaving the workhouse were offered a halfway house, a base to re-establish work and friendship groups, before once more attempting to make their own way in the town, in turn testimony to the way in which women were active in creating a seamless philanthropic web between private charity, organized charity and the poor law.

Yet, perhaps more important than the ideas and policies of the BLWVC themselves is the fact that they excited so little conflict with workhouse staff or male guardians. Three important tactical aspects of the organization appear to have been important in defusing the potential conflict that the historiography suggests ought to have emerged. *First*, the BLWVC was chaired by John Haslam, Mary's brother-in-law and a prominent philanthropist and cotton spinner. This effectively pitted a major male rate-payer against minor male rate-payers in the negotiation of authority over the workhouse. However, it would be wrong to imply from this that female involvement in public life had to be underscored by male sanctioning. John Haslam was a figurehead and, as we shall see, Mary Haslam was sufficiently skilled at manipulating the male guardians not to require his practical support. *Second*, most of the reforms suggested and achieved were undertaken after extensive consultation with workhouse staff on the one hand, and individual male guardians on the other. Indeed, ideas on rewards for help in the laundry and building work in the insane wards originated with workhouse staff themselves. It is notable that in November 1894 one of the senior nurses felt able to remark to Mary Haslam that, "the place was different and they all felt it. She wished it was 'our own ladies' who were candidates for the poor law guardian."[129] This positive and even affectionate attitude apparently contrasts with the reception given to such women by workhouse staff elsewhere.[130] A management style of co-operation and conciliation thus enabled the women of BLWVC to traverse potential hostility and dress up potentially radical changes in the clothes of consensus. *Finally*, it is important to understand the language that marked communication between the BLWVC and guardians. Their yearly report of May 1894, for instance, talked of the *necessity* of a nursing superintendent, a resident doctor (in which Bolton lagged behind other unions) and more paid labour in the workhouse; their *suggestion* that one cottage home be devoted to sick children, and of their *consideration* that reports suggesting the cook was idle and the doctor a drunk were worrying.

Reading meaning into language is of course fraught with difficulty, but this language and the strategy that underpins it appears so often in the working diary that we can and should analyze it. Thus, where they could call on precedents elsewhere (which they were active in uncovering) the women of the BLWVC were forceful in their recommendations of *necessities* to the male guardians. By the following year all of their necessities were in place. Where they wanted to achieve something for which there was less precedent, they offered *suggestions*. Where they dealt with an area where the seat of power was ambivalent (the employment of officers, for instance) they offered an opinion or *consideration*. This exposition of language is worthwhile because its character and range suggests a conscious strategy. Female activists were clearly acutely aware of the battles that could and could not be won, and of the consequences of failure. They were also clearly aware of the fault lines among male guardians themselves, and of the necessity of thorough research on all questions. The language that they employed might be regarded as somehow passive in a modern sense, but in practice the women of the BLWVC used that language, successfully, to implement a quite radical change and reform agenda.[131] Indeed, these were principles that were to underpin the campaign of the BLWVC in the board of guardians election of 1894/95, explored in the following chapter, and the strategies of female poor-law guardians over the next decade, explored in CHAPTER FIVE.

How far women in general, and Bolton women in particular, set out to use the Workhouse Visiting Committees as a Trojan Horse into local government is uncertain. While Levine claims that "it was necessary for women to understand fully the nature of the sphere to which they were denied access before they could begin to challenge the very ideology which posited their exclusion from it"[132], these Bolton women, each with a long history of shaping local philanthropic and local government initiatives and simultaneously involved in a whole range of public activities, had little need to understand the sphere from which they were excluded. Nor did they necessarily need the BLWVC as a vehicle to make inroads into local policy. There is no doubt, as Davidoff suggests, that "pillow talk should not be underestimated".[133] Mary Haslam had the ear of a family with a deep tradition of public service and very considerable wealth and she, along with other women in the same position, no doubt influenced the husbands, brothers, uncles and children who were at the core of male philanthropic, political and campaigning culture in Bolton. However, with their overlapping and complementary charitable, campaigning and other activity, their own wealth and an upbringing saturated with politics, public questions and philanthropy, it would be foolish to believe that these women were not capable in their own right of influencing policy on a range of issues in Bolton. Perhaps the really important function of the BLWVC was to contribute to the citizenship credentials of women ahead of the drive to elect female poor law guardians.

Conclusion

Bolton women philanthropists, campaigners and public servants worked in a complex arena, one that dripped philanthropy and one that, while notionally dominated by men, offered a core of women with very differ-ent socio-economic, personal and ideological backgrounds the chance to excel as donors, workers, organizers and instigators of charitable endeav-our, civic pride and social reform.[134] Their activities were significant from the end of the eighteenth century but really gathered pace from the 1870s and particularly after 1880, when traditional philanthropic work came to be combined with campaigning, public activism and public service on some scale. It is quite true that, as Jalland has shown, women could have a political influence behind the scenes, and that the wives and daughters of prominent local ratepayers and employers could, even if not active in public life, hold considerable sway over those who were.[135] There were women of this sort in Bolton too. However, this detailed survey of phil-anthropy and activism has revealed a much more complex picture than such conclusions allow. Some 50–100 female activists came to have very significant sway over philanthropic resources in the town and to have a direct route to social welfare policy through the BLWVC. Many of them had not started out as feminists, and there is little suggestion, at least before 1885, that they formed a conscious collective movement linked together by friendship and ideology.[136]

By the late nineteenth century, however, the situation was changing, and CHAPTER SEVEN will argue that whatever the motivations of indi-vidual women Bolton did indeed have a vibrant feminist community at this date. The philanthropic experiences of these women were very important. While in an abstract sense we might agree with Levine that English feminism was a conscious collective ideology and requires us to divorce it from the wider ideological concept of philanthropy and the idea that early feminists inevitably cut their teeth in the philanthropic movement first, it is certainly true for Bolton that the core members of the feminist movement did indeed have deep individual and family roots in philanthropy.[137] It may be this background that explains why female activism generated so little hostility in the town.

When Robert Heywood died, the Bolton Chronicle noted that he had "won the hearts of the community". Fifty years later the paper noted with pride the combination of the BWLGA and the BWSA to form the WCA.[138] All three movements were led by Robert Heywood's daughter, Mary Haslam, and at the time of her death, as we have seen, it had been proposed to make her a freeman of the borough. Vigorous feminist cam-paigning did not inevitably mean conflict and unpopularity then, and while it may be true that English feminists "were women who consis-tently and determinedly yoked public to private and private to public",[139] the evidence from Bolton suggests, in line with more recent feminist commentary, that this sort of dichotomy may mask as much as it reveals. Nowhere is this observation more pertinent than in the decision of women to stand for election as poor law guardians, the theme of CHAPTER FOUR.

CHAPTER FOUR

Fighting an Election

The previous chapter traced the way in which philanthropic endeavour merged into campaigning and public service. In this chapter we take up these themes, exploring the political, electoral and campaigning processes that underpinned the presence of a growing number of women on boards of guardians in the late Victorian and early Edwardian period. Focusing once more on Bolton, we will reconstruct the political background of female activists such as Mary Haslam, analyze the first election campaign (1894/95) in which women became practically able to stand as candidates for guardianship in some numbers, and investigate how the lessons of this early electoral work were drawn upon and developed in the 1890s and 1900s.

Context

Late Victorian and early Edwardian women were involved in local political and electoral processes at three levels: as voters, election workers and candidates. Thus, as we saw in CHAPTER ONE, single female householders regained the municipal vote in 1869. By the late 1880s "unmarried women ratepayers represented between 12 and 25 per cent of the municipal electorate".[1] The 1892/93 Local Government Act extended local voting rights to married women who were rate paying occupiers, and while many women remained disenfranchised the female vote could, if fully mobilized, be a potent force in many urban areas by the mid-1890s. Further reform in 1894 gave women the vote in parish and district councils and revised the structure of voting in municipal elections, so that by

1900, as CHAPTER ONE suggested, there were more than a million women voters at local level.[2] Potential voters or not, women were often involved in political campaigning and election work on behalf of men. This might be at an individual level: the wives and daughters of national and local politicians gained significant political experience and influence, for instance.[3] However, much more work was done by groups of women on behalf of local political parties. The 1883 Corrupt Practices Act ended well-established payment schemes that had funded male election workers and "A whole new election machinery began to develop, based on women volunteers".[4] Both the Conservative and Liberal parties moved rapidly to formalize women's practical involvement in local politics. The Conservative Primrose League (PL) was convened in 1883 to "exercise indirect influence on politics and to co-operate with men rather than rival them", being conceived as a campaigning group for national rather than local elections.[5] The Women's Liberal Federation (WLF) was formed in 1886 as a "woman's organization standing apart and sometimes aloof from male Liberalism, insisting on its independence and autonomy",[6] but it was nonetheless an important campaigning organization at local level. Both bodies, argues Rubinstein, gave women experience of organizing, speaking and campaigning and provided a bridge to wider political involvement.[7]

A further way in which women became involved in the political process was through their candidature for election to local bodies. As CHAPTER ONE noted, the first female poor law guardian was elected in 1875. By 1884 the *Westminster Review* was noting that there were thirty-one female poor law guardians "fourteen of these being in London, five in Birmingham, four in Bristol and eight in Edinburgh".[8] It is easy to be beguiled by the success stories, and while there were 136 female guardians by 1892 this amounted to a minute percentage of all the seats potentially available. There were good reasons for this seemingly muted progress: the roll call might include male, and male-governmental, opposition to an extended role for women in public life, the time requirements of the job, the fact that the franchise for guardian elections was tapered to give larger property holders more influence, lack of a campaigning machinery, and concerted attempts to beguile the electorate on the eligibility of female candidates. However, the real practical drag on wider involvement was the usual nineteenth-century Achilles' heel for women (and most men), property. Until 1894, guardian candidates were, as we saw in CHAPTER ONE, obliged to have property with a rateable value of £15 outside London, at once limiting the pool from which potential candidates could be drawn. Hence between the election of the first female guardian and the mid-1890s, women active in the poor law sphere were comparatively rare.

The property requirement fell to £5 in 1893, and was abolished in 1894, so that by 1895, and despite what Hollis, sees as considerable hostility to female candidates, there were 875 female guardians, or just over one per union.[9] By 1899 there were 975 female guardians but 300 boards had none at all, suggesting that there were around three female guardians per union that elected any women at all. Within this framework, successes in London and a handful of big cities such as Manchester dominated the headlines and the perspectives and experiences of those elected in such places have come to dominate the historiography, as we saw in CHAPTER ONE. There were, of course, electoral successes in other areas – School Boards, Vestries and so on – but for the purposes of this book it is the poor law elections that are really significant.[10]

Levine suggests that these figures represent "an impressive showing in so short a period of time", but in practice how to read them is a more difficult matter than such conclusions allow.[11] In order to ascribe success or failure what we really need to know is not the number of women elected but the number who stood for election in the first place. Even better would be the number that were minded to stand but never made it to the end of the election process, since withdrawal of both male and female candidates was common. Such analysis is rarely available, however, given the lack of systematic local studies highlighted in CHAPTER ONE. This said there are several reasons to think that the number of elected female guardians does reflect a significant achievement. Thus, most of those who stood in the initial wave of elections in the mid-1890s had few role models.[12] When they did get such models, later generations of candidates also received from them an inkling of what to expect if they stood and were elected. As we saw in CHAPTER ONE, there is a large body of historiography suggesting such women candidates would have heard little to encourage them. Hence, Hollis suggests that women "were feared to be generous with public money" and that "Countless women guardians wrote to the Women Guardian's Society and the women's press describing the rancorous hostility they met on the board".[13]

Moreover, potential candidates, even those with a considerable local record in campaigning or philanthropic organizations, are seen by most historians as having to construct a carefully crafted linguistic and practical case for active involvement in elected public life before they could ever enter the election process. Their strategies, at least in the later nineteenth century, also had to "manoeuvre within the constraints erected by state representations of femininity and the laws which embodied these".[14] We have seen that such strategies might involve emphasis on the need to extend women's domestic influence to public issues such as the poor and institutions such as schools and workhouses, making a virtue of their enforced domestic rituals of order, provisioning and cleanliness. They could, with some substance, argue that women had a place in public life because they understood how "public issues" affected the home and family.[15] More widely, women seeking election had to wrestle with, and come to individual and collective decisions on, the question of whether they framed their claims to represent and representation in terms of equality or difference. Should they, in other words aspire to elected office on the basis that women and men ought to be equal and had equal capacities, or should they aspire to office because while they might be equal to men, women were also different and had different, often superior, capacities? Feminist biography has revealed this dilemma as a key issue for individual women in the later Victorian period, and some have questioned whether the stance of equality and difference was logically possible.[16]

However individuals resolved this dilemma, it was just one of the angles that had to be considered when making claims to public office. A carefully crafted case might also involve the ability to quote a track record in organized charity, while at the same time acknowledging that this did not automatically give a woman the right to claim a public role.[17] Alternatively women might style themselves as part of what Yeo calls "a moral vanguard", asserting their particular (and sometimes religiously inspired) suitability to reform morals at the same time as they claimed a moral right to involvement in certain aspects of welfare.[18] Or they might use the linguistic and conceptual register of "the family" to assert their claims to expertise when dealing with children or the aged. Indeed, by the late nineteenth century, the language of family had elided with the languages of the labour market and citizenship as "Different groups of women created different versions of a mother-worker-citizen role for themselves in the public sphere" and motherhood itself became an argument for citizenship and thus representation.[19] Thus, Yeo claims that, "at the end of the nineteenth century such was the cult of motherhood that it would have been difficult for women to create public identities and strategies totally outside it".[20] Whether or not we agree with such conclusions, the key point is that the case for female participation in the electoral process had to be made, made consistently and made publicly. For many potential candidates this was likely to be a significant bar to participation.

A further reason to think that even a limited number of electoral successes represented a considerable achievement is that while some potential candidates had already successfully navigated the boundaries between public and private spheres in their previous voluntary or political work, this may not have equipped them for the very public forum of the election hustings. Indeed, the *Westminster Review* felt that the "publicity of the election" for the board of guardians was one of the reasons why more women were not drawn to stand, an idea that has been echoed by modern historians.[21] Even if women were not publicity-shy, many, including those who had been active campaigners on a range of local and regional issues, were often inexperienced public speakers. Some women themselves noted this problem, and it has become a commonplace in the modern literature.[22] More widely, though many women had long and effective experience of canvassing and electoral work by the 1890s, it has become an article of faith that women candidates were poorly equipped in terms of dress,[23] tactics and practical support[24] to enter contested elections. Hence, Hollis believes that, at least in the early days of female candidature for guardian elections, agents, canvassers and lawyers were a vital part of the female armoury, though even this could not stop around one-third of all female candidates dropping out in some areas.[25] Hollis has also suggested that voter apathy, combined with the deal-making of local political interest groups, gave women few realistically winnable openings in most unions.[26] Judged in the round, then, the task of getting elected as a female guardian must have been considerable. Hollis reminds us that "It required women to seek election; mobilize an electorate; gain the endorsement of political parties and the confidence of local interest groups; accept the drudgery of canvassing and committee work, the exposure in the press and on the public platform, and the discipline of accountability".[27] Unsurprisingly, the supply of potential candidates appears to have been a particular problem in some localities, and against this backdrop we ought to regard the steep rise in the absolute numbers of female guardians in the later 1890s as a success.[28]

Expanding on these broad conclusions is difficult. While the potential problems faced by women are clear, and are often given real weight by articles and letters in journals, there have been no published studies of the micro-detail of the election process for individual localities. Notwithstanding the work of Hollis, we know little about how women with years of experience in philanthropy and public service/activism, came together to frame campaigns, forge tactics and develop new linguistic registers in individual localities. We know equally little about the conduct of campaigns, the diversity of male attitudes and the nature of public responses to female candidature.[29] Thus, while Davidoff argued in 1995, that "the courage necessary to act in formal public arenas was formidable and it is encouraging that such efforts are being sought out and recorded", there is clearly still some distance to go.[30] The rest of this chapter presents a detailed case-study of guardian elections in Bolton during the immediate aftermath of the removal of property qualifications for candidature. In keeping with the conclusions of earlier chapters, the analysis will suggest that a core of female activists in Bolton, steeped in philanthropy, volunterism and the language of citizenship planned, organized and executed a highly effective campaign to obtain initial representation on the board of guardians. Thereafter, they honed an electoral machine that was more effective than any male candidate. In Bolton, at least, negative commentary on women and the election process will need to be revised.

Getting Elected: Bolton Traditions

Before we can engage with the election processes of 1894/95, it is important to acknowledge that this contest did not take place in an historical vacuum. Understanding the conduct, language and outcomes of that election is at least in part a function of understanding the conduct of previous elections from which women had been excluded. In this respect it is important to note that the core of the board of guardians, from the inception of the union in 1837 until the mid-1890s, comprised a set of men who were re-elected year after year. John Birley, MA, vicar of All Saints Church Bolton and vice-president of the Bolton Poor Protection Society, was elected continuously between 1839 and 1865. John Haslam (cotton spinner), John Fletcher (paper maker), James Edge (farmer) Daniel Bradshaw (Gentleman), Joseph Dearden (farmer), John Leyland (dyer) and Joseph Walch (land agent) served continuously between 1876 and 1894, while James Elliston (theatre manager) was a guardian for 27 years. The average length of service for a guardian in Bolton between 1870 and 1890 (excluding those who died in post) was eleven years, somewhat above comparable figures for Southport or Wigan unions.[31] Such stability and long service did not, however, mean that positions on the board of guardians went uncontested or unreported. In the decade prior to 1895 the *Bolton Chronicle* reported contests in 47 per cent of available seats. Such contests were vigorous, comprising several election meetings per candidate, published addresses, letters to the local newspapers, direct canvassing, teams to whip out the vote and cartoons and other material ridiculing opponents. Strong use was also made of the support of local political, social and cultural figures. We should not assume that the electorate were always impressed. In December 1890, the *Bolton Chronicle* reported that a recent bye-election had only managed an elector turnout of 25 per cent. While this was one of the lowest ever, it is nonetheless clear that contested elections for male candidates rarely attracted more than 50 per cent of those eligible to vote.[32] We return to this observation and to male tactics in the next section, where we explore the extent to which female candidates were influenced by the local history of election campaigning.

For now, it is also important to recognize that by 1894, Bolton women themselves had long and deep traditions of getting involved in public campaigns and philanthropic work. While this sort of activity did not equate to standing in an election, it is clear that few of the women activists identified in the last chapter would have been without experience of public speaking, campaign organization and committee work. Whether we focus on the letter writing, public appeals and open house meetings employed by the female organizers of the Toy Fund, the public meetings of the early suffragists in the 1880s and 1890s, the public debates fostered by the Bolton Improvement Trust, or the report writing of the Ladies Charity for Lying-in Women, it must be the case that all of the women who were eventually to stand for election in 1894/95 had a range of campaigning experiences to bring to the election process. While the same point has been made in some of the historiographical literature, rarely is it given the emphasis that it demands.[33] We might also do well to remember that many of these women were active in wider regional networks, such as the Committee for the Return of Lady Poor Law Guardians, which gave them opportunities to share campaigning experiences and develop their public speaking credentials. Nor should we forget that women's membership of organizations itself involved elections and public speeches. Mary Haslam notes in her diary that the women of the Bolton Ladies Workhouse Visiting Committee (BLWVC), "Went through 5 or 6 departments. Elected president [herself] and Miss Armitage Secretary of the committee".[34] The subsequent work of this group involved negotiations with male guardians, public speeches, dealing with workhouse staff and report writing, all of the skills that would be needed in the forthcoming elections and post-election strategy.

Women like Mary Haslam were also steeped in the politics of Bolton. As we began to see in CHAPTER THREE, and as becomes clearer in CHAPTER EIGHT, female activists in the town were usually drawn from families of birth or marriage (and usually both) that had rich traditions of male political activism. Mary Haslam was daughter to one of Bolton's premier Liberals and her childhood was suffused with the language, imagery and practice of politics. There can be no doubt that she, and other female activists like her, knew what it was to run a political campaign and could use the linguistic register of Liberalism and citizenship to frame political argument. In similar fashion, Hannah Bolling had experienced a childhood with a father who led the Conservative elite and who had employed her skills in organization for political and religious purposes. Both women were in turn to cut their political teeth, prior to, and alongside their philanthropic and local government work, through local political campaigning.[35]

Liberal women had long individual histories of support for national and local political campaigning. However, formal organization had to wait until the 1890s. Female ward associations had been started in 1890 and 1891, and these were brought together in the summer of 1893 as the basis for the Bolton Women's Liberal Association (BWLA). In October 1894, a large meeting was organised at which the two central aims of the BWLA – to educate women politically and to support Liberals, and Liberal women, at election time – were set out.[36] The names of those who attended and played an active part in the BWLA – Harwood, Hodgkinson, Heywood, Crompton, Cunliffe, Haslam, Mason, Davison, Waddington, and Taylor – will be familiar from earlier chapters as they comprised a large part of the campaigning and philanthropic elite of the town. In turn, this was a very active association, campaigning for male and female candidates in all wards in the 1890s and 1900s. The BWLA hosted the national conference in 1898, and by 1908 it had 600 active members.[37]

The Conservative women's organization, the PL, had a slightly longer history in Bolton, being initially formed in 1887 and reformed in 1889. As with the Liberals, a roll call of prominent members and activists comprises a significant number of late Victorian and early Edwardian female philanthropists and social reformers – Hulton, Thomasson Scowcroft, Hardcastle, Hesketh, Fletcher, Howarth – and some women who were to subsequently stand for election as female guardians. The *Bolton Journal* noted the considerable success in membership terms of the different Bolton Habitations of the PL in 1893, and membership was to remain buoyant into the twentieth century when an official count of 1908 numbered some 1,000 women.[38] For much of the 1880s and early 1890s, the PL had confined itself, as elsewhere, to supporting candidates in national elections. However, the advent of the BWLA changed the focus of female effort. At the annual meeting of the PL in 1894 the Chairman, Dr Mallett, noted the need to respond to the threat of the BWLA, explaining that

> there was a scheme on foot by which primrose dames would be associated with each ward in the borough, so that they might make themselves acquainted with the politics of every individual in the ward, and become a strong working body on behalf of the Conservative cause. He reminded them that the Ladies on the liberal side, particularly in Church ward, were displaying great energy and activity and he thought they might very well take a leaf out of their book (hear, hear).[39]

This change of approach led to two decades of intense female involvement with political and campaigning work in the locality, and in some areas women from the two organizations conducted rancorous campaigns for the municipal and other elections. In Farnworth, for instance, the *Bolton Chronicle* noted "Another of the earnest political fights for which Farnworth has for many years been noted was waged at this District Council election".[40] Such observations give considerable weight to recent feminist reinterpretations of the nature of women's political experience.[41] In Bolton, the women who were to underpin suffrage and poor law guardian campaigns had gained extensive and intensive experience of elections and electioneering. While it is probably true that nothing could prepare a candidate for the pace, cost, intensity and very public nature of an election campaign, as we shall see in the next section the experience of these women was used to good effect in the guardian elections of the 1890s.

1894/95: Anatomy of a Campaign

Unsurprisingly, there has been a tendency in the secondary literature on the election of female guardians to focus either on the initial pioneers or the nature of the electoral experience after the removal of property qualifications. This section too focuses on the latter period, but initially it is important to recognise that successes after 1894 did not simply emerge from thin air. The exact timing of the start of a campaign to actively promote the election of female guardians in Bolton is unclear, but we can learn from the *Bolton Chronicle* that as late as March 1891 candidature for female guardians was rare. Hence

> No department of the public service has suffered so flagrantly from the indifference and apathy of ratepayers . . . It is to be regretted that in Bolton there is not a branch of the Women's Poor Law Guardians Association , having for its object the bringing forward of lady candidates for election to the board. One great difficulty in the way is, of course, the property qualification, but it is quite conceivable that an easy way out might be found by the well-to-do even if there are not Ladies already qualified available. The advantage of having women Guardians must be evident to all who know anything of Poor Law administration. Where they have been tried they have proved a decided success . . . We can imagine nothing better than to have women represented on Board of Guardians, and it may be hoped that another year some action will be taken to supply the deficiency.[42]

The newspaper continued its commentary in April 1891, suggesting that

The public interest taken in the affairs of Bumbledom this year has been less than usual. In only three townships have there been contests, thus testifying once more to the masterly inactivity of the ratepayers as regards poor law matters . . . Monopolies are seldom free from reproach and sometimes positively injurious to the community. Nothing has yet been done in Bolton towards the election of women as Guardians.[43]

Certainly by 1892, the wishes of the newspaper had been met. On 19 March 1892 it reported a meeting to support lady candidates that, "was both unique and interesting, unique from the fact that it was a new departure in electioneering contests and interesting from the fact that it was principally composed of ladies". The men who were there comprised the Liberal and Conservative elite of the town and Mr Fullager spoke of

a brotherly interest in the subject because his sister had been a member of the Leicester Board of Guardians for three years. They didn't want ladies to preponderate on boards of guardians and he cautioned the candidates, if elected, not to expect a bed of roses. They must expect a great deal of unpleasantness for some boards were not quite inclined to welcome them at present. They must not try to boss the show because if they did it would only end in miserable failure. They must go at first to be seen and not heard.[44]

Such advice, as we saw in CHAPTER ONE, echoes the experiences that women are seen to have had by historians, and we return to the accuracy of these views in the following chapter. For now, it is important to note that the newspaper was enthusiastic, suggesting that the guardian election "promises to be more than usually interesting, judging from the list of nominations received up to last night . . . In Little Bolton, six Liberals have been nominated in opposition to six retiring Conservatives, whilst there are two other Conservatives in the field, in addition to two lady candidates. Mr Roocroft, the retiring representative for the urban portion of Halliwell, is also being opposed by a Lady candidate."[45] The editors also noted

The appearance of a larger number of Lady Candidates this year than previously, and the movement has perhaps received an impulse from the formation of a society in this neighbourhood for promoting the return of women Guardians. It is unnecessary any longer to urge the claims of women to a share in the administration of the poor law, for these are now pretty generally admitted. What is necessary is that active steps should be taken to secure the presence of at least one woman (though two or three would be better) upon every Board.[46]

Ultimately the female candidates were to be unsuccessful, but this material illustrates very well *three key points* that help us to frame the activity of the philanthropists and campaigners who were to underpin the drive to improve women's local government representation in Bolton in the 1890s. *First*, the supporters of female candidature for the board of guardians had formed a society, or more accurately a branch of the Society for the Return of Women as Poor Law Guardians, to formalize and organize their campaign work. This should not of course surprise us. As we saw in previous chapters, female philanthropists and campaigners in Bolton had no qualms about joining male organizations, forming branches of national organizations or developing their own societies and associations. Yet, if the formation of the society should not surprise us, it is important because it probably testifies to the considerable political and campaigning experience of the women involved. The formation of the society is also important because its initial membership list indicates that it brought together the talents and drive of the most prominent women in Bolton, from all sides of the political and social spectrum, to bring pressure to bear on the electorate and existing guardians.[47] *Secondly*, the very editorial material itself is testimony to a subtle educational campaign for potential voters, pointing to the obvious benefits of female guardians in the context of a moribund poor law. While we might question the political stance of this particular newspaper, the fact is that all of the Bolton newspapers threw their weight behind female poor law guardians. As we shall see below, the obvious benefits of female guardians is a theme to which public meetings, candidates and newspapers returned time and again. *Thirdly*, it is clear that, even prior to the dropping of the property qualification, Bolton women could identify a number of candidates willing and able to stand in the election process, and put up a good fight in their support. The successes of the later 1890s, therefore, must be seen as part of a very well-organized and deeply-rooted developmental process in Bolton. This point is rarely made in the secondary literature.

Yet, it was the prospect of the ending of the property qualification for election to the office of guardian that really stimulated an upsurge of campaigning and electoral activity, and it is to this issue that we now turn. Thus, Mary Haslam records in her working diary of 17 July 1894 that the members of the BLWVC had "Decided that steps must shortly be taken to bring out some Women Poor Law Guardians at the next election".[48] The entry is testimony to the forward planning that was to become the hallmark of the women who made it through the election process. In practice, "steps" meant the rejuvenation of the Association for the Return of Women as Poor Law Guardians (ARWPLG) after previous failed campaigns, and initial contact with elements of the female electorate. This diary entry also marked the start of a fact-finding process to establish the latent support for the election of women that had seemed to be demonstrated at previous elections and in the newspaper commentary highlighted above.[49] Thus, on 31 July 1894 the members of the BLWVC,

> Desired our Secretary to write to the different Women's organisations in the town, the British Women's Temperance Association; the Primrose League; the West Ward Women's Liberal Arm and the Association for Befriending Young Servants, and ask for their co-operation in furthering the cause of Women Poor Law Guardians.[50]

By 11 September, the secretary "Found that three of the associations alluded to above would give all help possible; Primrose League declined to act with us" despite the fact that the campaign was to be, as elsewhere, apolitical.[51] By way of an aside, we should not understate the difficulty of the decision to fight an apolitical campaign. As her autobiographical notes (CHAPTER EIGHT) show, Mary Haslam came from a long and active tradition of Liberalism. Moreover, at the very time she was organising the BLWVC and re-starting the campaign for female poor law guardians, she was active in supporting her husband at political functions and campaigning on a Liberal platform through the BWLA. She was not alone. Three of the women returned in the 1894/95 election came from a Liberal leaning tradition and were active campaigners. In this sense, the term apolitical does little justice to the complexity of the private and public lives that these women led.[52]

Nonetheless, on this apolitical platform Haslam "Decided to ask representations to meet at 21 Maudsley Street on Monday Sept 20th to decide on suitable steps. Mr John Harlow, Mr Brownlow, Mr Walker, and J.H. also".[53] This innocuous entry masks more than it reveals. John Haslam (JH) and George Brownlow were two of the longest-serving male guardians, and Haslam was the current chair of the board. John Harlow and James Walker were leading Liberals and also occasional board members. The idea that male boards of guardians had negative reflex reactions at the prospect of women joining them[54] can thus be questioned. Unfortunately, there is no record of the debate at this meeting, but Mary Haslam's working diary records, in an undated note,

The above meeting took place; and the following ladies were selected:

Miss Hardcastle to stand for Haulgh
Miss Armitage to stand for Little Hulton
Mrs Walker to stand for Bradford Ward
Mrs Howard to stand for Little Bolton
Mrs C. Taylor to stand for Halliwell
Mrs R. Ashworth to stand for Turton[55]

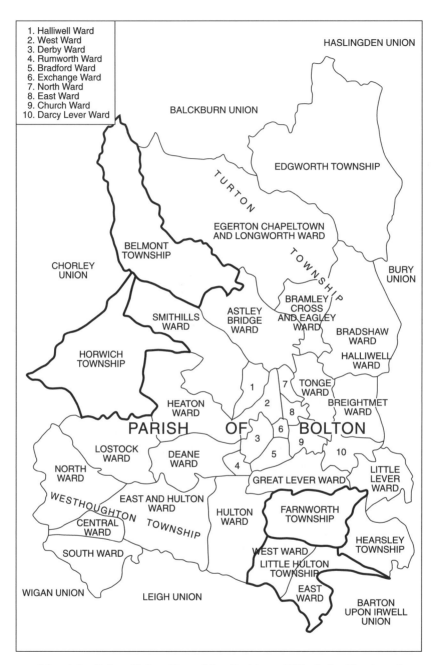

1. Halliwell Ward
2. West Ward
3. Derby Ward
4. Rumworth Ward
5. Bradford Ward
6. Exchange Ward
7. North Ward
8. East Ward
9. Church Ward
10. Darcy Lever Ward

HASLINGDEN UNION

BALCKBURN UNION

EDGWORTH TOWNSHIP

T U R T O N

EGERTON CHAPELTOWN
AND LONGWORTH WARD

BELMONT
TOWNSHIP

CHORLEY
UNION

T O W N S H I P

BURY
UNION

BRAMLEY
CROSS
AND EAGLEY
WARD

SMITHILLS
WARD

ASTLEY
BRIDGE
WARD

BRADSHAW
WARD

HORWICH
TOWNSHIP

HALLIWELL
WARD

TONGE
WARD

HEATON
WARD

BREIGHTMET
WARD

PARISH   OF   BOLTON

LOSTOCK
WARD

DEANE
WARD

NORTH
WARD

GREAT LEVER WARD

LITTLE
LEVER
WARD

WESTHOUGHTON
TOWNSHIP

EAST AND HULTON
WARD

HULTON
WARD

FARNWORTH
TOWNSHIP

CENTRAL
WARD

HEARSLEY
TOWNSHIP

SOUTH WARD

WEST WARD

LITTLE HULTON
TOWNSHIP

WIGAN UNION

LEIGH UNION

EAST
WARD

BARTON
UPON IRWELL
UNION

Map 4.1   Bolton Union: Townships, Parish, and Wards for Election of
Guardians

100

In short, and as map 4.1 shows, the Society planned to fight for six of the potential thirty-six seats in the union. Female candidates had stood previously in four of the six wards that were being contested. Of the six candidates, two were founder and another three were co-opted members of the BLWVC and four had stood in previous elections. This is testimony of the degree to which this organization had drawn together the most prominent female activists in Bolton by 1894, a point that we explored in the last chapter. Finding candidates, then, appears to have been rather easier than has often been suggested. Indeed, the situation is even better than these figures suggest, since a survey of the Bolton newspapers in 1894 reveals a further four women who were standing on political tickets.[56]

Mary Haslam then notes that, "Another meeting was arranged for Thursday next the 27th at 3pm. Miss Barlow is secretary and Mrs Nash treasurer. Mr J. Haslam to continue chairman". The formal structures of the ARWPLG had been rejuvenated, influential members of the existing board of guardians had been present at the outset of the campaign, and Mary Haslam's working diary has given us a window on a process that is all too often missing from the historiography.[57] The diary also provides some testimony as to the popular support that the candidature of female guardians might foster. Thus, on 20 November 1894, Mary Haslam,

> Had talk with Nurse Beesley She was very encouraging about the good our Committee was doing and said we should never know the help we were, but the place was different and they all felt it. She wished it was '*our own ladies*' who were candidates for the Poor Law Guardian, so I said two of them were.[58]

In common with the experiences of men, not all of the female candidates originally agreeing to stand or being formally nominated made it to or through the election itself. Personal circumstances, political deal making, fear and distaste for campaigning or a vicious electoral process could prompt withdrawals. Thus, on 1 December 1894, the Bolton Conservative Council met and

> The question of Lady Guardians was favourably considered, but the meeting did not pledge itself to any definite course of action, although as regards West Ward [where a lady candidate nominated by the Liberals proposed to stand] it was stated that an arrangement was likely to be carried out . . . A notice of motion will be submitted at an adjourned meeting to the effect that the Council favours the election of Lady Guardians but that it be left to the wards to settle . . . In North Ward the Liberals favour the adoption of a Lady candidate, but the other side is stated to be unfavourable, and prior to the question of lady candidates being brought before them they had chosen a candidate.[59]

In practice a deal was done and the potential Liberal lady candidate withdrew. Other women – Mrs Charles Taylor, Mrs Walker and Miss Hardcastle for instance – withdrew because of changes in their personal circumstances and had to be replaced. This turnover amongst female candidates must, however, be judged against appropriate yardsticks. Thus, if we analyze all of the material relating to elections for the board of guardians reported in the *Bolton Chronicle* between 1884 and 1894, we see that in seats that were contested, the turnover rate of male candidates was almost 23 per cent. There was, then, nothing unusual in the experience of women. It is also important to remember that the female candidates *were* replaced. The BLWVC clearly had extensive networks for finding potential candidates and we do not get any sense that Mary Haslam and her colleagues wanted to fight more wards but were prevented from doing so by lack of suitable women. This is a theme to which we return in the next section.

Meanwhile, on 8 December 1894, the *Bolton Guardian* attested to "Considerable interest" in the prospect of women standing for election as guardians and noted,

last night a public meeting in support of the Lady candidates – Mrs Haslam and Miss Howard (West Ward), Mrs Swan (North Ward), Mrs Ashworth (Turton) and Mrs Orrell – was held . . . There was an influential gathering of ladies and gentlemen, including, in addition to the Lady candidates, the Hon Canon Atkinson M.A. (who presided), Dr Rhodes J.P, C.C, Chairman of the Chorlton Union (who attended in place of Miss Bertha Mason, guardian for Ashton-under-Lyne Union), Miss Herts (guardian for the Manchester Union); Messrs John Haslam (Chairman of the Board of Guardians), J. Heywood M.A, J.P; G. Harwood M.A; W. P.Fullagar; W. Haslam; T. Walker J.P; W. W. Cannon Jnr; R. Ashworth (Turton); J. R. Barlow J.P; Dr Pauton; and councillors Broadbent, Cunliffe and Fletcher.[60]

This extract is worth quoting at some length both because those who attended this meeting were vital allies for female guardians on the board from 1895 onwards, and because they represent a very considerable spectrum of influential socio-political opinion and economic status. The Bolton philanthropic, campaigning and reforming elite had turned out in force for the meeting, just as they had done in 1892 when female candidates had stood in numbers for the first time. It is surely significant too that Cunliffe and Fletcher, implacable enemies in voting terms on the Bolton board of guardians, should turn up to the same meeting to support female candidates. Nor should we forget that others, including the leaders of the Liberal and Conservative parties in the town, sent letters of support. The female candidates had clearly learnt from the conduct of previous campaigns from which they had been excluded. There is little support here for the idea that in 1894 or previously "poor law women . . . stood on their own and stood for the most part silently, relying on one or two friendly letters in the press and perhaps a commendation from the local doctor and the local vicar".[61]

Of course, meetings like this were a usual part of the campaigning land-scape for men seeking election or re-election to the board. The Bolton newspapers are full of addresses in the five to six week period before elec-tions were held, reporting faithfully the credentials of male candidates, their past achievements and their aspirations for change once elected. Women too held election meetings, as we shall see below. However, this was a different sort of event, a meeting to establish the moral authority of women's place in the election process and to convince ratepayers of the appropriateness of female candidature. It was also a collective meeting for all of the female candidates across all wards, something that we do not ever see when examining the candidature of men. Above all this was a carefully planned and orchestrated event in which members of the BLWVC and the ARWPLG, individual women in their political campaigning role, and women of a higher social status such as Mary Haslam, had used their networks to engineer the gathering of a social, moral, philanthropic and leadership elite. These observations do little to support a historiographical literature that has emphasised conflict, minority positions, ad hoc and small scale organization and, in many cases, a hostile press.[62]

The meeting was strongly in favour of candidature. Hence "The Chairman . . . supposed the question was being asked, why should women be elected, and he would answer that question by another, why should not they be elected! . . . The thing was so self-evident that one was at a loss to know what arguments to bring forward". To return to the issue of how women themselves are seen to have justified their claims to wider influence, women's candidature was implied to be natural and a matter of equality. Noting that women had fought their way into universities, nursing and doctoring he felt that women should be fully supported and pointed out that other unions already had female guardians. Further extension of the female influence was thus inevitable. Indeed, if "prudent, sensible and thoughtful women were put on, nothing but good could result", though in this context he was talking mainly in terms of the relief that such women could afford to workhouse inmates. Such themes and language resonate with newspaper commentary in the early 1890s that had called for female candidates to come forward and the electorate to put them at the top of the poll.

Speakers returned to the areas of female competence later in the meeting, suggesting that "The work which the ladies would engage in divided itself into three heads, viz. Useful, economical and sympathetic", particularly or mainly to do with workhouse inmates and, within this group, particularly women and children. It is difficult to know how to read such language and the underlying inference that women were seen, even by their male supporters, as fit to work in only certain areas. The idea that women were confined, or confined themselves, to matters of municipal housekeeping and maternalism when seeking election or holding office is a commonplace of the literature. However, some commentators have urged us to judge such strategy and accompanying language against the correct yardsticks – many (male) electors and guardians were worried that women would be liberal with the rates and there was ingrained hostility to them as candidates and members of elected bodies. In this sense, agreeing with, using and sometimes subverting the language of the moral, maternal and domestic made considerable sense. Confining, or at least to be seen to be promising to confine, their attention to women and children also made sense against the backdrop of female experience in philanthropy, often but not always an asset in elections.

Yet, in the Bolton context we should certainly be wary of an overly negative reading either of the language or its use by male supporters. The language of usefulness, sympathy and (long-term) economy pervades Mary Haslam's working diary, reproduced and annotated in CHAPTER NINE, and was actually used for a fundamental assault on the policy and authority structures of the board of guardians after 1894. We must also be clear that the female candidates *themselves* used a related linguistic register, both in this meeting and in subsequent campaigning. Thus,

> Mrs Haslam, . . . in proposing a vote of thanks . . . said she had been asked why, so long as there was a Ladies' Visiting committee, she was not satisfied with them. They had been attending the workhouse regularly, and, their opinion that they wanted more opportunity *to be of service* at the workhouse was increased by what they had heard that night. The Guardians were *exceedingly kindly disposed to them*, but no matter how kind they were they (the ladies) wanted to go there as *representatives of the people*.[63]

This was a carefully crafted response on the part of Haslam. While we should beware of reading too much into these speeches, Mary Haslam invokes the important trio of rhetorics seen here in many other places, including her diary and suffrage writing (reproduced in CHAPTER ELEVEN). They thus deserve more attention. *First*, she (and other female activists) belonged to the town, to the workhouse, to public life and to philanthropic life. The ladies were *of* the people, implying a natural right to representation which would in turn be an unselfish act for the good of the poor. Language like this was used in a variety of contexts by nineteenth century-women activists.[64] *Secondly*, the female candidates had experience and wanted to bring their skills to the service of the community and the workhouse. By inference, and in common with the wider feminist literature on the way in which women used vehicles like Liberalism to justify their wider public roles, they had a moral duty to serve.[65] *Thirdly* the female candidates wanted to exercise their rights to represent men and women in elected office, as citizens of Bolton and on an equal footing with men. As Canning and Rose point out, and as we saw in CHAPTER ONE, citizenship was both an aim for nineteenth-century women and a vehicle for making claims on locality and state for civil, political and social rights. Claiming, taking up and practicing citizenship were tied up with the "politics of recognition" and the wider election process, and Mary Haslam's speech could and should be read in these terms. Yet, we should not go too far down this route. There is much evidence that in terms of their philanthropy and social activism in the town, the women who stood for election in 1894/95 had already established their theoretical and practical status as citizens. Thus, while it might be true that the ideology and linguistic register of citizenship provided a way of "claims-making", Mary Haslam and her colleagues were not simply using empty rhetoric. They were not making claims in the vague hope of recognition, but instead demanding the recognition of their hard-earned status. In many ways we might regard the rhetoric here as seeking to transcend the distinction of sex, a recurring theme as women negotiated power on the board after election.[66]

Mary Haslam's speech is also important for one other reason. She goes out of her way to show that she is not challenging either individual or institutionalized male authority. The male guardians had after all been very kindly disposed to her group. Indeed, arguing that women were well prepared to engage with the nitty-gritty day-to-day activities of giving relief (including we might note outdoor relief), she suggested "seeing the great amount of sin and misery, it was only by men and women joining hands in this matter that they could be successful in levelling it. It was not in any spirit of interference that they wished to join the men in their work". Once again, we see an attempt not to skirt gender boundaries, but to erase them. Miss Hulme, recounting her experiences in Manchester, reinforced the notion that "the work of the men guardians should not be separated from the work of the Lady guardians". Naturally, Mary Haslam had every intention of challenging men on the board, as she and her colleagues had challenged them on several occasions when presenting reports of the BLWVC, but the strategic posturing here is significant.[67]

The newspaper reporting of the meeting as a whole is very significant.

It advertised the social and experiential credentials of the female candidates and highlighted for all the potential electors that the existing board were already kindly disposed to female activists in their BLWVC capacity. Both ideas would have been given weight in the eyes of the readership by the attendance of prominent board members. Against this backdrop, it is important to note that none of the male candidates in the 1894/95 election could claim such high profile support in their public meetings. Moreover, the reporting implies that the idea of the women candidates that they could be more useful as formally elected members was actively reinforced – *increased by what they had heard* that night – rather than simply passively accepted by the meeting. The reporting of male election gatherings is much more passive than this. More widely, the implication of all sides of the reporting is that electing female guardians was natural. It had been done in other places, the electors would be voting for women with an active local profile and the candidates would be apolitical. The extent to which the language used in this meeting penetrated and reflected popular consciousness can perhaps be seen in a *Bolton Journal* report of 15 December 1894, when, at the meeting of the Conservative candidates for Bradford Ward, one of the candidates "advocated the election of Lady Guardians and hoped they would be well supported in the different wards [not his own!] where they were seeking the suffrage of the electors. His experience told him that Ladies would be distinctly *useful* members of the Board".[68] Finally, a self-confident speech like the one reported from Mary Haslam does not sit easily with the idea that potential candidates were under-confident in public speaking and inexperienced in electoral meetings.[69]

When the *Bolton Journal* reported the names of candidates, proposers and seconders for the whole union on 8 December 1894 it was clear that the election was to be keenly fought. The list of candidates and proposers is important both in the context of the election and the subsequent operation of the board. What all of the female candidates had in common was the high social standing of those who nominated them. Thus, both their supporters and the lady candidates themselves were somewhat above the run of the mill middling sorts who had made up the fluid part of the board up to 1894. This has also been observed of elections elsewhere, but in the case of Bolton what it meant was that women belonged to an upper-middling constituency on the board, and one that would be strengthened by the forthcoming election.[70] A second observation about the listings is that the female candidates were nominated/seconded by both Liberals and Conservatives.[71] We might contrast this situation with the accompanying *Bolton Journal* article that noted in several wards the prospect of a fierce battle between Liberal, Conservative and Independent members of the

Bolton political scene. The different political context for the candidature of men and women is significant. The rancorous male politics, first demonstrated in the election process, could split even late nineteenth-century boards of guardians and allow apolitical women, once elected, to pit male guardians against each other.[72]

Meanwhile, the individual meetings to support women candidates in their proposed wards took up many of the themes that we have been highlighting here. We start, though, with a brief analysis of a male campaign meeting. Thus, the *Bolton Journal* reported a meeting to support Mr Haworth in Westhoughton on 9 December 1894. The report was loaded with policy statements and called attention to his track record. Mr Haworth, it was noted, "was in favour of labour colonies for the unemployed, some scheme for the better assistance of the widows and the fatherless, the relief of the indigent sick, the housing of those wandering from town to town, provision for the aged poor other than the workhouse, and old age pensions".[73] The "well attended" meeting on 9 December to support the candidature of Mrs Orrell, by contrast, concentrated on the fact that she was apolitical and that she would be elected to serve the interests of ratepayers as a whole. Hence Mr Ainsworth suggested a "vote of confidence . . . and observed that they were not purposing to send a Lady who was going to represent anyone's . . . fancies, but the ratepayers generally". Once more, we see the idea that the female candidates were *of the people* and that ratepayers should put aside their conventional understanding of gender boundaries when voting.[74] The election meeting for Richenda Ashworth took a slightly different tack. The chairman, John Scowcroft, noted that Ashworth was standing on an apolitical ticket but then passed over to Ashworth herself who urged the electors "to recognize her work for the poor and excluded majority and elect her at the head of the poll, giving a message about what it meant to be a citizen of this town". This melding of local electoral politics with a record of experience and the rhetoric of citizenship is familiar from other studies, but we can at once see that the women and their supporters were running differentiated campaigns in individual wards.[75]

The meeting to support Susannah Swan took up more of the key themes from Mary Haslam's speech, quoted earlier. The chairman of her meeting, the prominent merchant John Kearsley, told his "enthusiastic audience" that "they ought to think carefully on the rights and duties of the Lady candidates for their previous good work in the town imposed a duty on them to offer their services to the union and a duty on the electorate to put them at the head of the poll as the local parties had suggested". This complex speech, emphasising enthusiastic support for female candidates, the apolitical nature of their campaign, the depth of support in the locality and the duties as opposed to the rights of female candidates, encompasses many of the justifications for claims to public life made by women on the national stage. It also suggests very clearly that there was little reflex hostility to female candidates.[76] Mary Haslam did not herself hold an election meeting (being supported by both parties in her ward), but she did host "home meetings" for prominent local employers in the run up to polling day.

Election meetings and addresses were just one strategic device. While there is certainly some truth in the generalization that female candidates approaching the elections of 1894/95 had much to learn in tactical terms, Bolton women appear to have been much more active and imaginative than those who underpinned Hollis's analysis of this issue. Female candidates, like their male counterparts, produced large numbers of posters and leaflets. Rather than adopting individualized checklists of where women could be of service in poor law work, as appears to have been he case in other areas, all of the women adopted the same posters, demanding simply that electors "Vote for the Lady candidates". The supporters of the female candidates in turn vied with those of rivals to paste up and distribute material.[77] In the immediate run up to polling day, the members of the BLWVC and the ARWPLG organized several small street parties, while on the day itself they employed baker boys to attend last minute canvassing parties with cakes and bread. They had clearly caught onto the mood of the voters, for as Annie Hulkin of Bolton noted in her autobiographical notes "On election days . . . gangs of lads with red and blue sticks [went round] singing voting songs; when rival gangs met there were good-natured tussles, but no really rough play".[78] Moreover, they also caught onto the mood of popular interest in this particular election (as evidenced by the newspaper coverage reported above), organizing "orange box" meetings in the town square where female candidates and their supporters standing on empty orange boxes would harangue the general public with the failings of the conventional approach to elections and extol the virtues of the female candidates. These were precisely the tactics that would be used in the suffrage campaign over a decade later, and in this context they suggest that prevailing historiographical notions of subdued and quiet female campaigning at the municipal level might need to be rethought.[79]

The electoral turnout for the December poll was the most substantial for over fifteen years. In her diary of 17 December 1894, Mary Haslam notes

Election of Board of Guardians
  Mrs Howard 1,356 votes

Mrs Swan 422 votes
Mrs Ashworth 580 votes
Mrs Orrell 1,296 votes
Myself returned 1,363 votes. [80]

In addition to these five women, who were all elected, Miss Mason had stood independently of the ARWPLG and BLWVC and was also returned, testimony once more to the need for reinterpretation of an historiographical literature that has usually pointed to the difficulty of getting candidates to stand and see through the whole election. Thus, in 1895 six female guardians took their seats in the board-room of Bolton union. While they were small in number compared to the male guardians (31), their election campaign had drawn in a significant spectrum of male guardians, won widespread political support, had the support of workhouse staff and resulted in a 100 per cent election rate for female candidates. Judged by the yardstick of what was possible rather than what was desirable, this first large-scale electoral campaign had been a spectacular success, a sentiment that we rarely see in the historiographical literature on women in local government. CHAPTERS FIVE and SIX deal with their reception and the impact that these women made.

Subsequent Elections

The presence of female candidates was both regular and substantial at every election after 1894, and the number of female guardians increased steadily into the twentieth century, reaching twelve by the mid-1900s. The voting public certainly got used to their presence as both new candidates and women seeking re-election. Thus, on 18 March 1897 Mary Haslam notes in her working diary,

> Day of nominations for election of Guardians. Mrs Howard and myself are supported by both parties on West Ward. Mrs Swan declined the Liberal Support offered in East Ward and stands as an independent candidate, Mr Myles and Mr Shaw being the two Conservative opponents. Mrs Ashworth is unopposed in Turton; Mrs Orrel opposed at Horwich. [81]

By 23 March, however, "Mrs Orrel's opponent has retired" so that female candidates were largely unopposed in the election of that year. [82] The determination of the candidates to remain apolitical (Mrs Swan could not accept Liberal support as she did not have that of the Conservatives) is familiar from the historiographical literature, but well emphasised in this contest. In turn, the 1897 election was very successful and on 5 April 1897 we learn that,

> Election of Guardians in East and West Wards. <u>East Ward</u> Mrs Swan 673 votes Mrs Shaw 386. <u>West Ward</u> M. H. 1464 votes, Mrs Howard 1452 Mr Chadwick 978, Mr Ward 940, Mr Eaton 903. Mr Rothwell out.[83]

Taking into account other independent or political female candidates, the number of female guardians had risen to eight. In turn, 1897 marks a further step change in the nature of female electoral politics and machinery. The Bolton Women's Local Government Association (BWLGA) was formed in May of that year with an executive committee consisting of middle and working-class activists, women from across the Liberal–Conservative–Socialist spectrum and women of very different religious and socio-economic standing. Its apolitical remit overlapped with the ARWPLG, with which it merged in April 1907, so that two major organizations were active supporters of female candidates in the 1890s and early 1900s. Moreover, the BWLGA had joint meetings with the Women's Co-Operative Guild (WCG) from November 1898, testimony both to a lack of class tension in the local women's movement and the capacity for rapid expansion of the campaigning base. None of these organizations were replicated on the male side of poor law politics.[84] This election machinery organized public meetings and posters, mobilized very considerable numbers of canvassers and other volunteers, incorporated prominent working-class female activists from an early date, and made use of home meetings in a way that was not open to men. Such strategies and organizations could put real pressure on other candidates and it is notable that men opposing female candidates in the 1890s usually withdrew, rather than vice versa. The female electoral machinery could also put pressure on political parties, and we might wonder whether cross-party support was offered to female candidates out of choice or necessity.

Unsuprisingly, the BWLGA and related organizations sought to extend their influence further over time. Hence, women contested two wards where they did not already have representation in 1901. The minutes of the BWLGA record the commissioning of 80 large posters and 4,000 small ones in preparation for the contest.[85] The reaction of male candidates was swift and furious. Its tone and thrust can be gauged by a letter from *No Politics* in the *Bolton Journal* of the 9 March 1901 about a meeting to support male candidates:

> It was painful to notice the distinct attempt of several of the speakers to drag politics into this election. They must know perfectly well that the lady

guardians now on the board were nominated and elected simply for their fitness for the position, politics being carefully excluded.[86]

Mrs Barnes, one of the sitting female guardians, also wrote for this edition of the *Journal*, noting that

> This Association [for the Return of Women as Poor Law Guardians] has never taken account of the politics of the candidate it has supported, at the first election at which there were women candidates – these were Mrs Howard, Miss Hardcastle and Mrs Charles Taylor – two out of the three being Conservatives: but all standing on non-political lines.[87]

Given the history of political bickering in Bolton, the charge of politicization of the poor law was an important one, and had to be rebuffed.[88] The charges had little impact on the electoral success of female candidates, however, and steady progress at election time continued to be achieved. By 5 April 1910, the *Bolton Evening News* was noting that contests in Exchange and Church Wards had resulted in the election of two further women guardians, "completing the dozen". In their thanks notice to electors in this year, the BWLGA gave particular praise to "the electors of Bradford and Derby Wards, whereby their candidates are elected without contests, and thus approving emphatically of the non-political policy of the Association".[89] However, the ability of lady guardians to call on smooth electoral machinery in addition to the attractiveness of their apolitical stance must also be acknowledged. Mary Haslam, for instance, continued to put great efforts into recruiting canvassers. Thus, the *Bolton Chronicle* of 19 May 1909 reported that "Mrs W.Haslam . . . held an at home at Hamer's Commercial Hotel on Tuesday evening . . . Forty two ladies present gave in their names as canvassers and workers on behalf of the association".[90] She was joined in her efforts by Sarah Reddish and other working-class female activists, who had been drawn into the BWLGA from its inception. Reddish organized factory meetings, deployed working class canvassers and made public speeches on behalf of female candidates. A prominent player in the Bolton WCG, Reddish's support was vital in a situation where, by 1905, 90 per cent of the female electorate in Bolton was working-class.[91] In the elections of 1909, then, the BWLGA was able to commission 2,500 posters, eighty canvassers and a team of women writers to deluge the newspapers. Since the local political parties were in large part dependent on the labours of the same women for their election machinery, no male candidate could match this level of support.

Of course, it would be foolish to suggest that local poor law politics was always unproblematic for female candidates, sitting guardians, canvassers or organizations. Female canvassers were often jostled, posters were ripped down, charges of political involvement and lack of experience or character were made against female candidates, and deals were done between political parties and male candidates. These are familiar experiences from the historiographical literature.[92] Enlisting candidates could also sometimes be more problematic than we have thus far allowed. On 11 February 1898, for instance, the minutes of the BWLGA note that all seven of the potential candidates approached for the forthcoming election had turned them down and that the political parties had refused to co-operate. Indeed, "there was a decided refusal to do anything in the matter of co-operation with the committee".[93] The BWLGA reported further problems getting candidates in October 1903 and March 1904 and even in March 1905 it took some persuasion for the formidable Sarah Reddish to stand. These instances do not, however, provide support for the idea that there were structural problems in the supply of female candidates. Thus, on 23 September 1902, "At Board resignation of Mrs Orrell on ground of health. At once took steps to fill her place, but found a fortnight too short so let the seat go". Subsequently on 4 November Mary Haslam recorded the "Election of Mr Lilley as P. L. G. in place of Mrs Orrell".[94] While it is impossible with any confidence to read sentiment into this language, there is at least a hint that the female guardians had after so long come to regard this as *their* seat, and they were distinctly unhappy about having to give it up. In both cases, the seats were eventually regained, and, as we have seen, women extended their influence to the round dozen. It would not be accurate, therefore, to read these instances as a sign of weakness or failure.[95]

Yet, it is also important to acknowledge that the electoral machinery we have celebrated above did not always run smoothly or succeed in getting women elected or re-elected. The minutes of the BWLGA in April 1905 noted that the Conservatives systematically opposed them. Though the Conservative candidates lost and "it was noticed with great satisfaction that in the wards where women had stood they were elected at the head of the polls", the point is that dedicated opposition remained.[96] Moreover, the *Bolton Chronicle* noted that in the elections of 1908/09, "Mrs Wilson . . . was nominated for Little Hulton but for the first time in the history of the [Bolton Women's Local Government] Association, the women candidate failed to secure a seat", though in this year there were eight members of the association plus Mrs Tonge and Mrs Caldwell, Liberal and Conservative interest, elected.[97] Further setbacks were to follow. In the guardian elections of 1909/1910, Mary Haslam, and Mary Ann Howard for West Ward and Sarah Cropper for Bromley Cross and Eagley Ward were elected without contest. However, Susannah Swan was third placed candidate by some distance in East Ward after being a guardian for fourteen years. The BWLGA placed this poor result down to loss of interest and activity on the part of the canvassers and it was agreed that organizing committees for elections should meet at least three months in advance thereafter. The *Bolton Journal* reporting of that meeting on 25 February 1910 noted that the failure of Mrs Swan to get re-elected was regretted but "the increasing influence for good brought about by the appearance of women in practically every department of public life" was celebrated. Looking forward to the subsequent re-election of Mrs Swan, the paper feted the contribution of women like her: "Able, business-like and active, they were showing themselves ready and willing to take their share in public labours".[98] Such setbacks have occupied our attention, however, precisely because they were unusual. Male candidates were often defeated and dozens of sitting male guardians in any five-year period would either lose or vacate their seats. Judged against appropriate yard-sticks, an increasingly well-organized and cross-class Bolton women's movement secured notable gains in the electoral politics of the town. In turn, and as we shall see in CHAPTER SEVEN, the foundations of a campaigning machinery that was to come alive in the twentieth-century drive for women's suffrage had been laid.

The Aftermath

The 1890s marks a step change in the nature of women's public creden-tials in Bolton. Philanthropic activism and campaigning on social welfare gave way to rather more direct and organized influence on policy, poli-tics and local government. This started with the BLWVC and BWLGA and carried on in the twentieth century to women's suffrage and associa-tions to promote women's citizenship. By the later 1890s female activists had extended and solidified their role in public life through four avenues. *First*, they had drawn on their shared networks and experience in philan-thropy to formally organize themselves. *Secondly*, these organizations were not exclusive. Working-class activists like Sarah Reddish were drawn in and given committee membership at the earliest opportunity, so that the Bolton women's and campaigning movements were probably less fractured along class lines than those elsewhere. *Thirdly*, while some women still fought on political tickets in guardian elections, most candi-dates fought on an apolitical basis, setting an important precedent for later campaigning work. *Finally*, the 1894 elections built upon and devel-oped the electoral machinery that had first seen the light of day in the early

1890s. While the machinery could not guarantee election or re-election, it was both efficient and large-scale. Its existence drew together those who wanted a role in public life and those who were happy to help but did not, fostering a shared collective consciousness that we will see manifested itself in the town by the early twentieth century,

Thus, it is quite true that even as late as 9 March 1910, the election notices placed by the BWLGA had to both justify their candidature at election time and did so in terms of maternalism and municipal housekeeping.[99] Newspapers also took up this theme, with the *Bolton Chronicle* of November 1907 suggesting that, "There are ten women serving as guardians for the Bolton union, and their work has commended itself to all who have the welfare of the poor at heart . . . the gradual growth of women's influence on local bodies cannot but make for improvement in municipal administration and a purer atmosphere surrounding public life.'[100] Yet, to concentrate on such reporting is misleading and underplays the nature of the achievements of women in the 1890s. They had managed to engineer a situation in which male guardians, political parties, the electorate and, crucially, the local newspapers, were usually supportive of a wider public role for women, however it might be justified. Moreover, the women who stood for election, the men and women who had canvassed for them and supported their meetings, and the organizations that had been formed around and for the election, were to underpin a much wider assault on public life in the 1890s and 1900s, including demands for representation on pension committees, boards of trustees, sanitation boards and extraordinary relief committees. The early 1890s also mark the start of a more focused women's suffrage campaign and the start of planning for women to sit on borough and county councils.[101] Some of these issues are taken up in CHAPTER SEVEN. For now, and as so much of the historiography points out, getting elected was just the first of many potential hurdles for women becoming engaged with the New Poor Law. What happened on the board of guardians also helped to shape the women's movement in Bolton, and to frame its strategies, linguistic register and the nature of communal support. It is thus to the negotiation of power after the 1894/95 election that we now turn.

CHAPTER FIVE

Negotiating Power

Context

CHAPTER ONE reviewed an historiographical literature that has largely portrayed elected female guardians as marginal influences on local welfare policy, facing the sustained hostility of their male counterparts. While poor law work offered "multiple languages within which women could advance their rights, plead their cause, pursue their duties, fulfill their mission, and lay claim to full citizenship",[1] many have argued that such potential was simply not realized. Rubinstein concludes that "The novelty of being an elected woman, her minority status and the inhibitions of education and socialization meant that it was often difficult to institute policies of aggressive reform."[2] Levine suggests that "women's presence on local government bodies . . . continued to disrupt the harmony of single-sex bodies", and that "the weight of formal oppression was burdensome". The small numbers of elected women were forced to tackle "the arduous and unremunerated committee work of local administration in a hostile and unrelenting environment".[3] Female guardians were consistently out-voted by a core of male guardians who resented challenges to their authority and argued that undertaking elected office was unwomanly.[4] As a rule, "men found it hard to take their contribution seriously or value it properly" and they resented "impediments to the dirty jokes and local politicking" that were characteristic of board meetings. More widely, "Party managers anxious to advance their party's fortunes, regarded local government women with little enthusiasm and wished they would go away."[5] This chapter will explore these broad generalizations, effectively the second core theme of this book.

Focusing on the particular experiences of Mary Haslam, it will consider whether female guardians in Bolton encountered sustained hostility, explore the broad remit that they carved out and the tactics used to consolidate and extend that remit, and address the question of the representativeness of these Bolton women.

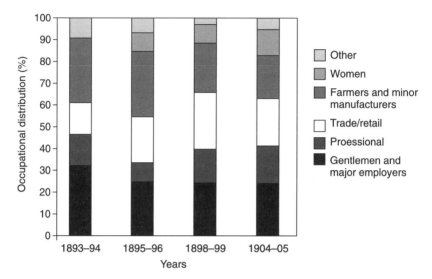

Figure 5.1   Occupational composition of the board of guardians,
1890s and 1900s

Source: BRO GBO 13, Lists of Officers and Guardians for Bolton Union.

As a precursor to such analysis, however, it is important to understand that when Mary Haslam and her female colleagues joined the Bolton board in 1895 they became part of a body that was, and had always been, fractured along many fault lines. Several are worth exploring in more depth. *First*, the male guardians were split along occupational and socioeconomic lines. Figure 5.1 records the occupational composition of the board in 1893–94, 1895–96, 1898–99 and 1904–5 and suggests that it had four broad, and broadly stable, occupational interest groups.[6] Membership of one or other occupational group is not a reliable guide to the attitude of individuals to the poor law or to female guardians. Nor can we say in any easy sense that the forum of the board pitted major against minor ratepayers, rate savers against rate spenders, major manufacturers against minor manufacturers or professionals against tradesmen, given that all occupational groups in the town had in the past shown a remarkable capacity to form temporary alliances.[7] Nonetheless,

116

there *were* distinct occupational groupings on the Bolton board and its membership had often split along occupational lines and argued over occupational representation on committees.[8]

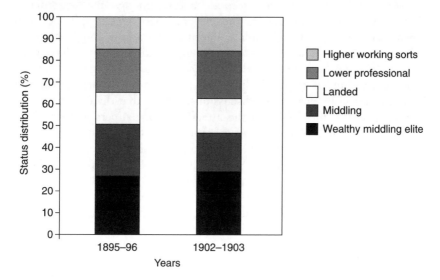

Figure 5.2 Crude social structure of Bolton board of Guardians, 1890s and 1900s

Source: Based upon a synthesis of BRO GBO 13, List of Officers and Guardians for Bolton Union and all surviving personal, professional, newspaper and official testimony on or by guardians in this period.

It is difficult to move from this measure of occupation to wider considerations of differences in socio-economic status on the board, not least because of the poor survival of family collections and rating lists. However, we cannot ignore the fact that such divisions did exist. From 1895 until Word War I, the board drew some of its male membership from the ranks of the Haslam, Heywood, Bolling, Kearsley and Watkinson families, all of them part of the wealthy middling elite. Moreover, there was also a solid representation of the wealthy professional classes. At the other end of the spectrum, we find tailors, drapers, theatre managers, coal dealers and artisans who formed the higher levels of the working-class in the town. Figure 5.2 attempts, for 1895–96 and 1902–3, a crude representation of the weight of these different interests, and we can see that there was little by way of a tendency for the socio-economic status of the board to be diluted over time, in contrast to the situation prevailing elsewhere.[9] Since the first wave of female guardians was all of higher social status, they would have joined a significant pre-existing interest group on the board. The potential for splits based upon socio-economic status rather than gender should thus be clear.

Meanwhile, religion was a *second* fracture amongst male guardians. While Anglicanism dominates the picture, there was a split between forms of worship, and Catholics, Baptists, Unitarians and Methodists also served office. The potency of such religious divisions may have been reduced in the later nineteenth century by inter-marriage, conversion and the waning of evangelicalism, but they were nonetheless real and could result in intense policy discussions. Topics that divided the board along religious lines included the attendance of paupers at town cele-brations and the introduction of more leisure activities into workhouse regimes. Religious tensions also surfaced on the issue of where to board out pauper orphans. In April 1898, for instance, "Mr Hoskyns said that the sect of Protestantism was as necessary to be attended as meals . . . and that he should object to a church child going to a Wesleyan home and vice versa."[10] And religious feeling ran particularly high when the board had to discuss the provision of religious ministry to workhouse residents.[11]

The Bolton board was also divided, *thirdly*, between those who attended regularly and those who came only when a particular issue was to be discussed or a vote held. Table 5.1 demonstrates that, in line with unions elsewhere, a relatively small core of guardians attended regularly over the period 1896–7 to 1911–12. The tendency for much of the real business of Bolton union to be done at the level of sub-committees would have exacerbated the potential tension between those who attended regu-larly, and thus served on the committees, and those who attended irregularly and occasionally had to vote on the recommendations of the sub-committees at board level.[12] We perhaps see this fracture played out on a *fourth* issue that divided guardians, that of temperance and drinking in the workhouse more generally.

Table 5.1   Attendance on the Bolton board of guardians

Year	Lowest attendance	Highest attendance	Average attendance
1896	32	48	37
1897	27	49	36
1898	29	49	37
1899	31	47	40
1900	28	47	35
1901	21	49	40
1902	21	49	37

1903	35	51	42
1904	36	54	46
1905	36	53	32
1906	33	50	38
1907	24	48	38
1908	36	52	43
1909	39	52	40
1910	39	53	48
1911	40	55	43
1912	35	51	39

Source: BRO GBO 23/4, Summary of Relief Returns 1892–1917.

A brief consideration of this issue through the pages of Mary Haslam's working diary illustrates the nature of the debate amongst the guardians:

> *Dec 21 1898*: At Board, question of beer at Xmas dinner discussed and voted upon 19 against beer and 13 for, so none this year.
> *Nov 29 1899*: At Workhouse – Enquiries as to whether Xmas should be without beer. Chairman advised waiting for resolution next week.
> *Dec 6 1899*: At Board, resolution to have no beer at Xmas dinner to workhouse inmates carried by 26, against 6. (Much progress since last year!).
> *Dec 5 1900*: At Board; resolution re inmates Xmas dinner without beer passed without an amendment!
> *Dec 4: 1901*: At Board resolution re Xmas Dinners. "A limited quantity of roast beef and plum pudding, with one pint of tea, coffee, cocoa or milk, snuff and tobacco for the adults and oranges and nuts for the children" Passed without dissent so we hope the question of beer is dismissed for ever.[13]

At the end of 1898 then, the guardians who regularly attended the workhouse sub-committee and raised the question about the availability of beer at Christmas were clearly out of touch with the less frequent attendees on the board, thirteen of whom voted against the resolution to curtail provision of beer. Over time, the temperance supporters won the day. After this victory they moved onto medicinal drinking. Thus, "Sept 23 1903: Mr Tonge asked for return of spirituous liquors in workhouse for past 5 years ordered by doctor".[14] The return was made and debated on 21 October and resulted in ongoing attempts to restrict the availability of alcohol in the workhouse. Temperance was, then a significant issue and one that paradoxically threw together female guardians such as Mary Haslam with those, such as Charles Tonge, who were actively opposed to many of the other causes espoused by female guardians.

A number of further fractures amongst the guardians must also be noted. Thus, the board was split along residential lines, with guardians from Bolton forming a block against those from the outer parishes. Legislative and organizational changes had taken some of the venom out of this division by the later nineteenth century, but even in 1899 it is possible to identify distinct policy blocks based upon the urban or rural residence of the guardians. Philanthropic traditions could also be divisive. Some guardians had rich backgrounds of, and were active in, philanthropic activity and campaigning on issues outside of the poor law. We saw in CHAPTER THREE that Mary Haslam was involved with campaigns over suffrage, sanitation, infant mortality and women's citizenship. John Haslam and John Heywood were also campaigning on the issues of suffrage and women's citizenship, and they were at the forefront of housing improvement in the town. Others, even some of the wealthy members of the board, did not have these credentials and the board often split between the more humanitarian attitudes of male and female philanthropist-guardians, and other male guardians. As just one example of many, the board was split over the abolition of uniforms for the deserving poor in November 1894.[15]

Nor should we forget that one of the biggest sources of tension between guardians lay in politics. While determined political in-fighting was a distant memory by the 1890s, CHAPTER FOUR showed that local parties often still saw the guardian elections as a political instrument. Male and female wings of the Liberal and Conservative parties were very active in Bolton from the 1880s to 1913, and they were augmented by a mushrooming male and female labour movement.[16] Uncovering political divisions on the board is difficult except where they break out directly over issues such as representation on the main spending committees, but a linkage exercise in which guardians present in 1891 or elected subsequently up to 1901 were traced to all surviving sources that might indicate political persuasion suggests that there were clearly entrenched political interests on the board, which was consistently split at 50–60 per cent Liberal, 30–40 per cent Conservative and 0–20 per cent of no known political standing. Some of the personal enmities that become apparent amongst the guardians were thus likely to have had a political foundation.

Meanwhile, we should not forget that the issue of personality rather than gender often dominated debate over resolutions. On 27 October 1897, Mary Haslam noted 'Great delay in [workhouse] business due to interruption by Dearden and Crompton; extreme tedium of latter'. The theme was resumed on 3 November when 'Proposal to proceed with Administration block of new Hospital, postponed one week on account of small number of Guardians left. Dearden again unbearable'.[17] Ellis

Crompton and Thomas Dearden were both farmers and, according to Mary Haslam's diary occasionally turned up intoxicated. Her irritation at the nit-picking parsimony of these men was shared by many other guardians, such that even their natural allies from the more rural out-parishes would often oppose them in voting.

This has been a lengthy but important discussion. While the tendency in the literature has been to counterpose the interests of men and women, we must recognize, in Bolton at least, that there were alternative and perhaps more important fault lines running through the board of guardians.[18] In these fault lines, as we shall see, lay female power and an opportunity to offer some reinterpretation of the dominant themes of women marginalized and underachieving in local government and a poor law that was in decline. We turn first to one of the articles of faith in the wider historiography, male hostility to new female guardians.

Negotiating Power: Male Hostility

We should not, despite the largely favourable reaction of the Bolton press and public to the prospect of women playing a formal role in welfare policy highlighted in the last chapter, automatically assume that female guardians in Bolton escaped male hostility once elected. On 9 January 1895, Mr Elliston "welcomed the Lady Guardians most heartily", but given the well-publicized experiences of other female guardians they must have been alive to the prospect of being sniped at in meetings, confronting ingrained forms of male behaviour on the board and facing an implicit questioning of their status and abilities.[19] Indeed, on the face of it the Bolton evidence reveals both explicit and implicit hostility. Let us start with explicit hostility. On 12 June 1895,

> Sectional relief 9.30–11. Board 11–12. Discussion whether ladies should be represented at north western Conference in Manchester in July. Vote 13 for and 15 against. Chairman gave casting vote in our favour. Proposed Mrs Ashworth and Mrs Orrel. Workhouse 2.30–5.10 . . . [A] New committee to be formed to consider old hospital scheme, 'one without ladies'.[20]

Both of the events described here are significant. Bolton had always sent representatives to the Northwestern Conference of Poor Law Guardians but we see clear male opposition to women extending their presence and influence onto the regional stage. Such opposition is famil-iar from the experiences of other early guardians.[21] It is also important to note, however, that the vote was close, with eight male guardians voting for the motion, that the defeat was reversed by the vote of the Chair, and that the Chair was the brother-in-law of Mary Haslam. While opposition to women can clearly be read here, its effectiveness was questionable in the context of a board split on kinship and socio-economic lines and against a group of women who had considerable experience as public activists. The other area of conflict – over rebuilding of the hospital facilities at the workhouse – more clearly demonstrates the petty nastiness that other contributors to the secondary literature have generalized to make common experiences. A further example of hostility to female guardians comes from a lowly parish clerk rather than the male guardians. Thus,

> Chairman called attention to remarks at Heaton parish council, by clerk re the lady Guardians' extravagance causing rise in rates. Voted by 20 against 19 that the board write and request explanation of the same. Got consent of lady colleagues to solicitors' letter being sent from us to Mr. Fearnhead. This done Mr. Cooper [the chairman] approved. Also several of the men.[22]

There are two points of interest in the response to this familiar charge leveled against the female guardians. *First*, those who voted for the letter to the clerk included some of those who were implacably opposed to the women on other issues, so that while the vote was close that closeness cannot be couched in terms of a latent hostility to women on the board. *Second*, the response on the part of the female guardians themselves was swift and severe, a measure of their confidence both in respect of their position as guardians and their status in the wider community. The fact that their letter gained the explicit support of the chairman and fourteen other male guardians suggests that this confidence was not misplaced. Indeed, the motion had been brought by male guardians and was largely discussed by them.

These instances are, of course, significant but we should not over-emphasize them. Mary Haslam's diary clearly suggests that the presence of female guardians in Bolton did not generate the sustained direct hostility of their male counterparts. She hardly comments on explicit male hostility and what commentary there is on this matter soon dissipates. Thus, in June 1896 she recorded a forthcoming absence from her buildings sub-committee, and "I asked for a lady to take my place as I shall be absent, and all four are added protection".[23] Just one year later the character of opposition had changed and she felt no similar compunction to cover her absences in this way. Even when men and women seem to directly oppose each other, we must be careful of our reading of the situation. Thus, on 10 November 1897, "Motion of Mr Leyland re Mrs Ashworth's remarks at a Manchester Conference this day fortnight".[24]

Leyland's motion, one of censure, followed upon newspaper reports of a speech, attributed to Richenda Ashworth, in which the poor diet in Bolton workhouse was highlighted and the fault was laid at the feet of farmer guardians. The motion was debated on 8 December and Ashworth denied the substance of the report. She was supported by other male guardians and, "Mr Leylands' motion re Mrs Ashworth fell through after a few remarks". [25] On 5 January 1898 Leyland renewed his motion and,

> Mr Leyland's motion of censure carried by 12 against 10. Mrs Howard spoke very well; I alluded to the disgraceful way the business at the workhouse is carried on. At Workhouse I was taken to task by Mr Shippobottom as implying fault lay with chairman and vice-chairman. I explained this not my meaning at all. [26]

This is a very interesting entry, implying as it does, that women were able to debate vigorously in public and private. On the face of it, the outcome, a censure for Mrs Ashworth, is an example of the hostility which women could face when overstepping the boundaries of their poor law roles.[27] However, the censure motion was only carried by twelve votes to ten, with Ashworth gaining the support of five male guardians. Moreover, we must remember that male guardians were censured in the same way if they "went public". Nor does Mary Haslam write of her outrage at the process of censure, suggesting that she recognized the need for collective liability. Moreover, the same Richenda Ashworth who was censured in January 1898 was drowned at Whitby a few months later and a motion of the board referred to her untiring work for them and recorded their considerable sorrow at her death.[28] The women guardian's motion of 15 June 1898 in memory of their colleague is not so different, suggesting that in tragedy at least the board was united,

> Sectional relief [committee]. We ladies met in one room at 1.45 to pass the following resolution: Dear Mr Ashworth, We the undersigned women Guardians of the Bolton Union desire to express our deep sympathy with the loss you have just sustained, and to record our high appreciation of your wife's services on the Board. We, who have worked with her so regularly during the past three years, know her untiring energy and ever-ready sympathy in every detail intended to bring greater happiness to those less fortunate than ourselves, and it is with heavy hearts that we face a future deprived of her presence. We remain dear Mr Ashworth, Yours faithfully, Mary Ann Howard, Susannah Swan, Marian Orrel, Mary Haslam.[29]

The same male-dominated board thought enough of Mary Haslam to send a Christmas card all the way to St. Moritz in 1897, and to openly support plans to give her Honorary Citizenship of the town. In short, the overwhelming impression is of the *lack of explicit gender tension* and the warm appreciation of the work of female guardians.

It is equally difficult to interpret the *implicit* male hostility that sometimes appears in sources such as Mary Haslam's diary. Thus, on 9 January 1895, immediately after the elections had taken place, the: "Workhouse committee at Fishpool at 2.30. [It] Decided by 18 against 14 votes to recommend continuation of the Ladies Visiting Committee till April next."[30] This was a significant victory, giving female guardians two fronts on which to shape local welfare policies, but it is notable that fourteen men voted against the proposal. Since, as CHAPTER THREE showed, the board had previously welcomed female volunterism in the workhouse, one explanation for this voting pattern might be that some male guardians wanted to clip the wings of women activists. That said, and very importantly, at least thirteen men must have voted for the motion as well as all of the female guardians. The Bolton Ladies Workhouse Visiting Committee (BLWVC) was to remain a source of contention, but not for long. Thus, on 12 May 1897, "Sectional relief 9.30–10.0 then left for other committee. Board meeting 11–11.35. Mr Fairclough moved that Ladies Visiting Committee be discontinued, but this negatived by 17 against 11."[31] Robert Fairclough was an insurance agent and his motivations in this case are unclear. However, the margin of victory was greater than it had been in 1895, and on 20 April 1898,

> First meeting of new Board of Guardians J. Heywood appointed chairman; first time this done from outside. He had been thrown out at the election of Bradford Ward last week, and so was put in under co-optative clause. Appointment of Ladies Visiting Committee also carried again.[32]

By April 1899 "Mr Watkinson paid tribute to the good work which the Lady Visitor Committee had done in the past – some amusement was caused by Mr Dearden exclaiming during the discussion 'oh put em all on'."[33] In April 1900 a further renewal resolution was considered and "As on previous occasions Mr Dearden offered a mild protest against the admission of outside ladies on such a committee, he remarking that he thought they were getting too many in connection with the workhouse affairs . . . J. P. Haslam humorously observed that if he had proposed to double the salaries of the ladies not members of the board he could understand Mr Dearden's objection (laughter)".[34] At the conclusion of the debate Mary Haslam recorded with evident satisfaction that "Lady Visitors re-appointed without opposition."[35] Apparent gender tension must thus be viewed with some sensitivity, and more widely we must beware of accepting the view that new female guardians were cowed into silence.

Other instances that might be read as implicit opposition to female guardians also look different when viewed in their proper context rather than via the medium of autobiographies, committee minutes or journal articles. On 27 May 1896, for instance, Mary Haslam was absent on a family holiday in Hampshire but "Mrs Ashworth moved for me that deputation attend Central Conference in London in June, to hear discussion re transfer of Pauper Schools to Educational Authorities under new Bill. Rejected by 19 v 17."[36] The defeated motion was subsequently reintroduced and won in a new vote, but the opposition of seventeen (all male) guardians on this occasion had less to do with the fact that the motion came from a woman and was supported by female guardians than it did with the long-term opposition to central direction by Conservative elements on the board of guardians. Mary Haslam, meanwhile, seconded a motion on 9 June 1897 "in favour of refusing £50 for illumination of P. L. Offices on Jubilee day, as being so transient and enough being done, at workhouse, and all out-door relief doubled for that week. Lost 19 v 15".[37] This issue generated debate (and a considerable turnout) because it sat at the intersection of local debates over civic pride, citizenship, the acceptability of rate levels and religious sensibilities over public celebrations, rather than because it was seconded by a woman. One final example of implicit tension from the many that could have been chosen is particularly illuminating. Thus, on 12 May 1897 "Mr Cunliffe gave notice that at next meeting he would move to rescind the spending of £50 on tools" in the workhouse. At the next meeting on 26 May 1897,

> Sectional Relief 9.30–11.0. Mr Cunliffe's motion re spending £50 on carpentering, carried by 20 v 19. So it was lost. Mr C. afterwards spoke to me about it, and after my explanation said 'Oh I did not know all that', to which I replied that two or three of us had gone into the question fully and might have been trusted! His other argument was that it was giving pauper boys advantages over others![38]

The opposition here was thus motivated by cost and the fear of encouraging pauperism, rather than any conflict with female guardians. Mary Haslam and the other (male and female) guardians were to subsequently engage with Cunliffe many times over issues of expenditure and it would be easy to misinterpret the nature of such disagreements as gender based if we did not have the clarity offered by Haslam's diary.

In short, implicit hostility was often insubstantial and we must question whether male guardians had reflex reactions against female intrusion to the board room. Episodes which might be interpreted as demonstrating gender tension and hostility are capable of many readings. What genuine hostility there was appears to have been muted, ineffective and transient, a reflection of the willingness and ability of female guardians to engage aggressively with male guardians and officials, and of the fact that the board itself was split along a number of lines on most issues. In turn, the relative absence of hostility enabled female guardians to stake a claim to a much wider sphere of influence over poor law policy and practice in Bolton than has been found in other areas.

Negotiating Power: Areas of Influence

From the day of their election Bolton female guardians approached their work with a vigour apparently lacking amongst the most prominent female poor law guardians whose experiences underpin much of our current understanding. Rather than being confined to single or marginal issues, they took an interest in, and helped to formulate policy on, the core business of the union. Their activities might be classified under five general heads:

First, initiatives to improve areas highlighted as "female responsibilities" – clothing, washing facilities, pregnant women, diets, nursing, inspecting child placements and arranging day trips for children.[39] Achievements in these areas are explored in CHAPTER SIX, but a brief review is needed here to suggest the range of female responsibility and to highlight the ways in which the influence and remit of the female guardians was firmed up. Thus, at the formation of the new board in 1895 Mary Haslam was placed on the School Committee, the Tramp Ward Committee and the Sick and Lock Ward Committees, confounding ideas that women were seen as too delicate to take on the dirty jobs in unions. She set about establishing her influence with gusto. On 30 January 1895 Haslam "Enquired into under clothing of children and thought we had better speak with the matron, with a view to substituting drawers for stays with the girls." This concern with the clothing of workhouse children was to be an enduring theme in the work of female guardians. In May 1901, for instance, suits for the workhouse boys, personally chosen by Mary Haslam, arrived but "found boys suits of clothes not quite as ordered. I asked to buy ties and bows".[40]

Moreover, the female guardians patiently extended their remit to encompass other aspects of child welfare, thereby allowing them to claim a voice in wider debates within the union about food contracts, the answerability of officers, and the built environment of the poor law. On 18 December 1895 the board formed a "Sub-committee re children's food." and Mary Haslam "made suggestions with help of Doctor and

Nurse". By 20 January 1897, she was taking a more direct interest in diet and food preparation, noting "Decided to try stove in number 2 cottage (Mr and Mrs Taylor) so that children may have more variety of cooking in their food than is possible by its being prepared in the boiler".[41] Unsurprisingly, by 1898 Haslam and two other women had become members of the food tendering committee. Their presence here was the outcome of the insistence of female guardians from the day of their election that they be involved in appropriations. Thus, on 21 March 1895 three women were placed on the stores committee which "met 2 – 4 Chose brushes, dress goods etc. and gave out tradesmen's contracts'. Tenders for the supply of the workhouse were submitted quarterly and the overall budget for the committee was £3,700 annually, suggesting that female guardians had managed to gain a significant foothold in the basic economic processes of the poor law.[42]

They also extended their interests to the residential conditions of pauper children. On 8 January 1896 the board meeting had "Nothing much of note except the appointment of sub-committee re 'housing of children in workhouse' Dr Gilchrist's motion of Dec 4 [1895]. Mrs Swan and I chosen from one Sectional Relief Committee". The ultimate outcome of the deliberations of the sub-committee was capital expenditure on a new children's ward, testimony to the fact, revisited below, that women could and did influence the "important" committees of their unions. Responding to national initiatives on children was a natural extension of this early interest, so that on 4 March 1898 "Committee re Infant Life Protection Act. Mr Leyland [a persistent critic of female guardians on other issues] moved that we ladies undertake either to do the work or find a deputy. This agreed to. I met the others with Miss Barlow and Miss Armitage representing the Boarding out Committee and we agreed that Miss Armitage should undertake the office". Then on 30 March "Sub-committee for Infant Life Protection Act accepted Miss Armitage as officer for 1 year. This confirmed at Board meeting which followed".[43] While this episode might be read as confirming the marginalization of women to "female tasks" were we to see it in isolation, in the context of Mary Haslam's diary it represents one aspect of a growing role for women in the whole business of the union.

That role also extended to the leisure activities of children and to the fate of pregnant women. At a meeting of 11 May 1898, Mary Haslam "proposed that boys from the cottage homes should go to the swimming baths in Bolton once a week. Deferred for further discussion until next week." On 18 May 1898,

At workhouse was resolved 'that the boys go at discretion of the schoolmaster to the Bolton swimming baths once a week during the summer months' and 'that instruction in swimming shall be provided for the first few weeks of the season'. Mr Ellis Lee and Mr Swan moved contrary amendment but did not press it.

The policy was implemented on 25 May and extended on 28 June 1899 so that "Girls to go to swimming baths as boys".[44] Lee and Swan were concerned that pauper children were being given opportunities not available to the independent poor but did not attempt to subvert the original motion, testimony to the influence of female guardians. This influence was also felt with regard to pregnancy and childbirth amongst the poor. On 29 January 1895, the BLWVC "discussed the difficulty of dealing with the girls who go to the workhouse for their confinements and decided on Mrs Watkin's suggestion that the Guardians be asked if before they leave the master let us know". On 30 January Mary Haslam "Spoke to Mr Haslam [her brother-in-law and Chair of the Board of Guardians] about matters alluded to yesterday and the master was told to write to one of us (myself for the present) giving the date of the cases leaving." Such practices built upon a long tradition of support for poor pregnant women, noted in CHAPTER THREE, and highlight the importance of family and other networks of support for female guardians in their initial attempts to establish an influence and power.[45] These brief examples give only a slight flavour of the extent to which female guardians engaged with "women's" issues. A cursory reading of the working diary of Mary Haslam (CHAPTER NINE) reveals that these took up considerable time, effort and money. Yet it would be wrong to regard such concerns as evidence that women were somehow marginalized. In practice, they reflected the long-term philanthropic and campaigning interests of women who went on to become guardians, so that the involvement of female guardians in "domestic" issues is not a sign of their marginality, but rather of their accumulated success.

A *second* area of intense and developing female activity was in union staffing. In terms of appointments, Mary Haslam was "put on subcommittee to select Nurse Superintendent candidates" in March 1895. On this occasion the sub-committee "Reduced number to 3 and Mr Dearden [a persistent critic of female guardians on other issues] afterwards moved that only the name of Miss Hughes be recommended. (Much astonishment!)."[46] While her postscript suggests that she expected the usual debates over finance with the often implacable Dearden, one reading of the events might be that Mary Haslam was seen as having a particular expertise in the area of nursing staff and was thus unlikely to be challenged by male opponents. However we explain this particular event, other entries in the diary suggest that sub-committees with a strong female representation were both relatively harmonious and very successful in expanding staffing. Thus, Haslam noted on 2 August 1899 that "proposal to appoint three additional charge nurses and five additional probationers carried without the expected opposition [to additional expenditure rather than female guardians]".[47] Female guardians appeared on the appointment panels for nurses, cooks, engineers, workhouse doctors, workhouse masters and matrons, and relieving officers, confounding the dominant view in the historiographical literature that they had little role in staffing. In turn they might use their experience in this area to push for increased numbers and better quality of staff in debates at board level. On 11 August 1897, for instance,

> Sectional relief 9.30–11.30; Workhouse 2.30–5.20. Sub-committee of Main Buildings and Hospital on question of new officers for Probationary Wards. Warm discussion. Chairman (Kearsley) contended there was pauper help in hospital and so might be in the new wards; contradicted by Mrs Ashworth. It was finally agreed to advertise for man and wife, and extra help to be given by Holden and Nurse Hevey. Agreement for and against pauper help in general.[48]

Bolton had been slow to abolish pauper nursing and portering in the workhouse and this resolution and agreement, moved, seconded and debated by female guardians and Liberal male guardians, marked the beginning of the end of the practice. Female guardians, then, were prime movers in the staffing trajectory that we identified in CHAPTER TWO.

However, it is in the management of staff that the board appears to have deployed female guardians to the greatest degree, something that is rarely highlighted in the secondary literature. The role is hardly surprising given that women guardians had experience of favourable relations with the workhouse staff through their workhouse visiting activities. Yet, the fact that their opinion was sought and that women were invited to take an active management role is significant both in itself and in the sense that management of ever more and more expensive staff was an increasingly important part of union business.[49] Female guardians were often called in to deal with complaints about union staff by paupers or other staff members, or to decide on disciplinary actions. Indeed, Mary Haslam's working diary is full of such instances. Some few instances must stand for many. Thus, on 8 April 1895, "A sub-committee of ladies [was formed] to enquire into complaint against nurse. Heard nurse Rayner had exceeded her duty by keeping a lunatic in a padded room all night without the doctor's order." Nurse Rayner had originally been vetted by the BLWVC and Mary Haslam was reluctant to take disciplinary action given the pressures of inadequate staffing. On 10 April she convened a "Sub-committee to consider overcrowding in infirmary and temporary use of Cottage homes. Dr Buck saw need for this measure",[50] effectively shifting the blame for this incident to the lack of space in the workhouse. She was less sympathetic to other officers, especially those of doubtful character. Hence on 5 February 1896, "Workhouse 2.30–5.30. Higginbottom desired to resign post as store-keeper because of disobeying the master's order as to changing room. In discussion other reasons came up why this should not be overlooked. Bad language at meals". However, on 12 February, "Further business with regard to Higginbottom. Sub-committee appointed to investigate charges made by different officials and letter of ditto written by H. as follows: Ward, Shaw, Fairclough, Kearsley, Haslam, Watkinson and myself." One day later "Sub-committee 2.30 to 4.45 to investigate case of Higginbottom. Concluded that he had failed at all points to prove his indictments"[51] and he was dismissed. The outcome was not always so easy. On 7 June 1899,

> At Board Miss Basket Superintendent nurse resigned. In future salary to begin at £50, with annual increase of £5 to a maximum of £100. At the board, the storekeeper is ordered to resign, but at workhouse he protests, and his wife interviews the house Committee on his behalf, and the matter is remanded. I moved an amendment that the original is kept to, and that his resignation is kept to, but there being no seconder, it fell through. A great disgrace, as no doubt about the man having cheated, using fake weights etc., etc.[52]

This extract is significant for two reasons. It suggests that Haslam was part of the committee that determined the salary levels of staff, indicating a very significant remit indeed. It also shows a sub-committee split not along the lines of gender but between those who wanted to avoid inconvenience and were willing to accept a lack of professionalism, and Mary Haslam who was not. Her commitment to professionalisation can be seen throughout the working diary and was shared by other, male, members of the board in the period after 1895. This commitment was recognized in many ad hoc ways by the board, as for instance when she was asked to oversee implementation of the Superannuation Act in 1896, culminating in a "Special meeting at Workhouse at 2.30 to explain to officers [the] decision about Superannuation Calculations".[53]

Female guardians were also active in a *third* and very important area of union policy: renewing and extending the built environment of the poor law. In contrast to the prevailing image of women bullied by male guardians, unwilling to speak and isolated from the important sub-committees, the female guardians of Bolton fought strenuously for influence over the fabric of the poor law. Between 1895 and 1906, women sat on all of the major building committees formed by the union and were vociferous in their condemnation where women were not initially included. Thus, on 31 January 1900,

> At Board, £8000 to be applied for repayable in 30 years, for the building of new nurses' Home. Had been decided to form small sub-committee to see after the work, but no ladies, so at this Board meeting I moved and got carried that Mrs Howard and Mrs Barnes be added.[54]

Such incidents were unusual, however, since by 1896, the point had been conceded that female guardians should be free to *choose* on which of these sub-committees they sat. Thus, on 16 April 1896, "First meeting of new Board. Mr. Watkinson appointed chairman. John Heywood appointed vice chairman at workhouse. Mr. Graveson chairman and Mr. Kearsley vice chairman. Committee appointed no-one to be on more than one. I *choose* main buildings only."[55] In turn, the role of women in renewing the poor law fabric is perhaps best demonstrated by a brief case study of the building of hospital and nursing accommodation.

On 14 May 1895 there was a "Meeting of Hospital Sub-committee 3.30–5. Vote 5 against 6 in favour of proposed new Hospital Scheme. Mrs Ashworth spoke well". Of the eleven members of the committee, four were women, testimony to the influence of female guardians in this key area. On this occasion, however, the full board of guardians rejected the scheme. Mary Haslam noted "Warm discussion on the new Hospital plans. Matter 'referred back to sub-committee and a smaller scheme to be brought forward instead', 15 against present scheme, 9 for". In response, the buildings sub-committee "Decided to propose part of the scheme to go on with at once; and discuss the possibility of altering old hospital as well", because after the board meeting of 27 November Mary Haslam had talked "afterwards with Mr S. Cooper who advised us to accept any proposal of new Committee for new Hospital so as to make a start." A further meeting took place on 11 December 1895 "to reconsider Hospital question and this time success. 23 against 15. 2 1/2 blocks therefore to be erected on the originally proposed site. Mr Smith much excited". Further extensions were attempted in 1899, when the hospitals sub-committee, still hosting four female guardians "moved the extension of present Hospital Pavilions and building of administration block. Mr Shaw seconded". However, "Mr Cooper saying that the cost now probably is £35,000, the resolution was withdrawn". Nonetheless, by 26 September "The previous week it was decided to build the nurses Home" and new buildings, further nurse accommodation and administration blocks and changes to the fabric of the workhouse itself flowed with relative ease throughout the later 1890s and early 1900s, as we saw in CHAPTER TWO.[56] Female guardians, then, were long standing and active members of the single most important sub-committee in the Bolton union, suggesting a very different role and experience to that which has dominated so much of the historiographical literature.

We might extend this observation to the *fourth* area of female activity. While Hollis suggests that female guardians were largely marginalized when it came to the determination and execution of outdoor relief policy, in Bolton they sat on the sectional relief committees appropriate to their wards.[57] Mary Haslam served on the Bolton township committee and her diary is littered with weekly references to long meetings considering outdoor relief applications. The development of out-relief policy in Bolton is a theme for the next chapter, but it is clearly significant that female guardians had such an entrenched role in this area. *Finally*, women involved themselves, and were involved in, the conduct of the board of guardians itself. Mary Haslam's diary records her private and public anger at wastefulness in the refitting of the boardroom, her distaste for drinking amongst some of the male guardians, her friendship with the clerk to the board, and, a subject to which we return in the next section, her public representation of the board at conferences and meetings. These are not the thoughts and records of a woman marginalized, cowed by male hostility, conditioned against public speaking and active participation and isolated in a male clubland world. They are the thoughts and records of a woman with deep experience of philanthropy and campaigning, a mandate from the people, complex networks of support, a set of equally forceful female colleagues, the support of a significant core of male guardians and, perhaps above all, an excellent grasp of strategy. Rather than experiencing hostility and achieving only on the margins, these women were mainstream players on the board, a fact that would not become apparent if we had to rely on autobiographical sources or even the detailed sub-committee minutes of the union. How, then, was this role carved out?

Negotiating Power: Strategies and Language

While there is very little evidence indeed in Bolton of the "deep-rooted prejudice from many male guardians" that Hollis believes to be representative of other places, neither in strategic or linguistic terms were the female guardians of Bolton passive and undemanding.[58] Indeed, they did much that could have excited more conflict than in fact we detect.

Reconstructing the linguistic strategies and substantive tactics that prevented conflict is fraught with difficulty, as we saw in considering the activities of the BLWVC in CHAPTER THREE. This said, a detailed reading of Mary Haslam's diary and the various union records that overlap with it reveals that, like some of those in Levine's sample of women activists, female guardians in Bolton had a firm grounding in "tactical reality".[59] There were several key characteristics in the making of a successful and, in policy terms, influential, female guardian and these can be traced in some detail via the working diary of Mary Haslam.

Initially, female guardians had to be well-informed. Mary Haslam attended regional and London-based poor law conferences, but also visited other poor law institutions in the north-west and elsewhere. Thus on 23 February 1895, "Visited Chorlton Workhouse with Mr H. and A", while on 18 July 1895 "Mrs Howard and I with Mr Watkinson, Mr Thwaites and Mr H. Cooper visited Lancaster Asylums the County and Royal Albert." On 4 March 1896, Haslam was "Absent from Board meeting on account of attending Central Poor Law Conference in London. Visited Whitechapel Workhouse Infirmary while away and had talk with Mr Vallance (Clerk)". This early flush of visiting in the company of men and women continued throughout the course of her recorded career, and some of it was very strategic indeed. On 6 August 1896, for instance, she "Visited Prestwich Asylum in company with Mrs Simpson Cooper, Mrs Howard and Mrs Swan"[60] giving her time with the wife of the clerk to the board (Mr Simpson Cooper) at a key juncture in debates over new hospital provision in the union, where the support of Cooper was very important. Mary Haslam was also active in canvassing the opinions, experiences and strategies of other Lancashire women involved in local government and local politics. She attended the Southport Annual Meeting for Return of Lady Poor Law Guardians in March 1895 and every year thereafter for instance. On 9 March 1898 she was "Absent all day; due to attending meetings of Women's Liberal Association, at which were debates on points of Poor Law".[61] Nor should we forget that Haslam actively pursued foreign perspectives on welfare and its organization.[62] She kept detailed diaries of her trips abroad (reproduced and annotated in CHAPTER TEN), and on a trip to Ireland in 1899 she noted:

> We passed the workhouse, just as we got to Westport and having time, after having lunched, went to pay it a visit! The master was most obliging and I considered him a superior officer. He had been there 10 years. The number of inmates is about 146. There is no oakum picking or stone breaking as punishments. The master finds forwarding a refractory one before the magistrates is the best deterrent. There is one paid nurse trained under the doctor but not in hospital and I saw a ward attendant with some

infirm and miserable old women, otherwise it is chiefly worked by the paupers. The food somehow very good. The soup has always vegetable in and not peas as with us. The old women sat on forms without backs and all the ground floors are flagged but there were cheerful fires and the standard of comfort, compared with what these inmates have in their cabins is a very high one.[63] It is a rough building with only whitewashed walls and one room was not plastered and another had no ceiling, but for an Irish Standard it struck me as clean and well managed. The children number 17 – 5 boys and 12 girls, who have separate schoolrooms and the master expressed much astonishment when I said the English system was mixed, in many schools as well as in the workhouse. This workhouse is a 'National School' and similar to the rest in Ireland and under its Education Department. The new Irish Local Government Act has made already changes and the master said Ireland had now one lady guardian and could hardly believe over 900 in England. A doctor visits daily – Outsiders are nursed with the rest – about 12 or 15.[64]

National and international travel of this sort reflected Mary Haslam's independent means and economic power, themes that chime well with a secondary literature that has generally portrayed women activists as enabled by the economic means of families and husbands to break out of the domestic sphere.

Such a depiction has unfortunate connotations, implying as it does an idle dalliance with philanthropy, social reform and local government. In practice, a comprehensive reading of Mary Haslam's diary suggests that undertaking this fact-finding was strategically important. It meant that the female guardians in Bolton were well-informed about national and regional poor law policies. In some key debates this gave them the strategic edge. Thus, at the time the guardians were most vigorously debating workhouse staffing and diets in the first part of 1896, Mary Haslam visited the workhouse in Ormskirk union. She was "Very much pleased. Almost 300 inmates; very few "able bodied" cases. Hired women employed as cleaners in men's wards and in laundry – wages 2/- and not food. No picking of oakum at all. Master and matron, Mr & Mrs Caine. Dietary table – 5 meals for children". It can be no coincidence that outside cleaners, children's dietaries and work regimes subsequently came up in the Bolton debate. Fact-finding was also important because it was exactly what some of the male guardians had always done. While it would be wrong to suggest that female guardians simply imitated men, the selective adoption of their best practices was undoubtedly a successful strategy, and one that had been put to good use, as we saw in CHAPTER FOUR, during the election of 1894/95. Yet, perhaps what is most significant is not simply that Mary Haslam and other female guardians undertook regional and national visiting, but that they did so in company with each other and with men. While we cannot be sure that this was a conscious strategy, its net effect must have been to foster solidarity amongst female guardians and to allow them the opportunity to influence their male counterparts. In a situation where the majority of votes on the Bolton board were close, the ability of women to influence men even on the margins was important.

This suggestion introduces a further strategic avenue in the making of a successful female guardian: assiduously networking other (male) guardians and being willing to give ground in order to make longer term gains.[65] When the proposals for a new hospital were in doubt, as we have seen above, Mary Haslam talked extensively with the chairman and clerk of the board, agreeing that they should force through the commencement of part of the scheme on the basis that the rest would then become undeniable. She visited institutions and cottage homes with Canon Wood, "Spoke to Mr Shaw" about his opposition to increased vocational training in the workhouse and quickly followed up the concerns and interests of her allies on the board. Thus, on 30 December 1895, Haslam and Mrs Swan were at the "Workhouse 2.30–4.45. Visited cellar and tower to see if occupied with beds as chairman has said. Cellar first used this winter on Dec 25. Beds in tower number sixty – and are in passages and wards." Subsequently, the female guardians sided with the chairman Mr Watkinson and other allies in a "Noisy meeting about cellar sleeping accommodation", against those with an interest in reducing the rates such as Mr Shippobottom.[66] Interestingly, however, Mary Haslam also tried to network her opponents. On 6 January 1897, for instance, the workhouse committee dealt with a "Proposal to enlarge Committee room. I moved amendment, that though new furniture is unsuitable, still it has cost so much, that we ought not to spend money on further alterations at present, but appoint sub-committee to consider if better ventilation could be devised".[67] On this occasion she worked with the rate savers. The following week, "Report of Committee to deal with increased expenditure, presented and received. (I wrote this week to Local Government Chronicle enquiring chances of placing workhouse school under Education Department)".[68] There can be little doubt that the latter action, which promised small economies, would have been welcomed by those concerned with rising expenditure, and, perhaps as a result, male guardians such as Shippobottom supported Mary Haslam's appointment to spending committees ever after. Rarely does one see such alliances in a secondary literature dominated by perspectives from generalized autobiographical and poor law records. They demonstrate that opposition to female guardians was unlikely to be monolithic, something that it is all too easy to assume.

Many other examples of networking, strategic alliance and giving of ground can be identified in Mary Haslam's diary. On 2 March 1898, for instance, Haslam, Hannah Barlow and Margaret Greg supported one of their otherwise implacable enemies, Mr Leyland, in his attempts to restrict consumption of whisky at the workhouse. On 4 May 1898 the same women were "At workhouse sub-committee re cook. Recommended that he (Roper) is allowed to keep office and live outside for 3 months on trial at 35/- per week. Mrs Swan and I disapproved but gave way to Kearsley and Shippobottom as only for a time".[69] In turn, male guardians gave way to them on other matters. In October 1898, for instance, Shippobottom removed his long-standing objections to the teaching of carpentry in the workhouse in recognition of "our fellow feeling", while on 18 May 1898, as we have seen "Mr Ellis Lee and Mr Swan moved contrary amendment [on swimming lessons for children] but did not press it."[70] Networking and getting to know their male opponents thus yielded dividends. The female guardians also networked the LGB Inspector Jenner Fust, with Haslam noting on 16 September 1896 that "At Board meeting Mr Jenner Fust present. He reported on his visit at the Workhouse, and gave places for improvements . . . The doctor and Miss Hughes made great changes in sick wards. Had a little talk with Mr J. Fust afterwards re children boarding out and cottage homes etc etc."[71] Fust was in turn to become a major ally in the efforts of female guardians to change conditions in the workhouse in the 1890s.

If being well-informed and well networked were important, another strategic device in the making of a successful and influential female guardian was to press a determined agenda of reform without using the language of confrontation and conflict. While Emmeline Pankhurst and Selina Cooper were *demanding* change in other Lancashire unions and alienating male board members,[72] Mary Haslam and her colleagues were *suggesting* change, *considering* issues and *asking* for specific things. Thus, Haslam "Objected to casual way in which children are hired out by any one wanting a young servant" in May 1895, but this was not an issue that was to be fought out at board level through confrontation and accusatory language. Instead, the female guardians moved motions at sub-committee level, sought to use external legislation on schooling to improve the lot of older children and *asked* for the formation of committees of investigation upon which women would sit. The strategy took time to succeed, and we see the frustration of Mary Haslam at several points in her diary, but at no point in this source or the union minutes do we see the language of conflict. There are many other examples: the female guardians *asked* to be allowed to invite workhouse inmates, imbeciles and children on outings, while on 19 February 1896, "Sub-committee re children's dietary. Decide to *ask* power to revise the same up to 16 years of age".[73] Certainly in the first years after their election asking rather than demanding was a conscious and subtle linguistic strategy on the part of female guardians. The art of suggestion was also important, as for instance on 30 April 1897, when "Workhouse 2.30–5.45. Brought forward [the] question of pauper attendants to fetch hospital cases (See March 25). [I] *suggested* that each R. O. should find out and employ respectable woman or women and pay them for going with [the] ambulance. This approved".[74]

The ability to step back, apologize and clarify was also an important component in the process by which women negotiated power, and should not be regarded as a reflection of their weakness. On 15 January 1896, for instance, "I corrected my remark about R. O. at previous Board meeting: Mr Ellis Lee 'now that's ladylike'". Similarly, on 5 January 1898, as we have seen already, "Mr Leyland's motion of censure carried by 12 against 10. Mrs Howard spoke very well I alluded to the disgraceful way the business at the workhouse is carried on. At Workhouse I was taken to task by Mr Shippobottom as implying fault lay with chairman and vice-chairman. I explained this not my meaning at all".[75] This heated debate did not poison relations between male and female guardians and, as we have seen, men were also alive to the issue of when to give way with grace. Female guardians in Bolton extended their influence through keen argument but rarely did they push issues beyond the bounds of what was reasonable. Of course, there are many ways of reading the linguistic subtleties of diary entries, minutes and other sources. Many commentators in the historiographical literature equate the language that I have seen as positive, with female weakness and ineffectiveness.[76] Judged in the round, however, and in the light of the achievements of female guardian's outlined in the next chapter, a reading which sees the language of compromise, asking, consideration and suggestion as weakness simply cannot be entertained for this case study.

Meanwhile, and at the danger of repeating slightly the concerns of the introductory section of this chapter, a major factor in the making of a successful female guardian was an early appreciation of, and ability to exploit, the fact that gender contests were only one, and often not the most important, fracture amongst guardians. Indeed, where we accept that union policy was the outcome of multi-layered power relations, generalizations on the experiences and role of female guardians lose much of their foundation. Thus, from the 1880s most important votes on the Bolton board were very close indeed, reflecting multi-level, but frequently unstable, interest groupings. There was little consistency in the voting patterns of guardians, even when they were faced by successive questions of the same broad type. On issues that involved increasing expenditure, Mary Haslam often found herself in opposition to Mr Shippobottom, reflecting very real tensions between different socio-political and economic groupings of ratepayers that had been evident for decades. However, on two occasions she voted with him against increasing capital expenditure, testimony to the shifting sands of alliance and mutual interest that we rarely see in studies based purely on the records of the board of guardians itself.[77]

Other important conflicts also overtook the issue of gender. There were persistent struggles between the Bolton board as a whole and some LGB inspectors running from the 1870s. Women shared this hostility. In early 1895, for instance, the LGB inspector Jenner Fust presented figures that appeared to show poor quality and quantity of staffing in the Bolton workhouse. He returned on 3 April 1895, when "Board meeting 11–12.15. Mr Jenner Fust [was] present. Mrs Ashworth spoke about nurses to number of patients", arguing that the figures had been wrongly constructed and that the board of guardians was best placed to decide staffing levels.[78] In this attitude, women guardians were allying themselves with the vast bulk of their male counterparts of all political and religious persuasions. They allied themselves with different groups of male guardians, as we have seen already, on issues of religion, temperance, morals and behaviour. Nor should we forget the issue of politics. While Mary Haslam was willing to court the support of the Primrose League to further the election of female guardians, it is clear that most of the elected women had Liberal leanings. They joined a substantial male Liberal grouping on the board, one which stood in opposition to the likes of Shippobottom, Dearden, Shaw and Crompton who were prominent Conservative voices. The election of male and female guardians drawn from the labouring classes during the late 1890s added another political and social dimension to this jigsaw. It is important not to overstate the practical impact of political divisions on local policy, but we can see from newspaper reporting that political contests over committee representation, chairmanship of the guardians, recurrent expenditure and the construction of new buildings were both real and intense.[79] Female guardians who, as we saw in the last chapter, could claim to be apolitical even if they were not, both accentuated the political fractures and retained the ability to navigate such political divisions, giving them opportunities to extend their influence.

Negotiating Power: Issues of Representativeness

On the occasion of Mary Haslam's death in 1922, the Bolton Women Citizens Association published an address "In gratitude for her life and influence, and in the affectionate remembrance of a truly great woman, and a loyal and devoted leader of the women's movement in Bolton." Mary Haslam, the address continued, "was a veritable tower of strength, and a most wise counselor on committees. She was unequalled for seeing all points of view, and her sound judgement none ever questioned . . . She consistently kept aloof from all the littlenesses and petty jealousies that so often beset the path of public life."[80] While we must beware of the rosy pictures painted in obituaries and remembrances, there can be no doubt that Mary Haslam had been a major figure in public life in general and on the board of guardians in particular. The idea that female guardians were silent, felt the weight of oppression and confronted men who found it hard to take their contribution seriously, does not fit this particular life story. Yet, this brief review of the ways in which Mary Haslam and others extended their influence over local poor law policy leaves four broad questions of representativeness unasked or unanswered. *First*, to what extent is it possible or desirable to use life stories such as that of Mary Haslam to explore the role of women in local government? After all, Poovey reminds us that there is a tension between looking at individuals as agents and exemplars of change and regarding individual or collective life stories as "merely points at which competing cultural forces intersect".[81] Biography and collective biography have been important tools for extending the reach and depth of women's history, so this remains an important question. For the purposes of this book we might make the distinction between analysis of *national* figures such as Emmeline Pankhurst, people in whose experiences cultural forces intersect and who underpin so much of the secondary literature, and *local* figures. At the local level it is possible, desirable and useful to focus on the individual exemplar whose life, strategies and achievements often drove the local processes that led to social reform, female political engagement and the creation of a case for women's citizenship. The Bolton Women Citizens Association certainly celebrated an exemplary life when they wrote about Mary Haslam.[82]

In turn this brings us to a second and related issue: to what extent does the diary of Mary Haslam reflect the wider ideological, linguistic, strategic and personal position of other female guardians in Bolton. As Purvis incisively notes, "the category 'woman' has a number of multiple fractures based on differentiation by race, ethnicity, social class, marital status, sexual orientation, culture, religion, able-bodiedness and age".[83] Divisions certainly existed amongst the core of Bolton women who underpinned the philanthropic volunterism and campaigning activism of the post-1850 period, as we saw in CHAPTER THREE. These facts do not, however, mean that Mary Haslam was unrepresentative in her local context. Two observations should act as a caution in respect of such assumptions. *First*, Mary Haslam's work for the poor law involved strategies and ideological perspectives which could have been, and were, shared by reforming guardians of *both* sexes. She observed and exploited numerous fault lines running through the task of poor law administration, pushing forward a clearly defined, and cogently argued, agenda of welfare reform. Like some of the women in Levine's sample, Haslam could "capitalize on inconsistencies and confusions" in local administrative structures and exploit "the vulnerabilities of the system".[84] Indeed, no amount of snippets from her working diary can convey the detailed calculation that underpinned Mary Haslam's poor law activities. *Secondly*, whatever their socio-economic, religious and residential backgrounds, it is clear that all of the female guardians were involved in a variety of overlapping and complementary campaigning and philanthropic activities. Most were active suffrage campaigners. While the other female guardians appear only relatively fleetingly in the working diary of Mary Haslam, their obituaries and other newspaper commentary points to a group of women with a high public profile in early twentieth-century Bolton. Haslam's obituary declared "to all such leaders success is merely the spur to greater efforts, and we have no doubt the memory and influence of the woman who led so many causes will be an inspiration to other women citizens of Bolton", and it would be wrong to regard her as anything other than representative of the drive, strategies and achievements of Bolton women in the public arena.[85]

The third question of representativeness concerns regionality. Were the activities of Mary Haslam and her allies unusual on the Lancashire stage? The lack of detailed research on women and local government at the level of individual unions (as opposed to ad hoc examples drawn from letters and autobiographies), makes this a difficult question to answer. However, if Mary Haslam is one of the best documented female activists, she was certainly not alone in her reforming zeal in the Lancashire context. The broad swathe of Lancashire unions from Rochdale in the east to Southport in the west contained a dense network of women – administrators and radicals – who were accelerating the process of social reform. Selina Cooper, Hannah Silcock, Sarah Reddish, Alice Collinge, Elizabeth Lees, Hannah Mitchell, Emmeline Pankhurst, Teresa Billington and Annie

Kenney are just a few of the many women engaging in Lancashire local government by the 1890s, and diaries, letters and other material wait to be explored in a number of local archives.[86] In this sense, it is unfortunate that the call of Liddington and Norris for a more complex appreciation of female radical activity in Lancashire has gone unheeded.[87] Undertaking such an exercise would have the added bonus of rescuing the late Victorian poor law from ignominy and obscurity, balancing the temptation to judge the New Poor Law and its administrators against national yardsticks in the late nineteenth-century where they had always been judged against local ones before.

A final question of representativeness necessarily follows: to what extent should this review of the strategies and policy successes of Mary Haslam and her peers lead us to question the older literature on women and local government? It would of course be claiming too much to say that the literature should be turned on its head. And there is a danger of counterposing one extreme against another by contrasting the lack of gender tension and the extent of female success in Bolton with the harsher experiences and limited successes of other female guardians such as Emmeline Pankhurst.[88] Yet, the story of Bolton women in general, and Mary Haslam in particular, does offer a useful corrective. Where we move away from the brief snippets offered by autobiographies, the writing of women who were prominent on the national stage, and the uncontextualised perspectives of journal articles, female agency and success emerges.[89] The correspondents and contributors to journals such as *The Westminster Review* who outlined negative experiences of public life are too numerous to think that the Bolton picture is representative. Yet, by July 1907 the formation of the BWLGA brought together a large group of female activists who were looking forward to extending their influence to county and borough councils, who had underpinned the management of the Bolton Distress Committee since 1905 and were forcefully extending their influence over the local poor law.[90] Only more studies of the sort conducted here will really tell us how representative the negative experiences outlined by Hollis really were. In the meantime, a natural extension of the observations on the lack of hostility to female guardians, their strategic successes and the policy reach that they managed to garner is that we should question the considerable literature that has seen the detailed achievements of female guardians as insubstantial, transitory and marginal to both the poor and a poor law undergoing stagnation and decay. These themes are taken up in CHAPTER SIX, where the detailed nature of female agency in poor law policy is explored.

CHAPTER SIX

Making a Difference

The previous chapter suggested that female guardians were not always subject to reflex male hostility, silent, marginalized and tactically naïve. Indeed, there is evidence that, in Bolton at least, female guardians participated in the full array of union business and purposefully sought to extend their reach and effectiveness. This chapter follows up these themes, and some of the lessons arising out of CHAPTER TWO, to discern the impact of female guardians on the range and level of poor law spending in Bolton and on the experiences of the indoor and outdoor poor.

Influences on Bolton Poor Law Policy and the Lives of the Poor

As we saw in CHAPTER TWO, both recurrent and capital spending increased substantially in Bolton during the later nineteenth century. While in headline terms the union lagged behind others in staffing, on almost all other indicators Bolton seemed to be making very considerable strides. By 1890 recurrent annual expenditure was almost three times higher than it had been in the early 1850s, and there was a further very significant rise between 1895 and 1910, broadly contiguous with the activity of the first wave of female guardians.[1] Some of the changes underlying these expenditure patterns are to be explained, as we saw in CHAPTER ONE, by wider, national, amendments to welfare legislation, the guidance issued by the Local Government Board (hereafter LGB), and central and local attempts to take some groups of paupers out of the ambit of the poor law. Thus, while it was not until the early twentieth century that Britain adopted continental models of collective security such as the pension, there was a significant impetus for better treatment of the elderly from at least the 1880s.[2] More widely, Harris reminds us that a proliferation of specialist government departments was accompanied by the rise of "new bureaucratic structures and managerial procedures" that began to undermine the "chrysalis of patronage, idiosyncrasy and circumlocution that had continued to dominate many aspects of public administration in the mid-Victorian years".[3] In terms of welfare administration, this meant a flurry of orders and circulars from the LGB. The range of initiatives from the 1880s is well described by Crowther and does not require detailed consideration here.[4] What these initiatives meant was a new round of visits to unions by inspectors armed with damning comparative statistics on all issues from average expenditure on sickness, to levels of staffing in poor law institutions. As one example of many, Mary Haslam's diary recounts the visit of the LGB inspector, Jenner Fust, in March 1895, when

> Sectional Relief 9.45–11 Board Meeting 11–12.15
> Present at L. G. B. offices Mr Jenner Fust on account of long registrar ship dispute. Allusion made to new arrangements at the Workhouse. Mr J. F. gave the following figures as showing the inadequacy of the nursing staff:

Average number of cases to 1 day nurse nationally	22.1
Average number of cases to 1 night nurse nationally	79.1
Average number of cases to 1 day nurse in Bolton	52.1
Average number of cases to 1 night nurse in Bolton2	40.1

The guardians took issue with these figures, as we saw in CHAPTER FIVE.[5] While there was little immediate outcome from this confrontation, there can be no doubt that staffing was pushed to the forefront of the minds of the guardians. Moreover, legislation and guidance on the conduct of the boarding out of children, child education and employment, lunatics and imbeciles, the able-bodied poor and pauper hygiene all worked to reduce the size of the pauper host under the control of guardians and influence the distribution and level of union expenditure on those who remained. The LGB also issued guidance on the qualifications of poor law staff and, through their use of veto over some aspects of staffing, sought to subtly influence its quality.[6] Hollis thus concludes that "By the later 1890s, the workhouse was being deconstructed."[7]

Meanwhile, another part of the explanation for the changing level and composition of poor law expenditure in Bolton was that the administration of the poor law continued to be tied up with issues of civic pride and civic leadership. The town seems, as we saw in CHAPTER FOUR, to have been insulated from an early twentieth-century trend for the businessmen who underpinned local government in the 1870s to be "replaced by a much more cautious and economical generation", thus ensuring the evolution of ideology and practice.[8] Nor did the increasing working-class involvement in issues of local government derail local policy. As Harris points out "Nonconformist progressivism . . . united much of middle and working-class Lancashire", and nowhere was this clearer than in Bolton itself".[9] Stable, sensitive and imaginative poor law governance by a board with local elites at its core had thus become an article of faith amongst Bolton people in the 1880s and 1890s and remained so into the twentieth century. Local newspapers took a keen interest in the work of the guardians and, as we have seen, elections continued to be solidly fought well past the time when interest in them had waned elsewhere. Against this backdrop, renewing the fabric of the poor law to improve the lot of the poor, to open up institutional help to those who would not otherwise seek it, and to stand as a reflection of the power and status of the town and the elites that underpinned its governance, became an urgent priority for many guardians. The passion that expensive building could excite has already been hinted at in CHAPTERS TWO and FIVE but the fact is that the poor law fabric was renewed and, as we have seen, at considerable cost. The importance of civic pride and civic leadership in this endeavour can be seen from newspaper reporting of the opening of the new nurse's home in 1901, in which the guardians were complimented for their foresight, thoughtfulness and their attention to civic duty.[10]

Patterns and levels of poor law expenditure also continued to be influenced by the nature of philanthropy. The range and scale of philanthropic resources was explored in CHAPTER THREE, but it is worth noting again that prominent industrialists and merchants continued to give very large sums indeed for the benefit of the dependent and independent poor. Thus, the obituary of William Haslam noted that "he took a keen interest in many social and ameliorative movements and assisted them liberally out of his means and in many phases of local life his influence and support will be missed".[11] Female philanthropic activity remained a particular influence on the lives of the poor and the nature of poor law policy, not least because all of the first wave of female guardians were prominent philanthropists. To some extent their continuing philanthropic work overlapped with their poor law functions and all of the female guardians made donations to the social and cultural life of the workhouse or cottage homes – from books and play equipment to fabrics and food – as well as inviting groups of inmates out of the institutions for special treats. Other elements of their philanthropic work had a more preventative focus. Hence, Richenda Ashworth was the single biggest donor to the Bolton Society for the Prevention of Infectious Diseases, and a vigorous campaigner on housing in the town, while Mary Haslam gave generously to the Bolton Civic Amenities Fund, the Bolton Society for the Clothing of the Poor and the Bolton Improvement Trust. She was a vigorous campaigner against slum housing, for the prevention and amelioration of tuberculosis, and a passionate advocate of providing clothing of sufficient quality and quantity to ensure that the poor were not marked out from their peers in daily life.[12]

The philanthropy of female guardians must in turn be set alongside that of Bolton women whose politics or personal situation militated against formal election.[13] As CHAPTER THREE suggested around fifty women stood alongside their elected peers and played a very active part in the lives of the indoor and outdoor poor during the 1890s and early 1900s. Three sorts of initiative that influenced poor law policy, the experiences of the poor or the nature and level of spending, are particularly noteworthy. *First*, these philanthropic women undertook visiting activities. On 6 December, 1899, for instance, Mary Haslam was "At Workhouse, decided to allow 4 ladies, including Mrs Butler, wife to Vicar of Farnworth, to visit Church of England inmates on Fridays and Sundays".[14] A detailed consideration of Haslam's working diary, the minutes of the board of guardians, newspapers and the manuscript and printed reports of various formally constituted organizations, suggests that between 1894 and 1904 at least twenty-three religious visiting committees were convened and attended to the religious needs of the indoor and outdoor poor.[15]

Female volunteers were also at the forefront of visiting linked to the distribution of advice and resources to poor people. The renewal of the Bolton Ladies Workhouse Visiting Committee (BLWVC) after 1895 meant that workhouse visiting continued, but even after the committee was wound down in 1901 the Bolton guardians allowed individual female visitors to attend the workhouse poor and children in cottage homes, to help with education, provide clothing or supplement and modify diets. Mary Haslam's working diary also indicates that she had a particular and enduring concern with what would happen to people discharged from the workhouse. Others shared this concern, to the extent that the names of those proposed to be discharged from the workhouse were forwarded to a Ladies Committee from 1897, with a view to the presence of lady visitors on discharge day. We have already seen in CHAPTER THREE that the mothers of illegitimate children were a particular target of this group, but disabled children, the elderly and able-bodied women were also subject to their attention and resources. Of course, women were also at the heart of other types of visiting. The records of organizations such as the Infant Life Protection Society trace the extensive activity of non-elected women in visiting the homes of those boarded out by the poor law, cottage homes

145

and the homes of poor people throughout Bolton. While such women might arrive with an agenda of advice and inspection, they also provided clothing, small cash allowances and opportunities for training and apprenticeship. Since many of them – Margaret Harris, Mrs Mothersole, Hannah Hulton and Jane Barlow – were well-connected in the town, we should not understate the importance of such visits.[16] As one example of many, we might refer to the Bolton Housing Improvement Trust, which employed the services of seven female inspectors to explore the living conditions of people in the Bolton slums. It is certainly true that this organization shared some of the surveillance credentials of other visiting organizations in Victorian England, but the female inspectors also offered practical help, using their social status to put pressure on landlords with respect of repairs, working with the council and other philanthropic groups for the renewal of the housing fabric, and using their connections to ensure the removal of nuisances.[17] In the sense that visiting activities and reports nudged guardians into particular forms of spending, and no doubt improved the lot of the poor, this sort of philanthropic activity is important for our understanding of the character of the poor law in Bolton.

Philanthropic women might also influence union spending and the experiences of the poor in a *second* way: how they chose to spend the resources under their control. The Bolton Society for the Clothing of the Poor, for instance, gave out clothing purchased from a subscription. Once per month, the poor were invited by leaflets and visits, to attend the market hall and to outline their clothing needs to five lady volunteers, who would then give out cloth and clothing as appropriate. We know little of the criteria that were employed in judging the neediness of the individuals, but the amounts spent on clothing reached a peak of almost £900 in 1901, suggesting a very significant contribution to the clothing economy of the poor.[18] This at once saved poor law expenditure but placed long-term pressure on the guardians to invest in the clothing of poor people. Women also continued to staff soup kitchens, to contribute financially to the Little Bolton Bread Charity and to contribute very substantially to organizations such as the District Nursing Association, all of which could keep people out of the workhouse or poverty altogether.[19]

In turn, the middle-class drivers of philanthropic activity were joined from the late 1890s by working-class women from organizations such as the Bolton Women's Co-operative Guild. This brought impetus to a *third* area of philanthropic work: that which would help mothers and women seeking employment.[20] Interestingly, and importantly, middle-class women such as Mrs Mothersole combined their energies with working-class activists like Sarah Reddish in the early twentieth century to start organizations including The Servant Exchange, which aimed to find work for unemployed domestic servants, and the Women Mill Workers Self-Help Committee, which aimed to provide impartial financial advice to working-class women on issues such as clothing and burial clubs, friendly societies and savings banks. The latter committee would help pay the society subscriptions of those women who had fallen into arrears as a result of illness, and would also pay for things like a stock of goods to help women who wished to pursue a career in hawking or retailing.[21] Whether they offered help to those already dependent on the poor law or put in place preventative structures to stop people reaching this position, female philanthropists were clearly an important influence on both poor law policy and the experiences of the poor.

These factors are significant, but for the purposes of this chapter the most important question is whether the presence and activities of female guardians had an impact on the level and distribution of poor law spending, and on the individual and collective lives of the poor. This issue has been the subject of considerable debate, as CHAPTERS ONE and FIVE suggested. In terms of the broad strategic influence of female guardians, the judgement has been largely negative. Rubinstein and Digby argue that women found "aggressive reform" difficult.[22] Wilson suggests that "any interference from women met with much resistance from Boards of Guardians and Masters of workhouses at the beginning."[23] Hollis takes up this theme, noting that female poor law guardians were "resented by many inmates, staff and male guardians"' because their very election presented a critique of male ways of ordering poor law business and their relationship to the poor. She suggests that female guardians faced "embarrassment, indifference, marginalization or outright hostility", and that they "were never allowed to forget that they were interlopers".[24] The early female guardians were faced with a situation in which "male guardians and male staff closed ranks against the women, kept them off the committees that counted and denied them access to the workhouse", and even by the early twentieth century this situation had not improved much.[25]

Moving away from the question of strategic influence, there is broad agreement that female guardians were able to soften the administration of the poor law. Rubinstein suggests that female guardians "improved the condition of children and the aged, providing more amenities in the workhouse, expanding the functions of guardians into other fields than the relief of destitution".[26] They began, in other words, to make good their election rhetoric which, for many, had concentrated upon where the social housekeeping skills of women could make a difference: in the standards of workhouse care offered to the poor and in the everyday administration of relief to a corpus of the poor that was largely composed of women, children, the old and the sick. Digby argues that female guardians became like friends and family to the poor and that their greatest achievement was to "domesticate the workhouse, mother pauper children, and humanize the arrangements for the sick and old".[27] Hollis takes up these themes. While suggesting that the process of acknowledging the contribution of women guardians was at best grudging, she notes that by the late 1890s "the more silent and tactful of them were beginning to overhaul their workhouses".[28] Female guardians introduced "toothbrushes, sufficient towels, decency and privacy in lavatory arrangements. They inspected the kitchens and the laundry for safety and cleanliness, and brought in new equipment", attempting to impose a "culture of domesticity and emotional warmth rooted in an endless attention to small details." Indeed, "Much of the change in poor law policy towards the young and old, the sick, the handicapped and the fallen, was woman-led" even in the most progressive of boards. Women "tried to domesticate the system, make it knowable, reduce it to a human scale, and see its inmates as an extended household", and "Where the women led, the inspectors and the LGB followed . . . dozens of LGB codes and circulars were largely authorizing best practice already urged by women campaigners and adopted by leading women guardians".[29] Such advances should be regarded positively argues Levine, for "the weight of formal oppression was burdensome . . . the individual victories which women were able to wrest from these institutions had enormous symbolic value as proofs of the successful challenge to the contradictory conservatism of venerated bodies".[30] In other ways, however, a concentration on the human side of the experiences of the poor "stopped them [female guardians] from standing back and seeing the system as a whole".[31]

In the Bolton context, CHAPTER FIVE suggested that female guardians gained a wide strategic and practical influence very soon after the elections of 1894/95. Indeed, women appeared in some numbers on most of the important standing and ad hoc sub-committees, where their influence was increased still further by the fact that female guardians were much more regular attendees than their male counterparts, giving them the opportunity to squeeze through votes, initiatives and spending plans that might otherwise have become bogged down in debate.[32] The rest of this chapter is concerned with how the female guardians in Bolton used this influence to shape poor law policy, spending and sentiment. It focuses not on buildings and committee work, with which we have already dealt, but on the ways in which women influenced the day-to-day experiences of being poor inside and outside the workhouse, on their attempts to "domesticate the system, make it knowable, reduce it to a human scale", and the impact of their activities on the level and pattern of poor law spending.

Women Making a Difference in the Poor Law

The prima facie case for female guardians in Bolton having a substantial influence on the lives of the poor has been made in CHAPTER FIVE. In common with the wider literature, however, much of the detail of that influence remains obscure. There was no shortage of advice on how female guardians should act and the areas that fell within their remit. Louisa Twining's 1885 guidance to female guardians noted that "Nearly all the details of the vast institutions which come under the care and supervision of guardians are such as women would naturally control in their own households". It went on to list clothing, diets, toys, schooling (by far the biggest element of the instructions), bedding, temperance, midwifery and the salvation of souls. This list, and the absence of items such as buildings, outdoor relief and external relations, is familiar from the work of other nineteenth-century commentators and much of the modern historiography.[33] It also reflects the experience of Emmeline Pankhurst, who suggested that the presence of women on the Chorlton board of guardians "had changed the face of the earth" for children and that "We had bought land in the country and had built a cottage home system for the children, and we had established for them a modern school with trained teachers. We had even secured for them a gymnasium and a swimming bath".[34] While the female guardians of Bolton cannot claim to have been instrumental in the building of a swimming pool, we will see below that their remit both reflected and extended these lists, with very significant implications indeed for the experiences of the poor, union spending and their own group identity.

Initially, however, it is important to take an overview of the character of the pauper population that such women had to deal with. Like their counterparts elsewhere, Bolton guardians faced a poor law under which the majority of recipients were people for whom the rigours of 1834 had never been intended. The admission books of the workhouse sub-committee give summaries of the number of people relieved indoors for each half year, and figure 6.1 records the proportion of *distinct* children, men and women admitted to the workhouse at indicative dates in the 1890s and 1900s.[35] While there were subtle variations between different parts of the union – the rural out-parishes had many more men in the workhouse than the Bolton itself, for instance – the key point is that women and children usually outnumbered men on indoor relief.

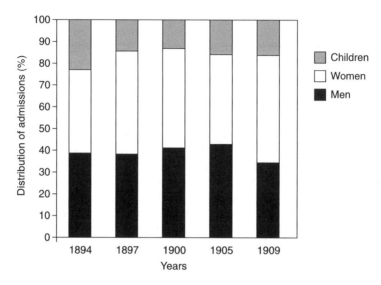

Figure 6.1   Composition of the Bolton workhouse admissions, 1890s and 1900s

Source: BRO GBO 9/151-154, Workhouse Sub-Committee Minutes; BRO GBO 7, Indoor Relief Registers.

The case books for the workhouse sub-committee offer more detail. They show that the committee was dealing with a very limited constituency indeed. Most of the adults that came before the guardians for indoor relief were old and/or sick, while those under the age of 50 admitted to the workhouse were often recorded as being sick. This said, unemployment and underemployment was also a consistent theme. Thus, in the fortnight beginning 7 September 1896, 67 people were admitted to the workhouse. Of these, Thomas Greenhalgh (47), was from Bolton and had delirium tremens, Mary McCormick (28) was placed in the work-house at her request because of her husband's neglect, Mary Green (56) was infested with vermin and in a fever, while Joanna Body (32) turned up to commit her four children to the workhouse to be picked up in two weeks' time once her husband's illness had passed. The rest of those admitted were sick, old or asked for temporary respite from lack of work.[36] This level of detail is intrinsically interesting, and illustrates well that a period in the workhouse could be actively sought by those facing serious problems in the outside world. Figure 6.2 shows the detailed causes of admission to the workhouse for a number of indicative dates, emphasising once more that indoor relief had become focused on those who were not supposed to be subjected to the rigours of 1834. While this is a familiar contention in the literature, more studies of workhouses are clearly needed.

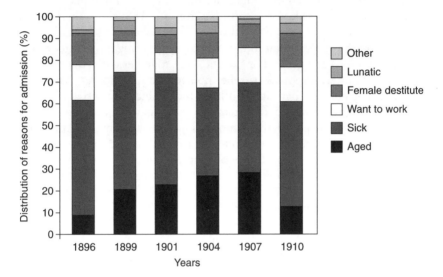

Figure 6.2   Distribution of the causes of Bolton workhouse admissions, 1890s and 1900s

Source: BRO GBO 9/151-154, Workhouse Sub-Committee Minutes; BRO GBO 7, Indoor Relief Registers.

Of course, none of this should surprise us. It is well known that the composition of the indoor population on a national basis was geared towards children, women and the aged.[37] Moreover, it is equally well known that most paupers were relieved outdoors for the entire duration of the New Poor Law period. Bolton was no exception. While the total number of people relieved fluctuated according to background economic conditions, the proportion on indoor relief remained both low and stable at 10–15 per cent over the period 1892–1917.[38] In terms of crude numbers this would still mean that the Bolton workhouse contained over 300 heavily dependent people at most dates. Thus, even if these observations should not surprise us, they do indicate the potential scale of the task facing Bolton female guardians attempting to change the experiences of the indoor and outdoor poor and inject their own agendas into poor law policy.

151

Their energies appear to have been directed along *nine* avenues in addition to membership of the major building and finance committees. *First*, and in a very general sense, one of the most important but least visible impacts of the work of the female guardians was to put constant change in the workhouse onto the union agenda and into the day-to-day experiences of the poor. Of course, male guardians in Bolton had taken a very active interest in workhouse conditions from the 1880s, but there was a step change after the election of the female guardians. The decade after 1895 witnessed no less than nineteen separate investigations into workhouse conditions at a general or specific level, together with twenty-seven special committees on outdoor relief policies, cottage homes,[39] staffing, staff training and remuneration, clothing, food, education and workhouse discipline. Many of these committees and investigations were fostered or suggested by female guardians, almost all had female representation and their effect was to keep the attention of guardians focused firmly on union policy and its impact upon the poor, and the attention of the poor on changing workhouse regimes.

Female guardians also worked beneath this aggregate veneer on matters that had a very direct impact on the lives of the indoor and outdoor poor. A *second* area of interest and initiative, for instance, was nutritional standards. Diets were perhaps the most immediate interest of female guardians in Bolton, taking up a theme that we see them exploring previously in the context of the BLWVC. While their concerns with the quality, balance and quantity of food may be regarded as simply an extension of domestic expertise, we should not understate the value of dietary reform to paupers, nor the significance of the sway that female guardians came to have over this area of indoor relief.[40] Thus, on 3 December 1895, Mary Haslam, "Visited workhouse in morning. Tasted pea soup and found it very good . . . Children in Mrs Matthew's house (babies) were having rice pudding for dinner, at Mrs Wolfendales' pea soup with peas taken out". These innocuous comments must be understood in terms of the criticism of poor law diets offered by female guardians in other forums. Thus, also on 3 December, Mary Haslam "Spoke with matron [to reassure her that criticisms were not levelled at her] about Mrs Ashworth's remarks on diet at Women's Lib. Association".[41] As a result of Richenda Ashworth's intervention, claiming that the workhouse diet was so poor as to endanger life, on 18 December 1895 a sub-committee on children's food was formed to redraw the dietaries. Moreover, on 19 February 1896 Mary Haslam made an ambitious attempt to redefine the notion of childhood in the workhouse rules, suggesting that the new dietaries should apply to all people up to the age of sixteen rather than the age of twelve as before. This amendment was accepted and in 1897 the female guardians turned their attention to the diets of children in the vagrant and admission wards, arguing that as a basic standard all children should be allowed milk, sugar and cheese. A letter on 21 May 1897 from Simpson Cooper to the workhouse master noted,

> Dear Sir, I send you herewith a print of an order of the LGB [order 35701] amending the regulations with respect to the diet of children under 7 years old admitted to the tramp ward. Mrs Howard and Mrs Swan have been deputed to arrange with Mrs Topp as to the supplies of milk required in pursuance of such an order and you better mention it to them when they next visit.[42]

Nor did the female guardians neglect adult diets, ticking off the cook in December 1896 when inmates complained to them about inadequate and poorly cooked food. Perhaps unsurprisingly, soon after this the female guardians began seeking extra cookery expertise in the workhouse and to raise the potential pay of the cooking staff in order to get better candidates to apply. They also sought to revise the rules on the conduct of cookery staff. Mary Haslam notes on 24 November 1897, for instance that "Appointment of Roper and wife £17 as cooks; duties to be defined by Sub-committee to revise rules".[43] While it is hard to know the direct impact of these actions on diets in relation to the everyday lives of the indoor poor, by the later 1890s the guardians were being consistently complimented for their general workhouse regime by newspapers and the LGB, and we see no complaints from the poor themselves about workhouse food after 1898. Thus, although nutritional standards may have been viewed as "women's matters", the impact of the actions of female guardians on the lives of the poor and the scale of poor law expenditure was potentially very significant.

A *third* major area of interest and initiative was childcare.[44] Like their counterparts elsewhere, female guardians in Bolton ranged widely across issues relating to children. They were active inspectors of cottage homes, the children's ward in the workhouse, foster homes and all places where children were housed. Mary Haslam's working diary (see CHAPTER NINE) is full of brief reports and criticisms of the cottage homes, fostering arrangements and the facilities for children who found themselves in workhouse infirmaries. In particular, she and the other female guardians dominated the sub-committees that established and equipped cottage homes, appointed cottage home keepers, and dealt with all aspects of the boarding out system. Their achievements in improving the general standard of childcare, and particularly in establishing a boarding out system that was a model for unions elsewhere, were reviewed in a *Bolton Chronicle* editorial of October 1901. This noted that at a recent conference on boarding out "Bolton union came out very well as compared with other Lancashire unions and Sir J. T. Hibbert, the president of the conference, spoke of them as a progressive board".[45] Moreover, in common with female guardians elsewhere those of Bolton were very active in the provision of leisure activities and treats for children inside and outside the workhouse. Hence, on 26 June 1895, Mary Haslam "Asked leave to invite imbeciles to a hay field tea next week", and on 1 July she noted "Had imbecile women and girls at White Bank (about 50). Heavy showers but fine between". Similarly, on 8 September 1898 "Had workhouse children at White Bank for afternoon. 30 unable to come from no 7 because of cases of measles. A beautiful day. 80 came. Returned in 2 minibuses".[46] Other trips organized by female guardians and open to workhouse children and the children of those in receipt of outdoor relief, included the Bolton flower show, an annual canal excursion, an annual outing to the seaside, Whit Walks, an annual picnic and an annual visit to the pantomime.

It is important not to understate the importance of these seemingly minor treats. Alice Foley, whose descriptions of her girlhood in Bolton we encountered in CHAPTER TWO, encouraged a friend, Annie Hulkin, to record her memories of early twentieth-century childhood in Bolton. As well as revealing intricate details of the street culture of the town, Hulkin notes a series of school trips and adventures that made up the life of a child just outside the ambit of the poor law. Thus, Annie and her fellow pupils "were taken to Chadwick museum and had lessons on the skeleton and allowed to roam about afterwards. We were also taken to Jumbles by special bus to Bradshaw and walked the rest of the way; we gathered plants and wild flowers and then sat round to listen to botany lessons. Once we were taken to Tigers Clough, Horwich . . . we had a review on Spa Road Recreation Ground where there was a band and mounted police . . . Boys and Girls wearing special caps though of different colours". Foley adds in her own words a note to the effect that Hulkin was heavily employed in childcare and domestic chores from the age of three and that neighbours used to complain that Hulkin had never had a childhood.[47] Treats, trips and parades were, therefore, an integral part of the childhood of even the most domestically captive of children, and it was important that female guardians had constructed a regular rota of such events by the later 1890s. Whether these reforms had "changed the face of the earth" for the indoor pauper children of Bolton is doubtful but the benefits of the reforms instituted by female guardians must nonetheless have had a very direct and immediate effect on standards of childcare.[48]

A related, and *fourth*, area of initiative for female guardians was education. As elsewhere, female guardians allied themselves with sympathetic male guardians to fight for better education, educational conditions and training for poor children both inside and outside the workhouse. Several developments are worthy of note. Thus, the very fact of regular inspection by female guardians highlighted problems and provided an impetus to consistent standards. Mary Haslam and the other female guardians were very active in this area, on average visiting the school rooms at least once per week. Indeed visiting was one of the very first subjects to be addressed after the elections, when on 23 January 1895, Mary Haslam considered "the visits of the Schools Sub-Committee of no use, being both formal and expected". This situation was to change quickly, with unannounced visits accepted by staff and male guardians in May 1895.[49] Female guardians also took an interest in, and visited, formal examinations. On 9 July 1896, for instance, a deputation of ladies: "Attended School Examination – Mr Mozley being examiner. Mixed school very good. Infants indifferent'.[50] The perspectives gained in such visiting led to a further set of initiatives as female guardians sought extended educational provision. On 3 December 1895, Mary Haslam led a deputation of women guardians and "Found in school in infants room 23 on gallery 16 writing 17 reading with Miss Ormerod, total 56. [An] Assistant mistress a necessity". The board subsequently employed a further teacher. On 18 July 1898 "At workhouse School Examination. Thought again that Mr Mozley [was] very dull and old-fashioned. Asked him would it be possible to get additional mistress in". Subsequently, on 10 August "At Workhouse the School Inspectors report re an additional mistress in the infants department discussed by schools and cottages sub-committee. I was asked to be present having gone into the question with schoolmaster and clerk", and then on 17 August "Schools and Cottages Sub-committee again discussed question of additional mistress".[51]

While on this occasion discussion proved fruitless, by 1900 there were no less than three qualified teachers in the workhouse, and seven more in the various cottage homes, suggesting a very significant level of educational provision when set against that likely to have been available to non-pauper children elsewhere in Bolton union.[52] Thus, while Hollis regards workhouse and district schools as an anachronism by the twentieth century, in Bolton at least they provided solid mass education. Indeed, not until 9 October 1900 had "Mr Shippobottom moved appointment of Sub-Committee to consider desirability of sending the children out to the public elementary schools", and only on 26 February 1902 was it "passed by 34 against 9 that the Cottage Home Children attend the public Elementary Schools. The Schools are St. Williams' and S. S. Simon and Jude. Victoria Schools said that at present they had not accommodation, so all Protestants go together. *My* one drawback to scheme is that we shall miss the Schoolmasters' interest and influence with the boys, but perhaps something will be done to meet this loss".[53]

As a natural extension of their education remit, the female guardians were active in shaping the conditions under which children left the workhouse for employment, investigating the experiences of those who left and inquiring into the circumstances of those, very many in the case of female children sent out to service, that came back. Their particular achievement, though long in coming, was the regulation of the criteria for employment, which must have had a significant policy and expenditure impact. When the female guardians took up their position, it was comparatively rare, even given the strides made by the union under the leadership of more radical male guardians, for children with particular problems (disability, upbringing etc.) to be provided with individualized solutions. The tendency appears to have been to ship children out to whatever employment was available at the earliest possible opportunity, something that infuriated the female guardians. Thus on 22 May 1895, as we saw in CHAPTER FIVE, Mary Haslam "Objected to casual way in which children are hired out by any one wanting a young servant". By 4 December, a "Small sub-committee appointed to visit the homes previous to children being sent out to service", and this was followed in 1896 by a new set of rules to govern who could be sent to work placements outside the boundaries of the union.[54] Female guardians were not always successful in their reforms. Hence on 5 August 1896 "Proposal to appoint Miss Barlow to visit children in situations instead of Relieving officers negatived". However, by March 1898 the union had a female-led boarding out and child employment committee. Further frustration was to be encountered, as for instance on 30 October 1900 when, "At Workhouse I moved a resolution 'that the children in the Cottages should not go out to service if the number left be not 3 over 12 years old' It was adjourned – nothing seems able to prevent these little girls going out to this miserable 'service' – !." Nonetheless, by 1901 Bolton union was alone amongst its peers in the northwest in having a formal employment policy for the children of indoor and outdoor paupers, while by 1911 it had set up housing for all children who had been apprenticed so as to give them an independent residence.[55] The corollary of such advances was a series of specialized treatments for those unable to enter employment, including epileptics, the mentally disabled, stunted, blind and deaf.[56] Collectively, such initiatives significantly raised the proportion of union expenditure allocated to children, as well, no doubt, as improving the day-to-day lives of poor children.

The female guardians also launched initiatives in a *fifth* area at the other end of the age spectrum, taking a concerted interest in the welfare of the elderly. Some of their touches were small but important, seeking to brighten the lives of elderly workhouse residents. Hence on 12 March 1895, a joint tour of the workhouse by the visiting committee and the female guardians was "Told no games allowed so agreed to enquire into it". Subsequently, Bolton workhouse was to have a specified games room and old people were treated once per month to a football match between workhouse inmates and local teams. In 1897, Margaret Greg seconded a successful motion to build a bowling green for the old people in the workhouse, while in 1898, Mary Haslam commissioned the Bolton Brass Band to perform once a quarter. The elderly were the intended users of a reading room paid for by the board and stocked with books donated by female guardians, who in turn also sought to provide treats for elderly paupers. Hence, on 11 July 1895 Mary Haslam "Asked leave for 'aged and infirm' to come out for afternoon. Mrs Howard ditto", and on 15 July "Had 100 'aged and infirm' men and women at White Bank. Day fine".[57] If small, these touches may nonetheless have appeared significant to the elderly.

Yet, it was in the general regime for the elderly indoor poor that female guardians had the most influence. Between 1896 and 1902, they sponsored the reallocation of workhouse space to give elderly couples more privacy and silence, re-outfitted all elderly paupers, proposed and had accepted the abolition of task work for the elderly and drew up formal rules guaranteeing set visiting times. On 1 November 1899, "At workhouse, proposal to start the Brabazon Employment Scheme there; by ladies outside, led by Mrs J. Hulton approved; the day to be Tuesday", and thereafter the elderly and disabled became part of one of the largest schemes in the northwest.[58] Meanwhile, the elderly also benefited disproportionately from changes to the fabric of the poor law (particularly hospitals), and staffing, with increased numbers of paid staff releasing elderly paupers from duties such as receiving the outdoor poor who came into the workhouse because of sickness. If these seem like small advances, cumulatively, they must have had a significant impact, and one elderly Bolton resident certainly recalled a conversation with their grandmother in which it was noted "the place was brighter after 1900, not that you'd want to be there but the food was decent and it was warm and dry, and they gave you out brand new clothing, and not a uniform mind, so a little time there was not so bad".[59]

This brief quote emphasises a *sixth* area of interest for female guardians, and one that they came to completely dominate: that of clothing. Between 1895 and 1905, a synthesis of sub-committee minutes, the working diary of Mary Haslam, newspaper reporting, and tenders and contracts issued by the poor law, indicates that there were thirty-nine separate initiatives on the clothing of the indoor and outdoor poor, almost all of them resulting from the activities of the female guardians. They ranged widely over the clothing of children, the sick, the aged, child workers and the outdoor poor. On 29 January, for instance, Mary Haslam, "Found in no.8 cottage (Mrs Colebourne) that the girls wear a most terrible kind of corset; begged her to discontinue it at once and promised to speak to matron. Find all the girl children wear the following clothes chemise, drawers (flannalette) 2 petticoats each with bodice, frock and pinafore. Think this adequate, but decided to ask matron to have all frocks made with long sleeves". Boys too came under scrutiny. Hence on 3 April 1901, "At Workhouse. I spoke to Mr Taylor about the boys clothes, and asked the committee to allow them to wear the composition collars on week days. Found Taylor would much like improvement in boy's clothes". Even the bed clothes of the sick were reviewed and renewed, with Haslam noting on 20 October 1897 that "Hospital Sub-committee brought in list of bed and patients' linen required in hospital and agreed to."[60] Nor did the outdoor poor escape. Richenda Ashworth instituted a survey of the clothing of the outdoor poor in 1896 with a view to a comprehensive renewal though a partnership between poor law and charity.[61] Unsurprisingly, then, clothing was a major item of non-core expenditure for the Bolton poor law.[62]

Meanwhile, female guardians also directed their energies to reform in a *seventh* area of poor law policy: facilities for pregnant women. On 25 September 1895, for instance, Mary Haslam "Spoke to Miss Hughes about privacy for Lying-in Ward",[63] after hearing complaints from nursing staff, workhouse inmates and presumably the many pregnant women who came into the confines of the workhouse just for the purposes of gaining medical attendance at birth. Over the next eighteen months, the female guardians worked tirelessly on the issue of maternity, eventually convincing the guardians to build separate birthing and convalescent rooms next to the old lying-in ward at a cost of over £2,000. As we saw in CHAPTERS TWO and FIVE, such expenditure marked out Bolton on the national scale as one of the most progressive unions when it came to maternity care.[64] A further advance was a trebling of the number of paid midwives available to the poor between 1896 and 1901, and this testifies to an *eighth* area of initiatives on the part of female guardians: the staffing framework of the union. While many of the questions they dealt with were apparently small – whether to have two laundresses or one, whether relieving officers should employ 'respectable women' to fetch hospital cases to the workhouse rather than ordinary (and often drunk) carters, the salaries and bonuses of officers, who should lead cottage homes, whether officers had the right to prevent the access of working paupers to fresh air during break times, how many new lunatic attendants to appoint and the appropriate level of experience to ask for – their impact on the level and professionalization of staffing was cumulative and profound. A brief consideration of the more than 1000 personnel files for the union over the period 1880–1929 suggests that the qualifications of paid staff were improving markedly in the 1890s and early 1900s. References were certainly more fulsome by the mid-1890s and staff turnover fell once the female guardians had been elected. This is testimony to the fact that the board generally used female guardians as mediators with paid staff given their experience and interpersonal skills in the area.[65]

The final and *ninth* area in which we see substantial female initiative was outdoor relief policy. While Hollis suggests that some of the early female poor law guardians (and many more female candidates) were exponents of the rigours of 1834, we see little evidence of this in Bolton.[66] It was unlikely to be otherwise given that almost all of the female guardians had grown up in households where trade or manufacturing were key determinants of income. Nor do we see any evidence that female guardians avoided membership of or were excluded from the committees that dispensed outdoor relief or formulated outdoor relief policy. Indeed, women served on 5 of the 8 union district relief committees. Their singular achievement in this area was to help foster a significant increase in the generosity of outdoor relief during the 1890s, particularly for female recipients. While Thane is scathing on the issue of out-relief policies for women, suggesting that "inadequate out-relief and the consequent unwillingness of many women to apply for a pittance which would be accompanied by a close investigation into the ways of life", undermined the social and economic position of women, in Bolton there was a clear and consistent uprating of female allowances.[67] Female guardians also supported measures to gather together a team of volunteers whose job it was to seek out need and recommend action to the guardians, and they voted in favour of every one of the sixteen measures put to the board between 1896 and 1906 aimed at increasing expenditure on food, clothing and allowances for the outdoor poor. On 26 September 1900 they joined with Liberal male guardians to fight off challenges "to [the] purchase of expensive drugs and medicines for outpatients",[68] and Mary Haslam herself was very active in tackling some of the causes of poverty amongst the outdoor poor. On 24 July 1901, for instance,

At workhouse. Report of sub-committee re Consumption presented and passed after much discussion by 13 against 9. Resolution to be sent to County Borough of Bolton Horwich and Farnworth Urban Councils. 'That notification of phthisis [to] be encouraged (if not made compulsory) and that full disinfection [to] be allowed after a removal or death.' Also a slight increase in out-door relief to be made if R.O. see that it is spent in extra beds, or food.[69]

The impact of these and other policies on the outdoor poor can best be judged by the observation that in Bolton, at least by the later 1890s, historiographical perceptions of the hostility of labouring people to contact with the New Poor Law through the outdoor relief system may have been overplayed. Short-term outdoor relief appears to have been factored into the expectations of a significant number of people at times of sickness or unemployment.[70] The sectional relief registers and admission and discharge books for the union are difficult to use, but a broad synthesis suggests that between 1895 and 1905 well over one-third of the nominal Bolton population came into contact with the poor law, the majority through outdoor relief. Interestingly, however, the average duration of relief (indoor and outdoor combined) more than halved over the same period. At the same time, and as we saw in CHAPTER TWO, union spending on sickness prevention and treatment, and on outdoor relief, rose substantially in the later Victorian and early Edwardian period.

Conclusion: Welfare Policy and Feminism

While this has been a brief exploration of the practical impact of female poor law guardians on poor law policy and the lives of the poor in Bolton, we might draw several key conclusions: These women were incredibly busy. While it is a commonplace that poor law work was time-consuming, Mary Haslam and her colleagues made their poor law work a vocation. Moreover, the extent of their interests and the intensity of their engagement with a spectrum of issues from out-relief and finance on the one hand to clothing and diet on the other, indicate that the female guardians had genuine power. They were involved in a web of interrelated decision-making, and they were there as of right either because they had the skills or because, as we saw in CHAPTER FIVE, they insisted on female participation.[71]

In turn, there is evidence that the injection of female agendas in local welfare policy had an important impact on the lives of the poor, the sentiment of the poor law and the nature of union spending. Given the progress made by male guardians prior to 1895, it would be wrong to suggest that female guardians somehow humanized the poor law, though there is no doubt that the lives of the poor became more comfortable and hopeful as a result of all of the small interventions and wider policy changes that these women promoted. In fact, their impact was more profound and multi-level. Thus, while it is difficult to construct counterfactuals to ask what would have happened if the female guardians had not been elected, a detailed synthesis of Mary Haslam's working diary and the financial records of the union suggests a very significant impact indeed. Without the female guardians, £36,000 of loans would not have been raised and isolation wards, maternity wards, nursing homes, libraries and cottage homes would not have been built. Without the female guardians, death rates in the workhouse would certainly have been higher, the clothing of the indoor poor would have continued to stigmatize inmates, pauper nursing would have clung on for much longer and the education of children would have been a lower priority. Without the female guardians, outdoor relief levels would have been materially lower, the guardians would have spent more on themselves, and the workhouse population would have been larger than it was. Without the female guardians, the influence of the middle-class in local government would certainly have waned.[72] This was more than humanizing the poor law, it was carving out a central role in the determination and execution of policy, the creation of a poor law that in experiential terms was doing anything other than falling into stagnation and decay.

Rather than being marginalized, then, the Bolton female guardians were at the very heart of union business, and this fact was recognised in numerous newspaper reports, obituaries of female guardians and testimonials to such women for their work. Thus, an editorial for the *Bolton Journal* of 25 February 1910 "paid a striking tribute to the value of the work of women guardians". The same edition of the paper reported a meeting of the Bolton Women's Local Government Association, where the chairman Dr Jeffries referred to

> the increasing influence for good brought about by the appearance of women in practically every department of public life. Able, businesslike and active, they were showing themselves ready and willing to take their share in public labours . . . the work done by their association as represented by the ladies on the Boards of Management of the guardians and infirmary, was not only practical, carefully considered and wise, but a great blessing to all concerned.[73]

Rebutting newspaper criticism of the state of some of the infirmary wards, he went on "these wretched assertions had no foundation in fact" and on the further criticism of the cost of their interventions "There were some things they could not pay too much for, and the money spent on the sick was well spent". In her vote of thanks, Mary Haslam noted "in public life it was character that almost told more than talent, and if they were to achieve their aims they must exercise self-control and be tolerant".[74] Haslam's particular contribution to changing the lives of the poor and helping to shape poor law policy was recorded in her numerous obituaries of 1922, one noting, for instance, that "It is perhaps as a Guardian of the Poor that Mrs Haslam will be remembered best by many people. She brought to her work as a Guardian a trained intellect, sane judgement and a sympathetic and conscientious understanding of her duties. Her efforts were for reform and improvement not only for the outside poor but for those in the Institution . . . Mrs Haslam was one of the pioneers in Poor-Law work in this town, and those who follow her and her colleagues are reaping the benefits of the work done by them".[75]

The achievements of female guardians in their professional lives were, then, considerable. They must have made a real difference to the experiences of being poor, though there is no doubt that the contemporary writers who identified grinding poverty in Bolton were tapping into a depressing reality. A final question remains, however, over the underlying motivations for the immense time commitment that these women made to their professional (and continuing philanthropic) work. In particular, and given the extent of historiographic comment on this issue, we might ask whether the female guardians of Bolton were driven by a broadly feminist agenda of the sort that we identified in CHAPTER ONE,[76] and whether local government work was a stepping stone to a much wider critique of a male dominated institutional and political system. This is a difficult question to answer, not least because so much of their work had an intimate personal angle. In December 1894, for instance, Mary Haslam visited the workhouse and,

> Heard that nurse Beseley was leaving and bid her goodbye. Visited hospital and Infirm wards. Talked with a Mrs Marsden (Green) who formerly lived in High Street and knew me as a child. Called mother 'such a nice little lady'. She has been in the workhouse 5 years and is in Hospital Ward 35.[77]

A brief reflection by Mary's son, Oliver, on the career of his mother continues the personal theme. He notes that while she was "Born to intellectual freedom out of material security", she was also "a woman of great character with ideas far in advance of the age in which she lived". The public activities of her father "left a deep imprint on his daughter, whose education fitted her, as her father inspired her, for a life of service dedicated to the community".[78] He concludes that "Hers were the days of Liberalism, and the fount of her energy lay in her idealism and her profound respect for lasting human values".[79]

There is little hint of feminism in this quote. Yet, personal and emotional motivations do not preclude wider feminist credentials. Hollis draws a distinction between philanthropic and local government women and those who moved from such work into women's suffrage and who "were feminists, insisting that women as women should posses equal citizen rights alongside men. They turned to local government not only as a place of political power in its own right but as a stepping stone to national power." Nonetheless, she insists, "When women's suffrage came in 1918 it owed little or nothing to women's local government work"[80] Levine also encourages us to make a functional distinction between feminism and campaigns for social and welfare reform, noting that "Feminism offered a consistent creed that functioned as a theoretically understood crossover from campaigning politics to philosophical stance". It involved " a collective understanding of oppression" and was not simply a natural extension of philanthropic or local government work. Moreover, she reminds us that that only 24 per cent of her sample of female activists had ties to local government as opposed to the 52 per cent who were involved with suffrage.[81] When approached from the angle of a local case study, such firm conclusions appear out of place. As Thane reminds us, women "fighting with little experience, against long entrenched structures of power", appear, when judged against appropriate yardsticks, to have made remarkable steps in the field of welfare, changing the lives of the poor and setting the foundations for a further leap into a wider political arena.[82] Were Bolton women, however, working with each other "to make active statements as to their vision of a feminist future"?[83] It is this question that we turn the final chapter of **Part I**.

CHAPTER SEVEN

Feminism, the Politics of Local Government and Suffrage

CHAPTER ONE showed that the issue of how to define "feminist" and "feminism" is complex and contested.[1] Nonetheless, the chapter suggested, if we take the term "feminism" to mean a conscious appreciation of the structural nature of women's oppression and the need to confront such oppression with collective woman-centred solutions, then we see the emergence of a national feminist movement in the 1850s. Those whose activities underpinned the movement engaged in multiple political, social and moral campaigns but soon came to voice the need for women to have the national vote as a means of undermining the central tool of male oppression. How to locate the election and work of female poor law guardians within this national framework seemed ambiguous, a reflection of wider doubts amongst historians about the success of women in their poor law work and the robustness of the connections between poor law work and other feminist issues. CHAPTER SIX took up some of these themes, suggesting that in the Bolton context the achievements of female guardians were profound and, tentatively, that engagement with the poor law may have been a springboard to the wider involvement of female activists in public life and politics, suffrage and the development of individual and collective feminist journeys. In this last chapter of **Part I**, we explore these issues further. It starts by emphasising the fact that the national feminist movement was multi-layered and experienced a number of key ideological, personal and tactical tensions. These tensions, allied with the still small numbers of systematic local studies of feminist networks and frequently ambiguous local evidence, means that it can be difficult to uncover and characterize the totality of local female agency. Thus, the chapter goes on to suggest key indicators of the existence and nature of local feminist movements before moving on to a detailed consideration of the feminist journeys of Bolton activists during three crucial periods: 1890–1906 (the local government period), 1906–1914 (the suffrage period) and 1914 onwards (the citizenship period).

A Multi-Layered Feminist Movement

It is not the purpose of the current chapter to explore the range and depth of feminist scholarship on the late nineteenth and early twentieth centuries. Such surveys have, after all, justified books in their own right. Nonetheless, it is clear from this scholarship that the multi-layered nature of the later Victorian and early Edwardian feminist movement generated implicit or explicit tensions between feminists and between feminist campaigning organizations. Many of these tensions have been explored in some depth in their own right. They are given brief elaboration here as a stepping stone to an understanding of what yardsticks we ought to use in judging the existence and depth of local feminism and feminist networks.

Initially, then, we can see that feminists were split on the existence and meaning of biological differences that gave women different capacities (mental and physical) to men;[2] on whether feminism and marriage were compatible goals and whether reform of the institution of marriage simply represented "a chipping away of the edges of patriarchy";[3] on how far the feminist movement ought to be associated with the more aggressive sexuality of 'New Women' in the 1890s;[4] and on the issue of class.[5] Late Victorian and early Edwardian feminists also debated the long-term and intermediate goals of their movement. Should women seek absolute equality, or should they simply seek to expand their (local and regional) sphere of influence, bringing maternalist, organizational and moral qualities to the public sphere inhabited by men? Doing the latter would allow women to portray their claims for wider involvement as essentially an unselfish act on the part of a group of people with public duties and a claim to citizenship, but would leave the fundamental structures of women's oppression in place. Or should women seek equality mediated by difference, making claims to specific areas of policy, governance and citizenship because they possessed qualities that men did not? Alternatively, should the feminist movement seek to re-invent the state and its notion of citizenship by campaigning for the vote and a formal presence for women in national public life? Or should feminists seek to systematically deconstruct the institutions of male power and re-invent the process of female socialization, questioning the very dichotomy between equality and difference?[6]

Variations of opinion between individual female activists on the national stage were marked. Lewis's discussion of the lives of Octavia Hill, Beatrice Webb, Helen Bosanquet, Mary Ward and Violet Markham shows how they challenged the boundaries between public and private spheres but resolutely defended the line that female activists should neither neglect the domestic sphere, nor seek absolute equality.[7] Other feminist biography reveals women with equally passionate views on the relative merits of equality and equality and difference, whilst new biographies of important figures such as Emmeline Pankhurst have re-emphasized the fundamental critique of female oppression that under-pinned the activities of some national activists.[8] In turn, these subtle disputes over long-term goals fed through into important debates about the ideological vehicles that feminists should use to stake their claims. Later Victorian newspapers, pamphlets, journals, and discussion groups hosted overlapping, complementary and competing feminist discourses on natural law, rationale morality, feminine virtue, historical rights to citizenship, female capacity,[9] experience in public service, maternalist qualities of women,[10] the duties of citizens, evangelicalism, socialism,[11] slavery,[12] Liberalism and constitutionalism.[13]

The issue of the goals of the feminist movement was tied up with a further tension point, that of national and local politics. While feminism and Liberalism have often been associated easily in the context of late nineteenth-century England – Rendall, for instance, suggests that "Liberal roots in nonconformity, in pressure group politics, in the politics of moral reform, offered women a basis for feminist claims"[14] – there is also a persuasive argument that Liberalism provided an uncertain basis for feminism.[15] At the same time Conservatism was not as antithetical to feminism as it might first appear, and modern feminist literature has drawn attention to the fact that Liberal and Conservative women could and did work together at both an individual and an organizational level throughout the late nineteenth and early twentieth centuries.[16] This said, there is also evidence that political division could be enduring and bitter, and Levine suggests that many feminists sought to short-circuit potential conflicts between feminism and political allegiance by seeing them as entirely separate entities.[17] Indeed, it has become a commonplace of the literature that feminist organizations eschewed formal linkages to political parties. Nonetheless, at an individual level it is clear from the work of commentators such as Hannam that the confluence of the two spheres of interest in everyday *local* life generated persistent and real tension in the feminist movement.[18] While such political tensions are clearly worthy of more discussion in their own right, the key thing for this chapter, which engages with how we might identify and characterize feminism and feminist networks at local level, is that the tensions exist in the first place.

Meanwhile, a further tension was experiential. Feminist activists often engaged in multiple campaigns but some generated divisions in the feminist movement. In particular, women activists might try to keep campaigns on issues like women's education or the poor law separate from the suffrage arena. National suffrage campaigners in turn tried to distance themselves from campaigns on issues such as women and contagious diseases.[19] More importantly for this chapter, the national activists brought very different registers of experience to national campaigns, something that we can see by focusing on local government work. Thus, for some women, local government work, social reform, social work and philanthropy was, and remained throughout the period, an end in itself and largely unaffected by feminism.[20] At another extreme, some of the most prominent feminists of the later nineteenth century had already been or were active in local government work and philanthropy. For them, such work was a strong and immediate inspiration for feminism and suffrage. As Bock and Thane point out, face-to-face engagement with the failures of male inspired welfare policies, either directly in the forum of local government or indirectly via philanthropy, convinced such women that only by influencing national policies and controlling national resources could they fundamentally change the nature of welfare, and this required the vote.[21] Nowhere is this more clearly expressed than in the words of Emmeline Pankhurst, who noted, 'I thought I had been a suffragist before I became a Poor Law Guardian but now I began to think about the vote in women's hands not only as a right but as a desperate necessity'.[22] Indeed, Rubinstein suggests that "many women moved naturally between politics and charity, with little consciousness of a dividing line between the two".[23] While the link was not inevitable, some commentators have seen philanthropy and local government work as providing the notional contacts, language and experience that made political campaigning easier and more effective.[24] We explore this theme further below, but for now the key point is that at national, and presumably local, level, experiential differences could be considerable and must have fed through into subtle differences of tactics, language and ideological focus amongst female activists.

Meanwhile suffrage was a definitive point of debate and conflict for the different parts of the feminist movement. While many men sympathetic to women's nineteenth-century public role took on board their successes in electoral campaigning and local government, male parliamentarians largely continued to believe that women really were different (and inferior) to men, and incapable of wielding the vote.[25] A women's

167

suffrage movement thus developed alongside the other campaigns conducted by feminists. The broad history of the movement itself between the formation of the London National Society for Women's Suffrage in 1867 (subsequently the federated National Union of Women's Suffrage Societies (NUWSS) in 1897 under Millicent Garret Fawcett), the formation of a Central Committee to co-ordinate the provincial societies in 1872, the Women's Social and Political Union (WSPU) and the dilution of middle-class impetus as the suffrage movement was joined by an increasing number of working-class women and working-class women's organizations,[26] has been well established and does not require extensive discussion here.[27] What does require slightly more comment are the divisions over suffrage that could emerge in the national feminist movement.

Thus, extended biographical work on individual suffragists has emphasized the centrality of friendships, shared values and jointly developed networks amongst women, to the success and endurance of the wider political movement of suffrage.[28] Much of the secondary literature has also, however, noted the complex personal fractures that suffrage could excite in the feminist movement. Caine and others have pointed persuasively to important generational differences in feminist attitudes, motivation and tactics, particularly after 1900.[29] Tensions also arose between women from the north and those from London, between women whose suffrage ideas were underpinned by economics or class and those whose ideas were underpinned by the wider visions of socio-political change,[30] and between women who were married and those who were not. Suffrage campaigners were also split according to their basic goals. Thus, we see a distinction between those who campaigned for the vote because its attainment would have wider benefits to society – better laws, moral improvement and more sensitive social justice – and those who campaigned for the vote as an end in itself, either as a remedy to entrenched male power or as a reflection of the natural rights of women. Moreover, the movement was also split along political/apolitical lines, between those who wanted a limited extension of the franchise based upon a property qualification and those who wanted full enfranchisement of all women, and between active and passive suffragists. From the formation of the WSPU in 1903, there was an additional split on the issue of tactics between feminists who accepted the views of male suffrage supporters in and around Parliament[31] that the suffrage movement had to frame its demands in terms of the virtue and character of women, not natural rights, citizenship or their demonstrable abilities and potentialities, and those who employed militant tactics.

Of course, some of the divisions ostensibly created by the suffrage cause were notional rather than real. The WSPU, for instance, has been the subject of sensitive rethinking. While militant activities have often been portrayed as directionless and opportunistic, a detailed consideration of the language of militants – including the concepts of "just war" and social oppression – suggests persuasively that there was a solid and important underlying rationale to the actions of the WSPU.[32] Purvis has likewise argued that we need to rethink the motivations of WSPU leaders, showing that they did not move to the right or become opportunistic, irrational man haters, but that they refused to work within the structures of society. Instead, they constructed a fundamental critique, rejecting the idea of liberal feminists that inequality was linked to exclusion from equal rights, and socialist feminist perspectives that inequality was linked to class, and arguing instead that inequality was directly linked to the privilege of men and the institutionalisation of their power.[33] In this sense, the formation and tactics of the WSPU ought properly to be regarded as just one point on the feminist spectrum and one segment of the feminist argument. As several scholars have pointed out, when one looks at the detailed underlying beliefs of many individual feminists who did not support militant suffrage, the distinction between their positions and individual WSPU members appears to have been largely one of tactics.[34] Of course, suffrage is a monumental issue and we could explore the secondary literature in considerably more depth. They key thing for this chapter, however, is that suffrage was potentially and actually a divisive issue for late Victorian and early Edwardian feminists. By implication, the nature of local suffrage organizations can probably tell us much about the character and role of local feminist networks.

This focus on the fractures of the feminist movement is not to question its unity of central purpose. After all, splits amongst feminists should hardly surprise us given that male political and campaigning groups were hopelessly split in the Victorian and Edwardian periods. Moreover, as Purvis cautions, a unified feminist movement is quite compatible with recognition that not "all women's shared experiences have been experienced equally".[35] Thus, Maynard argues that if we slip underneath the veneer of campaigning, individual personalities, and the numerous polarized debates in the Victorian feminist movement, we can see the development of a basic critique of the nature of female oppression and its cause. This critique, she argues, centred around the needs for equal rights, a reconceptualisation of the relationship between women and the family, access to employment opportunities, amelioration of economic dependency, and for women to take control of their sexuality. Its exponents sought remedy in changing the behaviour of men as individuals, alterations to the social construction of masculinity and femininity, and the deconstruction of systems of male power and authority.[36] Though their campaigns were diverse, they were also woman-centred and had overlapping membership and basic ideologies.[37] In turn, it is through an appreciation of this basic critique that we can make sense of the personal and institutional fractures, overlapping campaigning and intense debates in the feminist movement.

Meanwhile the focus on fractures and polarized debates should not deflect attention away from the achievements of the feminist movement. As many commentators have warned, it is important to judge the organizations, language, strategies and victories of feminism by appropriate yardsticks. Dominant boundaries and long-entrenched structures of power had, by definition, to be incorporated into organizational methods and strategic goals.[38] We might also remember that feminist campaigns were caught up with, and partially influenced, wider changes in issues such as the definition of citizenship,[39] the national and imperial status of motherhood,[40] the role and political importance of pressure groups,[41] and the representation of issues such as class, gender and feminism in legal and political discourse.[42] The rhetoric, ideology, organizational forms and strategies of feminists and feminist groups thus had to be mutable and fluid.[43]

From National to Local Feminism: A Framework

Of course, when we consider national figures and movements, mutability is not a massive problem; the proliferation of excellent biographical material on prominent feminist figures, analysis of articles and speeches in feminist journals and renewed discussions of the large-scale campaigning organizations, allows us to strip away the tensions, experiential variations and ambiguities of language to reveal the central beliefs, motivations and interrelated campaigning of feminists. The same task is much more complicated at local level. Systematic (and published) local studies of feminist networks that might provide an analytical framework remain surprisingly rare. While the provinces may have been a seedbed for feminist action on suffrage and other issues, the most visible focus of the important campaigns of the later nineteenth century and beyond ended up in London. Unsurprisingly, much of the feminist biography of the last thirty years has dealt with the lives, beliefs, experiences and writings of the relatively small, London-based, circle of feminists whose names have become synonymous with the movement. Consequently, how to read, and against what yardsticks to judge, the snippets of language, glimpses of biographical detail, conflicting or absent motivational detail and varying experiential profiles that often constitute our local information base on female activists, is very uncertain.

This said, our discussion of the tensions within the national feminist movement, allied with a reading of the voluminous secondary literature on feminism and feminists in the late Victorian and early Edwardian period, suggests six key yardsticks by which we might judge the meaning of such evidence. *First*, and notwithstanding the recent tendency of gender history to deflect attention from the particularity of women's lives, it is clear that local feminist networks, like the national movement, were likely to have been personality driven. Analyzing the lives, words, experiences and motivations of small core of local leaders can reveal much about the nature of feminism. The relationships between prominent individuals are also likely to be an important indicator of whether feminism became a way of life in a particular locality. Levine suggests that feminist activists were the product of a critical mass in the women's movement as "generation succeeded generation, each under the tutelage of the previous one", and of family systems that had a particular propensity to foster activism and feminist thought.[44] Historians disagree over how amicable the relationships were between such activists.[45] However, biographical work on national figures continues to stress that advances in feminist thinking and the development of feminist strategies was crucially dependent upon high profile individuals and groups bound together by friendship, upbringing and a shared history of personal development and campaigning,[46] who could "unite personal affection and political commitment, and provide the kind of informal networks" created by men.[47] Friendship networks could be supportive, protective, enabling, complements to a marriage,[48] and fulfilling, and they could both support and put strain on family relationships and marriages.[49] In turn, Hannam notes that strong personal networks were part and parcel of establishing a sense of identity that encouraged women "to emphasise women's authority and to value their own needs and experiences".[50] Thus, and as Rendall reminds us, our perceptions of the emergence of self-conscious feminist activity cannot rely on "the public record alone; it has to be related to the personal histories and to the networks of friendship which underlay the slow growth of that movement".[51]

A *second* and related theme is that however they were organized and whatever tensions were apparent, later nineteenth-century feminists were generally women with a history of campaigning on multiple and overlapping, but not always woman-centred, causes. Discerning the existence and character of local feminist networks is thus in part a function of tracing these multiple interests and tracing the interrelationships between them. Meanwhile, a *third* theme from the wider historiography is that identi-

171

fying the local linguistic register of feminism is an important task. While the language of historians characterizing feminists and the feminist movement in the late Victorian and early Edwardian period has become ever more precise – it is now possible to talk about "social mothers",[52] "Socialist feminists", "maternalist feminists", "welfare feminists",[53] "romantic feminists",[54] and "radical [working-class] feminists", as well as "feminists" and "women activists" – where to find and how to read the local linguistic landscape of feminism remains ambiguous. Can we, for instance, rely on letters to newspapers or newspaper commentary on the speeches at meetings organized by women, to identify the local linguistic register of feminism? Or is it the case that local feminists varied their language and conceptual thrust according to the particular forum in which they found themselves? On the national stage different groups of feminists varied their core linguistic register depending upon whether they linked feminist campaigns with the suffrage issue[55] and whether their motivations were an extension of the public sphere, equality or a fundamental reform of concepts of state and citizenship. Was the same true at local level? And how much weight should we give to the frank language about motivations and experiences found in diaries and autobiographies versus the often more tempered and usually neutral language found when the same women occupied their seats as guardians or charity trustees? There are no easy answers to these questions, but the fact is that at least a cursory analysis of linguistic registers is important for establishing the existence and character of local feminist networks.

A *fourth* yardstick for local studies might be the existence and succession, of female socio-political organizations. While the willingness to become involved in multiple overlapping campaigns on morals, social welfare and suffrage may be an indicator of feminist sentiment, this is not necessarily strong evidence of a functional feminist network. Nor is the existence or longevity of a particular campaigning organization. On the other hand, membership or foundation of organizations such as the Primrose League (PL) or Women's Liberal Association (WLA) alongside organizations working for the return of women poor law guardians, suffrage, female citizenship and social welfare reform, may well indicate a wider feminist network and sentiment. Related to this yardstick, a *fifth* might be that we should seek out and reconstruct the nature of public recognition (positive or negative) of feminism and feminist networks. *Finally*, it is clear from the secondary literature outlined in CHAPTER ONE and developed further here, that the conduct, scale and public reception of local suffrage campaigns provides a way for us to understand the depth, character and reach of local feminist movements. Of course, these crude yardsticks do not constitute an all-embracing analytical framework for local research. Yet, in the Bolton context they provide a useful pathway through the often ambiguous, sometimes contradictory and always patchy evidence on the feminist credentials, personal journeys and collective motivations of the women who became poor law guardians.

Feminism 1890–1906: The Local Government Period

As we saw in earlier chapters, the 1890s witnessed an upsurge in the extent and depth of female philanthropic and campaigning work. The chief focus of this book has been the planning and execution of strategies to increase the involvement of Bolton women in the sphere of welfare. In this, women like Mary Haslam were remarkably successful. We have seen that female guardians gained real power, with active participation in, and sometimes domination of, the web of debates that generated policy. They were not simply consulted, but by right and choice (sometimes their own, sometimes that of men) they actively shaped the whole tone of poor law decision-making. There can be no doubt that this sort of activity formed a real focus for the public persona of middle-class Bolton women, and there is equally no doubt that working-class women also saw involvement in welfare as a way of forging ahead with a radical, woman-centred agenda. Sarah Reddish, for instance, was a prominent member of the Women's Co-Operative Guild (WCG) and became a poor law guardian at the very end of the period considered here.

Yet, while the achievements of these women were profound, how to locate this poor law work in the context of their personal and collective feminist development, and indeed how to characterize the wider feminist movement of the 1890s, is ambiguous. There is no convenient feminist archive or contemporary discussion to point the way, and we are thus forced to rely on our admittedly crude analytical yardsticks.

Hence, this was certainly a women's movement dominated by a small core of personalities. The six female guardians elected in 1895 and the ten present in 1906 were, as we have seen, part of a group of fifty or so middle-class Bolton women whose public lives encompassed philanthropy, social and political campaigning, welfare reform or engagement with local government. Whilst Mary Haslam shared the philanthropic stage with other major donors and activists, such as Hannah Bolling and Hannah Hulton, there is no doubt that she was the heartbeat of the public women's movement. In this role, as we have seen from the biographies and obituaries reviewed in CHAPTER THREE, she was supported by women from

173

other prominent local families, including Richenda Ashworth and Margaret Barnes. The feminist credentials of these women in the early 1890s are difficult to see from any survey of their life histories. One of Mary Haslam's obituaries notes that "She has told with pride of how when a girl in her teens she paid a subscription to a society for women's suffrage out of her very first dress allowance".[56] Yet, as we can see in CHAPTER EIGHT, Mary Haslam herself suggested that she became involved in public life more as a way of coping with the death of her young daughter rather than because of any profound feminist sentiment. Nor is there evidence that any of the other middle-class female campaigners in early 1890s Bolton were driven by an upbringing that had installed feminism at their core, with the exception perhaps of Margaret Barnes who we encountered in CHAPTER THREE. Moreover, while these women had a shared educational experience, other evidence that they formed a self-conscious movement unified by friendship and shared background is slim. Indeed, the only time we get a sense from Mary Haslam's working diary (CHAPTER NINE) that these women had any real friendship is when the female guardians wrote to Mr Ashworth regretting the death of his wife. They were certainly not on intimate terms with the working-class Sarah Reddish, who, from the later 1890s, was using the language of class and feminism to make the case for socio-economic reform in Bolton.[57]

Other indicators that might point towards the existence of a broadly-based self-conscious feminist movement in early 1890s Bolton are also missing or ambiguous. Thus, while Rover traces the emergence of Manchester and other Lancashire centres as hotbeds of early suffrage activity, suffrage campaigning in Bolton was at best sporadic.[58] A meeting in 1894 sponsored by the "Manchester National Society" had been "largely attended and enthusiastic", hearing speeches like that of Miss Stacey that "Women were as much affected by politics as men could be said to be; and therefore they ought to have a share in the management of their own business – the business of the State".[59] Individual women also wrote letters on suffrage to the Bolton newspapers throughout the 1890s. However, attempts to establish formal suffrage organizations in the town failed and Mary Haslam, in her account of the Bolton Women's Suffrage Association (BWSA) notes that "In Bolton there had been at various times meetings held, and letters sent to the papers calling attention to the women's plea[60] but without any progress being made" before the BWSA was formed in 1908/09. This notwithstanding the fact that from her later teens Mary Haslam's "interest in the [suffrage] movement was unabated".[61]

The nature of public recognition of women's work and campaigning provides an equally ambiguous perspective. On 8 December 1894 a

Bolton Guardian editorial on parish and district councils suggested that,

> It will have been noticed that the claims of ladies to be members of Parish councils have received but little notice in most parts of the country. It may be that the electors consider ladies are more suited for the duties of poor law guardians, and, if so, they are probably correct. There may be exceptional cases in which ladies of experience in the management of property are qualified to render useful service in parish councils, but such instances are exceptional; while there can be no doubt of the great value of ladies in looking after the interests of poor women and children who need the help of the guardians. The District Council and the Board of Guardians are in most cases of greater importance than the parish council.

The paper went on to suggest that national politics should be kept out of these local elections and that if electors "have a predilection in favour of a class of candidates they will do well to let it be in favour of ladies, whose services at boards of guardians are almost always of great value".[62] Reading this contradictory set of comments is problematic, for on the one hand the paper praised women for their poor law work and suggested that they could make the leap into other spheres of government, while on the other it sought to restrain their ambition and to limit their citizenship. What this editorial does not do is give us a sense that Bolton had a unified, self-conscious and broadly-based feminist movement in the early 1890s. Our review of the nature of electoral campaigning for the poor law franchise in CHAPTER FOUR also seemed to demonstrate wide public recognition of the value of female involvement in public life, but little sense that their different campaigns should be linked together to make a wider feminist case. Of course, we might not expect to see such a case made in the forum of a newspaper. Yet, by the end of our period, 1906, the *Bolton Chronicle* was indeed making the point that "Our Lady Guardians have been involved in such a weight of campaigns that together have done much service for the locality, and one in particular, Mrs William Haslam, is the undisputed leader of the women's movement of this town".[63]

In short, the 1890s must be a period when we see the increasing public recognition of the variety of women's campaigning and an appreciation of its underlying rationale. Similar developments might be seen in the linguistic register of women activists. Mary Haslam's working diary (CHAPTER NINE) points persuasively to the existence of a multiplicity of female campaigning groups in the 1890s, but it gives little linguistic hint that the women involved were part of a conscious feminist movement. Her autobiography (CHAPTER EIGHT) is little more revealing. By 1906, however, the public linguistic register had changed.

Chairing a public meeting to begin thinking again about formal suffrage organization in Bolton (a gathering attended by female poor law guardians, members of the WLA and PL, prominent female philan-thropists and representatives of suffrage societies in London and Manchester) Mary Haslam noted,

> that 30 years ago she became a subscriber of the branch established in Manchester in connection with the women's suffrage movement. A gener-ation had passed since then, during which time they seemd to have been working in the dark and beating the air until just now, so to speak, they found themselves in the forefront of fashion . . . She explained that those who had called that meeting had done so in their private capacity, and not as nominees of any section of the large women's suffrage movement. They desired to show that whatever methods of urging on the cause might be adopted, the great mass of women were united in their desire for the fran-chise . . . Women had proved themselves useful on public bodies. There were women guardians in Bolton who had done great honour to the town (applause) and had worked on other public bodies with distinction . . . under laws made by men alone.[64]

Giving the vote to women, the meeting concluded, was central to the long-term socio-economic, moral and political development of the country. This complex speech draws attention to the diversity of women's public work, the longevity of claims to women's suffrage and the reason-able and patient methods of the women themselves. Above all, however, Mary Haslam's whole speech leaves us with the overwhelming feeling that politicians, activists and waverers ought to look at the collective public successes of women and recognize their right and duty to vote. By the early twentieth century, then, the undisputed leader of the Bolton women's movement was talking in feminist terms to a meeting of the most promi-nent women in the locality.

Further evidence of the presence and development of a functional and self-conscious feminist movement in 1890s Bolton can be inferred from the very considerable variety of overlapping causes in which Bolton activists were involved. As we have seen throughout this book, the campaigns for the return of female guardians dominated the long-term agenda of the 1890s, but they were not conducted in isolation. Middle-class women continued to be involved in a wide variety of charitable initiatives, including the Queen Street Mission, the foundation and running of orphanages, nursing associations, workhouse visiting, campaigns against prostitution, housing and public health reform, and the Poor Protection and Benevolent Society. Many of the same women were prominent members of the PL or WLA and, as we have seen, it is possible to see the first concerted stirrings of the middle-class suffrage movement by 1906. Table 7.1 provides a summary of the overlapping interests of eight prominent middle-class activists between 1892 and 1906. It is based upon an exhaustive gleaning of all references to these women in newspapers, charity records, the working diary of Mary Haslam, association and society minutes and personal collections. We can see that on average these eight women were involved in substantial number and variety of causes during the 1890s. There are few comparative figures for other communities, but it seems likely that table 7.1 does testify to a high level of public engagement. It certainly provides, in light of the national evidence on the multiple overlapping interests of feminists, interesting signposts to the presence of a self-conscious network of women activists. Moreover, we should also be aware that working-class women joined in some of these campaigns and developed their own. The Bolton WCG, founded in 1883,[65] had a membership of 80 by 1890, rising to 250 in 1926. Sarah Reddish was a member of the national Central Committee between 1889–91 and 1895–98, and was president in 1897, while Margaret Bury was on the Central Committee almost continuously between 1894 and 1908, taking the presidency in 1896, 1904 and 1908. Alice Collinge only joined the WCG in 1904 but she, along with Sarah Reddish, were important activists in the Independent Labour Party (ILP) branch at Bolton.[66]

Table 7.1 Overlapping interests of eight female activists, 1892–1906

Activist	Range of activities	Total 1892–1906
Mary Haslam	Poor law guardian; philanthropy, philanthropic campaigning, sanitation, WLA, suffrage, Women's Local Government Association, workhouse visiting, child welfare, home visiting, regional societies, aged poor.	43
Susannah Swan	Poor law guardian; philanthropy, philanthropic campaigning, housing, Women's Local Government Association, workhouse visiting, home visiting, self-help societies, nursing, regional societies.	28
Margaret Barnes	Poor law guardian; philanthropy, philanthropic campaigning, housing, sanitation, suffrage, PL, Women's Local Government Association, workhouse visiting, nursing, bible societies, education.	24
Hannah Barlow	Child welfare, home visiting, aged poor, philanthropy, philanthropic campaigning, self-improvement societies, PL.	17
Mary	Poor law guardian; philanthropy, philanthropic campaigning,	17

Howard	housing, sanitation, suffrage, WLA, Women's Local Government Association, workhouse visiting, nursing, education, child welfare	
Martha Moran	Housing improvement, sanitation, aged poor, child welfare, fallen women, orphans, suffrage, nursing.	14
Elizabeth Hughes	Aged poor, elections for female poor law guardians, child welfare, sanitation, women's employment, home visiting, working-class self-help.	11
Sarah Reddish	Trade unions, ILP, poor law guardian, women's employment, aged poor and children, libraries, women's local government, parish councils	11

These are intriguing perspectives. Two further observations make their inference, that there is evidence of a self-conscious feminist movement, more compelling. *First*, while it is tempting to focus on the sheer variety of female engagement with philanthropy, campaigning, suffrage and local government, what table 7.1 masks is the fact that those who were, or those who worked for the election of, female guardians dominated women's public life in Bolton. These were the women who formed the executive committees of philanthropic bodies, convened suffrage meetings, wrote to newspapers about women in local government and, in the later 1890s, brought together the WCG and the Association for the Return of Women as Poor Law Guardians (ARWPLG) to form one campaigning organization. Poor law work, therefore, was the focus for the early development of the Bolton feminist movement and an important stepping stone to other forms of campaigning activity. *Secondly*, and as we have hinted, what is also notable about the late Victorian and early Edwardian period in Bolton is the way in which the focus of women's public activity changes, becoming more formalized and organized. Sharing membership, interests and a desire to foster women's involvement more widely in the local public sphere, the WCG, ARWPLG and, from 25 May 1897, the Women's Local Government Association (WLG) provided a forum for women to develop their ideas, tactics and language, something that comes to fruition in the early twentieth century.[67] Organizations like this were also, in the post-war period, to provide the means by which the Bolton women's movement could move away from its personality-driven foundation.

Feminism 1906–1914: The Suffrage Period

The evidence for the existence, vibrancy and depth of the Bolton feminist movement is less ambiguous after 1906. It continued to be dominated by the guiding light of Mary Haslam. The foreword to her pamphlet on Bolton suffrage (CHAPTER ELEVEN), written by fellow members of the BWSA, noted that,

> All those who have been actively associated with the Society, know how much it owed to their inspiring faith and devotion, in the days when the cause was unpopular and the task of evolving a local society was one of the utmost difficulty.[68] Those who know nothing of its early history will never realise the dauntless courage and splendid tenacity of purpose with which Mrs Haslam and Miss Haslam – as she then was – pioneered the struggling movement.

More widely, Mary Haslam's obituaries drew attention to her status as a role model for local women, a status that was largely constructed in this period 1906–1914. One noted, for instance, that

> But it is as a leader of the women's movement in Bolton for many years that she will be best remembered. It was very near to her heart . . . it required considerably more courage in those days to fight for the freedom of women than it does today, and the present generation will never realize what a debt they owe her as one of a noble band of pioneers who first had a vision of a wider and fuller life for women, and worked mightily to secure it.[69]

As in her local government phase, however, Mary Haslam was not alone. Amongst middle-class campaigners she was joined by her daughter Mildred, Harriet Stacey, Margaret Barnes, Susannah Swan and Martha Moran. Working-class activists such as Sarah Reddish, Doris Chew, Hannah Staples and Elizabeth Browning were also prominent on the local and national stage, pushing for the rights of women workers, suffrage and, in combination with middle-class activists, a greater say for women in municipal politics. Moreover, a consideration of newspaper reporting, the minutes of associations and societies, personal collections and subscription lists for the period 1906–1914 suggests that the supporting cast of women campaigners had also increased, rising from the fifty or so of the 1890s to almost two hundred by the eve of World War I. Thus, while evidence that the leaders of the feminist movement shared common ground in terms of education, upbringing, socio-economic status, friendship or kinship[70] remains hard to find right up to 1914, it is clear that the movement reached a critical mass sometime after 1906. Feminist activists continued to be very active in a range of overlapping campaigns. Philanthropy and philanthropic campaigning dominated the scene in numerical terms as it had done in the 1890s, with housing improvement, clothing, nursing, child protection, education and visiting the key concerns of the ongoing philanthropic movement. The WLG and ARWPLG also remained a central focus for all the core of female middle- and working-class activists in Bolton as the process of getting female guardians elected and keeping them in position became harder in the 1900s. However, this second chronological stage in the development of the Bolton feminist movement saw women making much wider claims based upon their successes and experiences in local government and their rights to representation and citizenship. Thus, the *Bolton Evening News* of 7 November 1909 dealt with the formation of an Old Age Pension Committee in the light of the introduction of pensions of 1 January 1909. It noted,

> The Town Clerk read a letter from Mrs Taylor . . . hon. Secretary of the Bolton Women's Local Government Association, suggesting that . . . the Association be allowed to nominate a representative to serve on the committee. This course had been followed with advantage in London, Cardiff, Huddersfield, Southport, Chester, Otley, Oxford and Rochester.[71]

This was an important extension of the "precedent quoting" that had been so successful on the board of guardians and the resolution was adopted.[72] Feminist activists also held meetings in support of the idea that, having proved their worth in the forum of the board of guardians, they should be allowed to stand for election as borough councillors. A WLG meeting of February 1909 asserted, for instance, that "The work which women had done already might be sufficient . . . to clear away any hesitation in asking them to come forward officially. They had proved their worth as free lances and were WORTHY OF CONFIDENCE in the future".[73]

Yet, it was suffrage campaigning that marked the greatest advance of the Bolton feminist movement during this period and was a major reason for the expansion in the size of the underlying group of female activists in Bolton. We saw earlier (p. 174) the first stirrings towards formal organization had been felt in 1906. Mary Haslam's meeting had followed a visit to Bolton by Emmeline Pankhurst in July 1905[74] to address the local Trades Council, and was one of a series of ad hoc lectures, public meetings and informal gatherings to highlight the issue of women's suffrage.[75] Letters in support of women's suffrage began to appear in local newspapers in 1907 and the issue was raised at meetings of the WLA (where Mary Haslam argued that women should "not raise a finger for any candidate at an election who would not vote for women's suffrage.") and in meetings to canvass support for the NUWSS.[76] Then, on 7 March 1908, in a meeting at Haslam's home, thirty prominent female activists came together to

> form a branch of the North of England Society, which had for its object the granting of the parliamentary vote to women on the same terms as it is or shall be granted to men.[77] Shortly after this, a committee was formed as follows: Miss Dymond, Mrs Frankland, Mrs Howard, Mrs Jessop Hulton, Mrs Ernest Knowles, Miss Makinson, Mrs H Mason, Mrs Walter Musgrave, Mrs Rees, Mrs F Taylor, and Miss Winstanley; while the officers appointed were – Mrs Haslam, President; Mrs C V Thompson, Chairman of Committee; Miss Haslam, Hon. Secretary; and Mrs Knott, Hon. Treasurer.[78]

The NUWSS had 16 federated societies in 1897, 70 in 1909 and 305 in 1911, testimony to the regeneration of enthusiasm for suffrage nationally after 1900. However, given the extensive feminist network in Bolton by the 1890s and the explicit feminist sentiments expressed by Mary Haslam in 1894 the late development of a formal suffrage organisation is surprising, and may indicate that local feminists saw the need to consolidate their position in local government before taking the next leap, something which is implied in many of the early speeches on suffrage in the town.

Once started, however, the BWSA rapidly gained momentum. Mildred Haslam wrote to local newspapers in April 1908 to inform the public of the formation of the Association and to set out is committee and governance structures. The names can have come as no surprise either to the editors or their public. There were several female poor law guardians on the committee, as well as women who had stood as candidates but failed to be elected, and women – Taylor and Hulton for instance – who were at the very forefront of philanthropic activity in the town though they did not hold office, further testimony to the overlapping interests of many female activists by the early part of the twentieth century. The BWSA sent marchers to London and Manchester in 1908 and engaged in a series of public lectures to male and female church organizations.[79] The committee also organized large public meetings, using the publicity tactics pursed to great effect in poor law elections and calls for philanthropic donations. Mary Haslam notes

> But the crowning effort of the year was a public meeting in the Temperance Hall which was quite filled, over 2000 persons being present.[80] Mrs Haslam

presided, and Mrs Swanwich and Mrs Allanbright gave addresses. Miss Abadam was unfortunately prevented by an accident from being present. The meeting was very enthusiastic: it had been known by advertisements in the press, large posters on the walls, sandwich-men in the streets on the day itself, and by the distribution of leaflets.[81] Other meetings were held in October, December, and February, and the Committee felt encouraged by the result of the first year's work.

Suffrage activity expanded rapidly thereafter. Thus, in the 1909–1910 parliamentary election, members of the WLA, PL, WCG, the Women Textile and other Workers Representation Committee, and the Men's League for Women's Suffrage came together with the BWSA to campaign in Bolton. Mary Haslam notes,

> for three weeks, a shop in Deansgate (No.131) was taken and made gay with posters, and this formed the rallying ground of members and friends who obtained signatures to the Voter's Petition for Women's Suffrage. By canvassing the streets, attending candidates' meetings, and visiting in the dinner hour various works where men were employed, a large number of signatures were obtained.[82] Of course the candidates were not spared deputations and questions. On the election day at eight, out of the 22 polling stations, were stationed in relays, members of the committee or friends, who asked the men to sign our petition as they came out after registering their votes. The weather at first was fine, and large numbers signed our petition, but later the rain came on, and voters were not willing to be stopped. In one or two cases by the courtesy of the Returning Officer, we were allowed to stand inside the door, but in general, the undaunted women stood outside while the rain beat on their paper forms, and the writing of the blue indelible pencil became illegible. While the shop was kept open, 2657 signatures were obtained from Bolton. The same procedure was adopted at the County Election at Westhoughton and 1122 names were obtained there.[83]

These were by no means spectacular results, but the fact that all of these organizations campaigned together tells us much about the nature of the feminist movement in Bolton. In turn feminists in the town used their experience to good effect in shaping the female vote. Haslam notes of the 1910–11 phase of the suffrage campaign that

> Greater progress was made this year, and the goal came nearer into sight, by the formation of a Parliamentary Committee consisting of Conservative, Liberal and Labour members, with the Earl of Lytton as chairman, and Mr Brailsford as secretary. By this committee the Conciliation Bill was drawn up and it was introduced into the House of Commons by Mr Shackleton. A meeting was held in Bolton at which about 400 were present, explaining the Conciliation Bill and urging all members of the Association who could,

to go to London for the great demonstration in Trafalgar Square in favour of the Bill. The result of this was that 24 members joined the special train from Manchester, and helped to swell the audience of 15,000–20,000 women who assembled to hear speeches and resolutions from the plinth of the Nelson column. A report of this expedition was given to the Bolton Society and the Hon. Sec. followed up the enthusiasm with which it was met, by asking the members to unite in undertaking a canvass of the women municipal voters in the town and begging them to sign a petition in favour of the Conciliation Bill. There were 5750 municipal women voters of whom 3681 were interviewed, and of these, 2660 were in favour of the Bill.[84]

While a success rate of just over 50 per cent is not testimony to over-whelming support, what is important is the tactic of individual interviews in order to change opinion. Importantly, this tactic was to be extended and refined over the next year and in 1912

> Deputations to members and interviews at the House of Commons were frequent this year, and the social events included a garden party at Fernclough, and an At Home at the Spinner's Hall, and at this latter, the scheme of "Friends of Women's Suffrage" was explained. These "Friends" are those persons who, while not avowed suffragists, yet have some sympathy with the cause and at any rate do not speak against it, and to these, notices of public meetings will be sent. Forty-two members of the Bolton Society have each a circle of "Friends", and after little more than six months, 334 were enrolled under this title; needless to say, a proportion of these became in time members of the Society itself.[85]

Unsurprisingly, membership of the BWSA increased rapidly in the run up to World War I.

We should be clear, however, that the BWSA was interested in only a limited extension of the franchise, with Mary Haslam assuring public meetings that "only women ratepayers or those who possessed the qual-ifications necessary for men to have the vote, would be enfranchised". She also consistently assured the public from 1908 onwards that the BWSA campaign was, and would remain, non-militant.[86] Indeed, Haslam and the other members of the committee were strongly in favour of negotiated and agreed solutions to the suffrage issue, talking not in terms of the WSPU but of "the militant party" and noting in 1912 that "it is satisfactory to know that the law-abiding societies belonging to the National Union keep increasing in number, and that Bolton, which is one of the affiliated branches of a total of 400, has doubled its membership in the past year".[87] This is not to say of course that militant suffragism was unheard of in the town. Indeed, of a meeting in 1912 Mary Haslam records with regret that the audience was large, and Mrs Muter Wilson was given a good hearing, but Mr Parker, MP was frequently interrupted by militant suffragists who were seated in the body of the hall. It is worth mentioning that this is the only occasion in . . . life of the Bolton Society, where any confusion of incivility was shown between the various points of view on this subject.[88]

Nor were Bolton women absent from militant acts outside the town. Thus, the *Bolton Evening News* on 21 March 1907 reported the arrest of Mrs Kate Ford from Bolton at a demonstration in London, one of nineteen references to militant suffrage activity in Bolton newspapers between 1908 and 1912.[89] Yet, militant suffragists continued live in Bolton alongside their less militant sisters and by-and-large they managed to pursue their activities without real conflict. Indeed, by 1910, the activities of the two major wings of suffrage activity had been joined together by militants who pulled stunts rather than engaging in violence. Thus, the *Bolton Evening News* reported on 19 January 1910 the activities of Mrs Mary Lloyd, "a member of the Women's Social and Political Union, who holds that there are other ways of showing your pluck and taking in the suffrage cause than smashing windows in the Strand" and who gave a talk on votes for women while in a Lions den. Indeed, the Bolton papers carry many more stories on stunts like this than they do on the activities of violent militant suffragists in Bolton and surrounding areas.[90]

By the eve of World War I, the BWSA had grown into a very significant organization indeed, and in 1913 it was decided

> to increase the scope of our work, we took a shop in Bradshawgate as a suffrage office, where we could hold committee meetings and supply literature. A sign board was hung out, and the words "Bolton Women's Suffrage Society" painted below the window in green, white and red of the National Union; in fact it was determined that the attention of every passer-by should be caught by this announcement.[91] At the same time a full time organiser was engaged. This latter was Mrs Blincoe, who is still with us and has proved herself a tower of strength in all matters concerning the women's movement.[92]

The women's suffrage movement had come of age and begun to put in place the structures that would carry the third chronological phase of feminist development in Bolton.

We return to this issue below. For now, it is important to observe that the upsurge of suffrage campaigning alongside new initiatives to expand women's influence in local government and politics and the continuation of substantial philanthropic activity means that there was a quantitative and qualitative change in the nature of women's activity in Bolton. Table 7.2 traces the overlapping interests of eight prominent female activists for

Table 7.2 Overlapping interests of eight female activists, 1906–1914

Activist	Range of activities	Total 1906–1914
Mary Haslam	Poor law guardian; philanthropy, women's charity society, housing, WLA, suffrage, Women's Local Government Association, workhouse visiting, women's citizenship, child welfare, home visiting, regional societies, aged poor, female employment, Bolton distress committee, pensions.	58
Susannah Swan	Poor law guardian; parish and borough councils, philanthropy, women's charity society, orphanages, housing trusts, Women's Local Government Association, workhouse visiting, home visiting, self-help societies, nursing, regional societies, pensions toy fund, suffrage.	39
Margaret Barnes	Poor law guardian; philanthropy, women's charity society, housing trusts, sanitation, suffrage, political campaigning, parish and borough councils, Women's Local Government Association, workhouse visiting, nursing, bible societies, education, orphan children, pensions.	35
Hannah Bolling	Child welfare, education, orphans, women's charity society, school meals, home visiting, pensions, philanthropy, selfimprovement societies, PL and political campaigning, Women's Local Government Association, women ratepayer's association.	25
Mary Howard	Poor law guardian; philanthropy, women's charity society, orphans, housing improvement, Bolton distress committee, sanitation, suffrage, WLA, Women's Local Government Association, workhouse visiting, nursing, education, child welfare	23
Bertha Chew	Suffrage, women's charity society, women's employment, Bolton distress committee, pensions, orphan children, trade unions, ILP, temperance, women and marriage	16
Elizabeth Hughes	Suffrage, aged poor and pensions, elections for female poor law guardians, orphan and child welfare, sanitation, women's employment, home visiting, working-class self-help, toy fund, nursing and prevention of disease.	16
Sarah Reddish	Trade unions, ILP, poor law guardian, women's employment, aged poor and children, libraries, women's local government, parish and borough councils, regional and national associations, Women's Co-Operative Guild, Bolton distress committee, labour and servant exchanges	24

the period 1906–14, and we can see that the density of campaigning interests has expanded significantly even from the high levels of the 1890s and
early 1900s.

The scope of these campaigning interests was also wider than in the
1890s, and we see the continuation of the trend towards formal organizations as a focus for feminist activity. The BWSA joined the WLA, WCG,
PL, ARWPLG and WLGI and the Women's Charity Society as a
campaigning organization and almost 260 articles in the Bolton newspapers on matters from suffrage to female poor law guardians and the need
for women on town councils between 1906 and 1914 is testimony to
substantial development in the feminist public persona in this period.
Indeed, Mary Haslam notes in 1911 that,

> The Bolton press, which has always been favourable to our work, is now
> willing to accept paragraphs of Suffrage news which are being supplied to
> them regularly. As is said in our Report for this year, "The Editors have our
> best thanks for affording this useful opportunity: their action has given to
> Bolton the distinction of being one of the few towns where all the newspa-
> pers are friendly."[93]

Public recognition of the suffrage and wider feminist movements had
thus been heightened and refined since the 1890s. The linguistic register
of feminism had also expanded as women made the inevitable connections between their philanthropic and local government successes and
their rights as citizens to wider representation. As we can see, the cautious
language of the electoral campaigns of 1895 outlined in CHAPTER FOUR
was replaced in the later 1900s by the linguistic imperatives of success,
rights, duties, equality and female superiority.

We should not forget, however, that, without exception, the women
who led the formal organizations, expanded the linguistic range of feminism and sought to challenge the very power base of men at local and
national level, were or had been female poor law guardians. Whilst
pinning down causal relationships is difficult with patchy evidence, a
consideration of the membership, tactics, language and leadership of the
Bolton feminist movement between 1906 and 1914 can leave little doubt
about the centrality of poor law experiences to the wider campaigns of
the early twentieth century. Only after World War I did this central influence wane, and it is to this period that we now turn.

Feminism 1914 Onwards: The Politics of Citizenship

The war and postwar period was to see the Bolton feminist movement clearly and unambiguously cemented into public life, as feminists engaged with the politics of citizenship. However, the influence of Mary Haslam, strongly felt during the war, finally began to wane in the post-war period as failing health, the death of local family and ageing took its toll on her public persona. Other strong women were on hand to take her place. Amongst the middle-class, Margaret Barnes took over leadership of the female poor law guardians, becoming chair of the board and receiving an OBE. She was joined by Florence Blincoe, secretary of the Bolton Women Citizens' Association, the successor to the BWSA. At her burial on 1 August, 1932, the Revd Falconer offered the following assessment of her life and works,

> To this highest and noblest type Florence Blincoe belonged. She was one who loved her fellow men . . . Love shows itself in a thousand different ways – in an infinite tenderness for everything that suffers, a compassion for the sick, the crippled, the poor; a concern for the masses in their restless longing for greater happiness, and a high resolve to help them to a better life. This is the love that filled the big heart of Florence Blincoe, and forced her to spend herself, and be spent, in the service of man . . . Her work for 19 years is a record of self-sacrifice for good (and often unpopular) causes, and for individuals afflicted and oppressed. And to every task she undertook she brought an idealism, an enthusiasm and a practical genius for organisation rarely combined in one person. Every social worker admired her gifts and knew her worth, while hundreds of unknown individuals have reason to bless her name for wise counsel and help in times of uncertainty and distress.[94]

This is a moving tribute to a woman who had inherited much of the work of Mary Haslam as she withdrew from public life in the 1920s. While the Revd Falconer made no reference to Blincoe's feminism, the fact that she was secretary to the explicitly feminist Women Citizen's Association should lead us to rectify this omission. In turn, middle-class women like these continued to interact with and draw upon prominent working-class feminists like Sarah Reddish, Alice Collinge, Bertha Chew and Mary Hargreaves, all of them members of the ILP and working-class campaigning organizations such as the Northern Women's Trade Guild. Thus, in 1916,

> The Annual Meeting [of the BWSA] was held in May: this was followed by

a series of outdoor meetings, and a Garden Party was given by Mrs F. Taylor for munitions and other women workers, addressed by Mrs Anne Robinson. Later in the year, Mrs H. A. L. Fisher addressed a gathering of members and friends. Mrs Blincoe worked hard amongst the Trades Unions, the result of which was that the Trades and Labour Council, and seven large Trades Unions passed a resolution urging the necessity of the speedy enfranchisement of women. A Memorial was sent by the Manchester Federation to all members of parliament urging the necessity of enfranchising women in any proposed electoral reform, and in Bolton, 326 signatures of representative men and women were obtained.

Yet, this was also a perceptibly different feminist movement, one not so dominated by the personalities of a small core of feminist activists. The numerical gains to the underlying feminist movement made in the period 1906–1914 were built upon in the post-war period, and a comprehensive survey of surviving evidence such as minutes, diaries and newspaper reporting suggests that the underlying movement probably numbered at least 350 by 1918. And while Barnes, Blincoe and Reddish could bring much experience and wise counsel to existing and new campaigns, they were not as predominant in the feminist movement as Mary Haslam had become.

As in earlier periods, these women continued to be involved in a range of overlapping or contiguous activities, including local government, philanthropy, citizenship campaigns, suffrage agitation and post-war reconstruction. However, the nature, number and meaning of these activities had changed, and we might make four observations. *First*, the number of campaigns/organizations per female activists had fallen compared to even the 1890s. Table 7.3 traces the overlapping interests of eight key figures for this period. We can see that the absolute figures were lower than the period 1890–1906, and, incidentally, lower than the equivalent figure for 1890 itself. *Secondly*, and following on from this, we can see that middle and working-class activists were tending to focus their activities on different sorts of organizations compared to pre-1914. Hence, while philanthropy remained important, its emphasis shifted from sanitation, housing and nursing to broader political issues such as employment and unemployment, pacifism and education. Moreover, whilst it is clear that there was a continued emphasis on the need to elect and keep in office female poor law guardians, there had been a subtle shift in the nature of organizations aiming to increase the presence of women in public life, one that we began to see in the pre-1914 period. Increasingly, interest had turned to women's role in other areas of local government, councils for instance, and to the general citizenship rights and duties of women. We return to this theme below. *Thirdly*, the "female content" of many campaigning organizations had been diluted as women in Bolton sought political, social and economic allies in addressing a wider set of interests. In 1915, for instance, "no women were placed on the Relief Committee to administer the Prince of Wales fund". The pressure group formed to rectify this situation was largely male, though headed by Mary Haslam, and the credit for rousing public opinion so that "finally six women, all members of our [BWSA] Society, were put on" goes to a much more broadly-based organization than the BWSA itself. This should not, of course, surprise us, since nineteenth-century women had demonstrated a considerable capacity for joint work of this sort. *Finally*, it is clear that while individuals continued to be important to women's campaigning and pressure groups, the collective identity of these associations were beginning to take precedence. Certainly by the 1920s, then, we begin to see the emergence of a broadly based, mature and large-scale feminist movement in Bolton.

Table 7.3   Overlapping interests of eight female activists, 1914–1920

Activist	Range of activities	Total 1914– 1920
Mary Haslam	Poor law elections; philanthropy, women's charity society, housing, WLA, suffrage, Women's Local Government Association, women Citizen's Association, Prince of Wales Fund, child education, pensions.	12
Bertha Mason	Poor law guardian; parish and borough councils, orphanages, Women's Local Government Association, suffrage, Women Citizen's Association, women's employment, pacifism regional societies.	14
Margaret Barnes	Poor law guardian; philanthropy, housing trusts, Women Citizen's Association, political campaigning, parish and borough councils, Women's Local Government Association, education.	18
Margaret Mothersole	Child welfare, women's health, suffrage, Women Citizen's Association, school meals, women's employment, Women's Co-Operative Guild, factory reform, pacifism, women ratepayer's association.	17
Mary Howard	Poor law guardian; philanthropy, Women Citizen's Association, orphans, suffrage, WLA, Women's Local Government Association, child welfare.	11
Bertha	Suffrage, women's charity society, women's employment,	16

Chew	Bolton distress committee, pensions, orphan children, trade unions, ILP, temperance, women and marriage, prostitution, pacifism, servants, pensions and the aged, Royal Commission.	
Mary Ashton	Suffrage, pensions, PL, elections for female poor law guardians, orphan and child welfare, pacifism, town and borough councils, campaigns for female MPs, working-class self-help, nursing.	11
Sarah Reddish	Trade unions, ILP, poor law guardian, women's employment, aged poor and children, libraries, women's local government, parish and borough councils, regional and national associations, Women's Co-Operative Guild, suffrage, Women Citizen's Association, factory reform.	16

Unsurprisingly, the tendency for formal women-based organizations to multiply, grow, and succeed each other, exhibited in earlier phases of the development of the Bolton feminist movement, accelerated in the post-war period. The attainment of the limited national franchise in 1918 brought both euphoria and disappointment. Mary Haslam noted that "The feeling was universal, amongst suffragists throughout the country, that although the franchise now granted had not achieved the object we set out to get, namely, equality with the men's, it would be wise to let the matter rest here, and trust to public opinion for the future".[95] We know of course that such sentiments were not universal. Nor were they shared by many of the working women of the northwest.[96] However, in Bolton at least the period 1918–1920 was to mark a real time of co-operation between the different women's organizations. Hence, in June 1918, a conference was held, in which fifteen different women's organisations joined to discuss the future campaign priorities of the Bolton feminist movement. Energies that had been devoted to suffrage now transferred seamlessly, as had always been the case in Bolton, to other campaigning causes, including the establishment of a day nursery controlled by women and all other "such reforms, economic, legislative, and social, as are neces-sary to secure a real equality of liberties, status, and opportunities between men and women".[97] This was a powerful statement of feminist intent, the outcome of some forty years of local campaigning, local government involvement, engagement with the political establishment and the gradual broadening of the women's movement away from its middle-class base. Indeed,

> Bolton followed up this scheme by inviting all the women's societies in the town to come together and discuss the possibility of forming themselves into one large union or association, with due representation of the Committee

of Management. Altogether 25 Societies were invited to co-operate and of this number only three held aloof. There was much discussion and a little doubt on the part of some of the societies as to where this step would lead them, and whether they would be able to retain their independence, but by due regard to these points, and freedom of action not being interfered with, difficulties were smoothed away, and the present Women Citizen's Association was inaugurated.[98]

Haslam and her experienced feminist colleagues had not lost the appetite for further reform. She noted "those of us who had lived through the whole suffrage movement felt we could not rest satisfied with no woman under 30 having a vote while a youth of 19 or 20 had one, so we decided to continue our activities for the suffrage, and at the same time to join with the Women's Local Government Society in establishing the Women Citizens Association".[99] Finally, then,

as the history of the last two years shows, the ground which in the past had been covered by activities under the aegis of Suffrage, had now been monop-olised by the Women Citizen's movement. At the annual and final meeting held this year by the Bolton Suffrage Society, the following resolution was carried unanimously – "Now that a substantial measure of Women's Suffrage has been gained, this meeting of members, resolves to merge the Bolton Women's Suffrage Society into the Women Citizen's Association, which stands for complete equality of liberties, status, and opportunities between men and women."[100]

This was not the end of suffrage campaigning in Bolton, but the forma-tion of the WCA in 1918 does represent the ultimate coming of age of the Bolton feminist movement. The WCA itself had an underlying member-ship of 400 at its peak in the early 1920s, and to this we might add at least 100 more local activists who were not members. By the early 1920s the feminist movement could boast amongst their number Justices of the Peace, a chair of the board of guardians, councillors and members of a Royal Commission.[101] As Mary Haslam's obituary notes, "She lived to see the realization of some of her hopes. Women in Parliament; a woman on the Bolton town council; women magistrates etc. etc.; in all these her great heart rejoiced".[102] Organizationally, the WCA was a world away from the early 1890s, and the linguistic register of feminism had moved decisively towards asserting rights, making claims, defending achievements and demanding change. Public appreciation of the existence, reach and achievements of a self-conscious feminist movement can also be clearly seen in newspaper reporting of the foundation of the WCA and campaigns for council elections and further suffrage reform.

Conclusion

Chapter one started with the death of Mary Haslam, and it is appropriate that we should end at the same point. The formation of the WCA, of which she was president for the two years 1918–1920, represented the last hurrah of "a truly great woman, and a loyal and devoted leader of the Women's movement in Bolton".[103] Her obituary noted that,

> Too late comes the suggestion that the Town Council should recognize her fine citizenship by making her a freeman of the borough. This would have given her great joy, not for personal reasons, but as a recognition of women's citizenship . . . She was truly one of nature's freemen whom the truth made free, and needed not that others should confer it on her. Even through great personal sorrows that have crowded her life the last five years her spirit triumphed over all, and she continued to take and unflagging interest, not only in the cause of women but also in the great world problems and tragedies of the day.[104]

If she had not started out as a feminist and leader of a feminist movement, she was both at the time of her death. At the core of her activities and linking together her multiple campaigning fronts lay a keen appreciation of the need for equal rights and opportunities, a desire to see the recognition of the citizenship rights of women and a woman-centred view of the systems of male power and authority, honed initially through her work on the male-dominated board of guardians. She was part of a feminist movement which, starting its development in the early 1890s, was colonized by philanthropists, middle and working-class activists, social reformers, women with strong political views and those with none, moderate suffrage campaigners and militant suffrage campaigners. The movement was also characterized by a core of women who, like Mary Haslam, had a long history of engagement with the public sphere, local politics, campaigning and the formation and execution of a woman-centred agenda, but in its later stages it was joined by radical feminists and suffrage-focused women with much less experience. On the national stage, as we have seen, such diversity made for splits, but what is remarkable about Bolton is the capacity for these different interest and ideological groups to work together in the creation of a self-conscious feminist movement. Nowhere is this clearer than in the failure of local suffrage interests to fight over militancy.

While discussion of the national feminist movements has come by default to focus on just a few prominent activists because of the continued lack of local studies, in Bolton a set of excellent documentation has revealed the development of a vibrant women's movement, but nonetheless one centred very directly on a single personality, Mary Haslam. **Part II** of this book, "Born to Intellectual Freedom? The Records of Mary Haslam, Bolton Activist", reproduces key elements of her archive, including annotated versions of her working diary, autobiographical notes, travel diaries and a suffrage pamphlet. They paint a picture of a determined women, systematically trampling over the boundaries of public and private, male and female, philanthropic and campaigning, political and apolitical, domestic and institutional, Liberal and Conservative and, towards the end of her life, middle-class and working-class. All this was done with remarkably little conflict within the women's movement and between the women's movement and other interest groups in the town. Yet her greatest achievement, acknowledged so centrally in her autobiography, was to push women, women's interest and women's strategic vision to the very heart of the New Poor Law, a process that, as we have seen, changed the face of welfare practice and delivery in the town. For her and the other feminists who dominated the movement until the outbreak of war, the role of female poor law guardian was not an incidental part of a longer feminist journey, but a core stepping stone and staging post for a wider assault on public life and the structures of female oppression. While some commentators might downgrade or ignore the work of women with the poor law, in Bolton at least we cannot understand the scale and vibrancy of local feminism without it. Moreover, that work had a profound impact on the nature of poor law administration in Bolton, and should lead up to question the picture of New Poor Law stagnation and decay in the later Victorian and early Edwardian period.

Part II

Born to Intellectual Freedom? The Records of Mary Haslam, Bolton Activist

CHAPTER EIGHT

Brief Autobiographical Notes Written by Mary Haslam

Autobiographies and autobiographical are a difficult historical source.[1] On the one hand, they offer the perspectives on individual lives, decision making, motivations, beliefs and feelings that are rarely available to the historian unless in the form of oral histories. Yet, they also share many of the potential problems of oral histories. Those who reflect on their own lives may have selective or partial memories and their language, especially in written form, may encourage us to place emphasis where none was intended or ought to be. Moreover, the sorts of autobiographical notes reproduced here are not, and were never intended to be, a wide-ranging review of the life and experiences of the writer, nor to be an historical source. That said, the very brevity of Mary Haslam's birthday reflections should give us pause for thought, highlighting the central themes in the life of this important Bolton activist: family and marriage, the education of women, public action, feminist campaigning and the way in which women balanced their roles as daughters, wives, mothers, philanthropists and public actors.

The notes, however concise and potentially flawed, provide a window into the life of the sort of female activist who rarely makes it into the wider feminist or welfare historiography.[2] To the citizens of Bolton, who reflected on decades of public work by Mary Haslam when they proposed to grant her the status of freeman in 1922,[3] she was a powerful local figure. In the wider literature she is anonymous and this makes her

Full title: Brief Autobiographical Notes Written by Mary Haslam (née Heywood), my mother. Transcribed originally by W[illiam] H[aslam]. Bolton Record Office (hereafter BRO) ZHA 17/16, Autobiographical Notes.

domestic, political, philanthropic and campaigning life and her reflections on that life all the more valuable.

These notes reveal a very human, occasionally fragile and always reflective person. She was private, with a capacity for deep love of family. At the same time there was a drive to do public good, for which substantial time sacrifices were required.[4] Her initial feminist credentials are doubtful. Indeed, her active and enduring participation in the philanthropic, public and campaigning life of Bolton was prompted by a desire to "reduce the sum total of sorrow in the world" through philanthropic work. Such an entry trajectory, allied as it was with a close marriage and a supportive husband, is rarely seen in the more recent literature on nineteenth-century feminists, philanthropists and women campaigners.[5] While Dyhouse suggests that a dissatisfaction with Victorian bourgeois family life (during upbringing and marriage) informed and fuelled a feminist critique of women's socio-political and cultural position in the later nineteenth century, there is little evidence here or elsewhere that Mary Haslam found her family life "dwarfing", "stunting", claustrophobic or belittling, or that it informed her early public and campaigning activities.[6]

Mary's character and motivations were anything but static, however. She had in common with other women activists and feminists such as Helena Swanwick, Edith Morley and Emmeline Pankhurst a solid, liberating, education, and an inspirational teacher during girlhood.[7] By the 1880s she was active on a considerable variety of fronts in Bolton public life. Certainly by 1917 Mary Haslam was a high profile feminist activist, campaigning on suffrage, social welfare and citizenship issues. Evidence of her credentials in these areas can be found in the Foreword to her 1920 book (reproduced in CHAPTER ELEVEN) which refers to "the dauntless courage and splendid tenacity of purpose with which Mrs Haslam and Miss Haslam – as she then was – pioneered the struggling [women's suffrage] movement".[8] Throughout her development as a feminist, however, Mary Haslam's attachment to family was undimmed. For those with an interest in nineteenth-century feminism, women in public life and local government, and social welfare, these autobiographical notes provide a valuable pool of motivational detail where there is normally a desert. Moreover, and however briefly, the notes allow us to reflect on a variety of other themes: the closeness of intengerational and family relationships, education, socialization and the nature of marriage and childbearing. They particularly encourage us to think more carefully about some of the dichotomies – between feminist and non-feminist activists, between marriage and childbearing and public service, or between equality and equality with difference[9] – that inform the historiography of women in public life and local government.

198

The Autobiographical Notes

August 11, 1911

It is my birthday. I am 60 years old. I have been taking some long looks backward into my life, and will put down some of the mental pictures that come before me, one by one.

I am the middle one of my parents three children. My brother John was nearly two years older and my brother Robert, four years younger than myself.[10] We were fond of each other, and, moreover, through our lives never was there anything approaching a quarrel or even a coolness. My feelings towards my brother John was chiefly one of intellectual interest as he grew up and we had in common a large amount of public interest, so sympathy of tastes formed the bond between us. For my brother Robert I had, from childhood, a love that nothing could ever have shaken and, though we had few tastes in common, there is a "sympathetica" between us that has made the devotion of a lifetime on my side. Now we are left alone, for John died just a year ago,[11] and, until then, it had still seemed as if we were children together.

Picture 1

A little girl in a quiet home with dolls and books to herself each afternoon (lessons being only in the morning) a garden where it was always summer, John to play with and to be teased by till he went to school when I was nine, Robert still there till I left for school at 13 and a half. I had few friends, and those of my parents who visited us, seem elderly as I look back. My father was more grandfather than father to me, as he married late in life, and my sweet mother seems to have obliterated nursery out of consideration for him. It was a peaceful home, I do not remember a single angry scene between my parents, nor any but the most trifling punishments for us children, and these latter because we had been quarrelling between ourselves.[12] Life seemed a simple thing in that home life: there was no hurry, no unsettling coming and going. My father was constantly at meetings of either the Town Council or some other public body on which he served[13] and, as these were then held at night, our evenings were mostly spent with our mother alone and she read or played games with us. My father used to read aloud to my mother every morning the newspaper, the news and leading articles, and if we children stayed in the room, strict silence had to be observed. This was also the case when friends visited our parents and I think this blending together of young and old, and the former hearing the grown ups conversation, lead to a taste in

199

public questions, and an interest in the latter which developed in later years.[14] The end of the Crimean War with "Pam" and "Sebastopol" as constantly repeated words, is my first memory of public events, but the American Civil War, with the names of Lincoln, Jefferson Davis, Alabama claims etc. etc. seems to come before me in a long series of mornings with newspaper readings. Added to this there was a fair amount of coming and going at The Pike, for my father's public position made his house the centre of much of the life and thought of the Town[15] and there was constantly a guest staying the night, or a small party to meet someone, but of young people or what is meant by a frivolous element, there was not much. Then, as children, we did not question much: that would not have been thought "becoming" at our ages; duties were laid down and habits formed, in an indirect fashion which contrasts strangely with 50 years later when parents anxiously give their children direct instruction. But I belonged to the mid-Victorian period and kept many doubts and ponderings to myself lest my environment should be shocked.[16]

Picture 2
A day in January when my mother took me to school. The snow was on the ground and my father was sad at parting with me. I remained there 3 and half years and was happy. Miss Carbritt, who kept the school, was a large minded, large hearted woman, who chose this calling from interest in girls lives and the knowledge that the education at that time was deplorable. The teaching was excellent and intelligent, and what was taught or done was thorough. "A law to yourself" was one of her favourite phrases, and that being so, ordinary rules and regulations became commonplace, and, as such hardly existed. Our minds became open, and the habit of judging anything on its own merits strengthened our powers of reasoning and observation,[17] while the strong personal sympathy between Miss Carbritt and each one of "the girls" made the relationship of schoolmistress and pupil a quite common one. Let me here say that of this woman, my admiration as a girl and my friendship when grown up have made me realise that I owe the thought influences of which I have been conscious. Whatever I have done later in public work, or in the principles which underlie it I owe to her who was the inspiration of my youth (leaving aside the more direct influence of the home).[18]

Picture 3
I was summoned home on account of my father's illness, one Friday, and found him on the sofa. I sat on a low stool at his side and we talked, but he was rather tired. Ten days later he died, and I felt lonely. As a little child, sleeping in the dressing room, I had lain awake dreading the day

when he should be taken from me, and for years I could not listen to the begging tale of any old man, willingly finding pennies to give him, just because it was age and reminded me of my father. I was 17 when my father died.[19]

Picture 4

I had stayed at home six months with my mother but she, feeling I could not carry on any regular study at home, thought I had better go to school again, so I went to a Mrs Talor at Hampstead. This school was different from Brook House: the ladies who kept it were old, and there were many rules which chafed me and which I thwarted whenever possible. Consequently the evening before I left I was taken into Mrs Lalois private room and told that I should regret all my life the way I had set myself in opposition to all they had tried to do for me. I ought to say that at this school I enjoyed the lessons. I was just the age for study and did the required work with energy and interest, and the going in to London for lectures, concerts, picture exhibitions, etc. all helped to wake me up in many directions.

I was just 19 when I left school: the following spring I became engaged and, on September 17 I married as full of happiness and happy prospects as a girl could be.[20] On August 2nd 1873 my little Muriel was born, to be followed by Winifred and Robert. When she was five and a half years old a severe attack of scarlet fever tore her [Muriel] from us and all my life afterwards was a subtraction sum: she was a clever child with bright eager brown eyes and an understanding love between us made our relationship keener than is often the case.[21] For a long time I sorrowed a sorrow which my dear sweet mother understood; what roused me to activity after two or three years was the feeling that it should never be said that she, Muriel, had spoiled my life – no nothing sad or wrong should go into her memory, and so I would do what I could to help to reduce the sum total of sorrow in the world. This was the key to the different bits[22] of public work that afterwards became of so much interest in my life.[23] Two and a half years later Mildred was born: then two and a quarter Oliver and six and three quarters again Will. With different characteristics each one was just as dear as the others. I always had a thought that if, when they were grown up, they and their friends besides being parent and children I should not feel I had been a failure. With their father it was also thus, and I think no happier or more united family could have been formed and anything of the nature of quarrels or misunderstanding amongst the brothers and sisters was unknown. My mother lived to be 83 and her last years were spent near us. Her devotion and love of the children and grandchildren is shown by my diaries,[24] where the daily events of this household were my chief interest, and she was repaid by loving care from each member.[25]

Questions of education perplexed me much. If only there had been one best thing to do that might have done it. But it was all a groping after an ideal that was indefinite and I found so many of my contemporaries were prepared to be satisfied with just what was orthodox. Perhaps it was vanity and pride in our children that made me feel there was always something better to be had if only I knew the way to achieve it. I have often thought I should like to know what the children themselves thought, and whether they considered they had had the best chance.

August 11, 1917

Another birthday, and I have passed many milestones. Not only my little Muriel, but my beloved Mildred have been taken from me. My husband too and I am very lonely.[26] I miss the faithful companion of 45 years, always kind in unmeasured degree to me and to all others, always putting himself in the background and encouraging me to lead and do what I wanted. As I look back I see now how impatient I was and how little tolerant. I was keen and active and wanted to do so much, and I chafed at what I thought was his indifference. Now, when it is all over, I feel what a stout anchor that steady reliable trusting nature was and how much, all unconsciously I did lean on it, for now I am cut adrift and I want him very badly through all the trivial nothings of the day.[27] For him I am always glad he did not have an illness, but for myself I should have chosen a short one, that might just have shown with what love I would have tended him. And Mildred gone, a very special friend beloved and the sweet babe is in the old home and dear to all our hearts. He has cut his first tooth today, and as the dawn of intelligence is breaking through into sunlight. I ponder what life may have in store, and who and what will follow him when my love and care has to cease. His father is as a son to me, and if he is only spared little David will grow up into his sweet nature as a very real presence. My children are one and all most sweet and dear, and I am very conscious of what they are to me, but I don't want to live to be a burden and a constant thought to them. And I don't feel ready to be put on one side yet, but I want to find and go on with some of the things I have cared about so long – but – it just is all so difficult that I doubt and wonder.

I must write some more next August 11, if I can.[28]

CHAPTER NINE

Diary Kept by Mary Haslam of Her Work as a Poor Law Guardian

Context

Mary Haslam's working diary, combining the early minutes of the Bolton Ladies Workhouse Visiting Committee and her later perspectives on working as a poor law guardian, seems to be a very rare document indeed. As CHAPTERS ONE and FIVE suggested, most of what we know about the character, motivations and experiences of female poor law guardians is drawn from general autobiographies, where the poor law experiences of women are often brief, or briefly talked about, speeches at poor law conferences, articles in journals or newspaper reporting. Moreover, most of the historiographical literature melds together the experiences of female guardians over the whole period between the mid-1870s and the early 1910s. This diary offers a completely different perspective, tracing the week-to-week working activities of a woman who seems to confound many of the stereotypes of female guardians in the historiographical literature. Here was a woman who wanted to be heard and brought considerable philanthropic, campaigning and social authority to her position as a guardian, making sure that this aim would be realized. As we have seen in earlier chapters, Mary Haslam and her fellow female guardians claimed a wide remit over poor law policy, from children's

Full title: Diary kept by Mary Haslam of her work as a Poor Law Guardian between May 1893 and December 1904. Bolton Record Office (hereafter BRO) ZHA 17/17, Diary of a Female Poor Law Guardian. Unless otherwise stated, all supplementary information on people, decisions and debates is drawn from BRO GBO 1/25–33, Guardians Minute Books 1892–1906.

clothing through to outdoor relief and the rebuilding of the fabric of the poor law. What hostility there was to women on the board soon dissipated and it is clear that Haslam in particular had a tactical edge in a board of guardians split along all sorts of fault lines. The diary, contextualized with material from local newspapers to committee records, brings alive the achievements, tactics and experiences of the core of experienced women who claimed a place on the board in the 1890s and early 1900s. It is less good at showing the place of poor law work in the wider feminist journey of the individual women. As CHAPTER SEVEN showed, however, there is no doubt at all that individually and collectively these journeys were gathering pace in the 1890s. In this sense, the absence of a feminist critique of the board of guardians in the diary is interesting and important, suggesting perhaps that Mary Haslam was keenly aware of the need to press feminist claims on the back of solid achievement in philanthropy and social reform. Certainly her autobiography and obituary suggest this to be the case

Extracts from the diary have been used throughout this book, so that further review is unnecessary. However, a brief description of the diary and transcription conventions is important. The diary is written in flowing but dense and sometimes virtually impenetrable handwriting. Mary Haslam's shortsightedness is well known and we clearly see its impact here and in the travel diaries that are the subject of CHAPTER TEN. She appears to have written her diary entries on a daily basis, but there is no evidence from the outside bindings of the diary that she carried it around with her. This would have been possible, as it was kept in an A5 notebook containing 422 leaves. In addition, the diary contains seventeen loose postcards or pinned sheets. Its physical quality is excellent and while some words and sentences are obscured by smudging or written in illegible handwriting, there is very little damage to the pages or the bindings. This is the only diary extant in the archives, but the abrupt end of the entries suggests that there may have been at least one other volume that does not survive. Neither the Bolton archivist nor the author was able to contact surviving branches of the family.

The diary was transcribed by my research assistant Catherine Robertson, and quality checked by the author. Spelling, footnoting and punctuation were transcribed and reproduced exactly as they appear in the diary, though place and personal names were checked against alternative records and corrected where necessary. The layout of the diary has not been preserved because of space constraints. Annotations by way of clarification and extension have been offered throughout the text.

The Diary

1893: Visitors to the Workhouse[1]

May 9: Went through 5 or 6 departments. Elected president and Miss Armitage Secretary of the Committee.

May 23: Absent.

June 6: In fever ward. Had complaint of tea and two women who had been fighting.[2]

June 20: Hospital and lying in ward. Old woman died. Talked to nurse.

July 4: Hospital and lying in ward. Recommended to guardians to provide room for actual confinements only; the present one to be used for convalescents.[3]

July 18: Mrs Waterhouse read letter of complaint from Nurse Rayner, so she and Mrs Howard and I went to talk to the latter. Rations and washing found much fault with. We talked with Miss Healey also. The night nurse has charge of Infirmary and men's and women's wards, in all 156 cases. More paid help throughout the building required.[4]

August 1: Absent.[5]

August 15: Absent.

August 29: Absent.

September 12: Visited Hospital and Infirmary Wards. Found alteration to lying in ward had been made, and was found an improvement. Had some talk with Mrs Beesley the nurse, about separation of patients in Lock Ward.[6]

September 26: Heard continued complaints of Nurse Rayner and now the cook is implicated; the two both are R. Catholics and spend much time together to the neglect of their separate duties.[7] Talked with Mrs Westbury the task mistress and found her very nice and rational. She said how she often paid small rewards to the women who helped in the laundry, and wished some system of acknowledging extra labour could be adopted by the Board.[8] Mrs Davis absent.[9]

October 10: Heard further complaint against Nurse Rayner. Went into the Infirmary wards to enquire into them and talked with Mrs Davis.

October 23: Met deputation of guardians to talk about Nurse Rayner. It was decided to caution her about future behaviour. Saw Mrs Davis's work room and house laundress – Young, also Samuel Young, husband of the latter and furnace coalman at the Pike.

November 7: Visited the School. Find that Workhouse schools are under LGB not Education Department.[10] No Assistant mistress allowed. Discussed the advisability of allowing some tea or food to those women who willingly work at washing and give overtime. Suggested in the guardians book that £5 to £7 worth of stores be in the power of Mrs Westbury to give out in this way.

November 21: Visited the Infirmary. No answer has been received from the guardians as to suggestion entered for them in the minute book at the last meeting, but some of the ladies had read in the newspapers that they had decided not to grant the request.[11] Mrs Davis absent. We all signed the papers sent from the Local Government Board forming ourselves into a committee (with power to add to our number) for the "Boarding-out-of Pauper children".[12]

December 5: Visited the Infirmary. Talked with Nurse Henry about Nurse Rayner and found her still unsatisfactory. Discussed the case of Elizabeth Allen's unsuitability to go to the Blain Convalescent Hospital, and Miss Hardcastle undertook to get the necessary papers filled up. Mrs Davis ill in bed.

1894

January 2: Only Miss Armitage and myself. We talked with Mrs Davies about Nurse Rayner and the difficulties with her and the other nurses. Also about the cook and her inattention to her duties.[13] Lying-in-ward.

January 16: Absent.

January 30: Found that at the meeting on January 16 the necessary papers for the LGB had been received and the Boarding out of Pauper Children Committee was reorganised. Miss Hardcastle is chairman and Mrs Barlow secretary. I visited the school and talked a little to Mrs Ormerod and Miss Whiteside, afterwards going through Mrs Ormerod's Cottage Home. Mr Tomlinson, the school master was absent. Afterwards went with Mrs Davies into Infections Hospital, which has been cleaned and is henceforward only to be used for cases that break out in the work-house. All outside cases are being sent to Rumworth.[14]

February 13: I talked with Mrs Walker, Mrs Waterhouse, Miss Hardcastle and Miss Armitage. Visited the Lying-in ward, and talked with Polly Burns and Bridget Gormley. Learned that the inmates of this ward and those under title of "deserted wives" are <u>never</u> allowed to receive visitors.

27 February: Visited the Lying-in Ward again having tried to find out particulars of two of the women; one had left and the other had proved untruthful.[15] Visited feeble-minded room. Saw lunatics in bed. Talked with Nurse Henry. Our Committee suggested to the guardians the possibility of brightening the lunatics' surroundings by reversing a day and night room; we had some conversation as to whether occasional nurses could be provided.[16]

March 13: Visited ward 5 (Young Women's) and Children's Day room. Noticed that some of the children wear very heavy shoes. Helped Miss Armitage to interview adopted parents and select their children.[17] Signed papers for Mrs Seacombe and Mrs Kellett, who took away with them William Broadfield and Bertha Zorn. Mrs Walker mentioned that Mr Popplewell would remain at his Home (Mrs Bentley, 40 Davenport Street) girls who desired to be helped on leaving the Workhouse.[18]

March 27: Easter Tuesday, no meeting.

April 3: Visited Lock ward. Found no one ever went there to visit, but the priest and chaplain occasionally. Also visited the laundry and had some talk with Mrs Westbury. Visited the new Infirmary Ward (formerly infectious ward) and talked with new nurse. It was mentioned by some of the ladies that the doctor (Doctor Holden) was intemperate in his habits.

April 10: Meeting to get dates right though missing Easter week. Absent.

April 24: Visited the lock ward and put up pictures. Also children's day room and ward 5 (young women). Talked with nurse Grieves in new infirmary. Heard from Mrs Davies of difficulties with probationers, and Mrs Westbury.

May 8: Visited Lying-in ward and old women's. Discussed idea of sending in Report of our year's work to guardians. Decided to do this and mention the following points: Necessity of nursing Superintendent;[19] Necessity of resident doctor;[20] Necessity of paid laundress and more paid labour thoughout; Wish to know if rumours of doctor's intemperance true or false; Suggest that one cottage home be retained for use of sick children; Consider cook does very little work, and that some attempt at classification of cases might be made.

May 22: Met guardians who wished to discuss points mentioned in our report. The doctor's intemperance was denied by this committee.[21] Paid laundress should be considered.

June 5: Absent.

June 19: Discussed Guardians remarks as above.

July 3: Absent.

July 17: Decided that steps must shortly be taken to bring out some Women Poor Law Guardians at the next election.[22]

July 31: Desired our Secretary to write to the different Women's organisations in the town, the British Women's Temperance Association; the Primrose League;[23] the West Ward Women's Liberal Arm and the Association for Befriending Young Servants, and ask for their co-operation in furthering the cause of Women Poor Law Guardians. Talked with the new laundress Miss Harrison; and Mrs Westbury in the children's ward.

August 11: Absent.

August 25: Absent.

September 11: Found that three of the associations alluded to above would give all help possible; Primrose League declined to act with us. Decided to ask representations to meet at 21 Maudsley Street on Monday Sept 20th to decide on suitable steps. Mr John Harlow, Mr Brownlow, Mr Walker, and J.H. also. Visited lunatic ward and old women's.

The above meeting took place; and the following ladies were selected:

Miss Hardcastle to stand for Haulgh

Miss Armitage to stand for Little Hulton

Mrs Walker to stand for Bradford Ward

Mrs Howard to stand for Little Bolton

Mrs C. Taylor to stand for Halliwell

Mrs R. Ashworth to stand for Turton

Another meeting was arranged for Thursday next the 27th at 3pm. Miss Barlow is secretary and Mrs Nash treasurer Mr J. Haslam to continue chairman.

September 25: Absent.

October 9: Absent.

October 23: Visited young women's day room. Heard complaint of food, chiefly Thursday's dinners and the diseased state of the potatoes. Visited ward 29 (old women) and Children's ward. Spoke to Mrs Donolly the new task mistress; also to the matron, about the nurse's uniforms.[24]

November 6: Visited ward 29 (old women's) Visited Ward 15 (Infirmary) and talked with Mrs Elizabeth Banks. Visited Lock and Cancer wards, and interviewed the cook about the hash and tea. Consider that the time allowed for cooking the former (1 3/4 hours about) is not enough and this also true of the pea soup, the peas being usually quite hard. Answered Clerk's letter of enquiry by explaining this. Subject of nurse's uniforms waived for the present.

November 20: Found hash dinner was much improved. Tasted pea soup and found it good, but think it was probably better prepared because we were expected. Visited Lock, Cancer and Lying-in wards and hospital generally. Had talk with Nurse Beesley She was very encouraging about the good our Committee was doing and said we should never know the help we were, but the place was different and they all felt it. She wished it was "our own ladies" who were candidates for the Poor Law Guardian, so I said two of them were.[25] She spoke well of the doctor as far as her cases went. She and Mary had managed over 300 births during the 5 years she had been in charge and had had no accident or death with any.

December 4: Heard that nurse Beesley was leaving and bid her goodbye. Visited hospital and Infirm wards. Talked with a Mrs Marsden

(Green) who formerly lived in High Street and knew me as a child. Called mother "such a nice little lady". She has been in the workhouse 5 years and is in Hospital Ward 35.

December 15: Absent.

December 17: Election of Board of Guardians

Mrs Howard 1356 votes

Mrs Swan 422 votes

Mrs Ashworth 580 votes

Mrs Orrell 1296 votes

Myself returned. 1363 votes.[26]

1895

January 9: Board meeting at Poor Law Office at 11. Appointment of committees. Sectional Relief Committee at 12.[27] Workhouse committee at Fishpool at 2.30. Decided by 18 against 14 votes to recommend continuation of the Ladies Visiting Committee till April next.

January 14: At 3pm meeting of the Poor Law Board adjourned from January 9. Decided that appointment of workhouse staff be left to the Workhouse Committee and that Medical Officer of Health for district and Vaccination officer be 2 separate appointments.

January 16: At 9.30, Sectional Relief Committee till 11.45. At 2.30 Schools Committee at workhouse, followed at 3.30 by meeting of Workhouse Board. Went round Schools with Canon Wood.

January 23: At 9.30 Sectional Relief Committee; At 11 Board meeting. Appointment of resident doctor. Dr Buck chosen.[28] At 2.30 Workhouse Schools Sub-Committee. At 3.30 Workhouse Committee in Board Room. Consider the visits of the Schools Sub-Committee of no use, being both formal and expected.

January 29: Ladies Visiting Committee. Decided that Mrs Howard and I attend Poor Law Conference in London on February 12th and 13th.[29] Discussed the difficulty of dealing with the girls who go to the workhouse for their confinements and decided on Mrs Watkin's suggestion that the guardians be asked if before they leave the master let us know. Went with Mrs Swan into Hospital.

January 30: Sectional Relief Committee 9.30–12. Workhouse 2.30–5.30. Enquired into under clothing of children and thought we had better speak with the matron, with a view to substituting drawers for stays with the girls. Spoke to Mr Haslam about matters alluded to yesterday and the master was told to write to one of us (myself for the present) giving the date of the cases leaving. Canon Wood suggested that paralyzed women in number 8 cottage (Mrs Wolfendale's) be removed on account of the bad example for the little children; and this was carried.

February 2: Tramp Ward Sub-Committee at 10. Absent.[30]
February 6: Sectional Relief Committee 9.30–11.0 Board Meeting 11–1. Workhouse 2.30–5. Scarlet fever in Cottages 9 and 11. School very cold.
February 12: Visiting Committee. Absent in London at Poor Law Conference in Guild Hall 12th and 13th.
February 15: Tramp Wards Sub-Committee at 10. Absent.
February 20: Sectional Relief 9.30–11. Board Meeting 11–1. Workhouse 2.30–5.
February 23: Visited Chorlton Workhouse with Mr H. and A.[31]
February 27: Sectional Relief 9.30. Absent. Schools Committee. Absent but present 3.30–4.45 Workhouse Board.
March 2: Tramp Wards Committee 10. Absent.
March 5: Surprise visit to Tramp Ward went through and talked with Bloomer and wife.
March 6: Sectional Relief 9.45–11 Board Meeting 11–12.15. Present at LGB offices Mr Jenner Fust on account of long registrarship dispute. Allusion made to new arrangements at the Workhouse. Mr J. F. gave the following figures as showing the inadequacy of the nursing staff.[32]

Average number of cases to 1 day nurse nationally	22.1
Average number of cases to 1 night nurse nationally	79.1
Average number of cases to 1 day nurse in Bolton	52.1
Average number of cases to 1 night nurse in Bolton	240.1

Workhouse 2.30–4.45. Scarlet Fever in cottage homes. School closed. Did not go into the homes. Visited Lying-in and Lock wards with Mrs Swan. Spoke to M. Prior and M. Cane in person and enquired where they would go on leaving.
March 9: Special meeting of Tramp Wards.
March 12: Visiting Committee. Saw Margaret and men's Ward. Told no games allowed so agreed to enquire into it.
March 13: Workhouse Board Committee and previous visit to cottages. School still closed. At Board Committee put on sub-committee to select Nurse Superintendent candidates.[33] Reduced number to 3 and Mr Dearden afterwards moved that only the name of Miss Hughes be recommended. (Much astonishment!).[34]
March 16: Tramp Ward Committee 10.00. Absent.
March 20: Sectional Relief 9.30. Board Meeting 11. Appointment of Miss Hughes proposed and agreed to. Workhouse 2.30–4.45. Visited Cottages and enquired about cinder sifting which had been [the diary is smudged here] it was thought.

March 21: Stores committee met 2–4 Chose brushes, dress goods etc. and gave out tradesmen's contracts.[35]

March 27: Sectional relief at 9.30 and Workhouse at 2.30, absent from both. At Southport Annual meeting for return of L. P. G.s.

March 30: Tramp ward committee. Absent.

April 3: Sectional relief 9.30. Absent – Board meeting 11–12.15 Mr Jenner Fust present. Mrs Ashworth spoke about nurses to number of patients. First meeting in altered Board room. Thought carpet and curtains too good and expensive.

April 8: Went to Workhouse by 11.20 train and returned at 2.10. A sub-committee of ladies to enquire into complaint against nurse. Heard nurse Rayner had exceeded her duty by keeping a lunatic in a padded room all night without the doctor's order.

April 10: Sectional relief 9.30–12.10. At workhouse at 2.30 Sub-committee to consider overcrowding in infirmary and temporary use of Cottage homes.[36] Dr Buck saw need for this measure. Mrs Matthew's salary raised from nineteen pounds to twenty one. Girl A. E. Elston returned from service; ladies undertake to see about the case.

April 13: Tramp ward committee. Absent.

April 17: Sectional relief 9.30–11. Board meeting 11–12.15. Question of calf lymph for vaccination discussed. Workhouse 2.30–5.30. Applied for A. E. Elston on behalf of B. S. B. Y. S. and arranged for her to go to Mrs Bradshaw 288 Megan Road. Went over the new Nurse's Home.[37]

April 24: Sectional relief 9.30 Absent. Workhouse 2.30–5.30.

May 1: Absent.

May 8: Absent.

May 15: Sectional Relief 9.30–11 Board meeting 11–12.30 Workhouse 2.30–5.0. Introduced to Dr Buck and Miss Hughes.

May 16: Meeting of Hospital Sub-committee 3.30–5 Vote 5 against 6 in favour of proposed new Hospital Scheme. Mrs Ashworth spoke well.[38]

May 21: Ladies Visiting Committee. Went into children's ward. Cover ward and hospital generally. Left called on Dr Buck.

May 22: Sectional relief 9.30–12.30 Workhouse 2.30–6.30. Warm discussion on new Hospital plans. Matter "referred back to sub-committee and a smaller scheme to be brought forward instead". 15 against present scheme 9 for.[39] Objected to casual way in which children are hired out by any one wanting a young servant.

May 29: Sectional Relief 9.30–11.0 Board meeting 11–12.30 Workhouse 2.30–5.45. Decided to propose part of scheme to go on with at once; and discuss possibility of altering old hospital as well. Photograph of Board taken.[40]

June 4: Ladies Visiting Committee. Absent.

June 5: Absent all day. Whit week.

June 12: Sectional relief 9.30–11. Board 11–12. Discussion whether ladies should be represented at north western Conference in Manchester in July. Vote 13 for and 15 against. Chairman gave casting vote in our favour. Proposed Mrs Ashworth and Mrs Orrel Workhouse 2.30–5.10 Visited Mrs Pilling. Got help for her. New committee to be formed to consider old hospital scheme "one without ladies".[41]

June 19: Absent in London.

June 26: Sectional relief 9.30–11.0 Board meeting 11–11.45 Workhouse 2.30–4.15 Asked leave to invite imbeciles to a hay field tea next week. Signed lunatic register.

July 1: Had imbecile women and girls at White Bank (about 50). Heavy showers but fine between.

July 3: Sectional relief 9.30–12.30 Workhouse 2.30–5.

July 10: Sectional relief 9.30–11.0. Board meeting 11–11.45. Workhouse 2.30–5.0.

July 17: Sectional relief 9.30–11.45 Workhouse 2.30–5.15 Case of misconduct between inmates discussed, and passed over without punishment. Hospital sub-committee went through list of applications for 5 probationers. 9 names selected. Asked leave for aged and infirm to come out for afternoon. Mrs Howard ditto.[42]

July 15: Had 100 aged and infirm men and women at White Bank. Day fine.

July 16: Hospital sub-committee at workhouse 3–4.

July 18: Mrs Howard and I with Mr Watkinson, Mr Thwaites and Mr H. Cooper visited Lancaster Asylums the County and Royal Albert.[43]

July 24: Sectional relief 9.30–11.45 Board meeting 11–11.15 Workhouse 2.30–4.45 Suggested names of 5 probationer nurses which were passed by this sub-committee.

July 31: Sectional relief 9.30. Workhouse 2.30–5.30.

Aug 7: Sectional relief. Board meeting. Workhouse.

Aug 14: Sectional relief. Workhouse. Mrs Pilling to have leave of absence for 3 months.

Aug 21: Sectional relief. Board meeting. Workhouse.

Aug 28: Sectional relief – Workhouse.

Sept 4: Absent abroad.[44]

Sept 11: Ditto

Sept 18: Ditto

Sept 25: Sectional relief. Workhouse. Spoke to Miss Hughes about privacy for Lying-in Ward.

Sept 30: Extra Board meeting 2.30–4.0 to hear report of Committee; visit to the LGB with reference to proposed alteration to old fever hospital.

Proposal not entertained by the LGB Matter to be left for a fortnight for further consideration.[45]

Oct 2: Absent. (At Greenhill).[46]

Oct 9: Absent from sectional relief. Workhouse 3.30–5.

Oct 16: Sectional relief. Board meeting and relief continued after. Spoke to Mr Shaw about entry on Sept. 25. At Board meeting it was moved that Bolton join with other Unions to request power from LGB to dismiss its own officials. I moved amendment that the matter be considered that day fortnight as too important to be done so hurriedly. Amendment lost.

Oct 23: Sectional relief. Workhouse 2.30–5.45.

Oct 30: Absent (in London on R's account).

Nov 6: Ditto.

Nov 13: Sectional relief 9.30–11.0 Board meeting 11.0–11.30 Workhouse 2.30–4.45. Visited Male Hospital (Old Fever) (Lock and lunatic wards).

Nov 20: Sectional relief 9.30–12.30 Workhouse 2.30–5.15. Visited Mrs Pilling and talked with matron about required new laundress. Decided that Mrs Pilling return and have help equal to 8/ per week for the present.

Nov 27: Sectional relief 9.30–11.15 Board meeting till 11.30. Talk afterwards with Mr S. Cooper who advised us to accept any proposal of new Committee for new Hospital so as to make a start.[47] Workhouse 2.30–5.30. Saw the Pilling's and School, and went through R. C. children suitable to go to Tottington.[48]

Dec 3: Visited workhouse in morning. Tasted pea soup and found it very good. Found in school in infants room 23 on gallery 16 writing 17 reading with Miss Ormerod, total 56. Assistant mistress a necessity. Children in Mrs Matthew's house (babies) were having rice pudding for dinner, at Mrs Wolfendale's pea soup with peas taken out. Spoke with matron about Mrs Ashworth's remarks on diet at Women's Lib. Association.[49]

Dec 4: Sectional relief 9.30 At workhouse Dr Gilchrist moved that sub-committee be appointed to enquire into the "Housing of the workhouse children"; referred to Board meeting. Small sub-committee appointed to visit the homes previous to children being sent out to service.

Dec 11: Sectional relief at 9.10 (Resolved to meet at 9 on Board days). At Board Mrs Ashworth corrected her statement about children's food under 2. Dr Gilchrist's motion re housing of children. [I] advised that each Section of Relief should appoint 2 of its members to form the sub-committee to be appointed. Sectional relief again after Board meeting, as too many cases. Workhouse 2.30.

Dec 18: Sectional relief 9.30 *Workhouse 2.30 Sub-committee re children's food. Made suggestions with help of Doctor and Nurse.[50] *Special meeting of Board to reconsider Hospital question and this time success. 23 against 15. 2 1/2 blocks therefore to be erected on the originally proposed site. Mr Smith much excited.[51]

Dec 23: Sectional relief at 1.30 and Board at 3 On account of Xmas day on Wednesday.

Dec 30: Sectional relief 9.30–12.45 on account of end of quarter Workhouse 2.30–4.45. Visited cellar and tower to see if occupied with beds as chairman has said. Cellar first used this winter on Dec 25. Beds in tower number sixty – and are in passages and wards.[52]

1896

Jan 8: Present at Board meeting at 11.0 only. Nothing much of note except the appointment of sub-committee re "housing of children in workhouse" Dr Gilchrist's motion of Dec 4. Mrs Swan and I chosen from one Sectional Relief Committee. In afternoon laying of stone of new Porters Lodge and Probationary ward. Absent.[53]

Jan 15: Absent from Sectional Relief. At workhouse in afternoon. Noisy meeting about cellar sleeping accommodation. I corrected my remark about R. O. [relieving officer] at previous Board meeting: Mr Ellis Lee "now that's ladylike".[54] Felt that Father Brewer was not open about matter of Pheber's children going to certified home.

Jan 22: Sectional relief 9.30–11.0 At Board meeting, agreement passed for Boarding-out children beyond limits of Unions. Plans for 1st portion of Hospital Extension passed; now ready to be sent up to LGB.

Jan 27: Mrs Howard and I as a deputation, visited Rossendale Home. Much pleased certified for 18, at present has 15 girls. Charge 4/- per week. 3 elect from Bolton Union there.

Jan 29: Sectional relief 9.30–11.30 Workhouse 2.30–5.30. Spoke to Miss Hughes about little boys in men's hospital wards. Board granted a second laundress (£25 and Miss Hartland again).

Jan 30: Visited Ormskirk Workhouse. Very much pleased. Almost 300 inmates; very few able bodied cases. Hired women employed as cleaners in men's wards and in laundry – wages 2/- and not food. No picking of oakum at all. Master and matron Mr & Mrs Caine. Dietary table – 5 meals for children.

Feb 5: Sectional Relief 9.30–11.0 Board meeting 11–12.30. Decided not to send delegates to Central Poor Law Conference this year. Some opposition and matter to be raised next meeting. Workhouse 2.30–5.30. Higginbottom desired to resign post as store-keeper because of disobeying the master's order as to changing room. In discussion other reasons came up why this should not be overlooked. Bad language at meals.

Feb 12: Sectional relief 9.30–12.0 Workhouse 2.30–5.30. Further business with regard to Higginbottom. Sub-committee appointed to investigate charges made by different officials and letter of ditto written by H. as follows: Ward, Shaw, Fairclough, Kearsley, Haslam, Watkinson and myself.

Feb 13: Sub-committee 2.30 to 4.45 to investigate case of Higginbottom. Concluded that he had failed at all points to prove his indictments.

Feb 19: Sectional relief 9.30–11.0 Workhouse Board meeting 10.30–11.0 Board meeting 11–12.30. Warm discussion on result of yesterday's sub-committee. Decided that the whole Workhouse Committee investigate. Workhouse 2.30–3.30 Sub-committee re children's dietary. Decide to ask power to revise the same up to 16 years of age. 3.30–5.30. Ordinary worries.[55]

Feb 26: Sectional relief 9.30–12.30 Workhouse 2.30–5.0 visited Townley's and saw rooms occupied by storekeeper.[56]

Feb 27: Workhouse committee to enquire into storekeeper's case. 10.1.0 Found that charge of drink and disturbance against Mrs Macdonald put through – so others not enquired into.[57]

March 4: Absent from Board meeting on account of attending Central Poor Law Conference in London. Visited Whitechapel Workhouse Infirmary while away and had talk with Mr Vallance (Clerk).[58]

March 11: Absent from home.

March 18: Sectional Relief. 9.30–11.0 Board meeting 11–12. Workhouse 2.30–5.0.

March 25: Heard privately about Kenyon, driver of ambulance being often drunk, etc. and pauper women attendants also. Begged Mrs Swan to get particulars.

April 1: Absent from sectional Relief and Board meeting. Workhouse 3.30–5.

April 7: Sectional Relief for end of quarter 10.00–12.30.

April 8: Absent all day.

April 13: Absent from sub-committee re Labour of able bodied paupers.[59]

April 15: Sectional Relief 9.30–11.0.

April 16: First meeting of new Board. Mr Watkinson appointed chairman. John Heywood appointed vice chairman at workhouse Mr Graveson chairman and Mr Kearsley vice chairman. Committee appointed no-one to be on more than one. I choose main buildings only.[60]

April 23: Sectional Relief. 9.30–11.30 Workhouse 2.30–6.15 Inquiry into charge against Mrs Pilling about striking etc. 3 boys. Decided it was due if true at all to her ill-health.[61]

April 30: Sectional Relief 9.30–11. Board meeting 11–12. Workhouse 2.30–5.45. Brought forward question of pauper attendants to fetch hospital cases (See March 25). Suggested that each R. O. should find out and employ respectable woman or women and pay them for going with ambulance. This approved.

May 6: Absent from Sectional Relief. Workhouse 2.30–5.15 Mr Cooper raised question of laundry and more help required. Put on sub-committee to go into the matter.

May 13: Sectional Relief 9.30–10.30 Board meeting 11–12.30. Gave notice of motion next meeting that a deputation from Bolton Board attend Conference of Central Board in June re proposed changes by Education Bill.[62] Matter of pauper attendants referred back to workhouse. Workhouse 2–5.45. Carried point of pauper attendants. Deputed with Mr Ward to buy furniture for new cooks room.

May 16: Visited Workhouse, re furniture. Talked with matron about laundry arrangements.

May 20: Sectional Relief 9.30–11.30. Workhouse 2.30–5.0.

May 27: Absent (Lyndhurst).[63] Mrs Ashworth moved for me that deputation attend Central Conference in London in June, to hear discussion re transfer of Pauper Schools to Educational Authorities under new Bill. Rejected by 19 v 17.[64]

June 3: Sectional Relief 9.30–11.0. Workhouse 2.30–5.0.[65]

June 10: Sectional Relief 9.30–10.45 Board meeting 11.0–12.15. Guardians decided to visit in deputations lunatic asylums, homes etc. where pauper children are received. Workhouse 2.30–4.50 Sub committee main buildings to consider enlargement of Stores. Adjourned a week. Letter read from Dr Buck re visits to inmates in hospital on non-visiting days, and statement challenged by Mr Leyland.[66] Adjourned a week.

June 17: Sectional Relief 9.30–11. Workhouse 2.30–6.0. Sub committee re stores enlargement again adjourned. Men's lavatories to be proceeded with. Dr Buck came in to answer Mr Leyland's disgraceful remarks of latter. New rules re visiting of inmates adjourned a week. Miss Stirrup (2nd laundress) resigned. Talk about washing, and main building Committee to take it in hand next week. I asked for a lady to take my place as I shall be absent, and all four are added protection.[67]

June 24: Absent (Leicester).[68]

July 1: Sectional Relief 9.30–10.45 Workhouse 2.30–5.0.

July 5: Sectional Relief 9.30–11.0 Board meeting 11–12. Workhouse 2.30–5.0. Deputation of 4 to visit other Workhouses to see Laundry arrangements.[69]

July 4: Saturday. Had Cottage Home Children and officers (100) for afternoon.

July 9: (Thursday) Attended School Examination – Mr Mozley being examiner.[70] Mixed school very good Infants indifferent.

July 15: Sectional Relief 9.30–11.30 Workhouse 2.30–5.15.

July 22: Sectional Relief 9.30–11. Board meeting 11–12. Laundry deputation cancelled as being too many.

July 29: Sectional Relief 9.30–11.0 Workhouse 2.30–5.45.

Aug 5: Sectional Relief 9.30–10.45 Board meeting 11.0–11.50 Workhouse 2.30–5.45. Appointment of Miss Smith as Head Laundress. Rules for visiting workhouse inmates passed.[71] Proposal to appoint Miss Barlow to visit children in situations instead of Relieving Officers negatived Tenders for Building Contract of new Infirmary considered, and that of Mr Cunliffe accepted viz £9980 + £65 for woodblock floors.[72]

Aug 6: Visited Prestwich Asylum in company with Mrs Simpson Cooper, Mrs Howard and Mrs Swan.

Aug 12: Sectional Relief 9.30–11.0 Workhouse 2.30–5.30. Cunliffe's tender withdrawn. Special meeting to be called on Friday next to consider others.

Aug 19: Absent. (Brittany).[73] Workhouse Dietaries Sub-committee 2.30 At Board, appointment of Mary Smith as Head Laundress and Catherine Macdonald as charge nurse. Acceptance of building tender from E. D. Maginnis for new Hospital wing.[74]

Aug 26: Absent. (Brittany). Sub-committee re Mrs Pilling at 2.30.[75]

Sept 2: Absent. (Brittany). At workhouse, resignation of nurse Upton. At Board, agreed to superannuate Anne Pilling at 5/- per week, and appoint John Pilling as clogger to house at 25/- per week.

Sept 9: Sectional Relief 9.30–11.20 Workhouse Dietary Committee at 2.30. Afterward went in laundry with matron and talked with new laundress.

*Sept 3: Thursday. Visited workhouse with F. & M. Saw old Mrs Hesford, and talked to old women.

Sept 16: Sectional Relief 9.30–11.10 At Board meeting Mr Jenner Fust present. He reported on his visit at the Workhouse, and gave places for improvements. Made suggestions as to boys having single towels, epileptic beds to be provided.[76] The doctor and Miss Hughes made great changes in sick wards. Had a little talk with Mr J. Fust afterwards re children boarding out and cottage homes etc etc. Workhouse 2.30–4.30.

Sept 23: Absent from Sectional Relief. (M. going back to school). At workhouse 2.30–4.30.

Sept 30: Sectional Relief 9.30–11.10 Board meeting 11.10–11.45. Contracts followed at workhouse, allowed. Workhouse 2.30–5.15. Put on sub-committee to explain to officers the new Superannuation Act, and on what account it would be raised.[77]

Oct 7: Sectional Relief 9.30–12.0 Workhouse 2.30–5.30. Passed new Dietary Table for children. Discussed nurse Upton's superannuation fee and found discrepancy in age.[78]

Oct 14: Sectional Relief 9.30–11.0 Board meeting 11–12. Workhouse 2.30–5.30. Report of Laundry Sub-committee adopted and this committee to confer with that of main Buildings and get estimates.[79]

Oct 21: Sectional Relief 9.30–11.30 Workhouse 2.30–5.30. Laundry Sub-committee met. Decided to ask Bell & Co. of Bradford to send someone over to meet us next week, after he has first gone through present buildings. Discussions as to using cottage home when vacated by Pilling and wife as hospital for sick children. Matter referred back to school and cottages sub-committee.

Oct 28: Sectional Relief 9.30–11.0 Board meeting 11–12. Workhouse 2.30–5. Laundry sub-committee met Bell's man and discussed the schemes and suggested a third for next week. Mr Shippobottom moved that notice in future be given of all intended expenditure over £50 (passed). School and cottages Sub-committee recommend that boy's home is continued and Barber (£30) and wife (£15) is employed in place of the Pillings.[80]

Nov 4: Sectional Relief 9.30–11.30 Workhouse 2.30–5.0 Laundry sub-committee discussed scheme with Bell's man and decided on one to adopt. This recommended to Board and passed, to cost £700. Considered applications in place of nurse Upton. Hyam and Bishop to appear before Board next week.

Nov 11: Sectional Relief 9.30–11.0 Board meeting 11–12. Nurse Hyam appointed. Master and matron's salary to be raised from £245–270. Workhouse 2.30–4.30. Nurse Morris to come on trial for month.

Nov 18: Sectional Relief 9.30–12.30 Workhouse 2.30–5.0.

Nov 25: Sectional Relief 9.30–11.0 Board meeting 11–12.30. Chairman called attention to remarks at Heaton Parish Council, by Clerk re the lady guardians' extravagance causing rise in rates. Voted by 20 against 19 that the Board write and request explanation of the same. Got consent of lady colleagues to solicitors' letter being sent from us to Mr Fearnhead. This done, Mr Cooper approved. Also several of the men.[81] Absent from workhouse in afternoon.

Dec 2: Sectional Relief 9.30–12.0 Workhouse 2.30–6.0. Bishop recommended as charge nurse in place of Macdonald left. Inquiry into workhouse expenditure, Mr Shippobottom and Mr Ward.[82] Matter adjourned to sub-committee, consisting of Ward, Shippobottom, Gilchrist, Dearden, Watkinson, Leyland and chairman.

Dec 9: Sectional Relief 9.30–12.30 Board meeting 11–12.30. Reply and apology from Mr Fearnhead. Appointment of Barber and wife in place of Pilling and wife as cottage home keepers. (Edgar and Frances Colebourne). Nurse Bishop appointed. Workhouse 2.30–5.15. Main Buildings Committee interviewed laundress (Smith) on account of ill-health, and desired her to take fortnight's holiday at once. Children Murphy aged 8 & 4 applied for by mother, and refused until she could show she had a decent home for them. The Wolfendale's go to Pilling's cottage and Barber and wife come to them on account of child.

Dec 15: Sub-committee to consider new P.L. officers Superannuation Act, 4.30–6.0: adjourned.

Dec 16: Sectional Relief 9.30–11.15 Workhouse 2.30–5.15. Committee to consider Superannuation Act met again. Some complaints of inmates about the dinners; mentioned same to cook.

Dec 21: Special Board meeting, re proposed alterations to Manchester Royal Infirmary. Voted against rebuilding on present site. Special meeting at Workhouse at 2.30 to explain to officers decision about Superannuation Calculations.

Dec 23: Sectional Relief 9.30–11.0 Board meeting 11–12. Workhouse 2.30–5.0.[83]

Dec 30: Absent from Sectional Relief. Workhouse 2.30–5.

1897

Jan 6: Sectional Relief 9.30–10.30 Board meeting 11–12.30 Workhouse 2.30–5.30. Proposal to enlarge Committee room. I moved amendment, that though new furniture is unsuitable, still it has cost so much, that we ought not to spend money on further alterations at present, but appoint sub-committee to consider if better ventilation could be devised; carried but left to Main Buildings Sub-committee. Appointed on sub-committee to furnish Porter's Lodge.

Jan 13: Absent from Sectional Relief. Workhouse 2.30–5.35.

Jan 20: Sectional Relief 10.5–11.0 Board meeting 11–12.30 Workhouse 2.30–5.0. Decided to try stove in number 2 cottage (Mr & Mrs Taylor) so that children may have more variety of cooking in their food than is possible by its being prepared in the boiler. Report of Committee to deal with increased expenditure, presented and received.[84] (I wrote this week to Local Government Chronicle enquiring chances of placing workhouse school under Education Department.).

Jan 27: Sectional Relief 9.30–11.10 Workhouse 2.30–5.30. Case of Scarlet fever from Horwich to be returned, as fever Hospital is only for cases arising in workhouse proper.[85]

Jan 29: (Friday) Visited Workhouse and gave two Fitzroy pictures to the school. Talked with Schoolmaster about his wish to have the workroom of no.3 cottage (Pilling's shoe making room) made into carpenter's rooms, for training boys in joinery or carpentry. Found in no.8 cottage (Mrs Colebourne) that the girls wear a most terrible kind of corset; begged her to discontinue it at once and promised to speak to matron. Find all the girl children wear the following clothes chemise, drawers (flanellette) 2 petticoats each with bodice, frock and pinafore. Think this adequate, but decided to ask matron to have all frocks made with long sleeves. Deep snow. Suggested older children should sweep paths between the different houses.

Heard from matron that Scarlet fever case mentioned at last meeting had spent the first night in one of the female hospital wards. The order from Horwich requested the ambulance (not the fever van) but the certificate brought with the case notified the illness.

Feb 3: Sectional Relief 9.30–11.0 Board Meeting 11–12.15. Moved resolution in favour of attending Central Poor Law Conference on March 9 & 10. Carried. Workhouse 2.30–5.0.

Feb 10: Sectional Relief 9.45–11.40 Workhouse 2.30–5.45. Spoke in favour of using Pilling's late work room as boy's joinery room, and moved resolution that the Schools and Cottages Committee arrange details with schoolmaster and report to next meeting. Local Government Boards order re Instruction of children in Workhouse Schools referred to Schools and Cottages sub-committee.

Feb 17: Sectional Relief 9.30–11.0 Board meeting 11–12.15. Workhouse 2.30–4.45.

Feb 24: Sectional Relief 9.30–11.15 Workhouse 2.30–5.35. Sub-committee re furnishing Probationery Wards. Adjourned one week until master etc. get out particulars of what required.

March 3: Sectional Relief 9.30–11.0 Board meeting 11–12. Appointment of Alice Sanders as paying probationer in place of nurse Sawyers. Workhouse 2.30–4.45. Asked for Lizzie Grandine to be allowed to be sent to the Adcote Home for feeble-minded girls for 1 year £13. Granted. Probationary Wards sub-committee and discussed requirements.

March 10: Absent at Central Poor Law Conference Guild Hall.

March 17: Sectional Relief 9.30–11.0 Board 11–12. Appointment of Mary Hanson and Alice Mayole as probationers in place of nurses Neil and Seddon. Mr Watkinson and Mr Kearsley spoke on London Conference also myself.[86] Workhouse 2.30–5.0.

March 18: Day of nominations for election of guardians. Mrs Howard and myself are supported by both parties on West Ward. Mrs Swan declined the Liberal Support offered in East Ward and stands as an independent candidate, Mr Myles and Mr Shaw being the two Conservative opponents. Mrs Ashworth is unopposed in Turton Mrs Orrel opposed at Horwich.[87]

March 23: Date of withdrawals of P.L. candidates. Mrs Orrel's opponent has retired.

March 24: Probationary Ward Sub-committee. Absent through cold.

March 25: Sectional Relief 9.40–11.0 Workhouse 2.30–5.15. Probationary wards committee ordered tables and consulted with Chairman and Mr P. Boardman as to carpeting of committee room. Agreed to meet on Saturday at Boardman's shop. Mary Young complained that task mistress never allowed her to go out for fresh air. Main buildings sub-committee to enquire into it next week. Agnes Lang is paying probationer from Grimsby engaged.

March 31: Sectional Relief 9.30–11.0. Board 11–12. Tenders for Workhouse supplies 12–12.30. Workhouse 2.30–5.0.

April 5: Election of Guardians in East and West Wards. <u>East Ward</u> Mrs Swan 673 votes Mrs Shaw 386. <u>West Ward</u> M. H. 1464 votes Mrs Howard 1452 Mr Chadwick 978, Mr Ward 940, Mr Eaton 903. Mr Rothwell out.

April 5: Sectional Relief 9.30–12.0. Workhouse 2.30–5.45. Report of Sub-Committee re officers' Dietary.[88] Rather more costly so referred back.

April 4: Ladies Visiting Committee. Discussed future plans. Saw schoolmaster re carpentry.

April 12: Sectional Relief 9.30–11. Board 11–12.15. Grant of money to Nurses Institution 11gs. instead of 52gs. as heretofore. Supported thanks to retiring chairman on behalf of the ladies.[89] Workhouse 2.30–5.15. Officers Dietary Sub-committee report refused. Found officers in body indignant at any change in it.[90] Much discussion re teaching carpentry, finally voted for 9 against 8. Mr Ward chairman; a noisy distracting meeting. Last day of present Board's existence.

April 28: Sectional Relief 9.30–11.0. At Board meeting. Mr Watkinson reappointed Chairman and John Vice Chairman.[91] Appointment of Committees; 49 on workhouse. Expenditure of £50 for carpentry instruction passed. Workhouse 3.30–5.30. Re-appointment of Mr Kearsley as chairman and appointment of Mr Shippobottom as Vice, instead of re-appointment of Mr Ward. Mr Cunliffe moved that purchase of tools be deferred a month, and carried this, 12 for 9 against. Miss Hughes applied for testimonial. Very disorderly meeting, Mr Dearden worse than usual.[92]

May 4: Workhouse 2.30–5.20. Relieving officers and cases all the time.

May 12: Sectional relief 9.30–10.0 then left for other committee. Board meeting 11–11.35. Mr Fairclough moved that Ladies Visiting Committee be discontinued, but this negatived by 17 against 11.[93] Mr Cunliffe gave notice that at next meeting he would move to rescind the spending of £50 on tools. Workhouse 2.30–5.30. Found that too much bread in Cottage 8. 13 loaves on hand. Also too much dripping. Decided to write to Chorlton for particulars as to how they had dealt with the bread difficulty. Committee for furnishing porter's lodge and probationary wards re-formed and work distributed. Mrs Swan and I to do the bedrooms and ironmongery. Contractor appointed to meet Bell's man next week re laundry.

May 19: Sectional Relief 9.30–11.30 Workhouse 2.30–5.30 Arrangements for Jubilee day. Tea at 4 and supper after. Band and sports for children.

May 26: Sectional Relief 9.30–11.0. Mr Cunliffe's motion re spending £50 on carpentering, carried by 20 v 19. So it was lost. Mr C. afterwards spoke to me about it, and after my explanation said "Oh I did not know all that", to which I replied that two or three of us had gone into the question fully and might have been trusted! His other argument was that it was giving pauper boys advantages over others![94] Workhouse 2.30–5.0. Question of admission of inmates to Workhouse decided to come before the Committee in rotation, so as to save time; carried for a time on trial. Discussion on bread at Cottage homes; too much and therefore waste.

June 2: Sectional Relief 9.30–11.30 Workhouse 2.30–4.30. Resolution read and approved from Women's Guardians Association re homes for epileptics and feeble-minded.[95] Mrs Whittaker granted increase of salary.

June 9: Sectional Relief 9.30–11.0 Board meeting 11–12.15. Seconded an amendment in favour of refusing £50 for illumination of P.L. Offices on Jubilee day, as being so transient and enough being done, at workhouse, and all out-door relief doubled for that week. Lost 19 v 15.[96] Resignation of Miss Hughes read. Workhouse 2.30–5.0. Report of child Burns unsatisfactory.

June 16: Absent from Sectional Relief. Workhouse 2.30–5.30. Nurse Rotton to act in Miss Hughes' place until successor appointed. Nurse Haddon to come as paying probationer.

June 23: <u>Jubilee Day</u>. Absent from Sectional Relief and Board. Entertainment at Workhouse. Beautiful day: all went off well: Speeches in Board Room: photograph.

July 7: Sectional Relief 9.30–12.0 At Board meeting Miss Basket appointed nurse Superintendent in place of Miss Hughes. At Workhouse, Nurses Seddon and West appointed charge nurses.

July 14: Sectional relief 9.30–12.0 Workhouse 2.30–5.0. Nurses James and Grundy resigned. Remarks made as to cooking, cleaning, mending which need to be done by the nurses; the matter was referred to the Hospital Committee to be reported on.[97]

July 21: Absent. (London).

July 25: Absent. (Clifton).

August 4: Sectional relief. Board meeting. At workhouse discussed what new officers would be required for the new Probationary Wards.

August 11: Sectional relief 9.30–11.30 Workhouse 2.30–5.20. Sub-committee of Main Buildings and Hospital on question of new officers for Probationary Wards. Warm discussion. Chairman (Kearsley) contended there was pauper help in hospital and so might be in the new wards; contradicted by Mrs Ashworth.[98] It was finally agreed to advertise for man and wife, and extra help to be given by Holden and Nurse Hevey. Agreement for and against pauper help in general.

Aug 18: Sectional relief 9.30–11.0 Board at 11. At workhouse appointed Wolfendale and wife as caretakers as new Probationary Wards. Salary to be £50.

Aug 25: Sectional relief 9.30–11.30. Workhouse 2.30–5.0.

Sept 1: Sectional relief 9.30–11.0 Board meeting 11–12.15. I moved resolution toward discouraging sale of drink to children and offering of sweets as bribes to the latter. Carried by 14 to 12. Workhouse 2.30–5.0. Decided to appoint a laundry engineer to look after new machinery in laundry.

Sept 8: Absent. (Buxton).

Sept 15: Sectional relief 9.30–11.0 Board 11–12.30. Passed Workhouse Committee proceedings, raising charge nurses salary to £30 to commence and that Alice Greenhalgh be appointed Cottage School Keeper to house vacated by Colebourne and wife. Nurse Altman appointed paying probationer in place of nurse Hadden. Workhouse Board recommended Main Buildings Sub-committee to appoint experienced man as Engineer in laundry.[99]

Sept 22: Sectional relief 9.30–11.30 At workhouse. Examined list of candidates for offices of engineer and Cottage School keeper in place of Wolfendale and wife.* Resignation of Nurse Rotton accepted. Decided to send 21 boys to Buckley Hall. *James and Mary Guest appointed.

Sept 29: Sectional relief 9.30–11.0 Board meeting. At Workhouse Nurse Dix to succeed Nurse Rotton as paying probationer. Miss Smith laundress resigns. Mrs Watson, housekeeper at Townley's resigns.

Oct 6: Sectional relief 9.30–12. At workhouse. List of 81 candidates for post of engineer to be appointed.[100] 12 candidates to come before Board next week. Applications for 4 charge nurses considered.

Oct 13: Sectional relief 9.30–11.0. At Board Sarah E. Lloyd and Ellen Featherstone appointed as charge nurses. At workhouse, Hospital Sub-committee requested to consider the administration of new Hospital block, as it is approaching completion. Enquired about garden procedure at Townley's.[101]

Oct 20: Sectional relief 10.15–12. At workhouse interviewed three candidates for post of laundress and chose Fanny O' Malia 39 widow, from Risley Infirmary and Henshaws Asylum. Hospital Sub-committee brought in list of bed and patients' linen required in hospital and agreed to.[102]

Oct 27: Sectional relief 9.15–11.0. At Board resignation of Mrs Watson caretaker at Townleys. Resignation of Kenning and wife (Cooks) Workhouse 2.30–5.0. Great delay in business due to interruption by Dearden and Crompton; extreme tedium of latter.[103]

Nov 3: Sectional relief 9.15–12.15 Workhouse 2.30–5.15. Notice of new weak minded home at Springfield near Halifax, payment 5/- LGB notice re insufficiency of night nursing staff. Decided as Henry and Holden go to Probationary Wards, to advertise for charge nurse and probationer in their places. Proposal to proceed with Administration block of new Hospital, postponed one week on account of small number of Guardians left. Dearden again unbearable.*

Nov 10: Sectional relief 9.30–11.0 Board 11.0–12.15. Decided to send delegates to Poor Law Unions Association in London on Nov 23.

* Sub-committee of 7 to supervise rules of officers = myself one. At Workhouse discussion re new Administration block. Postponed one year, only 4 voted on going on at once. Discussion re sending boys to non-Catholic homes.

*Motion of Mr Leyland re Mrs Ashworth's remarks at a Manchester Conference this day fortnight.[104]

Nov 17: Sectional relief 9.15–11.30 Workhouse 2.30–5.0. New laundress came Nov 15. Considered applications of Cooks; and talked with matron about their work.

Nov 24: Sectional relief 9.30–11.0 Board 11–11.20. Leyland's motion deferred.[105] At Workhouse 2.30–5.30. Appointment of Roper and wife £17 as cooks; duties to be defined by Sub-committee to revise rules.

Dec 1: Sectional relief 9.15–11.15 Workhouse 2.30–5.0. Applications for housekeeper at Townley's; 3 so all to come before Board. Mary Jane Shaw 27 appointed Charge Nurse. Question of leave of absence to nurses, to be given by master or Superintendent, discussed Miss Basket called in, and told she must inform master in future, rather unpleasant scene Miss B. nervous.[106] Sub-committee of main buildings for hospital to define duties of the two cooks next week.

Dec 8: Sectional relief 9.15–11.0. At Board appointed Mrs Moffat housekeeper at Townley's. Mr Leyland's motion re Mrs Ashworth fell through after a few remarks.[107] Discussion re beer at Xmas dinner.[108] At Workhouse. Holden resigned as nurse. Decided to advertise for 2 lunatic attendants and return Miss Hevey to hospital Sub-committee re cooks decided that man cook take body and officers there; woman be at hospital; to be tried for 3 months. Annie Brown and Margaret Farmmond, a boarded out child, both to be sent to Park Road.[109]

Dec 15: Sectional relief 9.15. Workhouse in aft.

Dec 22: Sectional relief 9.15–11.0 Board meeting 11–12.15. Mr Leyland gave notice of motion answering Mrs Ashworth in fortnight.[110] At workhouse. Master absent ill. Mr Cranshaw apparently not sober, great interruption from him, re cooking for doctor.[111]

Dec 23: Sub-committee meeting re planning offices' rules 11–12.30.

Dec 29: Absent from Sectional relief. Workhouse 2.30–5.0. My turn on Rota.

1898

Jan 5: Sectional relief 9.30–11.0. Mr Leyland's motion of censure carried by 12 against 10. Mrs Howard spoke very well I alluded to the disgraceful way the business at the workhouse is carried on.[112] At Workhouse. I was taken to task by Mr Shippobottom as implying fault lay with chairman and vice-chairman. I explained this not my meaning at all. Child Donnelly girl aged 14 engaged as servant by Peter Heaton, Doulhill.

Jan 12: Sectional relief 10.15–12.15 At workhouse 2.30–6.45 much disturbance re Miss Basket and cook [three words obscured] from one section including chairman not over at 6.45 when I left. Saw candidates for lunatic attendants and recommended Arthur and Annie Bland for appointment.

Jan 19: Sectional Relief 9.30–11.0. At Board meeting. I am put on special committee re Infant Life Protection Act. Letter read from Liverpool Committee of Training ship "Indefatigable" desiring to recruit boys aged 14–15. At workhouse, carried that fresh cook is engaged for hospital salary £23. 7000lbs bread per week required in baking tender while oven is repaired.[113]

Jan 26: Sectional Relief 9.30–12.30. At Workhouse, child Meofrock returned by Mrs Tatlock of Church Bank as unsuitable. New lunatic attendants came Jan 24. Baby McGrath taken under control of guardians.

Feb 2: Sectional relief 9.30–10. At 10 meeting of sub-committee to carry out Infant Life Protection Act. Decided to ask Mr Blake (Office for Prevention of Cruelty to Children) to undertake the duty at salary to be fixed later. At Board 11–12.30 Dr Buck permanently appointed at workhouse by large majority. At workhouse. Elizabeth McLelland and Jane Macdonald engaged as paying probationers in place of Hogarth and Mills; also Mary Campbell as additional one.[114]

Feb 9: Sectional relief 9.30. Absent. At workhouse 3.30–5.0. Main building committee to enquire about room for refractory persons Hospital committee to enquire into large washer for hospital.

Feb 16: Absent. (Scotland).[115]

Feb 23: Sectional Relief 9.30–11.40. At Workhouse Mrs Burton appointed hospital cook. Annie Brown 12 and Bertha Oldfield 9 given to Park Road Home.

March 2: Sectional Relief 9.30–11.30 Board meeting. Discussion by Mr Leyland re: consumption of whisky at workhouse. At workhouse in afternoon.

March 4: Committee re Infant Life Protection Act. Mr Leyland moved that we ladies undertake either to do the work or find a deputy. This agreed to. I met the others with Miss Barlow and Miss Armitage representing the Boarding out Committee and we agreed that Miss Armitage should undertake the office.[116]

March 9: Absent all day due to attending meetings of Women's Liberal Association, at which were debates on points of Poor Law.

March 16: Absent from Sectional relief and Board meeting owing to bad cold. At Workhouse 3.30. Miss Barlow attended to explain about 2 children boarded out at the Cross Guns public house; explanation satisfactory. (Quantity of bread used per week 7600lbs.). Isa Russell appointed as probationary nurse in place of nurse Hope.

March 23: Absent from Sectional relief (cold). At Workhouse 3.30. Mr Aldred returned Mary Allen as unsuitable for her service.

March 30: Absent from Sectional relief (cold). Sub-committee for Infant Life Protection Act accepted Miss Armitage as officer for 1 year. This confirmed at Board meeting which followed. At Workhouse 2.30–4.45 (Robert went with me) nothing special.[117]

April 6: Sectional relief. At Workhouse. Nurse Lang resigned. Succeeded by nurse Kelly as P. P.[118]

April 13: Sectional relief. At Board rules for workhouse officers adopted. Increase of salary to J. Hume porter. Subscriptions to Manchester Eye Hospital £10.10.0, Bolton Infirmary £52.10.0, Bolton District Nursing Association £105. Absent from workhouse.

April 20: First meeting of new Board of Guardians J. Heywood appointed chairman; first time this done from outside.[119] He had been thrown out at the election of Bradford Ward last week, and so was put in under co-optive clause. Appointment of Ladies Visiting Committee also carried again. At workhouse re-appointment of sub-committees the "main buildings" is divided into two; main buildings proper and house. I am on latter. Elizabeth Skelton 12 1/2 applied for service at Littlewood of Farnworth local preacher. Mr Hoskyns said that the sect of Protestantism was as necessary to be attended as meals, the question of

Roman Catholic and Protestant and that he should object to a church child going to a Wesleyan home and vice versa.

April 27: Sectional relief. Board meeting. John in chair. Business routine. At workhouse appointment of Nurse Mills in place of Hope resigned. Sub-committee appointed to enquire into cook's duties and if 2 are required in main body.

May 4: Sectional relief. At workhouse sub-committee re cook. Recommended that he (Roper) is allowed to keep office and live outside for 3 months on trial at 35/- per week. Mrs Swan and I disapproved but gave way to Kearsley and Shippobottom as only for a time. Nurse Featherstone resigns.

May 11: Sectional relief. Board meeting. Discussion on vaccination re request of Leicester Board for Bolton to join them, in opposition.[120] At Workhouse I proposed that boys from the cottage homes should go to the swimming baths in Bolton once a week. Deferred for further discussion until next week.

May 18: Sectional relief. At workhouse was resolved "that the boys go at discretion of the schoolmaster to the Bolton swimming baths once a week during the summer months" and "that instruction in swimming shall be provided for the first few weeks of the season". Mr Ellis Lee and Mr Swan moved contrary amendment but did not press it. Man cook was told to send in resignation at once and leave premises this day fortnight June 1.

May 25: Sectional relief. At board, swimming decision was passed without comment. At workhouse Mr Richardson very impatient and restless, and finally went out in anger; (intoxicated) John's resolution re continuing with administration block at once, refused, and he was told to give notice to rescind former resolution and then proceed.[121]

June 1: Absent. (Yorkshire).

June 8: Sectional relief. At Board secretary of state for war in reply as to whether army pensions could be paid monthly instead of quarterly, replied that this difficult but that they were always glad to be informed of any who made bad use of their pension or became chargeable to the rates in between. 75,000 army pensioners in country. At workhouse discussed duties of new house committee.[122]

June 13: Saw death of Mrs Ashworth in Manchester Guardian. Drowned at Whitby the previous Friday June 8. A terrible shock.

June 15: Sectional relief. We ladies met in one room at 1.45 to pass the following resolution: "Dear Mr Ashworth, We the undersigned women Guardians of the Bolton Union desire to express our deep sympathy with the loss you have just sustained, and to record our high appreciation of your wife's services on the Board. We, who have worked with her so regularly during the past three years, know her untiring energy and ever-ready sympathy in every detail intended to bring greater happiness to those less fortunate than ourselves, and it is with heavy hearts that we face a future deprived of her presence. We remain dear Mr Ashworth, yours faithfully, Mary Ann Howard, Susanna Swan, Marian Orrel, Mary Haslam". At the Workhouse. Hannah Turner allowed to remain indefinitely at the Shibden Home Halifax (16 on May 19th).

June 22: Sectional relief. At Board, discussion introduced by Chairman (John) re proposal to proceed with building of administration Block and Nurses home in connection with new Hospitals. Dr Gilchrist moved amendment to negative this, which was carried by 29 for and 9 against it. Ellen Gardner accepted as Paying Probationer in place of nurse Hadden. At workhouse the furnishing of new hospital referred to Hospital Committee.[123]

June 29: Sectional relief 10–11. At workhouse T. J. Grundy resigns post as labour master (Inebriated of late).

July 6: Sectional relief. At Board meeting spoke in favour of Helston Union desiring to detain women with illegitimate children. A. R. [Annie Russell], Borthwick appointed Probationer. Mr Jenner Fust present. Workhouse. Nurse Hollis chosen as Probationer in place of Binnie.

July 13: Sectional relief. At workhouse discussed Helston Unions re July 6 and agreed further detention is necessary. Mrs Hydes extension discussed but refused.

July 18: At workhouse School Examination. Thought again that Mr Mozley very dull and old-fashioned. Asked him would it be possible to get additional mistress in.

July 20: Sectional relief. Board meeting. At Workhouse allowed that Elizabeth Grandine should remain at Adcote Home for the present.

July 27: Sectional relief. At workhouse Thomas Rainford appointed Labout master. Two cooks, man and woman, to be advertised for.

Aug 3: Absent from Sectional relief. At Board as usual, and at Workhouse.

Aug 10: Sectional relief. At Workhouse the School Inspectors report re an additional mistress in the infants department discussed by schools and cottages sub-committee. I was asked to be present having gone into the question with schoolmaster and clerk.[124]

Aug 17: Sectional relief. Board meeting. Workhouse. *Schools and Cottages Sub-committee again discussed question of additional mistress.

Aug 24: Sectional relief. Workhouse.

Aug 31: Absent from Sectional relief (Haigh). At Board. At Workhouse.

Sept 7: Sectional relief. At workhouse. Decided against additional assistant mistress. Discussed to make a bowling green by master; labour found so no expense.

Sept 8: Had workhouse children at White Bank for afternoon. 30 unable to come from no 7 because of cases of measles. A beautiful day. 80 came. Returned in 2 minibuses.

Sept 14: Sectional relief. At Board meeting review talks of statistics from Mr Jenner Fust re amount of in and out door relief in Bolton and other places.

Sept 21: Sectional relief. At Workhouse selection of cooks. Ball and wife recommended to Board.

Sept 25: Absent. (Clifton etc.).

Oct 5: Workhouse.

Oct 12: Sectional relief Board meeting. Question of Shoreditch Guardians re disfranchisement for out-door relief. Referred to future committee. At Workhouse carpentry for boys re-introduced by J. H. passed without difficulty; expenditure £50. See May 26 1897.

Oct 19: Sectional relief. Absent from workhouse. (at Wigan).

Oct 26: Absent from Sectional relief. Board meeting. Question from Birmingham re disfranchisement from out-door relief. Absent from Workhouse.

Nov 1: At Workhouse. Vestry Committee meeting.

Nov 2: Absent from Sectional relief. At Workhouse at 3.30. Miss Barlow present re boarding-out of children etc. Gertrude Lovett to be sent to Park Road, and to be transferred to Rossendale Home.

Nov 9: Absent from Sectional relief. Board meeting. Workhouse. Frances Todd taken out to service. Chairman notified mistress that the BSBYS would visit child.

Nov 16: At workhouse Gertrude Lovett and sister to be retained in workhouse until father gets home ready for them. Thomas J. Hunt appointed labour master.

Nov 23: Board meeting. Workhouse in aft.

Nov 30: At workhouse. Sub-committee's report as to officers' salaries given in.

Dec 7: Absent.

Dec 14: Absent.

Dec 21: At Board, question of beer at Xmas dinner discussed and voted upon 19 against beer and 13 for, so none this year.[125]

Dec 28: Absent. (Sidmouth).

1899

Jan 4: Absent. (Sidmouth).

Jan 11: Ditto.

Jan 18: Board meeting. On agenda Report of Bolton District Boarding-out Committee. Alfred Longworth appointed indoor labour master, and Eckersley (gardener) out-door labour master. At workhouse selection of 3 girls for Mrs Carlton Cross' Home at Whittle-le-Woods.[126]

Jan 25: At workhouse Elizabeth Grandine transferred from Adcote Home to Ashton House Home, Cheshire.

Feb 1: Board meeting. At workhouse, Margaret Ellen Wray returned from service.

Feb 8: Workhouse. Mrs Matthews applies for increase of salary £21 to be £24.

Feb 15: At Board question of midwifery fees by District Medical officers discussed. Decided that 2 guineas each and no extra, for special cases, instead of 1 guinea as before and extra when required.[127]

Feb 22: At workhouse. It was decided that a tablet (cost 14–5–0) be placed in the new Tramp Ward.

March 1: Absent. (Italy).[128]

March 8: Absent. (Italy).

March 15: Absent. (Italy).

March 22: Absent. (Italy).

March 29: Absent. (Italy). Termination of Miss Armitage's five months appointment as Inspector under Infant Life Protection Act. Re-appointed.[129]

April 5: At workhouse letter read from Launceston Union for detention of single women in Workhouses with children.

April 12: At Board Mr Tonge moved motion in favour of old age pensions. Discussion uninteresting and fell flat. Last meeting of present Board.[130]

April 19: New Board met. Committee appointed.[131] Learned that 1 1/2 oz. tea is put to 10 quarts of water and 5 oz. sugar.

April 26: At Workhouse, the cooks resign.

May 3[132]

May 10: At board letter from L. G. B. re Ball the cook. At Workhouse request of Whittaker the store keeper for a testimonial. Refused on account of enquiry about cook.

May 17: Workhouse, sub-committee appointed for the purpose, decided it would be well to engage women desiring out-door relief, to work in the laundry. Refused by Workhouse Board. Boys to go to swimming baths as last year

May 24: Board went to Town Hall and then to Church it being the Queen's birthday and thanksgiving service, no meeting at workhouse in consequence.[133]

May 31: At Workhouse, sub-committee appointed to enquire into charges brought against Whittaker the store-keeper decided he must resign, but the workhouse committee preferred that the chairman reprimand him.

June 7: At Board Miss Basket Superintendent nurse resigned. In future salary to begin at £50, with annual increase of £5 to a maximum of £100. At the board, the storekeeper is ordered to resign, but at workhouse he protests, and his wife interviews the house Committee on his behalf, and the matter is remanded. I moved an amendment that the original is kept to, and that his resignation is kept to, but there being no seconder, it fell through. A great disgrace, as no doubt about the man having cheated, using fake weights etc., etc.

June 14: At Workhouse Whittaker writes token of apology and resolution is carried that he be allowed three months trial.

June 21: Absent. (London). Board met.

June 28: Girls to go to swimming baths as boys.

July 5: At Board appointment of new Superintendent nurse. Miss Bayes from Brownlow Hill, Liverpool appointed.

July 12: Absent. (London conference).

July 19: Absent. (London. A. Knowles wedding).[134]

July 26: At workhouse my turn on Rota.

July 31: Special meeting in Mawdsley H. re nurses

August 2: At Board, proposal to appoint three additional charge nurses and five additional probationers carried without the expected opposition.[135]

August 9: At Workhouse. Request for Alice Wilson to stay on at 46 Bromwich St (Park St) home, and girls in general to be allowed to remain until 16. Great opposition and trouble from Mr Dearden. Finally decided that Alice should go to a situation as soon as possible, and that each future case should be decided on its own merits.

August 16: Got permission for onions to be supplied for the pea soup and meat broth. At Board meeting question re examination discussed.

August 23: Absent. (Ireland).

August 30: Absent. (Ireland). Whittaker's 3 months over – of course he remained.[136]

Sept 6: At workhouse Mr Watkinson moved the extension of present Hospital Pavilions and building of administration block. Mr Shaw seconded. Mr Cooper saying that the cost now probably is £35000, the resolution was withdrawn. The previous week it was decided to build the nurses Home.[137]

Sept 13: At Board resolution to build the Nurses Home at a probable expenditure of £6000 to £7000 passed. At workhouse application for 3 girls to go to Bromwich St. Farris, Cunningham and Riding. Farris had left and Cunningham being Roman Catholic only Riding available.

Sept 20: At Workhouse discussion on increase of salary to master and matron – Decided that £10 be given to matron, master's to remain the same.

Sept 27: At Board matron's salary to be raised from £70 to £80. Alice Hartland appointed Head Laundress. (On Sept. 26 Alice Riding was sent to Bromwich St.). At workhouse, house committee to enquire about washing machines.

Oct 4: At Workhouse, house sub-committee met about new washing machine. I was on Rota committee. Great waste of bread mentioned by farm sub-committee is it from Body in Hospital and can it be prevented.

Oct 11: Board meeting. Workhouse. Decided that Lizzie Grandine remain another year at Parkside Home. Committee to enquire into plans for new piggeries reports cost to be £500. Preston quote.[138]

Oct 18: At workhouse decided to recommend purchase of new washing machine from T. Bradford and Co. cost £164 and repair of old one by Bell and Co. £35.

Oct 25: At Board. Above re laundry passed. At Workhouse. Schofield's son to be sent to Huddersfield as a collier – Hospital and house sub-committees meet to discuss bread waste.

Nov 1: At workhouse, proposal to start the Brabazon Employment Scheme there; by ladies outside, led by Mrs J. Hulton approved; the day to be Tuesday.[139]

Nov 8: At Board, Brabazon Scheme passed. At Workhouse, further discussion re bread waste.

Nov 15: At Workhouse. Proposed to send 5 boys to Buckley Hall. Decided not by 16 against 10 votes.

Nov 22: At Board question of Lunatic Asylums accommodation discussed. Learned that 611 belong to Bolton (!) cost per head, per week 8/9. (See entry re boys to Buckley Hall: should be this day). Woman Schofield to be prosecuted for insulting Nurse Macdonald.

Nov 29: At Workhouse – Enquiries as to whether Xmas should be without beer. Chairman advised waiting for resolution next week.

Dec 6: At Board, resolution to have no beer at Xmas dinner to workhouse inmates carried by 26, against 6. (much progress since last year!). At Workhouse, decided to allow 4 ladies, including Mrs Butler, wife to Vicar of Farnworth, to visit Church of England inmates on Fridays and Sundays.

Dec 13: At Workhouse discussion on classification method by Mr Shippobottom

Dec 20: Board meeting. Workhouse committee.

Dec 27: Workhouse Committee not meet, on account of Xmas.

1900

Jan 3: Board meeting. Appointment of H. Chambers and A. Smith (Hilda Crook's) as probationer nurses. At Workhouse.[140]

Jan 10: At Workhouse, decided to raise age of children in Day room from 2 to 4 Mrs Swan and myself put on the classification sub-committee.

Jan 9: Meeting of Boarding-out Committee to hear report of children.

Jan 17: Board meeting. Report of Boarding-out Committee re children referred to workhouse. At workhouse.

Jan 24: At workhouse. Report of Boarding-out Committee, 55 children on list. Much talk re tenders for nurses' Home. One accepted (A. Atherton) for £6665 + £115.4.9 (counterceiling) + £76.16.6 for maple floors. Total £6857 – I protested and wished the total kept lower, but was quite over-ruled.

Jan 31: At Board, £8000 to be applied for repayable in 30 years, for the building of new nurses' Home. Had been decided to form small sub-committee to see after the work, but no ladies; so at this Board meeting I moved and got carried that Mrs Howard and Mrs Barnes be added. Workhouse.

Feb 7: At Workhouse. On Rota Committee. Estimate for new piggeries deferred a fortnight.

Feb 14: At Board. Continued Subscription to Poor Law Unions Association. At workhouse – nothing special.

Feb 21: At Workhouse. Sisters at Rumford St. Home ask for girl – Cassidy to remain another year as being of weak intellect although 14 years old (see Aug 9th); refused until she is brought before us and examined by Dr Buck next week. Boy at Buckley Hall refused another half year to have Compositors' trade, for same reason. Estimate for new piggeries £1500! Age of children in day room to be 3 instead of 4. (see Jan 10). £25 to be spent on trees for hospital grounds and cemetery.

Feb 26: At Board discussions on request of Band of Hope and Temperance Union as to sale of drink being prohibited to children; res in favour carried by 34 to 2. At Workhouse Rose Cassidy brought from Manchester; doctor certified she could not read and was defective so allowed to go back for another year. Mary Anford to remain another year at Epileptic Home in Essex.

*March 14: At Board expen. of £1500 on piggeries referred back to Committee. Deputation to attend Central P. L. Conference. Mr Shippobottom and Mr Knott.[141] At workhouse; children Foy to be detained till parents come out of prison.

March 7: At Workhouse Mary Anford to stay another year at Lingfield Home.

March 16: Visited Thomas Donolly, and 3 sisters Holt with view to Boarding them out.

March 21: House and Main Buildings Committee meet to discuss hot air drying closets in laundry, recommend that Bradford be asked to report.

March 28: At Board. At workhouse. I spoke to Winifred Chambers re her mother and eldest child.

April 4: At Workhouse.

April 11: At Board – resignation of Miss Armitage Inspector under Infant Life Protection Act. Deferred till new Board meets. At Workhouse; Nurse Hevey's resignation.

April 18: At Workhouse Classification Committee to meet in month hence, when the man's new shed for worst characters shall have been tried. New Board meets next week.

April 25: Meeting of new Board. Chairman of Board = Mr Ward; Vice " " " = Mr Knott; Chairman of workhouse Committee Mr Shippobottom; Vice " " " " Mr Cunliffe. At Board Lady Visitors re-appointed without opposition. At workhouse I leave the House Committee and join the Schools and Cottages.

May 9: Board and Workhouse. Absent. (London).

May 16: At Workhouse the question as to whether tailoring shall continue to be taught to boys, to be considered by Schools and Cottages Committee.

May 23: At Board consent passed for borrowing £8000 for building of Nurses Home. At Workhouse enquired into number of children in different cottages.

May 30: At workhouse Bradford and Co. to give another tender for drying closets.

June 6: At Board relieving officers to act in place of Miss Armitage re Infant Life Protection Act. Workhouse.

June 18: Workhouse. Porter's duties revised in consequence of classi-fication.

June 20: At Board. At Workhouse tender of Bradford's for drying closets accepted £389, less £121 for old materials; Total will cost about £400. £132 being for alterations to building.

June 27: Workhouse

July 4: At Board. J. Heywood resigned off Workhouse Committee being annoyed at delay re Nurses' Home. Society for Prevention of Cruelty to Children asks for help from Union; decided to ask the LGB. Workhouse.

July 11: At workhouse passed that all officers who live in the house should have a fortnights' holiday, instead of 5 days.

July 15: Absent on Continent.

July 25: Ditto

Aug 1: Ditto

Aug 8: Ditto

Aug 14: At Workhouse; in Cottages. Found again that no boys sleep in nightshirts. Girl Grace doing well at knitting.

Aug 15: At Board circular re deserving poor mentioned and to be supplied to guardians. At Workhouse, tender for new piggeries £790(!).

Aug 22: At Workhouse consideration of Taylors' position as LGB no longer recognises him as industrial trainer.

Aug 29: At Board, re subscription to Society for Prevention of Cruelty to Children, LGB forbids it, but allows payment for cases undertaken. Sub-committee appointed to consider matter, one from each sectional relief Committee. I chosen for Little Bolton.

Sept 3: Had workhouse children at White Bank.

Sept 5: Workhouse – Absent.

Sept 12: At Board salary of Pilling raised from 25/- to 30/- per week, on account of extra duties, driving, etc, etc. At Workhouse report of Sub-committee re classification, and agreed to be tried for 12 months.

Sept 13: Had old women and "fit" cases at White Bank.

Sept 19: At Workhouse.

Sept 26: At Board question raised as to purchase of expensive drugs and medicines for outpatients referred to sub-committee. At workhouse, request for permanent gardener refused.

Oct 2: At Workhouse. Cook [name illegible] resigns. Estimates for hearse and coffin carriage; Gordon's for £45 accepted.

Oct 10: Resignation of Miss Bayes as nurse Superintendent.

Oct 17: At workhouse. Sisters of Charity at Holly Mount request 6/- instead of 5/- as future charge there. Not agreed to.

Oct 24: At Board. Proposed readjustment of Salaries of Cottage home keepers. Circular from LGB re Workhouse dietaries. At Workhouse – tenders for new washing machine. Ada Owen to be knitter 1/2 time.

Oct 29: At workhouse.

Nov 7: At Board – Decided to purchase new washing machine for £167.15.0. Grant of £10.10.0 acknowledged by Secretary of Society for Prevention of Cruelty to Children. At workhouse.

Nov 14: Knitting of stockings not sufficient, so knitter to be engaged at 16/- per week, until required quantity is in stock.

Nov 21: At Board. Nothing special. At Workhouse. Enquired into numbers of stockings knitted.

Nov 27: At Workhouse; date of Xmas dinner fixed for Wed. after Xmas Day. Officers to have their own dinner at rate of 3/- per head purchased by the matron.

Dec 5: At Board; resolution re inmates Xmas dinner without beer passed without an amendment! At Workhouse – Hannah Turner to be allowed to remain 3 months longer at Shibden Home Halifax, at rate of 6/- (raised from 5/-). Applications for post of Superintendent Nurse.

Dec 12: At Workhouse. Maria Ball to be sent to Convalescent Home.

Dec 19: At Board. Appointment of Miss Archibald as Superintendent Nurse. At Workhouse. Lucy Ford, Winifred Mulligan and M. E. Murphey applied for by Rumford H. Home, but declined. Those of weak intellect can only be kept in workhouses at their own wish; there are 21 here who cannot be certified as lunatics. Mrs Whittaker (labour mistress) having undergone operation, matron empowered to get temporary help.

1901

Jan 2: At Board. Report re training ship Scamoulte. Annual charge for telephone between Workhouse and the Central. At Workhouse.

Jan 9: At workhouse. Application for increase of salary of Eckersley and wife, referred to workhouse.

Jan 16: At Board. Report of Boarding-out Committee. At workhouse 200lbs. of dripping accumulated.

Jan 23: At Workhouse. Application of Eckersley and wife refused. Report of Dietary sub-committee. Increased charge 5/- to be 6/- at Buckley Hall Orphanage requested, but refused.

Jan 30: At Board. Miss Cleghorn's (2nd laundress) salary to be raised from £27 to £30, according to scale. At Workhouse.

Feb 6: At Workhouse. Donolly brought back by mother.

Feb 13: At Board. I gave notice to move resolution re tubercolusis this day month. At Workhouse. E. Owen got leave to go out and visit son, earning 10/6. I proposed to get "Do-all" mops and pails. Deferred a month.*

Feb 20: At Workhouse, * meeting of sub-committee re classification. Further letter from Buckley Hall. Boys to be returned.

Feb 27: At Board. At Workhouse. Sub-committee appointed to consider officers dietary. Hannah Turner to remain at Shibden Home 6 months from March 22 -

March 6: At workhouse. Stores Committee to report if enough stockings in stock. Mrs Whittaker returned.

March 18: At Board. Adoption of revised duties of indoor and outdoor labour masters. I moved resolution re spread of consumption amongst the poor. Referred to Workhouse Committee. At Workhouse. Elizabeth Grandine to remain another year at Parkstone House Home.

March 20: At Workhouse. Officers dietary adopted.

March 27: At Board. Lancashire Asylums Board increase in weekly cost of maintenance from 5/9 to 9/4. At workhouse. Sub-committee appointed to deal with consumption question.

April 3: At Workhouse. I spoke to Mr Taylor about the boys clothes, and asked the committee to allow them to wear the composition collars on week days. Found Taylor would much like improvement in boys' clothes.

April 10: At Board. Mr I. H. Cooper "acting clerk" on account of father's illness. At Workhouse.

April 14: Death of Mr Simpson Cooper.

April 17: At Board, meeting of new Board. Lady visitors at workhouse abolished, with exception of Miss Barlow and Miss Armitage. At workhouse. Absent.

April 24: At Board. Appointment of Mr Barton as assistant R. O. to Little Bolton district. At Workhouse – Re-appointment of sub-committees.

April 22: Visited cottages. Dinners not sent up in time to cook so bacon and potatoes substituted, not enough. No.3 cottage.

May 1: At workhouse; sub-committee re consumption. Absent. (Glasgow).

May 5: Absent. (London).

May 15: At workhouse. Settlement of terms for appointment of workhouse master and matron.[142]

May 22: At Board. Salary of Master and Matron settled. Relieving officers to be appointed. Inspectors under Infant Life Protection Act in place of Miss Armitage resigned.

May 29: At workhouse; found boys suits of clothes not quite as ordered. I asked to buy ties and bows.

June 6: At Board. Adoption of new dietaries passed. At workhouse.

June 13: At Workhouse. Adoption of new dietaries. Amusement about Do-all mops with Mr Crompton.

June 20: At Board. At workhouse. Removal of H. Turner to Victorian Laundry Home at Liverpool.

June 27: Nothing special.

July 3: At Board. Nothing special. At Workhouse. I ordered to buy 3 more mops and pails and some looking glasses and trays for the cottage homes. Amusement amongst Mr Crompton's supporters.

July 10: At workhouse. Gertrude Duxbury went out to service with Mrs Ellison.

July 16: At Mawdsley St. Meeting of Consumption Committee. Drew up suggestions. This followed by meeting of workhouse committee to consider applications for posts of Master and Matron.

July 17: At Board. Proceedings of Workhouse Committee re appointment of Master and Matron. Mr and Mrs Booth of Preston appointed. At Workhouse. Absent.

July 24: At workhouse. Report of sub-committee re Consumption presented and passed after much discussion by 13 against 9. Resolution to be sent to County Borough of Bolton Horwich and Farnworth Urban Councils: "That notification of phthisis be encouraged (if not made compulsory) and that full disinfection be allowed after a removal or death." Also a slight increase in out-door relief to be made if R. O. see that it is spent in extra beds, or food. Mrs Greg and Sister make offer of £20 each for open-air shelter at the Workhouse. Applications for new Laundress.

July 31: At Board formal sanction given to the above.[143]

Aug 8: Absent.

Aug 15: Absent.

Aug 22: Absent.

Aug 29: Absent.

Sept 5: Absent.

Sept 12: At Workhouse – after September no further gratuities to be granted. Applications for increase in salary granted. Taylor and wife (cooks) £10 added to wife. Colebourne (barber) 1/- per week Walden (baker) not agreed to.

Sept 19: At Workhouse arrangements made for opening of new nurses' home next week.

Sept 25: At Board. J. Matheson appointed as Head Laundress, salary £30 to increase to £40 on afternoon opening of the new nurses' home. Mr Cunliffe opened, I seconded thanks to him. A very pleasant afternoon, and weather perfect. Band and masque.[144]

Oct 2: Absent. (Oliver ill – scarlet fever).

Oct 9: At Board. At workhouse Mr Shippobottom moved appointment of Sub-Committee to consider desirability of sending the children out to the public elementary schools. Agreed that Hannah Turner stay at Victoria House Laundry till end of year. Presentation of the service on to Mr and Mrs Davies.

Oct 16: At workhouse.

Oct 23: At Board. Report of Boarding-out Committee. Wages of stocking knitter to be 16/- per week. At workhouse. Discussed whether to cover day room and 2 bedrooms in cottages with linoleum to save so much scrubbing. Deferred until cottages be beautified. Asked that boys should wear celluloid collars and to enquire pieces etc at Peters.

Oct 30: At Workhouse I moved a resolution "that the children in the Cottages should not go out to service if the number left be not 3 over 12 years old" It was adjourned – nothing seems able to prevent these little girls going out to this miserable service!

Nov 6: At Board Local Government Board sanctions the appointment of Master and Matron at Workhouse.

Nov 13: At Workhouse. Frank Hopkins 14 went out to service with Mrs Almond Astley Bridge.

Nov 20: Resolution of Oct 30 agreed to. Matron and myself to get girls' new jackets.

Nov 27: At Workhouse.

Dec 4: At Board resolution re Xmas Dinners: "a limited quantity of roast beef and plum pudding, with one pint of tea, coffee, cocoa or milk, snuff and tobacco for the adults and oranges and nuts for the children". Passed without dissentient so we hope the question of beer is dismissed for ever. At Workhouse, request made for Assistant Sister or superintendent at the Nurses' Home, salary to be £40 and 3 servants at £18.[145] I to buy girls' jackets and linoleum.

Dec 11: At Workhouse. Details of various children.

Dec 18: At Board. Appointment of Assistant Superintendent and 3 general servants passed.

Dec 18: At Workhouse. Details of various children.

1902

Jan 8: At Workhouse. Details of various children. Mrs Hodkinson wanted leave to go and see daughter Alice Riding, promised she would not disturb the latter.

Jan 15: Heard the small cooking stove of no use except to boil on top. Heard that food for dinners not sent up in time from stores to cook that day. Roasting beef and boiling beef all alike, so [illegible word] is [illegible word] beef as stated in dietary table on Mondays and Thursdays. Salary of Bland and wife raised 10 £ = £60; Eckersley and wife 4 £ = 60£.

Jan 19: Sub-committee re Education of Workhouse children.

Jan 22: At workhouse. Details of children. Talk with Mr Knott and Matron about the Cottages. Mrs Hodkinson had kept her word about Alice.

Jan 29: Board meeting. At workhouse Mary Anford to remain another year at Lingfield Home. Little Hulton Urban Council accedes to one request to notify cases of phthisis as other infectious illnesses and disinfect afterwards.

Feb 5: [Blank]

Feb 12: Board meeting. A grant of £10.10.0 allowed to National Society for Prevention of Cruelty to Children from the period of Aug.1.1900 to Nov.30.1901. At workhouse proposal that sewing mistress be appointed.

Feb 19: At workhouse, applications for post of Assistant

Superintendent Nurse. Also duties of proposed sewing mistress defined.

Feb 26: Board meeting. Passed that a sewing mistress be appointed at salary of £20, to rise to £30 with furnished apartments and rations. Also passed by 34 against 9 that the Cottage Home Children attend the public Elementary Schools. The Schools are St. Williams' and S. S. Simon and Jude. Victoria Schools said that at present they had not accommodation, so all Protestants go together. *My* one drawback to scheme is that we shall miss the Schoolmasters' interest and influence with the boys, but perhaps something will be done to meet this loss. Miss Evans is the new L. G. inspector of B. O. children. Assistant Superintendent Nurse appointed. Miss Hopkins.

March 5: At workhouse. Letter read from Countess of Meath asking for patients to be sent to a Home for Epileptic girls "Meath Home of Comfort", 8/- per week.

March 12: Board Meeting. Notice from Lanc. Asylums' Board that charge of lunatics is to be raised from 9/4 to 9/11 per week. Workhouse.

March 15: Workhouse. Absent. Had it passed that E. Grandine be allowed another year at Parkgate Home and H. Turner to remain at Liverpool till end of June.[146]

March 25: Board Meeting. Ellen Tomlinson Cottage Mother resigns. Sub-committee cottages considered details of children going out to school, and fresh arrangements re cottage mothers as schoolmaster's cottage is vacant.

April 3: At workhouse sub-committee Cottages met again re last week's business. Candidates for Sewing Mistress interviewed. Miss Naylor chosen.

April 10: Board Meeting. Appointment of Miss Naylor as sewing mistress and appointment of Miss Whiteside, sister to the schoolmistress Miss W. as Cottage Mother. The two Miss Whitesides are to live in No 1 cottage and have about a dozen boys. Mr and Mrs Matthews to remove into No 10 cottage. No 9 remains empty. Since the older children have gone to school Miss Whiteside has been retained for the infants.

April 16: [Blank]

April 23: At Workhouse report re children at Holly Mount. Mr and Mrs Tomlinson [and doctor – partly obscured] had visited, and although not well satisfied did not feel justified in advising removal of children.

April 20: Board meeting. Abraham Wood appointed organist at salary of £5 to increase to £10. Appointment of Dr. T. G. Laslett of Farnworth as Examiner of Probationery Nurses at fee of 10/6 each. Passing of Finance Committee etc. including proposal to double the amount of outdoor relief in week of Coronation Celebration (£266) and illumination of Poor Law offices that night (£45). At the Workhouse, decided that Friday

June 27 is chosen as Coronation Day. This carried out in spite of King's illness.

May 7: At workhouse. Find Master very arbitrary with subordinate officers and objects to their speaking to guardians on sub-committee, as he ought to be asked first about any matter. Re [smudged] of school [smudged] of [smudged].

May 14: At Workhouse; man from the Fairy Hill Catholic Home applied to take Whittle and Shields; deferred a fortnight. Tender for open air shelters given by Mrs Greg.

May 21: Board meeting. Absent. (Italy).

May 28: Workhouse. Absent.

June 4: Board meeting. Absent.

June 11: Workhouse. Absent.

June 15: Board meeting. Absent. Transfer of Mr and Mrs Tomlinson to new duties re inspection of children in situations, and commencement of Miss Whiteside's duties as Cottage mother. About this time the girls were withdrawn from Holly Mount in con. of enquiry re Leigh guardians.

June 25: Workhouse. Absent.

June 27: Coronation celebration at Workhouse. A beautiful day. Sports for children.

July 2: Board meeting. Appointment of deputation to "International Congress for the Welfare and Protection of Children", in London. At Workhouse, Mr Edge to enquire about boys going to work in mills and live outside. Sub-committee appointed to consider question of babies going up to No 9 cottage (the vacant one) Ward, Shippobottom, Knott, Cunliffe, Swan, Haslam and Watkinson. Difficulty of separating the old women and the babies as they share the one officer Nurse Macdonald.

July 9: Workhouse. H. Turner engaged as housemaid at Nurses Home.

July 16: Board meeting. At Workhouse application of J. R. Airy as instructor in Manual training in woodwork, considered by cott. committee.

July 23: Workhouse. Nothing special.

July 30: Board meeting. Mr Jenner Fust present. At workhouse Sisters at Holly Mount beg that children be allowed to remain pending new certificate being granted by LGB.[147]

Aug 6: Workhouse. Absent (Keswick).

Aug 13: Board. Absent (Keswick).

Aug 20: Workhouse. Absent (Keswick).

Aug 27: Board and workhouse. Absent (Keswick).

Sept 3: Board and workhouse. Absent (Keswick).

Sept 10: Board meeting. At Workhouse Mrs Guest told me of the cruelty of the nuns at St. Williams School, a blow on the head last week

241

having been shown the doctor. Often marks on the body with stick. Report issued as follows, by request.

Widows under 40 years = 3 with 5 children
Deserted wives = 23 with 53 children
Single women = 24 with 36 children
Single women without children = 58

Sept 17: Workhouse.
Sept 24: Board meeting. At Workhouse asked that H. Turners' wages should be £14. £13 granted.
Oct 1: Workhouse. A case or two of smallpox, so visiting forbidden.
Oct 8: Board meeting. At workhouse. Cottages sub-committee suggest appointment of Alfred Ainscough as instructor in woodwork to boys, two nights a week, salary 5/- per night.
Oct 15: Workhouse. Absent (F. wedding).
Oct 22: Board meeting. Above appointment passed. Letter from Leeds Women's Suffrage Society, asking for support: rejected by 29 to 18. Workhouse. Officers request use of dining hall twice a month for recreation. Piano requested.
Oct 27: Workhouse.
Nov 5: Board meeting. At workhouse Mrs Barnes to purchase piano for use of officers.
Nov 12: Workhouse. Fresh kitchen ranges to be put in cottages.
Nov 19: Board meeting. Absent (Rome).[148]
Nov 26: Workhouse. Absent (Rome).
Dec 3: Board meeting. Absent (Rome). Piano to be bought.
Dec 10: Workhouse Sub-committee deals with differences between Master, Matron and Superintendent Nurse.
Dec 17: Board meeting.
Dec 24: Workhouse. Master to arrange for someone to meet children on return from school in afternoon.
Dec 31: Board meeting. At workhouse. H. Turner's wages to be £14.6.0 superannuation to be deducted.

1903
Jan 7: Workhouse. Heard 38 illegitimate children born in the Workhouse last year.
Jan 14: Board meeting. Talk of new footpath by Wash Lane; this frequently discussed. At Workhouse L. G. inspector wishes children to have hair brushes; decide that only the girls shall have them. Scale of officers' salaries revised.

Jan 21: Workhouse. Absent. (influenza). Application for Adam Salis, William Woodford and Joseph Sweeney to be sent to Catholic Working Boys Home, Manchester.

Jan 28: Board and workhouse. Absent (influenza).

Feb 4: Workhouse. Absent (influenza). Discussion on female classification.

Feb 11: Board and Workhouse. Absent (influenza).

Feb 18: Workhouse. Absent (influenza).

Feb 25: Board and workhouse. Absent (influenza). Payment of grant of £10.10.0 to Bolton Branch of National Society for the Prevention of Cruelty to Children.

March 4: Mary Anford to remain another year at Lingfield Home and Elizabeth Grandine at Park Gate.

March 11: Board and workhouse.

March 15: Workhouse. The LGB accountant warns that the cost of conveyances to the workhouse may have to be surcharged £36.3.6 per half year. Recommendation re officers salaries. Letter from schoolmistress re salary and age of children to be sent to school. Report of Catholic Guardians Association of visit to Canada.

March 25: Board and Workhouse. Resignation of Rev. G. Holden as Workhouse Chaplain. Report of ward instructor's classes; very satisfactory. Miss Whiteside's salary to be fixed at £50 and to be independent of grant.

April 1: Workhouse. Sub-committee re female classification deferred a month (until new Board comes in). Mr Shippobottom much opposed as scheme would require another officer. The clerk to write to LGB to enquire if they would approve vicar of Bolton leaving and appointing his curate to be Chaplain.

April 8: Board meeting. Letter read from the Mayor announcing meeting in Town Hall re tuberculosis and inviting representatives from Board of Guardians. First meeting after election of guardians. Mrs Howard again head poll in West ward.

April 16: Annual Meeting of Board, Appointment of Committees, etc. At workhouse appointment of Sub-committee. I remain on the Schools and Cottages.

April 22: Board meeting. At workhouse. Application of Eckersley (outdoor labourer) to remain as at present £60. Statement of admissions of Workhouse for quarter.

April 29: Workhouse. Report of female classification deferred another month. Question of heating old female hospital discussed.

May 6: Board and workhouse. Letter from Stamthwaite Colony re Ernest Woods an epileptic child. 12/6 per week.

May 13: Workhouse. Absent (London).

May 20: Board. At workhouse classification sub-committee to consider filling vacancies of store keeper and task mistress, Whittaker's having resigned.

May 27: Workhouse. Sub-committee appointed to consider raising of money for several improvements, to be over some years.

June 3: Board and workhouse. Absent. Appointment of Canon Keene as Chaplain. Resignation of J. Hulme porter.

June 10: Workhouse. Absent.

June 17: Board and Workhouse. Absent.

June 24: At workhouse. Mrs Guest pointed out that in regulations for cottage mothers, no mention of holidays or days off.

July 1: Board meeting. At workhouse hear that cottage mothers do not now take children out for walks. Question of tobacco and snuff; the last years allowance for same being [smudged] as against the previous year and sub-committee appointed to go into the matter.

July 8: Workhouse.

July 7: Paid surprise visit to Cottages. Found at no 10, children dining in kitchen and scullery and very untidy. On July 8 got it passed that in future cottage mothers should not have to pay their substitutes when on holidays.[149] Arrangements to be made for boys and girls to go to High St. Baths in holidays.

July 15: Board meeting. Workhouse.

July 22: Workhouse.

July 29: Board meeting. Roger Holdsworth appointed Porter at work-house. At workhouse. Cottage mothers to be provided with uniform. 2 dresses and 6 aprons yearly.

August 5: At workhouse. Found that Miss Walsh the temporary cottage mother and (sister to Mrs Matthews) had been most unsatisfactory in no. 2 cottage; now at no 8 but to leave after Miss Greenhalgh's return.

August 4: Tuesday. Children's treat, Drive to Rivington. Fine day; much enjoyed.

August 12: Board meeting. At workhouse. Children's Field Day. Fine day and much enjoyed. I gave present of 30 novels to Nurses' Home on August 10. (Value £5).

August 19: At workhouse. 3 boys, O'Brien 12, Orrell 10, and Hulme 11, ran away, home before next morning. O'Brien and Hulme to each receive 4 strokes of cane on hand, Orrell to be cautioned. Children to go to High St. Baths during holidays. 1d per child.

August 26: At Board. 1oz. tobacco weekly to be allowed to those employed in disagreeable work. Sub-committee had decided which these were; 75 in all Workhouse.

Sept 2: At Workhouse. Much conversation whether money (£4500) shall be raised on loan for following improvements

Bradford's washing machine	153.0.0
One [illegiable] up Boilers	88.7.6
Hot water supply to Old Female Hospital	352.
Bradford's machine for hot Wash	103.
New stoves	2500.
etc. etc. etc. total	4511.

Passed finally. We are told that the water pipes in Townley's quite useless and inadequate, after 5 years use. Mrs Bradshaw to enquire. Cuerden was the plumber employed.

Sept 9: At Board, letter read from Miss Bullan desiring that mothers be held responsible for their daughters to 16 years old. Deferred. Discussion re delegates to North Western P. L. Conference, res. carried that chairman, Vice and one other (Mrs Mason) chosen to attend. At workhouse find there are several big boys (14 yrs) whom we ought to find work for.

Sept 16: At Workhouse want to devise some plan of boys going to work and living outside. Discussion about tobacco for inmates.

Sept 23: At Board resignation of Mrs Orrell on ground of health. At once took steps to fill her place, but found a fortnight too short so let the seat go. Mr Tonge asked for return of spirituous liquors in workhouse for past 5 years ordered by doctor. Application by Hon. Sec. Girls Training Home Brook House. Sale for girls from the Workhouse to be trained as Servants.

Sept 30: At Workhouse [we] are told the LGB will no longer sanction the payment of omnibus seats to and from workhouse. Cottage mothers and other officers to have salaries raised according to scale without having to ask. Taylor and Matthews to be now at the maximum, and the latter £2 for knitting as hitherto.

Oct 7: At Board Miss Bullan's letter read again. See Sept 9. Decided that Board sympathises with it, but thinks imprisonment too drastic a step. At Workhouse a return had been made out according to resolution of House of Commons as to how many aged inmates would be able to live outside if they had a pension of from 5/- to 7/- per week. 83 in all. Afterward found that in 42 cases, the relations would not take charge of them at all. Linoleum is to be put on the bath rooms in the Cottages, having been asked for several times three months ago.[150]

Oct 14: Workhouse. Nothing special.

Oct 21: At Board. Return issued as to Spirituous Liquors used in workhouse.

Oct 28: Workhouse. Nothing special. Selection of candidates for Assistants at Casual wards.

Nov 4: Appointment of Special Committee re granting Relief by way of loan. Election of Mr Lilley as PLG. in place of Mrs Orrell. At Workhouse. Mr Jenner Fust was present and said he had found a cane on mantelpiece in No 10 cottage. Found Mrs Guest much troubled at Master's manner re reporting to sub-committee.

Nov 9: Surprise visit to workhouse.

Nov 11: 3 months leave of absence asked for Mrs Taylor (cook) Mrs O'Malia to do the work in the meantime at 13/ per week. I proposed that No 9 cottage be appropriated to use of children between 2 and 4; that cottage caretakers be advertised for, the wife to act as mother, and the husband to have control of the boys, teach carpentry, drill and music. Absent till Jan.6.04.[151] Miss Cleghorn appointed Head Laundress Dec.16.03.

1904

Jan 6: Isabella Ball taken out for service with Mrs Pennington Deane Rd; under control.

Jan 13: Representatives of Chorley, Leigh and Wigan to meet with Bolton re combination and Clarification of Workhouse. Ivy Virginia Lowe to go to Bromwich St.

Jan 20: Absent. (Oliver goes to S. America).

Jan 27: Girl E. Greenhalgh to go to Epileptic Home.

Feb 3: Absent. Ellen Todd applied for as servant on farm, but refused. Instructor in wood work (Mr Ainscough) complains of great heat in work room in school. Draft conditions drawn up for new foster parents at No 9 Cottage, the man to take charge of the boys in Nos. 1. 2. 3. out of school hours, to teach carpentry and drill and the wife to have charge of children between 2 & 4.

Feb 10: At Board Annie McKenzie appointed Assistant Laundress. I support again that Albert Todd (15) be found work under labour master.

Feb 24: Absent (London).

March 2: Find that 396 pairs of stockings and 37 [illegible], been knitted in last 3 months. Ellen Green made 16 pairs children's socks and Ellen Todd 11 pairs in one day. Hannah Turner's wages at the Nurse's Home raised for 5/6 to 6/- per week. Friction between Master and Matron and Superintendent Nurse re carbolic soap and condemned clothing.

March 9: At workhouse. 102 pairs socks knitted by the two girls in 1 week. Adam Sales brought back from Peter Heaton Willows Lane (he went there May 1903), on report from Inspector of Cruelty to Children; Explanation given by Heaton considered satisfactory. Sales came to workhouse in 1899, considered rather feeble-minded. Candidates interviewed as foster parents at [illegible]. Mary Anford to remain another year at Lingfield. Orders for admission to the workhouse to be in future for a limited time.

March 16: Foster parents Mark and Edith Russell recommended. A sub-committee was appointed to deal with difficulties between Master and Matron and officers; the chairman Mr Bolton and myself in addition to House Committee. Cottages Committee to draw up rules for new foster parents No 9.

March 23: At Board, received notice that Workhouse School's inspection is now transferred from the LGB to the Education Board. (Excellent!). Mark and Edith Russell appointed. At workhouse. Report of sub-committee as to worn-out Hospital clothing. Report of House Sub-committee as to Master's complaint in reference to want of discipline amongst officers of Main Building.

March 30: Report of Sub-committee re above complaint.

April 6: At Board. Report of conference of delegates as to combination and classification of workhouses; (children) 3 other unions. Tenders for tea. 1/8 and 1/4

April 13: [blank]

April 20: At Board Miss May Burt appointed dispenser, instead of Miss I. M. Dale. First meeting of new Board.

April 27: At Workhouse. Female Inmates Classification Sub-committee to meet and take up report of April 1 1903.

May 4: At Board. I proposed a grant being given to Bolton Poor Protection Society. Defeated. At Workhouse resignation of John and Alice Wolfendale, probationary Ward attendants. Miss Whiteside complained of children being sent errands in school time, and of greasy hair of some.

May 11: Gertrude Duxbury before guardians re leaving work at mill. Mr Knowles (guardian) promised to see into the matter; the mother had been interfering.

May 18: At Board, Sub-committees report re Classification on Women's Side approved. Thomas Hulme R. O. died from influenza. Deeply regretted. No meeting at Workhouse; (Rivington).

May 25: Absent (Paris). Application to sent Albert Todd to Kershaw Blind Asylum refused.

June 1: At Board. Proposed to send Thomas Rigby to the training ship, "Indefatigable". Workhouse.

June 9: At Workhouse. Cottages Committee to arrange about children's treat.

June 15: At Board. Mr Barton appointed R. O. in place of Mr Hulme, so assistant R. O. required. The "Case Paper" system introduced by Mrs Barnes.[152]

June 22: At Workhouse. Notice from Board of Education of inspection of Workhouse Schools.

June 29: At Board. Charles and Annie Evans appointed as Probationary Ward attendants. Appointment of special Committee to consider Case Paper system. I am one. At Workhouse. Cottages Committee to consider list of boys suitable for Training Ships. 6 were selected if doctor approves: Birtwistle, Ball, Comer, Dixon, Greenwood and Wiseman.

July 6: At Workhouse. Talk with Russell re making a hockey in playground on the green by the cottages.

July 12: Absent. Haysthenthwaite and Miss Hulme to marry and retain their present positions; granted now, I opposed it on previous consideration, and still think it unwise.

July 19: Workhouse.

July 26: At Workhouse. Mrs Matthews reported that 952 pairs of stockings had been knitted in last six weeks. 100 pairs had been sent to hospital that week. 12 doz. Men's and 12 doz. Women's ordered by matron. Mrs Guest says that Freddy Hall wants to be a shoemaker and H. Callaghan to be a joiner. The children to go to the baths; boys and girls one day each week at 1d charge. Question discussed of raising Charge Nurses' salary from £28 to £30 and holidays 1 month for Superintendent and 3 weeks for others.

August 2: At workhouse. Sub-committee to meet re classification of female inmates.

Aug 10: At workhouse no committee as it was day for children's sports.

Aug 17: Absent. Selection of 12 women for first class.

Aug 24: At Board and Workhouse. Question of Nurses' holiday postponed till Sept. At Workhouse found Miss J. Whiteside (Schoolmistress) ill; (fibroid growths) so must give up and go in hospital. Substitute to be provided, and leave of absence granted till Dec 31. Salary to go on. Miss M. Whiteside (cottage mother) wishes to take drill lessons for her sister, and to attend class of instruction for the purpose. Mrs Blandford appointed infant schoolmistress in place of Miss J. Whiteside.

Sept 7: At Board. At Workhouse. Discussion re doctor on question of nurses' salaries and holidays. Rise of salaries agreed to. Refusal of Comer to allow son John to go on "Indefatigable".

Sept 14: At workhouse. 4 boys to continue their swimming lessons, as being all who are in required standard.

Sept 21: At Board. Absent from Workhouse.

Sept 28: At workhouse.

Oct 5: At Board. Letter read from Socialist party re unemployed. Referred to Case Paper committee. At Board return showing number of paid scrubbers in other Workhouse hospitals.

Oct 12: At Workhouse. Support Tam O'Shanter caps for girls, and hoods for babies, but matron did not see need for latter.

Oct 19: At Board. At Workhouse. Said goodbye for winter. (St. Moritz). Heard by letter or post card the following:[153]

Nov 4: The matron said a large order was coming down next week for hospital requirement.

Nov 16: At Workhouse. Question of master's daughter residing there. Also stock of clothing and new sewing machine required. The "unemployed" committee met the Town Council on Monday last, and they promised to do all they could in finding of work. The Master asked for two sewing women in place of two washerwomen to cope with the sewing, and a new sewing machine, which were granted.

Nov 23: Consideration of Case Paper scheme deferred till New Year. Friction between Master and Superintendent.

Nov 30: Miss Whiteside asked for 2 months more leave of absence; granted until end of January with salary, but after that some fresh arrangement must be made. Superintendent Nurse gave her version of complaint and matter was left to 3 of Hospital Committee to devise some scheme of working smoothly with Master and Matron. The Schoolmaster at SS Simon and Jude reported that the children were not going regularly to school.

Dec 7: [blank]

Dec 14: Finance Committee re Mr F loan of land for Labour Colony, – their visit to Poplar and Lingfield. Suggested that Wash Lane is repaired by some of the unemployed. (This was done).[154]

Dec 21: [blank]

Dec 26 [blank]

1905

Jan 4: [blank]

Jan 11: Resignation of Dr. J. F. Wright as Medical Officer. Letter from secretary to the United Trades Council, re Unemployed.

Jan 17: [blank]

Jan 25: Discussion re Case Paper.

Feb 1: [blank]

Feb 8: Death of Mr Leish. Appointment of 2 members to act on the Executive Committee as to proposed Labour Colony, Blackburn. Wigan and Chorley to unite. Application for porter and sewing mistress to retain present posts after marriage in June. Granted.

Feb 15: Death of John Pilling clogger.

Feb 22: [blank]

Feb 29 [blank]

March 8: Further consideration of resolutions adopted Jan 23, re Case Paper system. I returned from St. Moritz having been absent since Oct. 04. Find the girls' playground being built.

April 4: Proposed scheme for Joint Labour Colony. H. Callaghan (14) wants to be a joiner, and Freddy Hall to be a shoemaker. Committee to consider putting them to these trades.

April 26: New Board. John Morton allowed to leave his four children in the workhouse, for 1 month while he seeks work, and reports back to R. O. each week.

May 3: Mr Cunliffe moves the re-consideration of Labour Colony scheme. Circular and Order of LGB re Underfed School Children. The children are to be referred from the Education Committee to the various Sections of out-door Relief.

May 10:[155]

CHAPTER TEN

The Travel Diaries of Mary Haslam

Context

Mary Haslam appears to have had a real thirst for travel, no doubt reflecting a childhood in which her father journeyed extensively across the world as a businessman and tourist. In later life she transcribed and edited his travel diaries to Russia, France, Italy and elsewhere, both as a tribute and memory to him and an encouragement to others.[1] We learn from her working diary that Mary Haslam herself traveled extensively in England, Scotland and Ireland, and also that she visited Italy, Brittany, St. Moritz and Spain. She was not like the women travelers who turned their backs on conventional lives to undertake long sexual, cultural or intellectual journeys.[2] Rather, Mary Haslam was more typical of that class of late nineteenth-century woman who had the means and motivation to take family holidays overseas, whose families had a long tradition of travel and whose aspirations were increasingly freed up by better communications, more sophisticated guidebooks and a new generation of newspaper reporters who filled the newspapers of provincial towns like Bolton with foreign exploits, sights and adventures.[3] As in other aspects of her life, such holidays and travels are keenly documented, and one of her travel diaries – to Ireland – is reproduced here.[4] The diary was kept in a small notebook containing squared paper and the handwriting suggests that it was updated daily. In common with diaries from holidays in Brittany and Italy, this from Ireland contains contextual material such as postcards, newspapers clippings, pressed flowers and other material. The text of the diary has been transcribed exactly as it appears in terms of spelling, grammar and content, but contextual material has been omitted.

In many ways Mary Haslam was a tourist, displaying all of the arrogance and disregard that commentators such as Buzard have seen as characteristic of tourists from the mid nineteenth century onwards.[5] Yet, this reproduction of one of her diaries, particularly where it is understood against the backdrop of contextual material from the Bolton archives, does fulfill three useful purposes. *First*, it adds further weight to calls for a breaking of the linkage between the word "travel" and "literary, male, bourgeois, scientific, heroic" achievements.[6] *Second*, the diary suggests that Haslam was not simply an idle tourist. Whilst in Ireland, for instance, she inspected the workhouse, made comparisons with Bolton and provided a social commentary on issues such as housing and diet. *Finally*, the diary adds weight to our picture of Mary Haslam, the woman and feminist. Transfixed by buildings and landscapes, amused or outraged by behaviour, conformist and nonconformist, mixing touristic commentary with penetrating observation and insight, we begin to understand the effusive obituary comments published in the newspapers at her death.

Diary of a Trip to Ireland, 1899 [7]

August 17th 1899: Left Bolton for Dublin via Holyhead – not impressed favourably with Dublin, the wide streets look very desolate and the houses everywhere want paint – and the windows soap and water. The names of streets are hardly legible and the whole depressing![8]

August 19th:[9] Left Dublin at 9.15 for Recess in Connemara. Several stations are mentioned as providing refreshments, but this did not amount to much more than drink. At Mullinger we got a few gingerbreads and pears – & at Galway we had a bread and butter lunch – I cut myself slicing the loaf on the table – There were no plates of buns or sandwiches etc. – but the drink of some kind or other attracted a good many of the passengers.

The country varies in appearance – some being long stretches of heather and bog where there are peat cuttings; some are cultivated fields and other parts again so full of loose stones that I wondered whether they could be the remains of villages from which the inhabitants had disappeared – either by famine or emigration. Our destination was Recess, where the Railway Co. has made a pretty and comfortable hotel adjoining the Station. The conversation here was entirely on the subject of fishing and we strolled up the hill, behind the hotel, to a marble quarry and brought away pieces of the green stone, that when polished we know as "Connemara Marble". Children came out to beg and followed us most of the way down.[10] They were nearly all pretty and had very nice teeth and many of them brown eyes. We heard afterwards that this marble is being cut out in columns, to be sent to New York – for the pillars in a new Roman Catholic Church which is being built there.

August 20th – Sunday: W., Will and I drove by car to Cashel by Ballinahinch and Inagh. R. and O. went on bicycles.[11] A beautiful drive – hills, lakes, one after another and wild flowers. An enormous specimen of the bell heather and saw also the Osmunda fern and honeysuckle purple loose drifts in quantities – and large blackberries. At Cashel an hotel (Littane Arms) much recommended in the Guide Books,[12] but dirty and untidy, though a comfortable building and well enough furnished – Strolled about a couple of hours and then back to Recess – Oliver's bicycle being tied up behind, having gone wrong.

I talked with an old man at Cashel and heard the following particulars – He and his wife live alone – farm 15 acres and rent £4 – Houses put up by tenants – 6 or 7 children some always go away "No young fellow who thinks a bit about himself would stay here; There is no living to be made on this stony ground". I asked if they eat the blackberries which are so plentiful. He replied "Once, in a while but you know what there is plenty of no-one takes much value on". Our car drivers on going home spend all they got in the summer. They spend in the winter – no matter whether it had been a good or bad season, they are neither better nor worse when the next spring came!

August 21st – Monday: Strolled by river for boys to fish – Very hot day.

August 22nd – Tuesday: We rest – Went to Clifden – Very hot day.

August 23rd – Wednesday: Very hot day.

August 24th – Thursday: Engaged a Johnny Jamey to go fishing and went to small mountain lake – Rain came on; an unappetising lunch sent from hotel, was eaten under difficulties and then we went back to where we had left the cars – In about 1/2 hours, the ground which was dry as moorland when we went onto it at first, had turned into bog and we were very wet on rejoining the cars. In a wet season what must these bogs be like?

August 25th – Friday: Still raining. So we had a landau, to take us to Leenane (16 miles). It is all beautiful with one small lake after another, and the 12 "Bens" looking very fine to our left – and the Masm Turk Mountains to our right. The rain stopped for the last six miles and we had a lovely view of the greater Killary as we drove into Leenane. The hotel is very full and somewhat rough and ready – but we were fairly comfortable.

August 26th – Saturday: In afternoon drove to Delphi, an enclosed valley across the Killary – It used to be reached by a ferry to Bundoera and then was two or three miles up the county – But last year a new road was opened. Crossing the river at Asebagh, at the head of the lough and running along the northern side. Before this, there was nothing but bridle paths down to the ferry and everything was carried on pack horses or donkeys. All along the roads are stones and vestiges of former dwellings – the outline of each holding being quite visible. The population had either died or emigrated. No farm had a cart, so bridle paths were all that were actually necessary.

Dorguort Lake is a little beyond Delphi and the lodge belongs to the Marquis of Sligo and just now is rented by the landlord of the Leenane Hotel. It might be a charming place but if an Englishman took it he would first want to put up the railings, that are all lying down everywhere, and through the garden, and were it not for flowers the desolation at present would be intolerable!

August 27th – Sunday: A wet morning – cleared up in afternoon and we hired a cart to take us to Salruck Burial ground. It was too wet until too late in the day for us to go round by Renogle and Kylemore Pass and Carl so we had to give up the idea of seeing these places. At Salruck the burial ground is up a winding, wet path, under trees and consists of a collection of stones more or less moss covered. There are fallen trees lying out and everything is damp and overgrown. After a closer look we can see there is a certain plan, about it all – Graves in the strangest confusion all covered with loose stones, some raised up, some on the level, but all looking as if they had been there for 2 or 3 hundred years. There are old wooden boxes containing pipes, which have been smoked during the "waking" and burial of those who lie under the stones! A little boy, who acted as our guide, showed us the last grave which was as recent as 2 or 3 months ago – but is equally rough. Altogether it is the most extraordinary and neglected place that could be imagined.

August 28th – Monday: Left Leenane for Mulrany. We left Leenane by car at 9.15 and reached Westport at 1 o'clock. The road is very level, open and the country varied, our road, following the Valley of the Erriff. There are the usual neglected buildings and ruins and signs of former holdings. As we approached Westport Croagh Patrick rose up looking very fine. The car man said the "Paltoni" (see MacKeroys sketch book), was still carried out. We met and passed many pack horses and donkeys and saw them carrying the peat in baskets to dry in wagons by the roadside. The women were reaping the corn with sickles and laying it in strips to be made into stooks. We passed the workhouse, just as we got to Westport and having time, after having lunched, I[13] went to pay it a visit! The master was most obliging and I considered him a superior officer. He had been there 10 years. The number of inmates is about 146. There is no oakum picking or stone breaking as punishments. The master finds forwarding a refractory one before the magistrates is the best deterrent. There is one paid nurse trained under the doctor but not in hospital and I saw a ward attendant with some infirm and miserable old women, otherwise it is chiefly worked by the paupers. The food somehow very good. The soup has always vegetable in and not peas as with us.[14]

The old women sat on forms without backs and all the ground floors are flagged but there were cheerful fires and the standard of comfort, compared with what these inmates have in their cabins is a very high one.[15] It is a rough building with only whitewashed walls and one room was not plastered and another had no ceiling, but for an Irish Standard it struck me as clean and well managed. The children number 17 – 5 boys and 12 girls, who have separate schoolrooms and the master expressed much astonishment when I said the English system was mixed, in many schools as well as in the workhouse. This workhouse is a "National School" and similar to the rest in Ireland and under its Education Department. The new Irish Local Government Act has made already changes and the master said Ireland had now one lady guardian and could hardly believe over 900 in England. A doctor visits daily – Outsiders are nursed with the rest – about 12 or 15.[16] Reached Mulrany about 5 o' clock.

August 29th – Tuesday: Annoyed with the hotel and dissatisfied with the food. The weather stormy so only took short walks. The hotel is well situated and Mulrany itself a beautiful spot. The sea bathing is about two miles off unless they want to wade out to it.

August 30th – Wednesday: Explored the neighbourhood still further.[17]

August 31st – Thursday: Left Mulrany at 12.30 for Achille Sound. At the latter station found a "long car" waiting to take us on to Dugort, about 12 miles. Trees may only be seen at a Major Pike's residence, near the Sound. The country boggy, with Silvermore Mountain rising before us, to the north-west. Arrived at Dugort – were hospitably received by Mr and Mrs Sheridan, who represented the almost extinct type of landlords – in looking after their guests and making arrangements for their pleasure. In the evening Mr Sheridan read us an account of his seal-hunting. He is much of a naturalist and botanist and has published many articles on these subjects. He also told us many anecdotes showing the Irish wit. Also an account of how he got the bridge across the Sound made, and of the deputation which went to London at the time of the "Fisheries Exhibition". He, with two more going from Achille Sound, and others from elsewhere in Connemara. The money was raised (£7,000) and the bridge built – now an immense boon!

September 1st – Friday: We joined with some others in an excursion to the Villages of Keel and Donagh and the Mountain of Croaghan. We went in a long-car accompanied by our landlord who had provided a lunch of lobsters, and which we ate at Capt. Boycotts' farm – The latter is empty now, but was the original property of Capt. Boycott – before he lived at his notorious house, near Galway Loch. After lunch Robbie and Oliver set off with four others, up the mountain. It was showery so they did not start till 2.30. The rest of us walked on to Keel Bay, having beautiful effects of colour on the sea and coast line which is very fine. Croaghan is about 2,200 ft. high and a stiff climb and on the west side goes sheer down into the sea! Oliver was glad a guide boy, whom we had sent to show them the way, just stopped him stepping over, so suddenly were they at the edge!

Our drive in the morning, took us through wild boggy country past the villages of Keel and Donagh, both of them entirely composed of the Irish cabins. We walked through Keel – It seemed entirely deserted, the inhabitants being out at work. There are scarcely any windows in these cabins. They are laid out in a kind of plan – with narrow paths and tumble down walls to divide them – with ducks and geese paddling in the more liquid filth. One door was open, so I went up to it and looked inside and in the far corner I discerned a figure, who came and tottered out, looking a most pitiable object – with deformed foot (of course bare) and yellow ancient witch like face. She looked about for the owner of the "beehive" hut – their one remaining example of what was formerly the common type of dwelling and presently he came. This hut is somewhat round and has stone walls like the rest, but the roof rests on a central pole starting from the ground and from which beams and planks rest on the walls. The room, lighted by a small lamp and after getting used to the dark and the smoke and the close smell, we saw in a corner a bed, with the roof almost touching its head and the remains of a turf fire, from which the smoke escaped through a hole where roof and wall joined. I saw no sign of furniture except a small rough table and a box of matches was on the shelf; there must surely have been a chair and a cooking pot or two but I saw no others. Man said, with apparent pride his father, grandfather and long enough before them, had all lived there! Last summer he began to receive money for showing his dwelling and one fears this will be against encouraging any change for the better in the community.[18]

At Cashel talked to old man and found he farmed 15 acres of land and paid £4 rent for it – very poor stony land. Had had seven children and one to England and America "him a young fellow that thinks a bit of himself would stay here – there is no living to be made".[19] I asked what they did with all the blackberries, which were in great quantity and was told they eat them, to which I said, none seemed to be gathered and that they should be got and cooked. "Well, it's just this way my lady – What we get plenty of, we don't think much about!"

I asked the car driver what they did in winter "Just nothing but mind our bits of land" "Then it depends on the fortune you make in the summer, how you live in the winter, and what you have left over by the spring?", "Oh no" he replied "Just whatever we get we spend – We don't think of putting any of it by". Another car man whom I asked something about the horses and what they did in the winter? "Just nothing at all, only our own bit of work", was the answer and when I suggested they must be quite frisky by April, he replied "Indaid no, They get no food!"

At Leenane saw the following announcement of public meeting: "Public Meeting – to be held at Tully Cross, Parish of Ballinakill on Sunday August 27th. Meeting under the auspices of the United Irish League. Several prominent speakers have promised to attend, amongst others.

Mrs W M O'Malley, M.P. etc. etc. (Long list -grim). The principal business of the meeting will be the demanding of more land and better land, for the people and the development of the Fisheries in the district. GOD SAVE IRELAND![20]

At Sligo, on Sunday September 3rd [21] was the unveiling of a statue in community – to the Martyrs who died in 1798 in their efforts to promote Irish political and religious liberty. The town was with flags, chiefly green and yellow (gold) and many had pictures of Robert Emett. There was allusion to a picture of Mr Gladstone. I noticed two small American flags – A green one bore the inscription 'Ireland a Nation'. There seemed to be a common form of decoration – Large branches of elm or small larches, were cut down and stuck into the roads, or fastened on to the tops of flag poles.[22] The meeting, we were told, was very orderly but we met many returning home, about 7 o'clock who were much the worse for drink.[23]

CHAPTER ELEVEN

Women's Suffrage in Bolton

Context

We have seen that Bolton could boast a large, active and complex campaigning group in favour of women's suffrage. It included a core of experienced middle-class women committed to non-militant campaigning, a small group of middle- and working-class women who espoused and practiced militant tactics, and an increasingly significant body of working-class radical suffragists. Their activities march through the Bolton newspapers from 1907 onwards, and the impact upon Bolton political and social circles must have been profound. The pamphlet reproduced here was written by Mary Haslam, probably sometime in 1919, and is her record of the rise and achievements of the twentieth-century suffrage movement in the town. While some of the perspectives are selective, the survival of newspaper records and the minutes and annual reports of the local suffrage society allow us a comprehensive window on the development, execution and purpose of a suffrage campaign. Four things in particular are worth noting. *First*, this was a campaign driven disproportionately by one personality, Mary Haslam, who brought to the suffrage issue a long-term commitment but also two decades of philanthropic goodwill, campaigning skills, electoral experience and networks. In a literature where the issue of personality has often been central to an appreciation of the national suffrage movement, it is interesting and important that we see a strong personality as a key factor in the development of local suffrage campaigns. *Secondly*, when judged in the round it is not at all easy to characterize the tactics of local suffrage groups. Vigorous campaigning and stunts melded at the margins into less extreme direct action, and women who were part of the non-militant Bolton women's Suffrage Society appear to have got themselves involved from time to time in more direct and militant action. While Mary Haslam notes with disapproval the heckling of speakers, others in her organization were much less opposed to such tactics. *Thirdly*, and in part following on from this, Bolton had a unified suffrage movement. Prominent working-class activists such as Sarah Reddish worked alongside middle-class women such as Mary Haslam and Margaret Greg. Moreover, this was not a group thrown together either by weakness or necessity. Whether it was in the forum of the board of guardians, the District Nursing Association or the municipal election process these women had worked together extensively in the 1890s. In this sense, their suffrage activities mark not a new departure but a natural extension of their campaigning activities and networks. *Finally*, while these women sought the vote on equal terms with men, we get no sense that the vote was supposed to be an end in itself. Claims for the vote were wrapped up in issues of duty and citizenship, and when it was won these Bolton campaigners formed the Bolton Women Citizens Association. In turn, this shared membership and sentiment with organizations from the 1890s dedicated to returning women as poor law guardians or improving the housing and life chances of infants. Suffrage cannot, then, be regarded as a discrete campaign in the town.

The Text[1]

Foreword
This history of the Women's Suffrage movement in Bolton has been compiled by Mrs Haslam, who as president of the Bolton Women's Suffrage Society through the whole period of its existence, knows more about its struggles and vicissitudes than anyone else. But the Committee feel, nevertheless, that the part played by Mrs Haslam and her daughter, the late Mrs Leggatt,[2] has been so lightly touched upon that it must be more fully described in this Foreword.

All those who have been actively associated with the Society, know how much it owed to their inspiring faith and devotion, in the days when the cause was unpopular and the task of evolving a local society was one of the utmost difficulty.[3] Those who know nothing of its early history will never realise the dauntless courage and splendid tenacity of purpose with which Mrs Haslam and Miss Haslam – as she then was – pioneered the struggling movement.

Through all the difficult later stages with their countless heartbreaking disappointments,[4] by which the triumph of 1918 was reached,[5] Mrs Haslam's wise and statesmanlike leadership never failed. Not only did she give unsparingly of herself, but was at all times the most generous financial supporter of the cause she had so much at heart.[6]

It is a source of the greatest possible satisfaction to the Society that Mrs Haslam, to whom we owe so deep a debt of gratitude for originating the Suffrage movement in Bolton – with all that it means for womanhood today and tomorrow – is also the first president of the new "Women Citizens' Association" into which the spirit of the old society has passed.

2 Fold Street, Bolton, 1920.

Women's Suffrage in Bolton
1908–9

Through the winter of 1907 and 8 a national impulse in favour of Women's Suffrage made itself felt.[7] Forty years earlier, John Stuart Mill had introduced his Suffrage Bill into the House of Commons,[8] and although there were kindred associations in both Manchester and London since that date, still the subject remained more academic than a vital force.[9] But in this particular year, some eager spirits began to interrupt the speakers at public meetings by the cry "are you in favour of giving the vote to women?" and a good deal of disturbance ensued in different ways.[10] In Bolton there had been at various times meetings held, and letters sent to the papers calling attention to the women's plea[11] but without any progress being made. However, on March 17th, 1908, a drawing room meeting was held at White Bank,[12] and out of a large number of invitations issued, about thirty accepted, and Mrs Allanbright gave an address. These thirty ladies were keenly interested, and it was resolved that Bolton would form a branch of the North of England Society, which had for its object the granting of the parliamentary vote to women on the same terms as it is or shall be granted to men.[13] Shortly after this, a committee was formed as follows: Miss Dymond, Mrs Frankland, Mrs Howard, Mrs Jessop Hulton, Mrs Ernest Knowles, Miss Makinson, Mrs H Mason, Mrs Walter Musgrave, Mrs Rees, Mrs F Taylor, and Miss Winstanley; while the officers appointed were: Mrs Haslam, President; Mrs C V Thompson, Chairman of Committee; Miss Haslam, Hon. Secretary; and Mrs Knott, Hon. Treasurer.[14]

We are glad to number six of these original members who are still with us, although not on the executive committee, with the exception of Mrs F Taylor, who has been an active committee member throughout, and a strong and unfailing supporter of our every effort.

In June of this year there was a Suffrage Procession in London, and although the Bolton Society was then in its infancy, at a social gathering where Mrs Swanwich explained the scheme, sufficient money was collected to send five delegates.[15] Later in the year there was a Procession in Manchester. By this time Bolton, like many other towns, had its banner of heraldic design, executed by the Artists' Suffrage League, and following this walked 30 members from Bolton, to an Open-air Meeting that was held in Alexandra Park.[16]

In order to arouse interest, the clergy and ministers, and all women's organisations in the town were asked if they would include Women's Suffrage in their list of winter lectures, and the Society offered to send a speaker if desired. The following is the list of organisations that responded, and the ladies who spoke at them:

Bolton Free Debate: Speaker: Mrs Haslam.
Astley Bridge Literary Society: Mrs Gibbon.
Emmanuel Church Men's Club: Miss Hutchinson.
Horwich Unitarian Church Women's Society: Miss Haslam.
Darcy Lever Wesleyan Young Men's Society: Miss Haslam.
Derby Ward Women's Liberal Association: Mrs F Taylor.[17]
Smithills Women's Liberal Association: Miss Haslam.
Derby St. Congregational Church Women's Guild: Mrs Knott.
West Ward Women's Liberal Association: Miss Haslam.
Bank Street Chapel Literary Society: Mrs Haslam.

But the crowning effort of the year was a public meeting in the Temperance Hall which was quite filled, over 2000 persons being present.[18] Mrs Haslam presided, and Mrs Swanwich and Mrs Allanbright gave addresses. Miss Abadam was unfortunately prevented by an accident from being present. The meeting was very enthusiastic: it had been known by advertisements in the press, large posters on the walls, sandwich-men in the streets on the day itself, and by the distribution of leaflets.[19] Other meetings were held in October, December, and February, and the Committee felt encouraged by the result of the first year's work.

1909–10
Another public meeting was held in the Temperance Hall, addressed on this occasion by Mrs Fawcett, Miss Margaret Ashton, and Miss Minna Rathbone who represented the Conservative and Unionist Women's Franchise Association.[20] A General Election took place this year, and for three weeks, a shop in Deansgate (No.131) was taken and made gay with posters, and this formed the rallying ground of members and friends who obtained signatures to the Voter's Petition for Women's Suffrage. By

canvassing the streets, attending candidates' meetings, and visiting in the dinner hour various works where men were employed, a large number of signatures was obtained.[21] Of course the candidates were not spared deputations and questions. On the election day at eight, out of the 22 polling stations, were stationed in relays, members of the committee or friends, who asked the men to sign our petition as they came out after registering their votes. The weather at first was fine, and large numbers signed our petition, but later the rain came on, and voters were not willing to be stopped. In one or two cases by the courtesy of the Returning Officer, we were allowed to stand inside the door, but in general, the undaunted women stood outside while the rain beat on their paper forms, and the writing of the blue indelible pencil became illegible. While the shop was kept open, 2657 signatures were obtained from Bolton. The same procedure was adopted at the County Election at Westhoughton and 1122 names were obtained there.[22]

It must not be overlooked that help was given in the above matter by the Women Textile, and other Workers Representation Committee, and also by the Men's League for Women's Suffrage, who asked questions at meetings which the women were debarred from doing because the candidates would only answer questions put to them by voters.[23] Two points on which the voters most wanted reassuring were – (1) That only women ratepayers or those who possessed the qualifications necessary for men to have the vote, would be enfranchised; (2) That we did not belong to the militant party.

1910–11

Greater progress was made this year, and the goal came nearer into sight, by the formation of a Parliamentary Committee consisting of Conservative, Liberal and Labour members, with the Earl of Lytton as chairman, and Mr Brailsford as secretary. By this committee the Conciliation Bill was drawn up and it was introduced into the House of Commons by Mr Shackleton. A meeting was held in Bolton at which about 400 were present, explaining the Conciliation Bill and urging all members of the Association who could, to go to London for the great demonstration in Trafalgar Square in favour of the Bill. The result of this was that 24 members joined the special train from Manchester, and helped to swell the audience of 15,000–20,000 women who assembled to hear speeches and resolutions from the plinth of the Nelson column. A report of this expedition was given to the Bolton Society and the Hon. Sec. followed up the enthusiasm with which it was met, by asking the members to unite in undertaking a canvass of the women municipal voters in the town and begging them to sign a petition in favour of the

Conciliation Bill. There were 5750 municipal women voters of whom 3681 were interviewed, and of these, 2660 were in favour of the Bill.[24] A garden party was given at White Bank this summer, at which about 100 were present, and addresses were given.[25] The Conciliation Bill passed its second reading, but time was refused for its further stages.

1911–12

This year a difference is noticed in the attitude of the public towards our cause; the growth of an Anti-Suffrage Society[26] is one proof of this, and Mr Asquith's promise of a week of Government time in the next session, and also his undertaking to allow an amendment to the proposed Government Reform Bill was as inspiring as it was unexpected. In consequence of this, much effort was expended in influencing Parliamentary voters, and the local members. Another Conciliation Bill varying slightly from its predecessor, was introduced by Sir George Kemp, and it also passed its second reading by a majority of 167. Mrs Mason and Miss Haslam attended a meeting in the Portman Rooms, London, to demonstrate in favour of the Bill. It may be here explained that the term Conciliation Bill, meant that no section of suffrage would oppose it, and the militant party would await its fate with patience. In June, there was a great procession in London, and 28 members from Bolton again with their banner, took part in it. The Hon. Secretary, this year wrote to the President of the Bolton Liberal Association, asking if they would pass a resolution in favour of the Conciliation Bill, to be forwarded to the Prime Minister. This was not agreed to, but later on the Association invited a Suffrage speaker to address them.[27]

The Women Textile and other Worker's Committee, asked the co-operation of the Suffrage members to help them in the agitation in favour of the Pit Brow women, of which the result was successful. Mr Asquith announced in the Autumn that he would next year introduce a Manhood Suffrage Bill and would allow an amendment to include women. Bolton and all other branches of the National Union, accepted Mr Asquith's proposal, so all energies were concentrated on this, and gatherings at which addresses were given were numerous, but money did not come in fast enough. Mrs Edward Crook gave an American Tea when £20 was raised and sent to the Manchester Federation which decided to hold a Bazaar, and Bolton undertook to be responsible for the greater part of the East Lancashire stall. The Bazaar was held the following February and was very successful, £2155 being raised.[28]

The Bolton press, which has always been favourable to our work, is now willing to accept paragraphs of Suffrage news which are being supplied to them regularly. As is said in our Report for this year, "The

263

Editors have our best thanks for affording this useful opportunity: their action has given to Bolton the distinction of being one of the few towns where all the newspapers are friendly."[29] This Autumn, Miss Haslam left Bolton on a long absence,[30] and under Miss Bridson, who took her place, the work of the society went on with unabated interest. Mrs Knott also resigned the Treasurer's office, and was succeeded by Miss Winstanley.

1912–13

In March of this year the Conciliation Bill was defeated by 14 votes. After the repeated failures to get a Suffrage Bill past its second reading, it is realised that nothing short of a government measure has any chance of success, and this, while an anti-suffragist Prime Minister remains in power seems impossible;[31] or unless the country shows a real demand for it. Consequently propaganda remains the chief lever, and it is satisfactory to know that the law-abiding societies belonging to the National Union keep increasing in number, and that Bolton, which is one of the affiliated branches of a total of 400, has doubled its membership in the past year.

The National Union now has decided to help the Labour Party at elections this being the only political party that has put women's suffrage in its programme. This decision taxed the loyalty of many branches, as away from industrial centres the Labour Party is less strong. An occasion for the exercise of this policy did not arise in Bolton.[32]

Deputations to members and interviews at the House of Commons were frequent this year, and the social events included a garden party at Fernclough, and an At Home at the Spinner's Hall, and at this latter, the scheme of "Friends of Women's Suffrage" was explained. These "Friends" are those persons who, while not avowed suffragists, yet have some sympathy with the cause and at any rate do not speak against it, and to these, notices of public meetings will be sent. Forty-two members of the Bolton Society have each a circle of "Friends", and after little more than six months, 334 were enrolled under this title; needless to say, a proportion of these became in time members of the Society itself.[33]

A bye-election took place in Bolton owing to the death of Mr George Harwood. As both the candidates on this occasion gave similar half-hearted support to our cause, it was decided that our efforts should be directed to general propaganda only. Four or more meetings were held every day, both in the shop which had been taken for a month, and outside in the dinner hour at public works, while the gatherings on the Town Hall Square attracted crowds and lasted two hours or more. A paid organiser was also engaged for this month. A crowded and enthusiastic meeting in the Spinner's Hall closed the campaign, during which much welcome help had been given by the local ILP, the Co-operative Society, the Progressive League, and other sympathisers.[34]

The second reading of the Reform Bill, for which suffragists had worked so hard for months and spent large sums of money was however now reached, and the Speaker ruled that the amendments to include women would so alter the Bill as to render a new one necessary, therefore Mr Asquith withdrew the Bill. The suffrage ranks were filled with amazement that the legal mind of the Prime Minister should have been allowed to lead them into this impasse.

A public meeting was held in the Spinner's Hall; the audience was large, and Mrs Muter Wilson was given a good hearing, but Mr Parker, MP was frequently interrupted by militant suffragists who were seated in the body of the hall. It is worth mentioning that this is the only occasion in the 12 year's life of the Bolton Society, where any confusion of incivility was shown between the various points of view on this subject.[35] In the autumn of this year, in view of her approaching marriage, Miss Haslam finally resigned her office of hon. secretary, and Miss Bridson became our permanent and able officer.[36]

1913–14

The only Suffrage Bill brought forward this year was Mr Dickenson's, which was defeated on its second reading. This was because it was brought forward by only one political party and the National Union decided not to waste any efforts over it. Questions have been asked in both Houses of Parliament; Suffrage amendments to other Bills have been put down for discussion; petitions have been presented; the action of the Government denounced in the Commons by Mr Snowden and Mr Keir Hardie, and in the Lords by Lord Lytton for the unfulfilled pledges to the women, and what remained to rouse a jaded public? But what seemed like a momentary set-back proved to be only a breathing space, for the Women's Pilgrimage in June and July, was the most ambitious and successful demonstration ever organised in connection with the movement. Little parties of women started on foot from near and distant parts of England with Hyde Park as their goal. About 30 members from Bolton (of course bearing their banner) accompanied the Pilgrims to Stockport.[37] Only a few of the whole number were able to complete the entire journey, and Bolton is proud to remember that one of their most loyal and indefatigable members, Mrs Mason, went the whole way, partly on foot and partly on her bicycle. For those who were unable to manage the long distances, vehicles were provided. The experiences favourable or hostile on the journey were either amusing or disagreeable to recall. Sometimes they were met by lavish kindness, at others stones and mud were their portion. It must be allowed that the science of organisation had become a fine art, when we remember that at 3 o'clock on the afternoon of July 26th all the Pilgrims entered the Park simultaneously by the different gates, and from 19 platforms, the object of the great gathering was explained by 60 or 70 speakers. After this, Mr Asquith was convinced of the sincerity of the women's desire, and consented to receive a deputation for the first time.[38] In this year in order to increase the scope of our work, we took a shop in Bradshawgate as a suffrage office, where we could hold committee meetings and supply literature. A sign board was hung out, and the words "Bolton Women's Suffrage Society" painted below the window in green, white and red of the National Union; in fact it was determined that the attention of every passer-by should be caught by this announcement.[39] At the same time a full time organiser was engaged. This latter was Mrs Blincoe, who is still with us and has proved herself a tower of strength in all matters concerning the women's movement.[40]

Small meetings at the shop and in cottages, and large ones elsewhere, filled up the year, and our numbers steadily increased.[41]

1914–15

The first six months of the year records the annual and the general meetings of our Society, and the formation of a branch of the Active Service League, which co-operated with the Manchester Federation tour in Derbyshire, where meetings were held in some twelve small towns and villages. Mrs Blincoe addressed many gatherings, and Bolton joined with Farnworth in a bazaar, money being badly wanted before a general election should occur.[42]

The outbreak of war in August, suspended most of the causes which has been dear to the hearts of women, and how to serve their country best was the paramount thought of everyone. The National Union desired that the various organisations should be devoted to the relief of distress that would be caused by the war, and to safeguarding generally the interests of women. Our committee offered the services of its society to the Mayor, but this was not taken advantage of, and no women were placed on the Relief Committee to administer the Prince of Wales fund, until public opinion was roused, when finally six women, all members of our Society, were put on.[43] Our Society then opened two kitchens for nursing mothers and young children. At one of these on three afternoons a week, the mothers stayed on after dinner to learn to make their children's clothes. Assistance was also given at the dinners arranged by the Education Committee for necessitous school children, and clerical or other help was accepted by the Poor Protection Society. Political work since July has been practically suspended for the rest of the year.

1915–16

The great feature of our work this year was the Scottish Women's Hospitals, with units in France, Serbia and Corsica. The Bolton Suffrage Society raised £227 10s. 4d., which supported 4 beds for one year. To raise money for this, a social evening and sale was held, a successful lecture was given by Miss Thurstan, who had been in Serbia, and a further public meeting was held in the Mayor's Dining Room. A good consignment of clothes was also sent, the result of weekly working parties held at the shop. Finally, an American Tea, given by Mrs F Taylor, completed our efforts for this national cause.

A feeling was expressed this year in the National Union as to whether the women's voice might not make itself heard on the side of humanity in this time of international conflict, and again as a means of influencing public opinion on questions that would arise when peace should come in sight, but it was difficult to avoid being misjudged or misunderstood on these points, and it was decided that only propaganda in favour of Women's Suffrage should be approved of. It may here be incidentally mentioned that this decision of the National Union caused the greater part of the Executive Committee of that body to resign, the result of which was a certain indefiniteness and confusion of issues, which was much felt by the various branch societies.[44]

At the end of April, two of the kitchens for nursing mothers, were closed, being no longer needed. £110 had been subscribed for this purpose (£42 of which was raised by an American Tea given by Mrs Bridson) and 6,600 dinners of two courses were provided at a cost of 4 1/2 d. per meal, of which the mothers paid 2d.[45]

A Study Circle was formed of the members of the Executive Committee for the consideration of questions relating to the war. "War and Democracy" was the book chosen and the discussions were most interesting. Mrs Blincoe continued to address various other societies: the subjects chosen were "The need of Organisation"; "Women and the War"; "Reconstruction after the War"; and "Women in the New Era".

A development of the Manchester Federation was the formation of a Women's War Interests Committee on which Mrs Blincoe was our representative. It concerned itself with women's labour in the new war-time occupations conferring with the men's trade unions, seeking representation on the various organisations that kept arising and which necessitated a constant watching of what concerned the women workers. Miss Bridson, hon. secretary, has left the town to take up war work, and we are grateful to Miss Hunter for kindly consenting to act temporarily.

1916–17

In this year the question of the franchise was again to the front because with so many men away the Voters' Lists were too inaccurate to be of any use, so a Registration Bill was introduced. The National Union then approached all the Cabinet Ministers with a resolution, that in the event of a Registration Bill including any fresh names, the claims of women's suffrage should be embodied in an amendment. It was then that Mr Asquith acknowledged that the claims of women could no longer be denied, and public opinion was so influenced by this pronouncement, that women's suffrage which had been suspended during the war, became again a living force.[46] So a campaign for this end began in the Spring, and Bolton was ready to take its share of the work. The Annual Meeting was held in May: this was followed by a series of outdoor meetings, and a Garden Party was given by Mrs F Taylor for munitions and other women workers, addressed by Mrs Annot Robinson. Later in the year, Mrs H A L Fisher addressed a gathering of members and friends. Mrs Blincoe worked hard amongst the Trades Unions, the result of which was that the Trades and Labour Council, and seven large Trades Unions passed a resolution urging the necessity of the speedy enfranchisement of women. A Memorial was sent by the Manchester Federation to all members of parliament urging the necessity of enfranchising women in any proposed electoral reform, and in Bolton, 326 signatures of representative men and women were obtained.

Activity on behalf of the Scottish Women's Hospitals continued, and an appeal for funds, and a "Bring one and Buy one sale" which was held at the shop, raised the sum of £84 3s 4d., many garments were also again sent, the result of continued working parties. Miss Hunter who had kindly agreed to fill Miss Bridson's post, was unable to continue this through bad health, so Mrs Blincoe undertook the secretarial work.

1917–18

On February 6th, 1918, the Representation of the People Bill became law, and quietly and unobtrusively, six millions of England's women citizens were thereby enfranchised. "Punch" immortalised the event by a drawing by Mr Bernard Partridge, "At last", and two members of the Committee waited upon Mrs Haslam and presented her with a framed copy of this, in token of her long-continued interest in the cause of women's suffrage, and being President of the Bolton Society. The feeling was universal, amongst suffragists throughout the country, that although the franchise now granted had not achieved the object we set out to get, namely, equality with the men's, it would be wise to let the matter rest here, and trust to public opinion for the future. In the meantime, we must concentrate our energies in the various directions to which Suffrage has opened the door.[47]

In June, a Conference was held, in which 15 different women's organisations joined. Mrs Thompson presided and the subjects discussed were "The need for Day Nurseries"; "Responsibilities and Opportunities for Women"; "Women in Industry"; and "Recreation for Boys and Girls". So successful was this conference that a few days later a request was received from the Vice-president of the Bolton Trades Council to hold a further conference on "Women in Industry", and this was carried out in November. The "Demobilisation of Women"; "Equal pay for Equal Work", and "The Right of Women to belong to Men's Trades Unions", when doing the same work, were thoroughly discussed. The Day Nursery now so well known in the town was the direct outcome of the June conference and a representative committee was formed consisting of eight members of the Suffrage Society, the Medical Officer of Health, three members of the Public Health Committee, and others under the chairmanship of Mrs Haslam.[48] The National Baby Week in Bolton was assisted by the loan of the Suffrage Office. We sent delegates to a conference in Manchester on "The Future of the Women's Movement", and our organiser attended a conference at Hampstead on "Problems of Reconstruction." In November a joint meeting for women, promoted by the Women's Local Government Association, the Suffrage Society, the Women Textile Workers and the United Suffragists was held, when Dr Gould gave an address on the "Medical Treatment of Venereal Diseases". Mrs Blincoe has continued to give addresses on points that arise through Suffrage work which have been very helpful and tended to throw light on many difficult subjects. The Annual Council Meeting in this year was an unusually important one. The chief feature of its work hitherto having been partially achieved, it was felt to be necessary to adjust its programme to the new conditions. It was therefore decided that while it should retain its title and continue to work for further suffrage, it should also interest itself in all other "such reforms, economic, legislative, and social, as are necessary to secure a real equality of liberties, status, and opportunities between men and women".[49] It recommended the formation of societies for this end, in those places where Suffrage Societies were disbanding, their chief work having been accomplished. The programme was a very comprehensive one, and in fact meant that the energies so long spent on Suffrage should now go to the reforms which it had shown the need for. Bolton followed up this scheme by inviting all the women's societies in the town to come together and discuss the possibility of forming themselves into one large union or association, with due representation of the Committee of Management. Altogether 25 Societies were invited to co-operate and of this number only three held aloof. There was much discussion and a little doubt on the part of some of the societies as to where this step would lead them, and whether they would be able to retain their independence, but by due regard to these points, and freedom of action not being interfered with, difficulties were smoothed away, and the present Women's Citizen's Association was inaugurated.[50]

1918–19

Now that the specific work of our Society was over, we discussed whether we should give up calling ourselves a Suffrage Society, and merge in the Women Citizen's movement for the education of the women voter in both national and municipal affairs. But again those of us who had lived through the whole suffrage movement felt we could not rest satisfied with no woman under 30 having a vote while a youth of 19 or 20 had one, so we decided to continue our activities for the suffrage, and at the same time to join with the Women's Local Government Society in establishing the Women Citizen's Association.[51]

In connection with our definite suffrage work, we helped in the campaign for putting the Maisons Tolerees out of bounds for British troops in France and prohibiting the establishment of these places in, or near British camps abroad. We also took part in a deputation to Mr Wilson, M.P., to consider the Criminal Law Amendment Bill and to urge the withdrawal of regulation 40D, under D.O.R.A. The protest raised by the united voice of the women's organisations, ended in complete victory in December 1918.

Then came a period of activity in connection with the voters' register. Posters were placed in the Suffrage Office window, reminding women of the dates for consulting the lists and making claims; many enquiries were answered and help and advice given. The Armistice was signed on November 11th of this year. In December there was a general election. In Bolton there was no contest, Captain Edge and Mr Tootill, being returned unopposed. We, however, requested interviews and put questions on matters of special interest to women; we were met with cordiality, and on the whole, the answers were satisfactory.

We assisted at a local conference on "Housing", and a resolution was passed urging that women should be co-opted on to the Housing Committee, a copy of which was sent to the Town Council. The reply was that only councillors were eligible, but that the Committee would consider the advisability of calling in women in a consultative capacity. Later, Mrs Agnew was appointed on to the panel of assessors to judge the plans of the new houses.

At the Annual Council Meeting of the National Union, to which we sent three delegates, an event of great importance occurred. Mrs Fawcett had decided not to offer herself for re-election as President, as she desired more leisure now that the principle of women's enfranchisement had been won. The whole suffrage world knows what it owes to Mrs Fawcett, and Bolton, with other towns, sent a letter of appreciation and admiration for what she had done.[52] Miss Eleanor Rathbone succeeded Mrs Fawcett as President and in future the National Union of Suffrage Societies, will be known by the title of National Union of Societies for Equal Citizenship.

Our Society this year regrets to record that Mrs C V Thompson is obliged to sever her connection with it as she is leaving Bolton. Her loss to the Society as well as to the town in general, will be felt by all, as she has been a consistent and faithful friend to all the women's interests.[53]

1919–20

Owing to the growth of the Women Citizen's movement, the time of our organiser was much absorbed, and the sewing classes for the mothers at Derby St. Congregational School had to be discontinued. The remaining surplus of the money that had been set aside for this, was appropriated to supplying to the office a telephone which had long been needed.

The National Union of Societies for Equal Citizenship, arranged to hold a Council Meeting in Glasgow in October, but the hands of the Committee here were full with work for the local municipal elections, and it was decided that no delegates could attend. Finally, however, the Council was abandoned owing to the railway strike. In fact as the history of the last two years shows, the ground which in the past had been covered by activities under the aegis of Suffrage, had now been monopolised by the Women Citizen's movement. At the annual and final meeting held this year by the Bolton Suffrage Society, the following resolution was carried unanimously: "Now that a substantial measure of Women's Suffrage has been gained, this meeting of members, resolves to merge the Bolton Women's Suffrage Society into the Women Citizen's Association, which stands for complete equality of liberties, status, and opportunities between men and women".[54]

The work, therefore, of the Bolton Women's Suffrage Society as such now, comes to an end. We leave the future in the hands of the Women Citizen's Association, in the belief that they will continue to progress and be animated by the ideals which, however imperfectly carried out, have been steadily kept before the Bolton Women's Suffrage Society.

July 13th, 1920.
Mrs William Haslam

AN APPRECIATION

On behalf of the Bolton Women Citizens' Association.
In gratitude for her life and influence, and in affectionate remembrance
of a truly great woman, and a loyal and devoted leader
of the Women's movement in Bolton.

The sudden and unexpected passing from this life of Mrs Haslam on
January 6th 1922, will inflict a sense of deep personal loss on a wide circle
of friends.[55] Bolton women, indeed all womanhood, have lost a faithful
and ever-loyal friend and guide.

The only daughter of the late Mr R Heywood, recently described as a
Bolton Giant on account of his multitudinous good works, of which Mrs
Haslam was justly proud; it will be seen that she inherited fine traditions
of public service to which in her own life she added in no small measure.[56]

A woman of large sympathies and wide knowledge and culture, a
leader of thought, she has left her mark in many spheres of public life. But
it is as a leader of the Women's movement in Bolton for many years that
she will best be remembered. It was very near to her heart. She has told
with pride of how, when a girl in her teens, she paid a subscription to a
Society for Women's Suffrage out of her first dress allowance, and from
that time onward her interest in the movement was unabated.[57]

It required considerably more courage in those days to fight for the
freedom of women than it does today, and the present generation will
never know what a debt they owe to her, as one of a noble band of
pioneers, who first had a vision of a wider and fuller life for women, and
worked mightily to secure it. Here in Bolton for many years she gave freely
in time, strength, and money towards that end, and no sacrifice was
counted too great.

In her early work as Poor Law Guardian, as in her later activities as
President of the Women's Local Government, Women's Suffrage and
Women Citizen's Associations, she was a veritable tower of strength and
a most wise councillor. On committees she was unequalled for seeing all
points of view, and her sound judgement none ever questioned. Her
memory can never fade from the minds of those who were privileged to
work with her. She consistently kept aloof from all the petty jealousies
that so often beset the path of public life.[58] In the radiance of her own
great spirit such could not exist.

In all her work Mrs Haslam was far ahead of her time,[59] and like all
pioneers, suffered disappointment and disillusionment, and did not win
the recognition she deserved from her own generation. But her dauntless

272

spirit triumphed over these as over the many obstacles in the path of progress. Having put her hand to the plough she never looked back, though the furrow she ploughed was a long and strenuous one. The seed sown by her will as surely come to a glorious harvest as that the day will follow the night; and knowing that, we honour her and give her grateful thanks.

Too late comes the suggestion that the Town Council should recognise her fine citizenship by making her a Freeman of the Borough. This would have given her great joy, not for personal reasons, but as a recognition of women's citizenship;[60] but those who knew her best know that she found her greatest compensations in giving and not in receiving. She was truly one of Nature's freemen whom the truth made free, and needed not that others should confer it on her.

Even through great sorrows that crowded her life the last five years, her spirit triumphed over all; and she continued to take an unflagging interest not only in the cause of women, but also in the great world problems and tragedies of today. She lived to see the realisation of some of her hopes: The Enfranchisement of women; Women in Parliament; A Woman on the Bolton Town Council; Women Magistrates, etc., etc., and in all these her great heart rejoiced.

Although she had left Bolton, and found in London an atmosphere of art and culture in which she delighted, her love for her native Town and her interest in its welfare and progress remained unchanged to the end.

The loss of her guiding spirit lies heavily upon us. It is such an overwhelming loss that words are feeble and meaningless to describe it. The woman's movement has lost a leader of great personality, high courage, and lofty ideals; and in the depths of our sorrow we know not where to look for comfort. But just as her whole life was a triumph of the spirit, so must we be strong in spirit and justify the faith she had in us. She believed in women as an effective and spiritual force in the world. Higher purpose, greater endeavour, must be the keynote of our efforts if we are to be true to the memory of our beloved friend and guide who has now joined "the choir invisible to those immortal dead who live again in minds made better by their presence".

Notes

CHAPTER ONE

The New Poor Law, Female Agency and Feminism

1   Bolton Record Office (hereafter BRO) *Bolton Chronicle*, 13 January 1922. My italics.
2   While female engagement with local government in Britain was about much more than the poor law – including for instance agitation over, or activity in, the provision of education, sanitary reform, housing improvement, factory improvement, the elimination of prostitution or public health – this volume will suggest that poor law work was a central driver for the personal and collective journey of local activists.
3   Hollis, *Ladies Elect.*
4   Eastwood, *Governing Rural England*, p. 186. On competing models for reform, see Henriques, "Jeremy Bentham", pp. 42–51; Brundage, *The Making*; Mandler, "Tories and paupers", pp. 81–103; Lubenow, *The Politics.*
5   On the Welsh New Poor Law, King and Stewart, "Death in Llantrisant", pp. 69–87. On the importance of appropriate yardsticks and on their diversity, see Williams, *From Pauperism*, pp. 136–44; Gazeley, *Poverty*; Fraser, *The Evolution*; Anne Crowther, *The Workhouse*, pp. 52–53.
6   The literature on the transition between Old and New Poor Law is substantial. See Thane, "Introduction", pp. 11–20; Harris, *The Origins*, pp. 40–58; Brundage, *The English Poor Laws*, pp. 61–89; Kidd, *State, Society*, pp. 23–47; Hollen Lees, *The Solidarities*; Crowther, *The Workhouse*, pp. 11–29.
7   Henriques, *Before the Welfare State*, p. 42.
8   Crowther, *The Workhouse*, pp. 30–87; Digby, *Pauper Palaces*; Digby, "The labour market", pp. 69–83; Crowther, "Health care", pp. 203–19.
9   King, *Poverty*, pp. 227–53; Harris, *The Origins*, pp. 1–14, 40–58, 91–103.
10 Digby, *Pauper Palaces*; Crowther, *The Workhouse*; Williams, *From Pauperism.*
11 Hollen Lees, *Poverty and Pauperism*; Hollen Lees, *The Solidarities.*
12 Hurren, "Labourers are revolting", pp. 37–55; Hurren, "'A pauper deadhouse'", pp. 69–94; Hurren, "The 'Bury-al Board'".

13 Dryburgh, "Individual, illegal"; Dryburgh, "The mixed economy".
14 Midwinter, *Social Administration*; Proctor, "Poor law administration", pp. 145–66; Boyson, "The history"; Apfel and Dunkley, "English rural society", pp. 37–68; Dunkley, "The hungry forties", pp. 329–46; Caplan, "The new poor law", pp. 267–300; McCord, "The implementation", pp. 90–108; Wood, "Finance", pp. 20–55.
15 Marland, *Medicine and Society*; Thane, *Old Age*.
16 Thane, *The Origins*, p. 23.
17 Stapleton, "Inherited poverty", pp. 339–55.
18 Ashforth, "Settlement and removal", pp. 58–91; Martin, "From parish", pp. 25–56; Driver, "The historical geography" pp. 269–86; Driver, *Power and Pauperism*.
19 Harris, *The Origins*.
20 Finlayson, *Citizen, State*.
21 Pugh, "Working class experience", pp. 775–96; Pedersen, *Family, Dependence*.
22 Wood, *Poverty*.
23 Rose, "The crisis", pp. 50–70 and Fraser, "The English poor law", pp. 9–31. Also Hennock, "Poverty and social theory", pp. 67–91; Thomson, "The welfare of the elderly", pp. 194–221.
24 Evans, *Social Policy*, pp. 211–71.
25 de Schweinitz, *England's Road*.
26 Finlayson, *Citizen, State*, pp. 68, 198.
27 Fraser, *The New Poor Law*, p. 23.
28 Crowther, *The Workhouse*, p. 269; Crowther, "The later years", p. 121; Ausubel, *In Hard Times*, p. 65.
29 Gazeley, *Poverty*.
30 Hollen Lees, *The Solidarities*, pp. 231–2; Williams, *From Pauperism*.
31 Vincent, *Poor Citizens*, pp. 41, 44–5.
32 For the 1834 legislation, see Brundage, *The Making*.
33 Crowther, "Health care"; Flinn, "Medical services", pp. 45–66.
34 Thane, "Government and society", pp. 1–62, 17; Crowther, "The workhouse", pp. 183–95.
35 Williams, *From Pauperism*, p. 87.
36 Rose, *The English*, p. 222.
37 Ashforth, "Settlement and removal". On the general background of political reform, extension of the franchise, and the rise of feminism see Ogborn, "Local power", pp. 215–26.
38 George Goschen was president of the Poor Law Board.
39 For general surveys see Thane, "Government and society", p. 37; Hurren, "'The 'Bury-al' board". On the relationship between poor law practice and the activities of the provincial Charity Organisation Society, see Humphreys, *Sin, Organised Charity*.
40 Mackinnon, "English poor law policy", pp. 603–25.
41 Fraser, "Introduction", pp. 12–13. Potentially path-breaking forthcoming

work from Elizabeth Hurren suggests that the crusade had a far longer and more complex hold than such statements allow. I am grateful to her for sharing this work.

42   Kidd, *State, Society*, p. 30.
43   Finlayson, *Citizen, State*, p. 148.
44   Though see Henriques, *Before the Welfare State*, p. 59, who argues that not until changed attitudes toward unemployment and the extension of the working class franchise in the twentieth century did the "principles of 1834 start to lose their grip".
45   Roberts, *Victorian Origins*; Rose, *The English Poor Law*, p. 236; O'Day and Englander, *Mr Charles Booth's Inquiry*; Englander and O'Day, *Retrieved Riches*.
46   Thane, "Non-contributory", pp. 86–106; Pugh, "Working class experience"; Hennock, "Poverty and social theory", pp. 67–91. For documents on the contemporary discussion, see Evans, *Social Policy*, pp. 161–73. On international dimensions, see Thane, *The Foundations*, pp. 270–87.
47   Johnson, "Risk, redistribution", pp. 225–48. On the Fabians, see Clark, "The new poor law", p. 273.
48   Koven, *Slumming*; Davies, "The health visitor", pp. 39–59; Moore, "Social work".
49   See Thane, *Old Age*, p. 172, who argues that only 5 per cent of all people aged 65+ were receiving relief in workhouses in the decade 1891–1901, though there were important regional differences.
50   Rubinstein, *Before the Suffragettes*, p. 76, suggests that the civil servants responsible for implementing the drive for more humane treatment, particularly after the 1893 Commission on the Aged Poor, were steeped in the traditions of less eligibility and were thus fundamentally unsuited to the task.
51   Harris, *The Origins*, p. 55.
52   Crowther, *The Workhouse*; Harris, *Unemployment and Politics*; Harris, *Civil Society*, particularly chapters from Harrison and Goldman.
53   Kidd, *State, Society*, pp. 30–32.
54   Crowther, *The Workhouse*, p. 271.
55   Fraser, "The English poor law", p. 29.
56   Rather than being the outcome of re-rating and re-financing, as in Sunderland. See Wood, "Finance", p. 35.
57   Crowther, *The Workhouse*, pp. 193–221; King, "We might be trusted", pp. 27–46.
58   See Bock and Thane, "Introduction", pp. 6–7; Bolt, *Feminist Ferment*, p. 28. For a discussion of American, French and other literature, see Pedersen, *Family, Dependence*.
59   Koven, "Borderlands", pp. 94–135. Of course, women were increasingly involved in welfare at a range of levels, from nurses and administrators, through matrons and teachers, to guardians and inspectors.
60   Bock and Thane, "Introduction", p. 7; Kanner, "The women of England", p. xvi; Levine, *Feminist Lives*, p. 117.
61   Thane, "Women and the poor law", pp. 29–51.

62 Lewis, "Gender, the family", pp. 37–55; Pateman, "The patriarchal", pp. 231–60. On women and their role in anti-poor law activism, see Clark, *The Struggle for the Breeches*.

63 For contextual material, see Clifton, *Professionalism*.

64 Crowther, *The Workhouse*.

65 Levine, *Feminist Lives*, p. 20; Hollis, *Ladies Elect*, p. 204.

66 Crowther, *The Workhouse*, pp. 68–69; McCrone, "Feminism and philanthropy", pp. 123–39; Hollis, *Women in Public*, p. 243; Deane, "Late nineteenth century philanthropy", pp. 122–42.

67 Hollis, *Ladies Elect*, p. 27.

68 Prochaska, *Women and Philanthropy*.

69 On the nature of these fractures, see Caine, *Victorian Feminism*.

70 Hollis, *Ladies Elect*, p. 200.

71 Summers, "A home", pp. 33–63, 47.

72 Crowther, *The Workhouse*, p. 69; Hollis, *Ladies Elect*, p. 199.

73 Summers, "A home", p. 33.

74 Lewis, *Women in England*, p. 92.

75 Summers, "A home", p. 45; Lewis, *Before the Vote*, pp. 218–19.

76 Banks, *Faces of Feminism*, p. 94; Bolt, *Feminist Ferment*, p. 9.

77 Nym Marshall, "The rhetorics of slavery", p. 63; Rendall, "Citizenship, culture", pp. 127–50.

78 We should remember that this was an agenda being played out on the international stage. See Corrada Pope, "Angels in the devil's workshop", pp. 296–324;

79 Harris, *Private Lives*, p. 190; Clarke, "Gender, class", pp. 230–53. On School Board suffrage and its importance, see Hollis, *Ladies Elect*, pp. 71–190.

80 Hollis, *Ladies Elect*, p. 235.

81 Rubinstein, *Before the Suffragettes*, p. 116; Hollis, "Women in council", pp. 192–213.

82 Hollis, *Ladies Elect*, p. 65.

83 Fuchs and Thompson, *Women*, pp. 152–3.

84 Though as Caine, *English Feminism*, points out, a claim for wider influence based upon the language of separate spheres and different capacities constrained as well as expanded the limits of female action. For the views of contemporary activists, see Lewis, *Women and Social Action*.

85 See Digby, "Victorian values"; Koven, "Borderlands"; Davidoff, *World's Between*, p. 56. On state hostility to women who came out of the borderland, see Jones, *Women in British*, p. 5.

86 Yeo, "Introduction", p. 8.

87 Rendall, "Women and the public sphere", pp. 475–88; Rendall, "The citizenship of women".

88 Rubinstein, *Before the Suffragettes*, p. 169.

89 Hollis, *Ladies Elect*, p. 40.

90 Hollis, "Women in council", p. 198. For comparative perspectives, see Urquhart, *Women in Ulster*, p. 126.
91 Hollis, *Ladies Elect*, p. 209.
92 *Ibid.*, pp. 213–14.
93 *Ibid.*, p. 197.
94 Davidoff, *World's Between*, p. 176.
95 Crowther, *The Workhouse*, p. 78; Lewis, *Women and Social Action*, pp. 10 and 204.
96 Rubinstein, *Before the Suffragettes*, pp. 167–8.
97 Levine, *Feminist Lives*, p. 72; Summers,"A home"; Liddington and Norris, *One Hand*.
98 Jones, *Women in British*, p. 10.
99 Harris, *Private Lives*, p. 195.
100 Hollis, *Ladies Elect*, p. 198.
101 Roberts, *The Radical*.
102 Twining, *Recollections*. Also Perkin, *Victorian Women*, p. 217.
103 Bartley, *Emmeline Pankhurst*; Purvis, *Emmeline Pankhurst*.
104 For a fuller list of prominent feminists and poor law guardians, see Banks, *A Biographical Dictionary*.
105 Pankhurst, *My Own Story*; Murray, *Strong Minded Women*, pp. 289–91.
106 Though see Ross,"Women in poor law administration".
107 For comparative Irish figures, see Urquhart, *Women in Ulster*, pp. 124–6.
108 Hollis, *Ladies Elect*, p. 202. My italics.
109 Digby, "Victorian Values", p. 214.
110 Summers, "A home", p. 48.
111 Her representativeness is considered in CHAPTER FIVE.
112 See Riley, '*Am I That Name?*'. Also Lewis, *Women and Social Action*, p. 9.
113 For an excellent review, see Stanley Holton, *Suffrage Days*.
114 de Larra Beiti, "Conspicuous before the world", pp. 106–26.
115 Rendall, "The citizenship".
116 For variants of this definition and a review of wider debates about how to define and locate feminism, see Levine, *Victorian Feminism*, pp. 14–15, 18, 156; Caine, *English Feminism*, pp. 89–97, 113–20, 134–46; Levine, *Feminist Lives*, pp. 39–40, 60, 176–77; Alexander, *Becoming a Woman*.
117 For interesting early work on this issue through the medium of feminist biography, see Forster, *Significant Sisters* and Jalland, *Women, Marriage*. For a useful timeline Harrison, *Prudent Revolutionaries*, pp. 4–5. Also McFeely, *Lady Inspectors*, and for more of an overarching framework, see Levine, *Victorian Feminism*.
118 Kanner, "The Women of England", p. xiv; Caine, *Victorian Feminists*.
119 Martin Pugh, *The March*. On anti-suffragism see Bush, "British women's anti-suffragism". On individual women who did not make the leap from charitable, campaigning and local government work to suffragism, see David, *Intellectual Women*.
120 While the primary material for this book comes from Bolton, the recent

publication of the journals of Lady Knightley opens up equal possibilities in a very different spatial context. See Gordon, *Politics and Society*.

121 Vickery, "Golden age", pp. 383–414; Landes, "The public", pp. 135–63; Davidoff, *World's Between*, pp. 227–76.
122 For an important overview see Rendall, "Women and the public sphere".
123 See Mort, "Purity, feminism", pp. 209–25.
124 Hall and Schwarz, "State and Society", pp. 7–32.
125 Banks, *Faces of Feminism*, p. 7.
126 Levine, *Victorian Feminism*, p. 16.
127 Perkin, *Victorian Women*, p. 214.
128 Hall, *Sex, Gender*, p. 1.
129 John and Eustance, *The Men's Share?*, p. xv.
130 Rubinstein, *Before the Suffragettes*, pp. xi–xv.
131 Harris, *Private lives*, p. 200. On social reform campaigners and their relation to feminism, see Levine, *Feminist Lives*, pp. 39–40.
132 On the USA, see Bolt, *Feminist Ferment*. On Ireland Urquhart, *Women in Ulster*. For France, Clark, *The Rise of Professional Women*.
133 Lewis, *Before the Vote*, p. 470.
134 Bartley, *Prostitution*.
135 Lewis, *Women and Social Action*.
136 *Ibid.*, p. 9.
137 Caine, *English Feminism*, p. 89; Caine, *Victorian Feminists*, pp. 8–17.
138 Though as Summers, "A home", p. 59 points out, some of the women engaged in poor law work and visiting were explicitly anti-feminist.
139 Jane Rendall, *The Origins of Modern Feminism*.
140 On women and marriage-related campaigning, see Shanley, *Feminism, Marriage*, pp. 22–78 and 103–30; Perkin, *Victorian Women*, pp. 212–13.
141 Harrison, *Prudent Revolutionaries*, p. 9.
142 Rogers, *Women and the People*, pp. 198–228. Also Jeffreys, *The Spinster*. For more negative commentary on Butler and the social purity movement, see Bland, *Banishing the Beast*.
143 Jane Rendall, "Friendship and politics", pp. 136–70, 137.
144 Caine, *Victorian Feminists*; Parker, *Women and Welfare*; Levine, *Feminist Lives*; Levine, *Victorian Feminism*.
145 Perkin, *Victorian Women*, p. 205. On the positive training given to working class women, see Liddington and Norris, *One Hand*, p. 134.
146 Caine, *English Feminism*, p. 131.
147 Purvis, "Reassessing representations", pp. 96–112.
148 Bock and Thane, "Introduction", p. 6.
149 Liddington, *The Life and Times*. Also Lawson, Savage and Warde, "Gender and local politics", p. 205, who emphasise that the working-class women's organizations ran classes to train women for municipal work.
150 Looking at Bolton gives us access to one of the second rank cities that Thane thinks is missing from a literature that has tended to focus on the biggest cities or on rural areas. Thane, *Foundations*.

151 Davidoff, *The Best Circles*, p. 14; Caine, "Feminist biography"; Urquhart, *Women in Ulster*, p. 123.
152 For a similar perspective see Perkin, *Victorian Women*, p. 217.
153 Hannah Mitchell of Ashton, Selina Cooper of Blackburn, Mrs Lees of Oldham, Alice Collinge, Margaret Greg and Sarah Reddish of Bolton, Hannah Hargreaves and Dorah Grey of Southport, Margaret Atherton of Burnley, Mary Asheton of Lancaster, Ellen Clark of Manchester and Susan Lee of Rochdale.
154 Caine, *English Feminism*, p. 89.

CHAPTER TWO

The Poverty and Poor Relief in Lancashire and Bolton

1 This is a considerable topic. See Harris, *The Origins*, pp. 40–58; Rose, *The English*, p. 236; Hollen Lees, *The Solidarities*.
2 See King, *Poverty*, pp. 83–7; Williams, *From Pauperism*, pp. 148–55.
3 Smith, "Ageing and well being", pp. 64–95; For comparative material see Tanner, "The City of London", pp. 153–87.
4 Midwinter, "State intervention", pp. 111–12.
5 Boyson, "The history", pp. 163–8. Contrast Henriques, "How cruel", p. 370, who argues that communities like Bolton petitioned against the New Poor Law because they felt that a lifetime of labour generated rights to relief.
6 Hitchcock, King and Sharpe, *Chronicling Poverty*; van Voss, *Petitions*, pp. 8–10; King, "'It is impossible", pp. 1–29.
7 Cooke Taylor, *Notes*, pp. 40–1. On the impact of trade depression in Lancashire, see Treble, *Urban Poverty*, p. 288.
8 Cooke Taylor, *Notes*, p. 43.
9 King, *Poverty*, pp. 93–104.
10 Boyson, "The history", p. 60.
11 Cooke Taylor, *Notes*, p. 38.
12 King and Timmins, *Making Sense*, pp. 328–60.
13 See Bowley, *Wages and Income*; Horrell and Humphries, "Old questions", pp. 849–80; Wood, "The statistics", pp. 128–63, 411–34.
14 Hunt, "Industrialisation", pp. 935–66; Hunt and Botham, "Wages in Britain", pp. 380–99; Walton, *Lancashire*, pp. 283, 290.
15 Lyons, "Family response", pp. 45–91; Timmins, *The Last Shift*.
16 For a more extensive discussion of the development of the Lancashire economy see Stobart, *The First Industrial*; Timmins, *Made in Lancashire*; Phillips and Smith, *Lancashire and Cheshire*.
17 Snell, *Annals*; Lee, *British Regional*; Lane, Raven and Snell, *Women, Work and Wages*.
18 Timmins, *Made in Lancashire*.
19 In 1848, for instance, Bolton had 40 per cent of the population dependent upon relief.
20 Cooke Taylor, *Notes*, p. 42.
21 Burnett, *Idle Hands*.

22 Hurren, "Agricultural trade unionism", pp. 200–22.

23 Huberman, *Escape From the Market*.

24 King, *A Fylde*; Huck, "Infant mortality", pp. 528–50. Recent studies of mutual organisations such as friendly societies and sick clubs have also emphasised the concentration of such organisations in Lancashire. See Gorsky, "The growth", pp. 489–511.

25 King and Timmins, *Making Sense*, pp. 134–62.

26 Englander, *Poverty and Poor Law Reform*.

27 Neild, "Comparative statement", p. 26.

28 Horrell and Humphries, "Old questions".

29 Simey, *Charity Rediscovered*, p. 7.

30 *Ibid.*, p. 43.

31 Foster, *Class Struggle*. For comparative material on Bradford see Ashforth, "Settlement and removal", p. 62. Also Chinn, *Poverty Amidst Prosperity*, p. 49.

32 For a review of these surveys, see Kidd, "Outcast Manchester", pp. 48–73.

33 Butler, *Poor Relief*, p. 14.

34 Bowley and Burnett-Hurst, *Livelihood and Poverty*, pp. 234–39; Walton, *Lancashire*, p. 293.

35 Not vastly different from the 56 per cent of household heads in Colyton who received poor relief between 1851 and 1881. See Robin, "The relief of poverty", pp. 193–218.

36 Foley, *A Bolton Childhood*, pp. 7, 13, 44, 60. For earlier perspectives, see Brigg, *A Lancashire*.

37 Quoted in Walton, *Lancashire*, p. 301.

38 For the last decades of the Old Poor Law in Lancashire, see King, "It is impossible"; King, "The English", pp. 1–23.

39 See the extensive discussion of the arrival of the New Poor Law in newspapers such as the *Bolton Chronicle*, 1833–1837; Dryburgh, "The mixed economy", pp. 93–103.

40 Wood and Wood, *A Lancashire Gentleman*, p. 387.

41 Midwinter, *Social Administration*.

42 Hollen Lees has characterised the period 1834–1860 as a period of "Residualism refined" where communities more generally "turned away from the more generous welfare regimes that had developed in the later eighteenth century". Hollen Lees, *The Solidarities*, p. 15.

43 For comparable material see Crowther, *The Workhouse*; Song, "Continuity and change", pp. 314–38; Brundage, *The Making*.

44 Edsall, *The Anti-Poor Law*; Rose, "The anti-poor law", pp. 41–73; Hill, *Nelson*.

45 Midwinter, "State intervention", p. 106.

46 Midwinter, *Social Administration*, pp. 20–8; Kidd, *State, Society*, p. 30.

47 Fraser, "The poor law as a political institution", pp. 111–27; Fraser, "Poor law politics", pp. 23–49.

48 Boyson, "The history", p. 124.

49   Midwinter, *Social Administration*, p. 30.
50   Boyson, "The history", p. 289.
51   *Ibid.*, pp. 284–90.
52   Driver, "The historical geography", pp. 269–86; Proctor, "Poor law administration", pp. 145–66.
53   Ashforth, "The urban poor law", p. 133.
54   Boyson, "The history", p. 297.
55   Wood, *Poverty*.
56   Midwinter, *Social Administration*, pp. 51, 57.
57   Williams, *From Pauperism*, pp. 60–66, tables 4.5 and 4.9. In 1846, the percentage of paupers recorded as able-bodied and under or unemployed and relieved outdoors in Bolton, Rochdale, Oldham and Garstang was 11.6 per cent, way above the 1.6 per cent national average.
58   Roberts, "How cruel", p. 104.
59   Midwinter, *Social Administration*, p. 61.
60   Crowther, *The Workhouse*, p. 50
61   Boyson, "The history", pp. 368–72.
62   *Ibid.*, "The history", pp. 387–8.
63   *Ibid.*, p. 144.
64   For comparable figures see Williams, *From Pauperism*, pp. 169–70.
65   Midwinter, *Social Administration*, p. 62.
66   Bolton Record Office (hereafter BRO) GBO 8/184–282, Sectional Relief Registers.
67   Boyson, "The history", p. 177. See also the specific justifications of this practice given by Clitheroe Guardians on fifteen occasions between 1840 and 1852. Lancashire Record Office (hereafter LRO) PUC 1/1–3, Minute Books.
68   For a good example, see the correspondence of Haslingden Union, the last of the Lancashire Unions to apply any sort of test to outdoor relief. LRO PUH 3/1–2, Letter Books. Contrast this with the records of Blackburn Union, the most enthusiastic to introduce restrictions on outdoor relief in the early days of the New Poor Law. LRO PUK 1/4, Minute Book. Also Boyson, "The history", p. 187.
69   For some of these issues see Hewitt, *The Emergence*; Lawton, "Regional population trends", pp. 29–70; Pooley and Pooley, "Health, society".
70   Driver, *Power and Pauperism*.
71   *Oldham News*, 18 January 1884.
72   Kidd, *State, Society*, p. 94.
73   Williams, *From Pauperism*, p. 105.
74   Guardian minute books and union correspondence files for all Lancashire unions were sampled by way of background.
75   Ashton, *Economic and Social Investigations*.
76   Brundage, *The English*, pp. 90–108. It should be noted that rural Lancashire poor law unions also saw radical progress. See Williams, *The New Poor Law*.
77   Gadian, "A comparative study", pp. 167–9.

78 Walton, *Lancashire*, p. 300.
79 Taylor, *Popular Politics*, pp. 57–103.
80 Mitchell, *The Hard Way up*, p. 43.
81 Foley, *A Bolton Childhood*, p. 59.
82 Walton, *Lancashire*, p. 284.
83 *Bolton Chronicle*, May, June and July, 26 June 1891.
84 *Bolton Chronicle*, November 1900. This extract is from 17 November 1900.
85 See the retrospective in *Bolton Evening News*, 2 June 1931.
86 For work on the early Bolton poor law, see King, "Locating and characterising", pp. 11–37; King, "We might be trusted", pp. 27–46; Dryburgh, "The mixed economy", pp. 46–92.
87 Taylor, *Popular Politics*.
88 Boyson, "The history", p. 112.
89 BRO GBO 1/1, Guardian Minute book, 25 March 1837.
90 *Bolton 1838–1930*; Cummings, *An Examination*.
91 BRO GBO 1/ 2, Guardian Minute book, 3 December 1842.
92 BRO GBO 1/9, Guardian Minute book, 3 June 1856.
93 BRO GBO 1/3, Guardian Minute book, 17 January 1843; Crowther, *The Workhouse*, p. 50. Dryburgh, "The mixed economy", suggests that only 12 per cent of union expenditure was on the indoor poor in 1850 and that a failure to take up the principles of 1834, resulting in poor workhouse conditions, was in itself a disincentive to applicants.
94 Boyson, "The history", p. 386.
95 Dryburgh, "The mixed economy".
96 BRO GBO 1/10, Guardian Minute book, 11 August 1857.
97 BRO GBO 8/192, Sectional Relief Book, 1 December 1855. The figures of Midwinter for per capita relief in Lancashire (4s. 7d.) quoted earlier in the chapter refer to regular pensioners only. This figure for Bolton includes the transient outdoor poor and is thus lower. Dryburgh, "The mixed economy", p. 91, argues that the continuation of such practices reflected the vested interests of guardians.
98 Mencher, "Introduction to the poor law reports", pp. 37–90.
99 BRO GBO 12/13, Newspaper Cutting Book 1901–1911.
100 *Bolton Chronicle*, 5 June 1890.
101 *Bolton Chronicle*, 29 September 1861.
102 Detailed by Driver, *Power and Pauperism*; Ashforth, "The urban poor law"; Crowther, *The Workhouse*, p. 50.
103 All material on loans and capital spending is gathered from BRO GBO 14/6–10, Guardian Financial Summaries 1871–1912.
104 Only 200 cottage homes were authorized for the whole country between 1870 and 1914.
105 *Bolton Chronicle*, 17 January 1891.
106 BRO GBO 14/2–10, Guardian Financial Summaries 1868–1912. For comparative national figures, see Williams, *From Pauperism*, pp. 170–1; Wood, "The poor law", p. 21; Crowther, *The Workhouse*, pp. 60–1.

107 *Bolton Chronicle*, 7 March 1894.
108 For comparative figures see Williams, *From Pauperism*, p. 232; Humphreys, *Sin, Organized Charity*, pp. 36–44. Excluding the costs of pauper lunatics would mean that the proportion of resources devoted to staffing almost doubles between 1868 and 1912.
109 BRO GBO 12/11–13, Newspaper Cutting Books 1890–1912.
110 Though census entries can provide us with an anchor point.
111 Thane, *Foundations*, p. 78.
112 BRO GBO 9/61–80, Workhouse Admission and Discharge Registers 1890–1900.
113 BRO GBO 9/67–94, Workhouse Admission and Discharge Registers 1894–1907. For official figures see copies in BRO GBO 23/4, Summary of Relief Returns 1892–1917.
114 Though the absolute per capita figures remain substantially below those set out by Williams as a national yardstick. Williams, *From Pauperism*, pp. 170–1.
115 *Bolton Chronicle*, 29 February 1888.
116 For wider context see Crowther, *The Workhouse*; Harris, *The Origins*.
117 On staffing, see Crowther, *The Workhouse*, pp. 135–55.
118 Dunkley, "The hungry forties", pp. 329–46; Midwinter, *Social Administration*; Boyson, "The history".
119 BRO GBO 21/1, Register of Nurses 1889–1914. For other staffing in Bolton union see BRO GBO 14/1–10, Guardian Financial Statements, which give detailed lists of staffing and costs. Also Crowther, *The Workhouse*, pp. 177–9.
120 Crowther, *The Workhouse*, p. 153.
121 BRO GBO 22/8, Scale of Officers' Salaries; BRO GBO 22/1, Statements by Union Personnel under the Superannuation Act. Context is provided by Crowther, *The Workhouse*, pp. 135, 137.
122 BRO ZHA 17/17, Diary of a Female Poor Law Guardian. Such dinners were a familiar part of the social and labour relations landscape for local employers.
123 BRO GBO 12/10, Newspaper Cutting Book 1887–1889.
124 BRO GBO 12/12, Newspaper Cutting Book 1894–1901.
125 Midwinter, *Social Administration*, p. 62.

CHAPTER THREE
Preparing the Ground? Philanthropy, Public Service and Activism

1 Harrison, "Philanthropy"; Owen, *English*; Kidd, "Outcast", p. 66.
2 van Leeuwen, "Histories of risk", pp. 33–8; Johnson, "Risk redistribution", pp. 225–48; Englander and O' Day, *Retrieved Riches*.
3 Kidd, "Outcast", p. 52. Also Kidd, "Philanthropy", pp. 180–92; Treble, *Urban Poverty*, chapter 2; Seed, "Unitarianism", pp. 1–25; Shapley, "Charity, status", pp. 157–77; Harrison, *Peaceable Kingdom*.
4 On the COS and the ideological debates leading up to its formation, see

Collini, *Public Moralists*, pp. 80–90; Harris, *Private Lives*, pp. 230–50; Roberts, "Reshaping the gift relationship", pp. 201–31; Rose, "The crisis", pp. 50–70; Humphreys, *Sin, Organised Charity*; Lewis, *The Voluntary Sector*; Kidd, "Charity organisation", pp. 45–66; Kiesling, "The long road", pp. 219–43; Moore, "Social work"; Vincent, "The poor law reports", pp. 343–63.

5 Kidd, *State, Society*, p. 67; Mandler, *The Uses of Charity*, pp. 1–37; King and Tomkins, *The Poor*, pp. 1–38, 100–36 and 258–80.

6 Kidd, *State, Society*, pp. 67–8; Shapley, *Charity and Power*; Gorsky, *Patterns of Philanthropy*; Prochaska, *The Voluntary Impulse*.

7 Kidd, *State, Society*, p. 92.

8 Kidd, *Manchester*, p. 153

9 Ashton, *Economic and Social*.

10 Harris, *The Origins*, pp. 60, 63, 184–96. Contrast this to Kidd, *State, Society*, pp. 95–102, who traces a polarisation in the nature of the charitable imperative into utilitarian and evangelical wings. Also Fraser, *The Evolution*, p. 115.

11 Finlayson, *Citizenship, State*, p. 63.

12 Gorsky, *Patterns*, p. 138.

13 Prochaska, *Women*.

14 Walton, *Lancashire*, pp. 229, 304 and 317; Levine, *Feminist Lives*, pp. 9 and 11.

15 On this issue see Kidd, *State, Society*, pp. 109–59.

16 Owen, *English*, p. 86; Walton, *Lancashire*, pp. 42–3.

17 Shapley, *Charity and Power*, pp. 23–56; Phillips and Smith, *Lancashire and Cheshire*, pp. 85–101; Walton, *Lancashire*, p. 332.

18 Shapley, *Charity and Power*; Simey, *Charity Rediscovered*; Burn, *Charitable Effort*; James, *A Wigan*, p. 16; Vase, *A Quaker*, p. 179.

19 Manchester Record Office L1 2/24/1–67, Ecroyd Papers; Burn, *Charitable Effort*, p. 86; Raybould, *A Survey*.

20 Kidd, *Manchester*, p. 150.

21 The Manchester Statistical Society kept detailed records of charities in the town. See Rose, "Culture, philanthropy", pp. 103–17.

22 Walton, *Lancashire*, 193–94; Shapley, *Charity and Power*, pp. 78–89. For comparable initiatives in Coventry, see Harris, *The Origins*, pp. 70–1.

23 Kidd, "Outcast", p. 57.

24 *Ibid.*, p. 151

25 Harris, *Private Lives*.

26 Prochaska, *Women*; Kidd, *State, Society*; Harris, *The Origins*. Harrison, *Peaceable Kingdom*, p. 223, notes that "Individual philanthropists naturally gravitated into social reform on seeing the personal altruism was not enough."

27 See Prochaska, *Women*, pp. 1–14; Prochaska, "Women", p. 431.

28 Roberts, "Head versus heart?", pp. 66–86; Walton, *Lancashire*, p. 236; Summers, "A home", pp. 33–63.

29   For early work on the multiple and overlapping campaigns see Rover, *Women's Suffrage*, pp. 2 and 61.
30   Koven, "Borderlands", pp. 94–135.
31   Davidoff, *World's Between*, p. 56.
32   Lewis, *Women and Social Action*, pp. 1–2 and 9.
33   Vicinus, *A Widening Sphere*, p. x.
34   Hannam, "Women and politics", p. 220.
35   See Maynard, "Privilege and patriarchy", pp. 221–47; Banks, *Faces*.
36   Kidd, *State, Society*, p. 84.
37   Prochaska, *Women*.
38   Kidd, *State, Society*, p. 84.
39   Banks, *Faces*; Lewis, *Women and Social Action*; Murray, *Strong-Minded Women*; Parker, *Women and Welfare*.
40   For sceptical views on the role and significance of women's philanthropic work, see Rover, *Women's Suffrage*, 1–3. However, see also Perkin, *Victorian Women*.
41   Davidoff, *Worlds Between*, p. 70. Also Phillips, *Divided Loyalties*.
42   Finlayson, *Citizenship, State*, p. 68.
43   Jones, *Women*, p. 10.
44   Levine, *Feminist Lives*, p. 117; Harrison, "Philanthropy", p. 233.
45   The literature on these issues is considerable. See Shanley, *Feminism*; Caine, *Victorian Feminists*.
46   Hannam, "Women and politics", pp. 221–2.
47   Hall, *Sex, Gender*, p. 1.
48   King, "Locating and Characterising". For contextual material see Slack, *From Reformation*.
49   Ainsworth, *An Inquiry*. On the small scale of charitable resources available elsewhere in Lancashire at this date, see Walton, *Lancashire*, pp. 42–4.
50   BRO 362 REP, *Further Report of the Committee for Inquiring Concerning Charities, 1828*; Dryburgh, "Mixed economy", argues that the importance of charity was limited both by the level of resources and philanthropic particularism.
51   Hollen Lees, *The Solidarities*, p. 68.
52   Laybourn, *Popular Politics*, p. 21.
53   Bolton Record Office (BRO), ZZ 410/1, Illuminated Address. The link between philanthropy and citizenship is important here. Dryburgh, "Mixed economy", suggests that in 1860 poor law expenditure was forty-five times greater than charity endowment income. The philanthropic imperative clearly increased notably after this date.
54   For Robert and John Heywood: BRO ZHE 71, The Diaries of Robert Heywood 1818–1868; BRO ZHA 3, Haslam Family Scrapbook; BRO ZHE 68/2, Newspaper Cutting Book; *Bolton Chronicle*, 23 October 1908; *Bolton Journal and Guardian*, 19 August 1910. Also Brown, *Robert Heywood*, and Hamer, *Bolton*, pp. 39, 50, 54, 56, 62, 65, 72, 73, 76, 83–7, 91, 93.
55   Hamer, *Bolton*, p. 62.

56 I am grateful to Peter Ainsworth for allowing me access to the private papers of the family during the course of writing this book.

57 McCord suggests three typologies – organized, transient and individual. See McCord, "The poor law", pp. 87–110.

58 *Bolton Chronicle*, 17 January 1891; *Bolton Chronicle*, 24 November 1894; *Bolton Chronicle*, 23 October 1908; BRO 361 BOLL, Bolton Poor Protection Society 69th Annual Report, 1909. Also Dryburgh, "Mixed economy", pp. 221–64.

59 *The Jubilee Report of the Bolton Society for Preventing Destitution*. I am grateful to Peter Ainsworth for sight of this volume. Also BRO GBO 4/60, Minutes of the Bolton Distress Committee, 1905–1912.

60 BRO ZHE 35/52, Charity Dinner Agenda.

61 For the 1842 and 1860s collections, see Hamer, *Bolton*, pp. 112–19. BRO 362.5/HOL, *Poor Relief in Bolton*.

62 See BRO HBO 1/10/1, Report of the Bolton Infirmary and Dispensary 1858–1860; BRO HBO 1/10/2, Report of the Bolton Infirmary and Dispensary 1860–1861. Also the retrospective and historic donation listings in BRO HBO 1/10/4, Report of the Bolton Infirmary and Dispensary, 1890–1901 and BRO HBO 1/10/5, Report of the Bolton Infirmary and Dispensary, 1901–1911.

63 BRO 371 BOL, *History of the Blind Welfare Association, 1866–1955*.

64 For John Haslam see BRO ZHA 11, Charitable Donations 1920; BRO ZHA/16, *John Haslam and Co. Ltd: A History*; *Bolton Chronicle*, 18 February 1921. On Mary Haslam see *Bolton Chronicle*, 4 December 1908; *Bolton Chronicle*, 11 December 1908.

65 For the role of Heywood in the Mechanics Institute, see *Bolton Chronicle*, 22 November 1907 and Brown, *Robert Heywood*. Also BRO, *Laws and Regulations of the Bolton Mechanics Institute 1825*.

66 On Bank Street Chapel see *Bolton Guardian*, 8 June 1856; Ramsden, *A Responsible*. I am grateful to Peter Ainsworth for material on Hick and Chadwick. For the work of Hick see also BRO 361 BOL, Bolton Benevolent Society Report and Rules 1859–60.

67 Hamer, *Bolton*, p. 62.

68 The initiatives emerge in a gleaning of all newspapers for the period synthesized with sources such as Mary Haslam's working diary. For the Toy Fund, *Bolton Chronicle*, 22 November 1911; Hospital Work Society *Bolton Chronicle*, 16 November 1905; Nightingale Fund BRO FZ 38/1, Subscription Lists for the Nightingale Fund, 1856; District Nursing Association *Bolton Chronicle*, 12 March 1892.

69 BRO ZHE 62/10, Deed of Gift; BRO ZHE 63/7 and 8, Correspondence.

70 These examples are listed in Hamer, *Bolton*, and can also be found in the indexes to Bolton newspapers.

71 Innes, "State, church", pp. 15–65. However, see Dryburgh, "Mixed economy", who argues the opposite for the period to 1860.

72 Kidd, *Manchester*. On the general experience of a core of philanthropists see Harrison, "Philanthropy", pp. 247–8.

73 For context, see Porter, "Health care", p. 26.

74 See William Haslam's obituary in *Bolton Journal*, 2 February 1917. Also BRO FCH 2/79, Membership Roll of the Queen's Street Mission, 1896–1912; BRO ZHA 3, Newspaper Cutting book.

75 BRO ZHE 26/3/118, Letter re. Hulton Trustees Book; BRO ZHE 26/3/220, Letter re. the Widows Fund; BRO ZHE 42/41, Letter re. contribution to the Athenaeum.

76 *Bolton Chronicle*, 14 June 1868.

77 Laybourn, *Popular Politics*, 63–9.

78 I am grateful to Peter Ainsworth for this reference.

79 BRO B367.76 App, Report of the Queens Street Mission; BRO FZ 38/1, Subscription and Collecting list for the Nightingale Fund; BRO FZ 6/1–16, Visiting Notes of the Bolton Evangelical Revival Committee, 1860.

80 Blackwood Hall Archive, BOL 64, 1851 Charity Reports.

81 BRO B3621 REP, Report of the Ladies Charity, 1838.

82 On the Ormrod's and their work for the Bolton Society for the Abolition of Slavery, see Ormrod, *Up Our Street*. On the wider importance of anti-slavery campaigns for female activists, see Nym Marshall, "The rhetorics of slavery", pp. 55–71; Billington and Billington, "A burning zeal", pp. 82–111.

83 BRO GBO 4/60, Bolton Distress Committee, 1905–1912; *Bolton Chronicle*, 9 March 1901, Bolton Adult Deaf and Dumb Society; *Bolton Chronicle*, 23 October 1908, Bolton Poor Protection Society; BRO FZ 6/1–16, Visiting Notes of Bolton Evangelical Revival Committee.

84 BRO FW 6/1, Minutes of the Bolton Committee for the Reclamation of Unfortunate Women; BRO FW 2/4, Annual Report of the Bolton Women's Suffrage Association; BRO FW 2/1, Minutes of the Bolton Women's Suffrage Association 1908–1914; *Bolton Chronicle*, 24 November 1894; *Bolton Chronicle*, 21 December 1906.

85 For a useful time-line of women's organisations 1888–1934 against which to set the experiences of Bolton women, see Harrison, *Prudent Revolutionaries*, pp. 4–5.

86 BRO ZZ 324/1, Newspaper Cutting Book, p. 189.

87 *Ibid.*, p. 231

88 See Bolt, *Feminist Ferment*.

89 BRO NUB 1/6/6, Letter to Mr Scowcroft re. the Ladies Sewing School.

90 BRO B3621 REP, Report of the Ladies Charity.

91 BRO 367.76 App, Report of the Queens Street Mission; BRO FCH 2/79, Membership Roll of the Queens Street Mission; BRO ZAL 232, Plan of Land in Queen Street.

92 BRO FW 1/1, Minutes of the Bolton Women's Local Government Association.

93 Ormrod, *Up Our Street*.

94 BRO FW 6/1, Minutes of the Bolton Committee for the Reclamation of Unfortunate Women; *Bolton Chronicle*, 18 April, 1867.

95 BRO FW 1/1, Minutes of the Bolton Women's Local Government Association.

96 BRO FW 2/4, Printed Report of the Bolton Women's Suffrage Association.

97 BRO FW 5/1, Minutes of the Bolton Women's Co-Operative Guild.

98 On the importance of economic independence, see Lewis, *Women and Social Action*.

99 For the History of Bolton Women Citizens Association, see *Bolton Chronicle*, 20 January 1922.

100 On the biographical approach to feminist lives and achievements, see Rose, *Parallel Lives*; Harrison, *Prudent Revolutionaries*; Lewis, *Women and Social Action*.

101 All of the succeeding quotes are drawn from this source. For a full annotated version of the notes see pp. 197–202.

102 On early family life for other female activists see Jalland, "Victorian spinsters", pp. 129–70; Levine, *Feminist Lives*, pp. 15–20.

103 On the influence of schooling on women activists see Caine, *Victorian Feminists*, pp. 15–17.

104 Levine, *Feminist Lives*, pp. 15–32.

105 Holt, *The Unitarian*.

106 On the importance of family deaths as a motivation for female philanthropy and public service, see Harrison, "Philanthropy", pp. 227–8. Contrast this stated motivation with the frustrations of family life, humanitarianism and feminist leaning that drove other prominent activists in Caine, *Victorian Feminists*.

107 Whether this refers to domestic tension and opposition to her work is doubtful, since Haslam was himself a prominent philanthropist and public figure and had a commitment to women's public action that predated his marriage.

108 Brown, *Robert Heywood*, p. 6. See also her obituary in *Bolton Chronicle*, 20 January 1922.

109 BRO FW 2/4, Annual Reports of the Bolton Women's Suffrage Association, 1910; BRO FW 5/1, Minutes of the Bolton Mother and Child Welfare Association.

110 I am grateful to Thomas Barnes for access to his mother's letter collection.

111 *Bolton Chronicle*, 18 June 1898, Obituary of Richenda Ashworth; BRO ZHA 17/17, Diary of a Female Poor Law Guardian. Other material is drawn from a survey of charities, political organisations and campaigning groups in the Bolton newspapers.

112 BRO 362 Coll, Autobiographical notes of Alice Collinge; *Bolton Evening News*, 2 June 1931.

113 Liddington, "Women cotton workers", pp. 103–4; Liddington and Norris, *One Hand*, pp. 22, 59, 112, 125, 134–9, 291.

114 Levine, *Feminist Lives*.

115 BRO ZHA 17/17, Diary of a Female Poor Law Guardian, June 1898.
116 *Ibid.*
117 BRO FW5/1, Minutes of the Bolton Women's Co-operative Guild.
118 See Banks, *Faces.*
119 Kidd, *State, Society*, p. 74.
120 Hollis, *Women in Public*, p. 243; Davidoff, *World's Between*, p. 257.
121 BRO ZHA 17/17, Diary of a Female Poor Law Guardian.
122 None of the Bolton female guardians were as active as Louisa Twining or Jenny Foster Newton, poor law guardian for Richmond at 36, but Mary Haslam in particular provides records somewhat richer than any other collection of which I am aware. See Deane, "Late nineteenth-century philanthropy", pp. 122–42.
123 Coleman, *Sussex*, p. 18.
124 The fact that the committee included the wives of some of the biggest ratepayers in the town may have smoothed their passage, but this was also the case in many other places where hostility was more marked.
125 BRO GBO 12/12, Newspaper Cutting Book.
126 Unless otherwise stated, the data which follows is drawn from BRO ZHA 17/17, Diary of a Female Poor Law Guardian, which also includes minutes of the BLWVC.
127 King, "We might be trusted", p. 27–46.
128 See Thane and Bock, *Maternity.*
129 BRO ZHA 17/17, Diary of a Female Poor Law Guardian, 20 November 1894.
130 Deane, "Late nineteenth-century philanthropy".
131 Jones suggests that such strategies reflect the powerlessness of women, arguing that it is not enough that women were able "to offer opinions which may or may not be taken into account, or be consulted on an arbitrary basis". To have power meant active participation in a "web of decisions". Jones, *Women*, p. 3. In this case, however, what is remarkable is how the absence of an automatic right to be heard did not prevent fundamental reform, nor the exercise of considerable power, in objective terms and in the minds of women activists themselves.
132 Levine, *Feminist Lives*, p. 82.
133 Davidoff, *World's Between*, p. 258.
134 Prochaska, *Women*, p. 42.
135 Jalland, *Women.*
136 Levine, *Feminist Lives*, pp. 9, 15, 20 and 32.
137 *Ibid.*, p. 121.
138 *Bolton Chronicle*, 19 May 1918.
139 Levine, *Feminist Lives*, p. 179.

CHAPTER FOUR
Fighting an Election

1 Ugolini, "'By all means'", p. 84; Clark, "Gender, class", pp. 230–53.
2 Harris, *Private Lives*, p. 190. On the importance of exercising the local franchise for women, see Lydia Becker, quoted in Lewis, *Before the Vote*, p. 348.
3 See Rose, *Parallel Live*.
4 Perkin, *Victorian Women*, p. 214. For a sceptical view of the importance of this development see Rogers, *Women and the People*, p. 213.
5 Hannam, "Women and politics", p. 227.
6 Hollis, *Ladies Elect*, p. 58.
7 Rubinstein, *Before the Suffragettes*, pp. 150–2.
8 Hollis, *Ladies Elect*, p. 204.
9 *Ibid.* National figures are surprisingly hard to reconstruct, not least because of re-run elections. Levine suggests a figure of 887 for 1895. See Levine, *Feminist Lives*, p. 71. There were 675 unions in England.
10 Contrast the slow gains made here with the more rapid progress made in areas such as School Boards. See Hollis, *Ladies Elect*, pp. 71–194.
11 Levine, *Feminist Lives*, p. 72. On yardsticks see Lewis, *Before the vote*, p. 2.
12 Hollis, *Ladies Elect*, p. 205,
13 *Ibid.*, pp. 208–14.
14 Hamilton, "Images", p. 79.
15 Perkin, *Victorian Women*, p. 216; Hollis, *Ladies Elect*, p. 472; Hollis, *Women in Public*, p. 247.
16 The literature on this issue is considerable. See Bock and James, "Introduction: Contextualising equality", p. 10; Poovey, *Uneven Developments*, p. 6; Pateman, "Equality, difference", p. 20; Hannam, "Women and politics", p. 224.
17 Davidoff, *World's Between*, p. 55. On the wider importance of linking philanthropic experience and public service see Fuchs and Thompson, *Women*, pp. 139, 152–3.
18 Yeo, "Introduction", p. 8.
19 *Ibid.*, pp. 14–15.
20 *Ibid.*, p. 18.
21 Hollis, *Women in Public*, p. 247.
22 Lidington and Norris, *One Hand*, p. 134.
23 Davidoff, *World's Between*, p. 57
24 *Ibid.*, pp. 222–3.
25 Hollis, *Ladies Elect*, p. 470.
26 *Ibid.*, p. 222.
27 *Ibid.*, pp. 7 and 65.
28 *Ibid.*, pp. 10 and 227.
29 Emmeline Pankhurst was elected guardian for Chorlton in a campaign that involved her taking on male rate savers, but we learn little about the election process itself. See Pankhurst, *My Own Story*, p. 23.
30 Davidoff, *World's Between*, p. 262.

31 For Southport and Wigan, see Knowles, *A Study*.

32 Bolton Record Office (hereafter BRO) GBO 12/11, Newspaper Cutting Book 1890–93, 17 December 1890. I am grateful to Elizabeth Hurren for pointing out that voting papers distributed and collected by the union clerk were not usually counted in turnout figures.

33 Perkin, *Victorian Women*, p. 216.

34 BRO ZHA 17/17, Diary of a Female Poor Law Guardian, 9 May, 1893.

35 On traditions of public activism in the families of feminists, see Perkin, *Victorian Women*.

36 *Bolton Chronicle*, 13 October 1894; Rendall, "Introduction", p. 22.

37 *Bolton Journal*, 12 March 1898. For some of the many other references see *Bolton Chronicle*, 29 January 1898; 5 March 1898; 2 March 1901; 11 October 1901; 14 February 1908; 20 March 1908. On the importance of the WLA election machinery for female candidates see Hollis, "Women in council", p. 212.

38 *Bolton Journal*, 22 April 1893. See also *Bolton Chronicle*, 29 January 1898; 30 July 1898; 20 April 1901; 26 April 1907; 1 May 1908; 14 May 1892.

39 *Bolton Chronicle*, 28 April 1894.

40 *Bolton Chronicle*, 7 April 1898.

41 Hannam, "Women and politics".

42 *Bolton Chronicle*, 28 March 1891.

43 *Bolton Chronicle*, 18 April 1891. While such low turnout was relatively rare, see Urquhart, *Women in Ulster*, p. 131, who argues that electoral enthusiasm was limited.

44 *Bolton Chronicle*, 9 April 1892. See Hollis, "Women in council", p. 197, for the challenge to male authority that simply standing posed. Hollis may be mistaken in her statement (p. 195) that it was not until the later 1890s that women candidates stood in Bolton.

45 *Bolton Chronicle*, 26 March 1892. This is not the indifference that Hollis believes to have been demonstrated by political parties to poor law elections. See Hollis, "Women in council", p. 197. On the notion that poor law elections were often hotly contested see Perkin, *Victorian Women*, p. 215.

46 *Bolton Chronicle*, 2 April 1892. Such enthusiasm tempers widespread arguments that fashioning a public role was often done in the face of considerable opposition.

47 The Society for Promoting the Return of Women as Poor Law Guardians was founded in 1881 and lasted to 1904. The Women's Local Government Society, which increasingly moved into poor law elections, was founded in 1888. See Hollis, *Ladies Elect*, pp. 40, 231; McCrone, "Feminism and philanthropy", pp. 128–9, 134. For the initial membership lists see the separate sheet of paper in BRO ZHA 17/17, Diary of a Female Poor Law Guardian.

48 BRO ZHA 17/17, Diary of a Female Poor Law Guardian. This is precisely the situation that some male guardians had hoped to head off by sanctioning the visiting committee in the first place. See BRO GBO 12/11, Newspaper Cutting Book, 8 February 1893. Also Levine, *Feminist Lives*, p. 73

49 On the importance of philanthropic networks see Hollis, *Ladies Elect*, p. 462. For the importance of mobilizing the women's vote see Levine, *Feminist Lives*, p. 120.

50 BRO ZHA 17/17, Diary of a Female Poor Law Guardian, 31 July 1894. On groups such as those for young servants, see Bartley, "Preventing prostitution", pp. 37–60.

51 For background on such a decision see Walker, "Party political women", pp. 165–91.

52 Hollis, "Women in council", p. 212, suggests that an apolitical stance meant that women "chose the women's constituency over party loyalty". See also Summers, "A home", p. 47. However, it is clear that Haslam and the other activists remained very much politically engaged and did not form a different political grouping.

53 BRO ZHA 17/17, Diary of a Female Poor Law Guardian, 11 September 1894.

54 Hollis, *Ladies Elect*, p. 220. However, the board had been split as early as 1892 on the desirability of lowering the property qualification. See BRO GBO 12/11, Newspaper Cutting Book, 30 November 1892.

55 BRO ZHA 17/17, Diary of a Female Poor Law Guardian.

56 Hollis, "Women in council", p. 197, suggests that women stood for wards far distant from the poor. This is clearly not the case in Bolton.

57 BRO ZHA 17/17, Diary of a Female Poor Law Guardian, 20 September 1894.

58 *Ibid.*, 20 November 1894, my emphasis. Contrast this with the prevailing assumption that such committees were toothless and only operated at the whim of the guardians.

59 *Bolton Journal*, 1 December 1894.

60 *Bolton Guardian*, 8 December 1894. There is little support here for Hollis, *Ladies Elect*, pp. 222–3, who argues that seats were not fiercely contested, that "political parties kept a low profile", and that women did not have a substantial constituency. There is more support for Summers, "A home", p. 48, who argues that elections were experienced as "a contest between one class of women and another class of men". We should remember that voting papers signified the "Quality or Calling of the Persons Nominated".

61 Hollis, *Ladies Elect*, p. 223.

62 *Ibid.*, p. 65.

63 *Bolton Guardian*, 8 December 1894, my emphasis.

64 Yeo, "Introduction", p. 10.

65 Bolt, *Feminist Ferment*, pp. 9–10.

66 Hollis, "Women in council", p. 209. On transcending gender boundaries see Alexander, *Becoming a Woman*, p. 145.

67 For clashes with the male guardians prior to 1894 see various entries in BRO GBO 12/11, Newspaper Cutting Book.

68 *Bolton Journal*, 15 December 1894, my emphasis.

69 Hollis, *Ladies Elect*, pp. 208–9.

70 Hollis, "Women in council", p. 197.

71 Though for sceptical comments on the level of local political support for female candidates see *Ibid.*, p. 212.

72 The rancorous politics of the mid-Victorian urban poor law are a familiar part of the welfare historiography. Political division amongst late-Victorian guardians has been the focus of much less empirical attention, though for an excellent first step see Hurren, "Agricultural trade unionism", pp. 200–22.

73 *Bolton Journal*, 9 December 1894.

74 *Ibid.* This sort of rationale had the added advantage of not promising too much to the electorate.

75 I am grateful to Peter Ainsworth for access to his broadside collection.

76 *Ibid.*

77 On posters and campaigning see Hollis, *Ladies Elect*, pp. 222–7 and figure 12. Competition over posters is reported in *Bolton Journal*, 15 December 1894. The only posters known to survive from the 1894 election are owned by Peter Ainsworth and I am grateful for access to this collection.

78 BRO ZFO 7, Autobiographical Notes of Mrs A. Hukin.

79 On Bolton orange box meetings see BRO ZAC 14, Notes of Alice Collinge.

80 BRO ZHA 17/17, Diary of a Female Poor Law Guardian, 17 December 1894. This equates to a turnout of almost 60 per cent once all the votes are added up.

81 BRO ZHA 17/17, Diary of a Female Poor Law Guardian, 18 March 1897.

82 *Ibid.*, 23 March 1897.

83 *Ibid.*, 5 April 1897.

84 BRO FW 1/1, Minutes of the Bolton Women's Local Government Association. See also Hollis, *Ladies Elect*, pp. 225–6, who suggests that these minutes are from the ARWPLG.

85 *Bolton Journal*, 9 March 1901; BRO FW 1/1, Minutes of the Bolton Women's Local Government Association, 15 March 1901.

86 *Bolton Journal*, 9 March 1901.

87 *Ibid.*

88 See CHAPTER THREE.

89 *Bolton Evening News*, 5 April 1910.

90 *Bolton Chronicle*, 19 May 1909; Hollis, "Women", pp. 208–9.

91 Hollis, *Ladies Elect*, p. 32. On Reddish, Liddington and Norris, *One Hand*.

92 Hollis, "Women in council", p. 210, suggests that election hostility was rare. This does not appear to have been the case in Bolton.

93 BRO FW 1/1, Minutes of the Bolton Women's Local Government Association, 11 February 1898.

94 BRO ZHA 17/17, Diary of a Female Poor Law Guardian, 23 September 1902 and 4 November 1902. One interpretation might be that the ARWPLG was unwilling to fight a poorly organized campaign and thus jeopardize their momentum.

95 As, for instance, does Hollis, *Ladies Elect*, pp. 225–6.

96 BRO FW 1/1, Minutes of the Bolton Women's Local Government Association, 4 April 1905.
97 *Bolton Chronicle*, 26 February 1909.
98 *Bolton Journal*, 25 February 1910.
99 *Bolton Chronicle*, 9 March 1910.
100 *Bolton Chronicle*, 12 July 1907; 24 November 1907.
101 Hollis, *Women in Public*, p268, likewise reminds us that commentators such as Lydia Becker had seen women's role in municipal government as a stepping stone to just this sort of wider horizon. Also Rendall, "Introduction", p. 23; Caine, *English Feminism*, p. 131; Lewis, *Before the Vote*, p. 465. Contrast this with the view that Victorian women did not slip easily into positions of decision and policymaking in Parker, *Women*, p. 309. On the issue of when and how a variety of campaigns and organizations might come together to form a local feminist movement, see Levine, *Victorian Feminism*, pp. 14–18, and Maynard, "Privilege and patriarchy", p. 224.

CHAPTER FIVE
Negotiating Power

1 Hollis, *Ladies Elect*, p. 7.
2 Rubinstein, *Before the Suffragettes*, pp. 167–8.
3 Levine, *Feminist Lives*, pp. 107, 119.
4 Digby, "Poverty, health", p. 74; McCrone, "Feminism and philanthropy", p. 133.
5 Hollis, *Ladies Elect*, p. 14; Hollis, "Women in council", pp. 197, 212.
6 Some of the interest groups identified by Crowther as representative on boards of guardians elsewhere are absent here. See Crowther, *The Workhouse*.
7 Taylor, *Popular Politics*.
8 See for instance the disputes over representation of the farming interest in 1892. Bolton Record Office (hereafter BRO) GBO 12/11, Newspaper Cutting Book 1890–1893.
9 On social dilution elsewhere see Summers, "A home", p. 47; Hollis, *Ladies Elect*, p. 209; Crowther, *The Workhouse*, pp. 75–6.
10 BRO ZHA 17/17, Diary of a Female Poor Law Guardian, 11 April 1898.
11 *Bolton Chronicle*, 28 August 1889.
12 There was persistent newspaper criticism at the poor attendance of many male guardians. See, for instance, BRO GBO 12/10, Newspaper Cutting Book 1887–1889 and BRO GBO 12/13, Newspaper Cutting Book 1901–1907.
13 All instances are drawn from BRO ZHA 17/17, Diary of a Female Poor Law Guardian.
14 *Ibid.*, 23 September 1903.
15 BRO GBO 12/13, Newspaper Cutting Book, 1894–1901, 28 November 1894.

16   On the particular importance of Sarah Reddish to the Bolton labour move-
      ment, see Liddington and Norris, *One Hand*, pp. 134–5, 291.
17   BRO ZHA 17/17, Diary of a Female Poor Law Guardian, 27 October 1897
      and 3 November 1897.
18   Similar conclusions have been drawn by other authors, but they can only be
      given the emphasis they deserve when underpinned by local studies such as
      this. See Levine, *Feminist Lives*, p. 178; Rendall, "Introduction", p. 4; Hollis,
      Ladies Elect, p. 473.
19   BRO GBO 12/13, Newspaper Cutting Book, 1894–1901, 9 January 1895.
      For the context in other unions see Hollis, *Ladies Elect*, pp. 211–12.
20   BRO ZHA 17/17, Diary of a Female Poor Law Guardian, 12 June 1895.
      While this is evidence of direct conflict, it is also important to note that the
      implication is that women had garnered too much power on the previous
      hospital sub-committee.
21   Hollis, *Ladies Elect*, p. 222.
22   BRO ZHA 17/17, Diary of a Female Poor Law Guardian, 20 November
      1896 and BRO GBO 12/13, Newspaper Cutting Book, 1894–1901, 25
      November 1896. Also Hollis, *Ladies Elect*, p. 214, for context on the criti-
      cism of female guardians by officials.
23   BRO ZHA 17/17, Diary of a Female Poor Law Guardian, 3 June 1896.
24   *Ibid.*, 10 November 1897
25   *Ibid.*, 8 December 1897. Also *Bolton Chronicle*, 8 December 1897.
26   *Ibid.*, 5 January 1898.
27   Digby, "Poverty, health", p. 81.
28   *Bolton Chronicle*, 18 June 1898; BRO GBO 12/13, Newspaper Cutting
      Book, 1894–1901, 22 June 1898.
29   BRO ZHA 17/17, Diary of a Female Poor Law Guardian, 15 June 1898.
30   *Ibid.*, 9 January 1895.
31   *Ibid.*, 12 May 1897.
32   *Ibid.*, 20 April 1898.
33   BRO GBO 12/13, Newspaper Cutting Book, 1894–1901, 19 April 1899.
34   *Ibid.*, 25 April 1900.
35   BRO ZHA 17/17, Diary of a Female Poor Law Guardian, 25 April 1900.
36   *Ibid.*, 27 May 1896.
37   *Ibid.*, 9 June 1897.
38   *Ibid.*, 12 May 1897 and 26 May 1897.
39   Contrast this with the marginalization that Hollis, *Ladies Elect*, p. 219, sees
      as the representative experience of most pre- and many post-1895 female
      guardians.
40   BRO ZHA 17/17, Diary of a Female Poor Law Guardian, 30 January 1895
      and 11 May 1901.
41   *Ibid.*, 18 December 1895; 20 January 1897. We have already seen in
      CHAPTER FOUR that the BLWVC were successful in carrying workhouse staff
      with them.
42   *Ibid.*, 21 March 1895. A female presence on such committees may also have

disrupted corruption in the awarding of contracts. In this sense, it is surprising that their presence caused so little conflict.

43 *Ibid.*, 8 January 1896; 4 March 1898; 30 March 1898.

44 *Ibid.*, 11 May 1898; 18 May 1898; 28 June 1899.

45 *Ibid.*, 29 January 1895 and 30 January 1895.

46 *Ibid.*, 12 March 1895.

47 *Ibid.*, 2 August 1899.

48 *Ibid.*, 11 August 1897. For context, see BRO GBO 28/1–1077, Personnel Files for Bolton Union; BRO GBO 21/1, Register of Nurses Employed; BRO GBO 15/8, Correspondence and Local Government Board Circulars, Order 35,540

49 Crowther, *The Workhouse*, p. 135.

50 BRO ZHA 17/17, Diary of a Female Poor Law Guardian, 8 April 1895 and 10 April 1895.

51 *Ibid.*, 5 February, 12 February, 13 February 1896.

52 *Ibid.*, 7 June 1899.

53 *Ibid.*, 23 December 1896.

54 *Ibid.*, 31 January 1900.

55 *Ibid.*,16 April 1896. My emphasis. Watkinson was a chemist, Heywood a cotton spinner, Graveson an ironmonger and Kearsley a butcher. This mix of substantial and petty ratepayers introduced an alternative focus of dispute within guardian relationships. BRO GBO 4/22, Minutes of the Workhouse Committee April 1896–April 1897.

56 BRO ZHA 17/17, Diary of a Female Poor Law Guardian, 14 May, 27 November and 11 December 1895, 4 June 1899 and 26 September 1899.

57 Hollis, *Ladies Elect*, p. 221; BRO GBO 8/272-366, Outdoor Relief Registers March 1885–March 1914.

58 Hollis, *Ladies Elect*, p. 227.

59 Levine, *Feminist Lives*, p. 110. However, see also BRO GBO 12/12, Newspaper Cutting Book, 1894–1901, 3 January 1900 where one guardian doubts the knowledge of female guardians when it came to building work.

60 BRO ZHA 17/17, Diary of a Female Poor Law Guardian, 23 February and 18 July 1895, 4 March and 6 August 1896. Also Levine, *Feminist Lives*, p. 14, who argues that the feminism and social activism of women such as Haslam was a way of life.

61 BRO ZHA 17/17, Diary of a Female Poor Law Guardian, 9 March 1898.

62 National debates about poverty and the appropriate state and charitable responses were increasingly informed by a pan-European and international information network. Philanthropic tourism was common from the 1850s as were formal delegations sent out from English parishes and unions to investigate alternative welfare systems. The fact that Haslam took time out from a family holiday to investigate the state of the local workhouse is a reflection of the importance she attached to her work with the poor, her humanitarian sentiment and a desire to garner information. For philanthropic tourism and the development of pan-European information

networks, see Cunningham, "Introduction", pp. 1–14; Hennock, *British Social Reform*; Cox, *The Development*, p. 76. Bolton union sent formal information gathering parties as far afield as the United States of America.

63   See Brandes, "'Odious, degrading", pp. 199–228.

64   For context see Crossman, "Welfare and nationality".

65   See also Jones, *Women*, p. 10, who argues that women could "network effectively, and offer a distinctive contribution to the public, although still local, world".

66   BRO ZHA 17/17, Diary of a Female Poor Law Guardian, 30 December 1895.

67   *Ibid.*, 6 January 1897.

68   *Ibid.*, 13 January 1897.

69   *Ibid.*, 4 May 1898.

70   *Ibid.*, 18 May 1898.

71   *Ibid.*, 16 September 1896.

72   Liddington, *The Life and Times*, p. 264.

73   BRO ZHA 17/17, Diary of a Female Poor Law Guardian, 19 February and 17 June 1896. My emphasis.

74   *Ibid.*, 30 April 1897. My emphasis.

75   *Ibid.*, 15 January 1896 and 5 January 1898.

76   Hollis, *Ladies Elect*, pp. 227–46.

77   Derek Fraser, *The New Poor Law*, has called for this sort of detailed analysis of shifting alliances in boardroom politics.

78   BRO ZHA 17/17, Diary of a Female Poor Law Guardian, 3 April 1895.

79   BRO GBO 12/1-13, Newspaper Cutting Books 1887–1908. On the aspirations of the Independent Labour Party for representation in Bolton see *Bolton Chronicle*, 11 June and 10 September 1892. For training schemes aimed at increasing female working-class involvement in local government, see BRO FW 5/1, Minutes of Bolton Women's Co-operative Guild.

80   *Bolton Chronicle*, 20 January 1922.

81   Poovey, *Uneven Developments*, p. 20.

82   For other examples of local success see Hollis, *Ladies Elect*, p. 233

83   Purvis, "From women worthies", p. 14.

84   Levine, *Feminist Lives*, p. 178.

85   *Bolton Chronicle*, 13 January 1922.

86   See King, "We might be trusted", pp. 27–46.

87   Liddington and Norris, *One Hand*.

88   See Murray, *Strong Minded*, pp. 289–91.

89   On the importance of the local picture, see Lewis, *Women and Social Action*, p. 16.

90   *Bolton Chronicle*, 12 July 1907; BRO GBO 4/60, Minutes of the Bolton Distress Committee 1905–1912.

CHAPTER SIX
Making a Difference

1 On disentangling union accounts see Crowther, "The later years". These broad trends are reconstructed from Bolton Record Office (hereafter BRO) GBO 14/1-9, Financial Statements of Bolton Union.
2 Hennock, *British Social Reform*, pp. 211–96.
3 Harris, *Private Lives*, p. 205.
4 Crowther, *The Workhouse*, pp. 54–87, 135–55 and 222–31.
5 BRO ZHA 17/17, Diary of a Female Poor Law Guardian, 17 March 1895. For nursing in Bolton see BRO GBO 21/1, Register of Nurses Employed. On the issue of workhouse nursing more generally see Crowther, *The Workhouse*, pp. 157–83 and Deane, "Late nineteenth-century", p. 129.
6 On issues around nursing qualifications and practice, see Rafferty, *The Politics*. For the tide of orders affecting Bolton see BRO GBO 15/8, Correspondence and Local Government Orders for Bolton Union.
7 Hollis, *Ladies Elect*, p. 278.
8 Harris, *Private Lives*, p. 201. On the social dilution of boards see Summers, "A home", p. 48.
9 *Ibid.*, p. 195; Hollis, *Ladies Elect*, p. 209.
10 BRO GBO 12/12, Newspaper Cutting Book, 26 September 1901.
11 *Bolton Journal*, 2 February 1917.
12 *Bolton Chronicle*, 4 December 1908; *Bolton Journal*, 11 December 1908; *Bolton Journal*, 18 February 1921.
13 For context see Lewis, *Women and Social Action*.
14 BRO ZHA 17/17, Diary of a Female Poor Law Guardian, 6 December 1899.
15 BRO GBO 10/1-25, Creed Registers, 1869–1930.
16 See *Annual Report of the Bolton Infant Life Protection Society*, 1899. For context on visiting Lewis, "Women and late nineteenth", pp. 78–99.
17 On the Bolton Housing Improvement Trust, see *Bolton Chronicle*, 28 June 1900. For context, Koven, *Slumming*.
18 *Report and Rules of the Bolton Society for the Clothing of the Poor*, 1901.
19 On the District Nursing Association see *Bolton Chronicle*, 9 March 1901.
20 BRO FW 5/1, Minutes of the Bolton Women's Co-operative Guild.
21 *Ibid.*
22 Rubinstein, *Before the Suffragettes*, pp. 167–8; Digby, "Poverty, health", p. 74.
23 Wilson, *Women*, p. 52
24 Hollis, "Women in council", p. 197; Hollis, *Ladies Elect*, pp. 15, 221.
25 Hollis, *Ladies Elect*, p. 219.
26 Rubinstein, *Before the Suffragettes*, p. 168.
27 Digby, "Poverty, health", p. 74.
28 Hollis, *Ladies Elect*, p. 197.
29 *Ibid.*, pp. 250–1 and 282–6.
30 Levine, *Feminist Lives*, p. 107.
31 Hollis, *Ladies Elect*, p. 286.

32 See BRO GBO 23/4, Summary of Relief Returns January 1892–October 1917, which contains annual lists of guardian attendance. For context see Deane, "Late nineteenth-century", p. 137; Crowther, *The Workhouse System*, p. 75.

33 Hollis, *Women in Public*, pp. 243–47.

34 Pankhurst, *My Own*, pp. 25–31.

35 BRO GBO 7/126-27, Indoor Relief Registers; GBO 3/9, Parochial Ledgers 1894–1910, which trace the accounting relationships between the union and its constituent parts. On the database constructed for this project to find distinct recipients, see the previous chapter.

36 BRO GBO/9/151-158, Workhouse Case Books 1895–1910.

37 See Crowther, *The Workhouse*; Williams, *From Pauperism*, pp. 152–232.

38 BRO GBO 8/297-684, Outdoor Relief Lists; BRO GBO 23/4, Summary of Relief Returns January 1892 to January 1917. For context see Hage, Hanneman and Gargan, *State Responsiveness*, figures 1–8.

39 For the history of committees on cottage homes see *Bolton Chronicle*, 11 April 1911.

40 On the general dietary background amongst the Lancashire population see Walton, *Lancashire*, pp. 293–4. Dietary reform did not end the practice of paupers selling surplus food.

41 BRO ZHA 17/17, Diary of a Female Poor Law Guardian, 3 December 1895.

42 BRO GBO 15/8, Correspondence and Orders for Bolton Union, Order 35, 701.

43 BRO ZHA 17/17, Diary of a Female Poor Law Guardian, 24 November 1897.

44 Rose suggests that around a third of all paupers in the later nineteenth century were children. See Rose, *The English*, p. 178.

45 *Bolton Chronicle*, 9 October 1901. Hollis, *Ladies Elect*, p. 260, notes that by 1914 there were 12,000 children boarded out by unions. See also Crowther, *The Workhouse*, p. 70 and Summers, "A home" for a review of the history of boarding out from its origins in 1871.

46 BRO ZHA 17/17, Diary of a Female Poor Law Guardian, 26 June and 1 July 1895.

47 BRO ZFO 7, Some Memoirs of the Early 1900s.

48 Pankhurst, *My Own Story*.

49 BRO ZHA 17/17, Diary of a Female Poor Law Guardian, 23 January and 4 May 1895.

50 *Ibid.*, 9 July 1896.

51 *Ibid.*, 3 December 1895, 18 July, 10 August and 17 August 1898.

52 For the credentials of teachers see BRO GBO 28/1-1077, Personnel Files.

53 BRO ZHA 17/17, Diary of a Female Poor Law Guardian, 9 October 1900, 26 February 1902; Hollis, *Ladies Elect*, p. 263. It is also important to acknowledge that female guardians made many more minor changes to enhance the learning environment, making sure, for instance, that the class-

room was properly heated and convincing the proprietors of the *Bolton Chronicle* to supply the workhouse free of charge.

54 BRO ZHA 17/17, Diary of a Female Poor Law Guardian, 22 May and 4 December 1895.

55 *Ibid.*, 5 August 1895 and 30 October 1900. Also *Bolton Chronicle*, 11 April 1911.

56 BRO ZHA 17/17, Diary of a Female Poor Law Guardian. The history of treatment for these groups can be traced on numerous occasions in the working diary.

57 *Ibid.*, 12 March, 11 July and 15 July 1895.

58 *Ibid.*, 1 November 1899.

59 Annie Beswick, interviewed by John Peacock on 4 January 1977.

60 BRO ZHA 17/17, Diary of a Female Poor Law Guardian, 29 January 1895, 20 October 1897, 3 April 1901. For context see Hollis, Ladies Elect, pp. 247 and 251.

61 I am grateful to Richard Ashworth for access to his family collection.

62 On the clothing of the poor as an indicator of the sentiment of the poor law see Steven King, "Reclothing".

63 BRO ZHA 17/17, Diary of a Female Poor Law Guardian, 25 September 1895.

64 On the importance that female guardians attached to improving facilities in this area, on their use of the rhetoric of motherhood to extend their public role and their criticism of maternal and child welfare policies as a means of critiquing male authority, see Yeo, "Introduction", pp. 1–24; Jones, *Women*, pp. 4–5.

65 BRO GBO 28/1–1077, Personnel Files. The equipment used by these staff also improved markedly. Mary Haslam and Mrs Swan were both on the tenders and contracts committee and so had a substantial say on what equipment was purchased and from whom.

66 Hollis, "Women in council", p. 197.

67 Thane, "Women", pp. 29–51.

68 BRO ZHA 17/17, Diary of a Female Poor Law Guardian, 26 September 1900.

69 *Ibid.*, 24 July 1901. These were measures to deal with tuberculosis. For the developing contemporary thinking behind these policies, see Eyler, "The sick poor", p. 193.

70 For suggestions that this was a wider experience, see Mandler, *The Uses of Charity*; Robin, "The relief", pp. 193–218.

71 This matches up with the definition of power offered by Jones, *Women*, p. 3.

72 On this issue see Summers, "A home", p. 51.

73 *Bolton Journal*, 25 February 1910

74 *Ibid.*

75 *Ibid.*, 20 January 1922

76 This is not a term I use lightly, as indicated in CHAPTER ONE. For a discus-

sion of the term and its contested meaning, see Levine, *Feminist Lives*, pp. 8–73.
77 BRO ZHA 17/17, Diary of a Female Poor Law Guardian, 14 December 1894.
78 On the importance of the education afforded to Unitarian women in their subsequent development of feminist and philanthropic campaigning, see Banks, *Faces of Feminism*, pp. 29–30; Hannam, "Women and politics", pp. 220–1.
79 BRO ZHA 17/8, *Born to Intellectual Freedom*.
80 Hollis, *Ladies Elect*, pp. 462–3.
81 Levine, *Feminist Lives*, pp. 39–40, 60 and 176–7.
82 Thane, "Visions of gender", p. 114.
83 Levine, *Feminist Lives*, p. 73.

CHAPTER SEVEN
Feminism, the Politics of Local Government and Suffrage

1 See Riley, '*Am I That Name?*
2 Digby, "Women's biological straitjacket", pp. 192–220; Jordanova, "Natural facts", pp. 42–69; Lewis, *Women in England*, pp. 81–4.
3 Hamerton, *Cruelty*, p. 164; Levine, "So few prizes", pp. 150–74.
4 Tosh, "The making", p. 54; Purvis, "Reassessing", p. 83;
5 Levine, *Victorian Feminism*, p. 70; Poovey, *Uneven Developments*, pp. 2–3 and 20.
6 On this important issue, see Pateman, "Equality, difference", pp. 17–31, 20; Bock, "Challenging dichotomies"; Alexander, *Becoming a Woman*, p. 145.
7 Lewis, *Women and Social Action*, p. 9.
8 Bolt, *Feminist Ferment*, p. 21.
9 Banks, *Faces*, p. 94.
10 Lewis, *Women in England*, pp. 88–104.
11 Banks, *Faces*, p. 7.
12 Midgley, *Women Against Slavery*.
13 Nym Marshall, "The rhetorics", pp. 55–71.
14 Rendall, "Introduction", p. 22
15 Morgan, *Suffragists*; Caine, *English Feminism*, p. 103.
16 On the links between Liberal and Conservative activists, see Parker, *Women*, p. 306.
17 Levine, *Victorian Feminism*, 70.
18 Hannam, "Women and politics", pp. 228–9.
19 Rover, *Women's Suffrage*, p. 2.
20 Lewis, "Women and late-nineteenth century", pp. 78–81. Of course, some who limited themselves to these spheres nonetheless had as their driving force a woman-centred emphasis and a fundamental critique of the subordinated position of both middle and working-class women. They were in the widest sense of the word "feminist".
21 Bock and Thane, "Introduction", p. 6.
22 Quoted in Murray, *Strong Minded Women*, p. 291.

23 Rubinstein, *Before the Suffragettes*, p. 152.
24 Levine, *Feminist Lives*, p. 82.
25 Holton, *Feminism and Democracy*.
26 See Liddington, *The Life and Times*.
27 See Holton, *Feminism and Democracy*; Pugh, *The March*; Nym Marshall, *The Militant Suffrage*; Rover, *Women's Suffrage*.
28 Holton, *Suffrage Days*.
29 Caine, *English Feminism*, p. 132.
30 Hannam and Hunt, *Socialist Women*. Also, Liddington and Norris, *One Hand*, on working class women in the regions.
31 Symonds, *Inside the Citadel*; Harrison, *Separate Spheres*, pp. 13–24.
32 Jorgensen-Earp, 'The Transfiguring Sword'.
33 Purvis, "Reassessing", pp. 85–6.
34 For a summary see Nym Marshall, *The Militant Suffrage*.
35 Purvis, "From 'women worthies'", pp. 1–22, 14.
36 Maynard, "Privilege and patriarchy", pp. 221–47; Pateman, "The patriarchal".
37 Levine, *Feminist Lives*, p. 73.
38 On this issue see particularly Thane, "Visions of gender", p. 114.
39 See Porter, "Health care", p. 26.
40 Yeo, "Introduction", p. 18.
41 See Hollis, *Pressure From Without*, p. 26.
42 See Hamilton, "Images of femininity", p. 79.
43 John and Eustance, *The Men's Share?*, pp. 5–6.
44 Levine, *Feminist Lives*, 9–15.
45 Sutherland, *Mrs Humphrey Ward*; Herstein, *A Mid-Victorian*; Rubinstein, *A Different World*; Murray, *Strong-Minded Women*; Banks, *Becoming a Feminist*; David, *Intellectual Women*.
46 Rendall, "Friendship and politics", pp. 137–9.
47 Rendall, "Introduction", p. 13.
48 Balshaw, "Sharing the burden", pp. 135–57.
49 Rose, *Parallel Lives*.
50 Hannam, "Women and politics", p. 234.
51 Rendall, "Friendship and politics", p. 163.
52 Hall, *Sex, Gender*, p. 67.
53 On these terms, see Bolt, *Feminist Ferment*, p. 28.
54 Holton, "In sorrowful wrath".
55 Indeed, Spring has suggested that the suffrage campaign was as much a linguistic battle as a real political one. See Spring, "The political platform", p. 160.
56 *Bolton Journal*, 20 January 1922.
57 Liddington and Norris, *One Hand*.
58 Rover, *Women's Suffrage*, p. 61; Kidd, *Manchester*, pp. 180–3. On other important regional concentrations of suffrage activity see Neville, *To Make their Mark*.

59 *Bolton Journal*, 24 November 1894.
60 Bolton Record Office (hereafter BRO) ZHA 23/1, *Women's Suffrage in Bolton*.
61 *Bolton Guardian*, 20 January 1922.
62 *Bolton Journal*, 8 December 1894.
63 *Bolton Chronicle*, 11 November 1906.
64 *Bolton Chronicle*, 21 December 1906. For the activities of Sarah Reddish in 1906, making similar points to a rally in Hyde Park, see *Bolton Journal*, 25 May 1906.
65 Webb, *The Woman*, pp. 96–104.
66 For context see Lawson, Savage and Warde, "Gender".
67 BRO ZHA 23/1, *Women's Suffrage in Bolton*.
68 Unpopular with women as well as men. On the general difficulties of starting or restarting a campaign see Hollis, *Pressure from Without*, p. 16. On the particular difficulties of getting suffrage societies established, see Caine, *English Feminism*, pp. 146–65. These comments, in line with the wider literature, also highlight the importance, even at local level, of personality in advancing feminist causes.
69 *Bolton Journal*, 20 January 1922.
70 See Levine, *Feminist Lives*.
71 *Bolton Evening News*, 7 November 1909.
72 Pugh, "Working class", p. 791.
73 *Bolton Chronicle*, 26 February 1909. Also *Bolton Journal*, 12 July 1907.
74 *Bolton Chronicle*, 21 July 1905.
75 See for instance reports in *Bolton Chronicle*, 31 August 1906.
76 *Bolton Chronicle*, 13 September 1907; 22 March 1907; 8 March 1907.
77 There is a considerable literature on the birth of the national suffrage movement, though less on the role of local societies like this. For a brief introduction, see Smith, *The British*, and for a useful time-line of women's organisations Harrison, *Prudent Revolutionaries*, pp. 4–5. Also Hulme, *The National*. For recent feminist reinterpretations see Joannou and Purvis, *The Women's Suffrage*. On the different theoretical approaches to justifying the female vote – equality, equality with difference, the women's mission, maternalism – see Bolt, *Feminist Ferment*, pp. 8–48 and 90. An excellent regional study is Liddington and Norris, *One Hand*.
78 BRO ZHA 23/1, *Women's Suffrage in Bolton*.
79 *Bolton Chronicle*, 12 June 1908.
80 The annual report of the Society puts the figure at 2200. See BRO FW 2/4, Printed Annual Reports of the Bolton Women's Suffrage Association.
81 These were exactly the sorts of tactics used by Liberal women in their campaigning and electoral canvassing work on behalf of the Liberal party and in elections for poor law guardians in the later nineteenth century. See Levine, *Feminist Lives*, pp. 107–20.
82 What does not come out from this text or the annual report was that Mary Haslam and her daughter divided the town into four divisions, with

campaign teams rotating between the divisions on a weekly basis. The Association also took on a paid organiser, Jane Schofield. See BRO FW 2/1, Bolton Women's Suffrage Association Minute Book.

83 BRO ZHA 23/1, *Women's Suffrage in Bolton.* The campaign was supported by a series of publicity stunts on the part of Bolton suffragists. See *Bolton Evening News*, 19 January 1910.

84 The Minutes for this year noted that "only 318 were indifferent or against votes for women". BRO FW 2/1, Bolton Women's Suffrage Association Minute Book. In comparison with other places, this was an excellent return. See Holton, *Feminism and Democracy.*

85 BRO ZHA 23/1, *Women's Suffrage in Bolton.* Helped by the fact, not acknowledged here, that such associate members had a lower subscription rate. See BRO FW 2/1, Bolton Women's Suffrage Association Minute Book.

86 *Bolton Journal,* 6 November 1908.

87 BRO ZHA 23/1, *Women's Suffrage in Bolton.*

88 This statement reflects strongly Mary Haslam's view that considered and reasoned argument, carefully applied to situations in which there were fault lines other than gender, would eventually achieve more than radical action. The relative absence of militant suffragism (though see below) in Bolton should not really surprise us, for as Banks in 1981 and Holton subsequently have pointed out, both wings of the movement shared by the late 1900s the same basic goal in terms of a limited extension of the franchise, diverging only on tactics. Banks, *Faces of Feminism,* p. 126; Holton, *Suffrage Days.* Also Caine, *English Feminism,* who argues that radical working-class suffragists from the north of England disliked militant tactics.

89 *Bolton Evening News,* 21 March 1907.

90 *Ibid.,* 19 January 1910.

91 There was also a more radical side to the campaign, which included pouring oil into post boxes and defacing public property. See *Bolton Evening News,* 15 March 1913.

92 BRO ZHA 23/1, *Women's Suffrage in Bolton.* The pool of applicants was "considerable". See BRO FW 2/2, Bolton Women's Suffrage Association Minute Book. Mrs Blincoe was the activist who dogged A. H. Gill M.P. at all of his public meetings in Bolton. See *Bolton Evening News,* 27 Feb. 1913.

93 BRO ZHA 23/1, *Women's Suffrage in Bolton.* The annual report notes that "From the Manchester Federation Report on the newspapers in this district it appears that twenty-four are friendly, twenty not particularly friendly, but giving fair reports, while only six are unfriendly". See BRO FW 2/4, Printed Annual Reports of the Bolton Women's Suffrage Association. On newspapers and suffrage more generally, see Harrison, *Separate Spheres.* The Bolton suffragists were skilled at giving the newspapers juicy headlines. Mrs Lloyd repeated her 1910 escapade with the lions in 1912 and got front page coverage. *Bolton Evening News,* 5 March 1912.

94 BRO B324.3, *Pioneers! O Pioneers!: A Survey of the Bolton Women Citizens' Association 19181–1950.*

95 BRO ZHA 23/1, *Women's Suffrage in Bolton*. For context see Nym Marshall, *The Militant Suffrage*; Pugh, *The March*.

96 Liddington and Norris, *One Hand*.

97 There is support here for Maynard's conclusion that members of the women's movement were not simply 'doing' on a variety of fronts but instead constructing an overarching critique of women's position, seeking "an interrelated framework of explanation" and seeing the solution in absolute equality. See Maynard, "Privilege and patriarchy", pp. 237–42.

98 BRO B324.3, *Pioneers! O Pioneers!: A Survey of the Bolton Women Citizens' Association 19181–1950*. Of course, the formation of the society must be seen in the context of the development of a much wider concept of national and local citizenship between 1900 and 1914. See Harris, *Private Lives*, pp. 180–4; Finlayson, *Citizen, State*.

99 For the national context on the fate of local suffrage societies, see Hannam, *Isabella Ford*, pp. 188, 196, who notes the disappointment of Ford that young post-war women did not campaign for a lowering of the voting age for women. Also Pugh, "Politicians", p. 372 and Bolt, *Feminist Ferment*, pp. 54 and 61.

100 On the overarching theoretical framework, see Caine, *English Feminism*, p. 166.

101 BRO B324.3, *Pioneers! O Pioneers!: A Survey of the Bolton Women Citizens' Association 19181–1950*.

102 *Bolton Journal*, 20 January 1922.

103 BRO B324.3, *Pioneers! O Pioneers!: A Survey of the Bolton Women Citizens' Association 19181–1950*.

104 *Bolton Journal*, 20 January 1922.

Part II
Born to Intellectual Freedom? The Records of Mary Haslam, Bolton Activist

CHAPTER EIGHT
Brief Autobiographical Notes Written by Mary Haslam

1 On the source genre and its problems, see Vincent, *Bread, Knowledge*; Burnett, *Destiny Obscure*, pp. 1–16; Rogers, *Women and the People*, pp. 242–6.

2 For the biographical approach to women and public activism, see Lewis, *Women and Social Action*; Harrison, *Prudent Revolutionaries*; Levine, *Feminist Lives*. For more complete autobiographical work, see Pankhurst, *My Own Story*.

3 The proposal to make Mary Haslam a freeman of the borough was curtailed by her death. Only eleven men, all of then prominent philanthropists, had been proposed for or granted freeman status by 1922. See Hamer, *Bolton*, p. 156.

4 Mary Haslam's working diary indicates that she attended 586 meetings and

conferences between 1894 and 1900, in addition to hosting dinners and her other political, campaigning and philanthropic work.

5   See, for instance, Levine, *Feminist Lives*; Nym Marshall, *The Militant Suffrage*; Deane, "Late nineteenth century", pp. 122–42.

6   Dyhouse, *Feminism*, pp. 5–6, 14–16.

7   *Ibid.*, pp. 19–21, 28–33.

8   Haslam, *Women's Suffrage*, Foreword.

9   Banks, *Becoming a Feminist*, p. 35; Dyhouse, *Feminism*.

10 For contextual material on the events of their childhood, see the comprehensive Heywood diaries. BRO ZHE 71/1-51, The Heywood Diaries. Also Lancashire Record Office DDX 492/2/23 and 51, Haslam Genealogies.

11 *Bolton Journal*, 19 August 1910. For negotiations over his monumental inscription, see BRO ZHE 72/81, Draft Monumental Inscriptions.

12 This brief sentence indicates one of the major problems with autobiographical sources as it is inconsistent with the opening statement.

13 Born in 1786, Robert Heywood had inherited his father's quilting business. From 1822, when he got his first partner, Heywood was involved in travel and local philanthropic work. As we saw in CHAPTER THREE, he was a magistrate, borough councillor, Alderman and Mayor of Bolton 1839–40. See Brown, *Robert Heywood*.

14 The word "taste" and the later observation that that habits were "formed" chimes with Levine's conclusion that most activist women came from family backgrounds that inculcated an interest in public duties, citizenship and philanthropy. See Levine, *Feminist Lives*, p. 15.

15 An assertion borne out by the variety of documents signed and meetings held at the Heywood home and recorded in BRO ZHE 63, 68, 70 and 72.

16 For contextual literature on growing up in Victorian families, see Jordan, *Victorian Childhood*; Dyhouse, *Girls Growing up*; Mintz, *A Prison*.

17 It is this essential pragmatism that we see played out in Mary Haslam's working diary, and in her work on the board of guardians.

18 For more on the general context of women's education, see Purvis, *A History*; Hunt, *Lessons for Life*; Hunt, *Gender and Policy*. For a comparative perspective, and on women attending lectures and seminars, see Fuchs and Thompson, *Women*, pp. 84–100.

19 See BRO ZHE 72/78, Records of the Burial of Robert Heywood 1868 and his Widow Elizabeth. This was clearly a heartfelt loss. Later in her life, Mary Haslam would fund plaques to her father's memory and she privately published some of his many travel diaries. See Heywood, *A Journey to Italy*; Heywood, *A Journey to America*; Heywood, *A Journey to the Levant*; Heywood, *A Journey in Russia*. How to interpret this sense of loss is complex. While her father was a supporter of more access to education and health care for women, there is little evidence of the close and supportive father–daughter relationship that fostered the development of feminist ideas amongst other nineteenth-century women activists. See Banks, *Becoming a Feminist*.

20 For the marriage notice, see BRO ZHE 70, Marriage Notice. On the economic context into which she had married see BRO ZHA 16, John Haslam and Co. Ltd., 1816–1920. Dyhouse, echoing Banks, suggests that feminist women "sought husbands broadly sympathetic to their views". There is little evidence here that Mary had done much by way of active seeking. See Dyhouse, *Feminism*, pp. 39–40.

21 For the genealogy of the Haslam family, see ZHE 70/9, Typescript Notes by Mary Haslam and Sir S. H. Scott Relating to Haslam Family Origins. For contextual literature on parent-child and other intra- and inter-generational relationships in the Victorian period, see O'Day, *The Family* and Abbott, *Family Ties*.

22 Such a phrase, suggesting that Haslam could compartmentalise her public and campaigning work into different boxes, rather than identifying them as one collective activity, suggests the necessity of switching our attention from the best known and most public campaigners if we are to understand the nuances and feminist credentials of the nineteenth- and twentieth-century women's movement.

23 On the life histories and experiences of other feminist and women activists, see Gordon and Nair, *Public Lives*; Hollis, *Ladies Elect*; Banks, *Becoming a Feminist*; Dyhouse, *Feminism*.

24 These personal diaries have not apparrently survived.

25 Her mother lived in Newton Terrace, Whitebank, Bolton. Caine's view that "cross-generational relationships between feminists and their mothers are only just beginning to be explored" remains as valid today as in 1999. We know little about the nature of the mother daughter relationship here. Mary's mother was active in Bolton philanthropy in the 1840s and 1850s, but her feminist credentials were strictly limited. There is little evidence of the "generational gap in outlook and aspirations" between mother and daughter traced for other feminists by Dyhouse, *Feminism*, p. 28. See Caine, "Mothering feminism", pp. 295.

26 Died aged 72 in 1917. See *Bolton Journal*, 2 February 1917. In 1915, William Haslam had transferred 1,000 £10 shares in his company to each of his three sons. See BRO ZHA 1, Letter and Agreement, 19 February, 1915.

27 The phrase "indifferent" hints at some of the tensions generated by balancing personal and family life with public duty. In this case, however, both parties were prominent public activists. For contextual material see Dyhouse, *Feminism*; Tosh, *A Man's Place*.

28 Any further notes do not survive.

CHAPTER NINE
Diary Kept by Mary Haslam of her Work as a Poor Law Guardian

1 The diary initially records the activity of the Workhouse Visiting Committee. On the workhouse visiting movement, see Summers, "A home", pp. 33–63.

2 Workhouse discipline remained a key problem in the later nineteenth century. See Crowther, *The Workhouse*.

3   The guardians acceded to this request. See BRO GBO 14/9, Guardian Financial Statements. On maternalist policies more generally see contributions to Bock and Thane, *Maternity*.

4   For context see Abel-Smith, *A History*. While provincial unions in general came in for sustained criticism of their treatment of sick paupers in the 1890s, those in Bolton were among the 16 per cent of the 73,000 sick poor nationally to be located in separate infirmaries. See Wood, *Poverty*, pp. 137–8. Also BRO Hfa 1/1, Register of Patients Admitted to the Farnworth Infectious Diseases Hospital 1896–1924.

5   In Ireland.

6   The segregation unit for those with venereal disease. It is perhaps important to note here how Mary Haslam generates consensus not conflict over reform by talking extensively to those most interested or affected.

7   The question of staff quality was a vexed one in the public forum of pamphlets and newspapers and the private forum of the board of guardians.

8   On perceptions of the need to give workhouse residents respect, dignity, comfort and stimulation, see Koven and Michel, "Womanly duties".

9   Mrs Davis was the matron.

10 On pauper education, see Crompton, *Workhouse Children*.

11 This was an erroneous report.

12 In 1870, one of the last acts of the Poor Law Board was to issue an order that allowed boarding out. By the late 1870s official sanction had also been given to another method of coping with pauper children: cottage homes. These were small-scale residential units overseen by foster-parents. By 1893, this idea had been refined further with the introduction of scattered homes, which placed children in individual units within the wider community. Crompton, *Workhouse Children*. On the history of cottage homes in Bolton see *Bolton Chronicle*, 11 April 1911. Also BRO GBO 9/133a, Register of Children Adopted 1888–1947.

13 Even at this date, many unions employed no paid cook.

14 In 1911, still only 48 per cent of sick paupers nationally were housed in separate infirmaries, and Bolton was one of the few unions to instigate the isolation of consumption cases before 1900. For context Hodgkinson, *The Origins*.

15 While pauper lives are not in the direct focus of this book, this episode demonstrates a significant point: that many of those experiencing indoor relief were doing so only temporarily.

16 The question of how to treat pauper lunatics was the fourth major issue for the poor law alongside children, the sick and the old. For context Peter Bartlett, *The Poor Law*.

17 These and other measures to govern the boarding out of children had been circulated regularly to boards of guardians by the LGB since the mid-1880s.

18 Mainly servants and the mothers of illegitimate children. See also BRO FW 6/1, Minutes of the Bolton Committee for the Reclamation of Unfortunate Women and BRO FW 6/5, Case Histories.

19   By 1897, the LGB had issued orders that all infirmaries with more than three nurses had to employ a superintendent nurse with three years training. The demands of the Workhouse Visiting Committee clearly predate this. By 1901, Burnley had four qualified nurses and thirty-two probationers. The figures for Bolton were eight and forty respectively. Burnley did not get a resident doctor until 1902, seven years after Bolton. See Crowther, *The Workhouse*, and BRO 362.1/B01, Bolton District Nursing Association Annual Reports.

20   Crowther, *The Workhouse*, p. 157, suggests that even by 1900 just forty-four unions had resident medical officers. The successful outcome of this demand, outlined later in the diary, places Bolton at the forefront of medical provision at union level.

21   It appears to have been usual to defend the union doctor simply because conditions were often so bad as to make it hard to find someone else in the event of dismissal.

22   See CHAPTER FOUR for more detail.

23   *Ibid.*

24   The pay and conditions of workhouse nurses was poor throughout the late nineteenth century. Louisa Twining had founded the Workhouse Nursing Association in 1879 to provide trained nurses to workhouses, but demand out-stripped supply and dropout rates were marked, leading to initiatives to enhance the pay of nurses and their hours, clothing and lodgings in an attempt to attract better recruits.

25   Contrast this with the ideas outlined at various points in this volume that female visitors and guardians had a tense relationship with workhouse staff.

26   See CHAPTER FOUR, which offer more details on the campaign.

27   Sectional relief committees were established – against the will and advice of the LGB which feared divergence of practice, a weakening of the union and indiscriminate alms giving – to allow the guardians of each district to deal with applications for outdoor relief. In effect this gave women a much smaller forum in which to develop an influence on the important issue of relief policies. Other women do not appear to have been able or interested in extending their influence in these spheres. See Lewis, *Women in England*.

28   As per the recommendations of the Workhouse Visiting Committee in the previous year.

29   In other unions, women appear to have been excluded from these key fact finding conferences.

30   The tramp/vagrant was a perennial thorn in the side of poor law unions and the LGB by the later nineteenth century. For a survey, see Vorspan, "Vagrancy".

31   This was a private visit, and reflects Mary Haslam's desire to be familiar with the best or worst poor law practices.

32   Jenner Fust was the LGB inspector. In fact, the overall average of paupers to nurses was only around 30:1. For the new arrangements see BRO GBO 9/151, Workhouse Admission Register 1895–97.

33 As per the recommendation of the Workhouse Visiting Committee in the previous year.

34 Mr Dearden frequently opposed expenditure. The astonishment was not the sudden paring of the short list, but the fact that Mr Dearden had dropped his opposition to this post per se. For more on Dearden and the other guardians see BRO GBO 13/4, List of Guardians 1896–97.

35 This extremely important committee, on which half the members were women, absorbed a significant minority of union expenditure.

36 Again, an important sub-committee on which female guardians constituted one half of the membership.

37 See BRO 361/BOL, Reports of the Bolton Society for Befriending Young Servants.

38 It is significant that the sub-committee shaping the single most important piece of expenditure after 1880 contained four women. See BRO 362.5/BOL, Bolton Union Year books, 1880–1948.

39 For an extended discussion of this incident, see CHAPTER FIVE.

40 See BRO ZZ 474, Board Photograph.

41 Such hostility is not framed in the guardian minutes on this issue. In the end both Haslam and Orrell sit on this committee, testimony to the expert way in which they managed gender tension when in broke out.

42 Along with entertainments offered by theatre companies, local businessmen and others, the activities of female poor law guardians in taking people out of the workhouse for these special treats suggests that pauper lives in Bolton were not as rigid and dull as they appear to have been in some nineteenth-century rural unions.

43 Watkinson and Thwaites were male guardians. Cooper was the son of the clerk to the board.

44 In France.

45 This is a key decision, and one that highlights the complexity of the power relationships on the board, which were rather wider and more divisive than just gender. The guardians united in their condemnation of the LGB on this matter.

46 The workhouse in Ashton, presumably a fact-finding trip.

47 Cooper was the clerk to the board, and a key player in much poor law activity. Mary Haslam appears to have courted Cooper as an ally against some of the more intransigent guardians.

48 Religious groups like the Roman Catholics proved eager to remove children of their denomination from the odour of the workhouse. Tottington, near Manchester, was home to a large Catholic school. See BRO GBO 10/1-25, Creed Registers, 1869–1930.

49 This statement is the first indication of implicit tension within the ranks of female guardians themselves. Richenda Ashworth was an outspoken critic of indoor relief structures in Bolton and her attacks were often in very public forums.

50 Again, evidence of Mary Haslam's strategy of carrying workhouse staff with

her. For more on the hostility evoked elsewhere, see Lewis, "Women, social work".

51 BRO GBO 362.5 BOL, Bolton Union Year Book, 1895.

52 This reflects the perennial problem of the seasonality of relief, which in a bad winter – as this was – could overwhelm even the best run poor law administration.

53 Financed with a loan of £2,371. See BRO GBO 14/9, Financial statements, 1905–1908, which contains a full listing of all loans drawn down and repaid from 1876.

54 Ellis Lee was a guardian and small machine maker. RO in this case means the relieving officer, who she had accused of being corrupt and incompetent. This willingness to acknowledge mistakes was perhaps a key factor in stimulating the respect that the board came to have for Mary Haslam.

55 See BRO GBO 4/22, Minutes of the Workhouse Committee 1896.

56 The union nurse's home at this time.

57 For context on the management of staff, see Crowther, *The Workhouse.*

58 More information gathering. Despite the resolution that the board should not send a deputation to this conference (which she supported), Mary Haslam went under her own impetus.

59 Mary Haslam's membership of this committee confirms the perspectives of CHAPTERS FIVE and SIX that female guardians in Bolton were not confined simply to matters of "municipal housekeeping".

60 Watkinson was a chemist, Heywood a cotton spinner, Graveson an ironmonger and Kearsley a butcher. This mix of substantial and petty ratepayers introduced an alternative focus of dispute within guardian relationships. Haslam's prioritization of the fabric of the union in her endeavours is clearly reflected here. However, she was co-opted onto other committees because of her vigorous pursuit of reform. Interestingly, the fact that this meeting also sanctioned the purchase of 6 corn mills and an oat crushing machine to put the able-bodied poor to work appears to have escaped the recording process. See BRO GBO 4/22, Minutes of the Workhouse Committee 1896.

61 But the cottage school keeper was still warned about physical punishment of those consigned to her care. See GBO 4/22, Minutes of the Workhouse Committee 1896.

62 The female poor law guardians seem to have been much more active in proposing, supporting and opposing motions than it has become usual to allow.

63 A union in Hampshire.

64 Subsequently overturned by a new vote.

65 This bland entry disguises the fact that the workhouse sub-committee on this day agreed to buy six water beds. In addition, permission was given for children from cottage homes to be entertained by Mary Haslam and Richenda Ashworth, and the annual seaside holiday for pauper children was approved. See BRO GBO 4/22, Minutes of the Workhouse Committee 1896.

66 A spindle maker.

67 A clear sign of gender antagonizm. However, in the totality of the diary these instances are comparatively rare.

68 In her absence, it was agreed that Susannah Swan and Richenda Ashworth should form part of a deputation to Blackburn, Chorlton and Bradford unions to investigate ways of improving the laundry process in Bolton.

69 In Southport, Ashton and Manchester.

70 Mozley was the union teacher.

71 The workhouse sub-committee had suggested new rules on visiting after an incident on 15 July when a visitor has assaulted the superintendent nurse. The new rules specified that visits must be in public and could only happen on the first and third Saturday or second and fourth Wednesday in the month, between the hours of two and four pm.

72 Cunliffe was himself a guardian.

73 See BRO ZHA 17/10, Account of a trip to Brittany.

74 Also at this meeting a proposal that the midget Minstrels entertain the paupers at the Temperance Hall was accepted. Workhouse children were allowed to attend the Lostock agricultural show.

75 This cottage home keeper was ill with breast cancer. At this meeting, the Great Lever Gardener and Poultry Keepers Association invited the workhouse children to their first annual show.

76 BRO GBO 15, Bolton Union Correspondence and LGB Circulars.

77 This was an important sub-committee in terms of staff relations and management, testimony once again to the reach of the female guardians compared to those who form the core of the sample in Patricia Hollis, *Ladies Elect*.

78 Guardians were not obliged to contribute to superannuation or given power to levy a contribution from the officer until 1894.

79 The offer of St Marks Sunday School Athletics Club to give an entertainment at the workhouse was also accepted at this meeting.

80 An expansion in the range (if not the pay) of officers, meant that there was a more or less continuous absolute increase in the amount spent on salaries

81 See discussion of this issue in CHAPTER FIVE.

82 Francis Shippobottom, clothier and outfitter, and Thomas Ward, wholesale smallware merchant, were the archetypal "rate-savers" highlighted by Emmeline Pankhurst as dominating other boards. See Pankhurst, *My Own Story*.

83 At the meeting of the workhouse sub-committee this day, the offer of Dole Street Mission choir to give an entertainment at the workhouse was accepted. There was also an uprating of salaries as per the recommendation of a special committee on this matter meeting over the previous two months. BRO GBO 4/22, Minutes of the Workhouse Committee 1896.

84 See reporting of this in BRO GBO, 4/22, Minutes of the Workhouse Committee 1896.

85 BRO Hfa 1/1, Register of Patients Admitted to the Farnworth Infectious Diseases Hospital 1896–1924.

86 Mary Haslam had given a speech on the administration of outdoor relief.

87 All but six of the seats on the board were opposed at this election. See *Bolton Journal*, 23 March, 1897.

88 Part of a larger review of the terms and conditions of union officers, originally instigated by Mary Haslam.

89 For reporting of this see BRO GBO, 4/23, Minutes of the Workhouse Committee 1897.

90 The proposal was to scale back allowances of bacon, beer and bread but increase the input of cheese, meat and potatoes.

91 John Watkinson, chemist and druggist. John Haslam, cotton spinner and brother-in-law to Mary Haslam.

92 Cunliffe was adamantly opposed to giving pauper children an advantage in education or training compared to children of the independent labouring poor, testimony to wide ideological divisions on the board.

93 Robert Fairclough, insurance agent. This substantial vote in favour might be seen to make the final turning point in gender relations on the Bolton board.

94 Much of Cunliffe's dogged opposition is mollified after this episode.

95 The national association rather than the local society.

96 In this Mary Haslam allied herself with people like Cunliffe and Dearden, testimony to the shifting sands of alliance at board level.

97 Job specifications for nursing staff were very imprecise. See GBO 28/1-1077, Bolton Union Personnel Files; BRO GBO 21/1, Register of Nurses Employed by Bolton Union.

98 Mrs Ashworth was of course correct. Pauper help in the hospital and the workhouse more generally had been slowly wound down in line with the expectations of the LGB. These comments are perhaps an index of the degree to which butchers and other minor tradesmen found it difficult to keep up with the actual practice of their own poor law institutions.

99 Also at this meeting, Mr Samuel Hough was thanked for entertaining the workhouse children with tea and games.

100 Only three other unions in Lancashire had a paid and resident engineer at this date.

101 The guardians had purchased the estate adjoining the workhouse (Townley's) for £10,000 in November 1894. Much of the land was used for new building (including the nursing homes referred to earlier in the diary), but working gardens were also laid out.

102 At an eventual cost of £384.

103 Ellis Crompton was a farmer. The exchanges at the board indicate that even the minor urban ratepayers were strongly critical of the farming lobby.

104 For a discussion of the motion and the remarks see CHAPTER FIVE.

105 Though for bitter opening remarks see BRO GBO 4/24, Minutes of the Workhouse Committee 1898.

106 There were no written rules on line-management for staff in Bolton union.

107 See BRO GBO 12/12, Newspaper Cutting book 1894–1901.

108 The issue of whether or not to grant paupers beer at Christmas is one which appears to have attracted annual dispute in many unions and points to

entrenched temperance interests on many boards. See McCord, "Ratepayers", pp. 21–35.

109 At the same meeting it was agreed to allow an extra 3oz bread, half oz of butter and 1 pint of tea to women who volunteered to work in the laundry.

110 A continuation of his personal crusade started earlier in the year.

111 William Cranshaw was a hop merchant. See BRO GBO 13/4, Bolton Union List of Guardians and Paid Officers 1878–1902.

112 See discussion of this incident in CHAPTER FIVE.

113 No children were found for the Indefatigable. The guardians *asked* prospective candidates, but all declined.

114 For context on the expansion of nursing provision, see CHAPTER SIX.

115 In her absence, the Board accepted the offer of Miss Barnett to supply a library for the tramp ward and noted the recommendation of Jenner Fust that vagrants should be subject to a labour test and that there should be a separate room for sorting in the laundry.

116 At the Board it was also noted that "the large increase in the number of sick poor admitted to the workhouse renders it desirable that every possible care should be exercised by the sectional relief committees with a view to only such being sent to the workhouse as cannot be treated at their own home". The corollary of this was generous outdoor medical relief in the union.

117 Mary Haslam's son.

118 This short note belies an important contextual event: a motion from Leyland and Dearden that expenditure on drugs in the last three years had been excessive was defeated by fifteen votes to seven.

119 Co-option to the board of guardians had been an option since 1894 and other unions appear to have adopted it willingly.

120 In opposition to compulsory vaccination.

121 George Richardson was a Cooper.

122 They also discussed new work tasks for indoor and outdoor paupers, as per the instructions of the LGB, and the annual seaside holiday for children in cottage homes was approved.

123 The Gilchrist amendment said "It is undesirable, irrational and illegal for this board to make or advise any structural changes to be made at the workhouse without first having a recommendation from the workhouse committee to that effect".

124 A letter was received from the LGB suggesting this measure on the 24 August. See BRO GBO 15, Bolton Union Correspondence and Orders.

125 See discussion of this resolution in CHAPTER FIVE.

126 This entry fails to mention other important business. First, new rules for giving outdoor relief were framed and transmitted to sectional relief chairs. This in effect liberalized criteria for out relief and would have allowed more people to remain outside the workhouse. Second, James Tonge instigated a debate on the issue of old age pensions and whether Bolton union should support the need for them. For context see Martin Pugh, "Working class".

127 £10 was also given to the Horwich District Nursing Association.

128 In Genoa.
129 But only after a motion to defer the decision until the April meeting (proposed by Dearden and George Richardson) was defeated.
130 Tonge was a brewer. A subscription of £5 5s. to the Little Hulton Distrct Nursing Association was also renewed.
131 In the appointment round, female guardians failed to gain a place on just three of the twelve sub-committees. These were the assessment, finance and stationary committees. Mary Haslam was subsequently co-opted onto the finance committee.
132 Entry missing. The guardian minutes suggest that the only significant event was the passing of a motion calling on the government to frame pension legislation by twenty-three votes to five.
133 The new vagrant ward was opened this day. The board also framed a motion "to tender to Mrs Greg their sincere sympathy on the loss of her most highly respected husband, the late Mr Arthur Greg who for some years was the guardian for the Turton township of this union and for many years an ex-officio member of the assessment committee".
134 The only significant item of business was in Mr Shippobottom's motion to know the per capita cost of workhouse care for the last half year and that regular reporting of this matter should become usual. See BRP GBO 24/7, Bolton Union Workhouse Costs Per Capita 1885–1911.
135 The board also agreed to send a deputation to Whttingham Asylum to look at their "Disinfectors", to see whether the same could be used in the Bolton Tramp Wards.
136 The frustration with a refusal to confront failing on the part of some salaried staff is palpable, and a regular feature of this diary.
137 Mr Shaw was an oyster dealer.
138 Deputations of guardians had been visiting union piggeries all over the north-west for the previous six months to identify the best design!
139 On the Brabazon scheme see *Bolton Journal*, 19 January 1901.
140 At this meeting the proposal to build a new nurses home was referred back yet again to the workhouse sub-committee on account of cost (£200 per nurse accommodated) and probable increase in rates, with the suggestion that the project is either postponed or re-modeled. This ongoing saga was not resolved until later in the year.
141 Percy Knott was a chemist.
142 Clipped into the diary at this point there is a newspaper cutting which reads as follows: "Workhouse Committees proceedings of the 8th & 15th instant, including: (a) Proposed purchase of new engine for Laundry, £198; (b) Fixing the value of the emoluments of Master and Matron of the workhouse at £100 for furnished residence, and allowing £70 per annum as at present in lieu of rations; the salary for the Master to be £150 per annum, with annual increases, if the Guardians so determine, of £10 to a maximum of £200; and for the Matron £80 per annum, with annual increases, if the Guardians so determine, of £5 to a maximum of £100". *Bolton Chronicle*, 15 May 1901.

143 Reported in *Bolton Journal*, 2 August 1901.
144 Reported in *Bolton Journal*, 27 September 1901.
145 Subsequently granted. By this date there were sixteen patients to every nurse, significantly below the figure for other Lancashire unions.
146 The language is significant here, suggesting that Mary Haslam had real power.
147 See the report on withdrawal from this institution in *Bolton Journal*, 18 July 1902.
148 BRO ZHA 17/11, Diary of a Trip to Italy 1902.
149 The language is again important here.
150 See Pugh, "Working class".
151 BRO ZHA 17/12, Diary of a Trip to Italy.
152 In practice, the union had been running a version of the case paper system for the last three years. For background on the system, see Crowther, *The Workhouse*.
153 Sent by male and female guardians. These letters and cards are pasted into the diary.
154 In short, Haslam was still writing back to Bolton about poor law matters when she was on holiday.
155 The diary ends here. There was clearly a subsequent volume, but it does not appear to have survived.

CHAPTER TEN
The Travel Diaries of Mary Haslam

1 See CHAPTER EIGHT.
2 There is an extensive literature on intrepid women travellers. For their own words and perspectives, see the excellent volume by Morris, *The Virago Book*.
3 Revill and Wrigley, "Introduction", pp. 1–23.
4 There are other travel diaries. These have been transcribed but lack of space prevents their reproduction. Transcripts are available in electronic form from the archive of the Centre for Health, Medicine and Society. See Bolton Record Office (hereafter BRO) ZHA 17/10, Diary of a Trip to Brittany, 1896; BRO ZHA 17/11, Diary of a Journey to Italy, 1902; BRO ZHA 17/12, Diary of a Trip to Italy, 1903.
5 Buzard, *The Beaten Track*.
6 Clifford, "Travelling cultures", p. 106.
7 BRO ZHA 17/2, Diary of a Trip to Ireland, 1899.
8 Though Bolton at this time was not in a much better state, as we saw in CHAPTER TWO.
9 While there is no entry for 18 August, William Haslam (Jnr), who kept a diary on the same journey, notes that the Haslam party went to see Trinity College and buy fishing tackle. During the excursion William noted the "queerest street I have ever seen", where "The roofs of the houses had holes in them not a single house had glass in the windows . . . The people had made

the houses larger by adding another room on the ground floor so blocking up the footpath". See BRO ZHA 17/3, Diary of a Journey to Ireland by William Haslam.

10 The disparity with William Haslam's diary entry of the same events is important. He notes that on the way up to the quarry "a crowd of little children ran out and saw that we were picking up pieces of marble and tried to give us some", while on the way back "the children following us and picking flowers to give us". In light of the institutionalized nature of welfare in Ireland and a denuded economy of makeshifts, it is likely that such gifts were indeed a begging mechanism. See Crossman, "The humanization", pp. 229–50.

11 (W)illiam Haslam, Mary's husband, (R)obert Haslam and (O)liver Haslam, both her sons.

12 On travel in the nineteenth century, see Revill and Wrigley, "Introduction".

13 There is no reference to this visit in the diary of William Haslam.

14 National debates about poverty and the appropriate state and charitable welfare responses were increasingly informed by a pan-European and international information network. So called "philanthropic tourism" was common from the 1850s as were formal delegations sent out from English parishes and unions to investigate alternative welfare systems. The fact that Haslam took time out from a family holiday to investigate the state of the local workhouse is a reflection of the importance she attached to her work with the poor, her humanitarian sentiment and a desire to garner information that might be of use in subsequent welfare debates in Bolton. For philanthropic tourism and the development of pan-European information networks, see Cunningham, "Introduction", pp. 1–14; Crossman, "The humanization"; Hennock, British Social Reform.

15 A point also made by Crossman, "The humanization"; Brandes, "'Odious, degrading", pp. 199–228.

16 For a chronology of Irish legislation and the function of workhouse infirmaries and open general hospitals, see Crossman, Local Government; Crossman, "Welfare and nationality".

17 William Haslam notes that they "grumbled at the Hotel".

18 Once again, testimony to Mary Haslam's deep interest in questions of social welfare. As CHAPTER THREE showed, Haslam had equally strong interests in the housing situation of labouring people in Bolton.

19 On Irish emigration, see Fitzpatrick, Irish Emigration; Kennedy, The Irish; Kinealy, The Great.

20 On the United Irish League and the wider landscape of Irish politics, see Rees, Nationalism; Mitchell, Labour; O'Brien, William O'Brien.

21 According to William Haslam's diary entry, the party were journeying to Sligo for most of the day.

22 The day had been spent, according to William Haslam, driving around Loch Gill. He noted "The cottages were nicely kept compared to those we had seen in Conemara". Of course, it is no surprise that national politics should take

up so much of this diary entry given Mary Haslam's growing suffrage work and work for the Liberal Party in Bolton at this time.

23   The diary ends here, though the family stayed in Ireland until 5 September, when they traveled back to Holyhead.

CHAPTER ELEVEN

The Women's Suffrage in Bolton

1   Haslam, *Women's Suffrage*.

2   Mildred Haslam. There is some support here for Levine's view that there was an intergenerational aspect to nineteenth and early twentieth-century feminism. See Levine, *Feminist Lives*, p. 9.

3   Unpopular with women as well as men. On the general difficulties of starting or restarting a campaign see Hollis, *Pressure*, p. 16. On the particular difficulties of establishing suffrage societies, see Caine, *English Feminism*, pp. 146–65.

4   Some of the numerous failed bills are described below. For a definitive listing of the bills and their sponsors, see Rover, *Women's Suffrage*.

5   On the achievement and limitations of the extension of the franchise, see in particular the commentary of Caine, *English Feminism*, p. 166.

6   The local financing of the suffrage movement has been little explored, except in the context of the lack of funding of the working-class radical suffragists. See Caine, *English Feminism*, pp. 132–60; Holton, *Feminism and Democracy*, pp. 1–8.

7   On the reasons for and nature of the renewal of support for women's suffrage, see Shanley, *Feminism*, pp. 189–96, who argues that campaigning on issues related to marriage obliged feminists to address anew the issue of the wider system of state enforced male power. Levine, *Feminist Lives*, pp. 114–19, makes the same point. Also John and Eustance, "Introduction", p. xv, who argue that suffrage was caught up with major upheavals in the conception of gender, state and civil society in the period 1880–1920. For a more overarching commentary see Caine, *English Feminism*, pp. 131–59 and Nym Marshall, *The Militant Suffrage*.

8   On the large number of women activists and suffrage campaigners who engaged with the publications of Mill, see Rendall, "Friendship and politics", p. 146; Nym Marshall, "The rhetorics", pp. 55–71; Rendall, "'A moral engine?'", 112–40. For the limitations of Mill as appreciated by mid-Victorian feminists, see Caine, *English Feminists*, pp. 104–8.

9   We might usefully contrast this contemporary opinion with Rubinstein's attempt to revive the 1890s as a decade when key steps were taken to underpin twentieth-century suffrage activity. See Rubinstein, *Before the Suffragettes*. For later work building upon the importance of linguistic advances – "New Woman" or "Feminism", for instance – see Caine, *English Feminism*, pp. 134–44.

10   The *Bolton Evening News* carried a leader on 21 March 1907 highlighting a siege on the House of Commons in which "Lancashire lasses" were

involved. There has been a considerable increase in the literature on militant suffragism in recent years. See Rosen, *Rise up Women!*; Nym Marshall, *The Militant Suffrage*. Also Purvis "Reassessing", pp. 79–83, who argues that historiographically militant suffragism has fallen between socialist feminist representations, which have seen the Pankhurst's and their supporters as separatist traitors to the socialist cause, and Liberal feminist representations which have seen them as opportunistic, uncivilized, autocratic and irrational, such that the "good feminist" has become "non-militant, patient and controlled, willing to work within the structures of society rather than seeking to transform them". Such views, she claims, misrepresent the ideological basis of militant suffragism and ignore the "women-centred approach" of the Pankhurst women. See also Purvis, *Emmeline Pankhurst*, pp. 96–112.

11 See for instance *Bolton Journal*, 24 November 1894.

12 Home of the Haslam family. The use of domestic meetings of this sort informed female activism, electioneering and philanthropy in Bolton throughout the later nineteenth century, as we have seen elsewhere in this volume.

13 There is a considerable literature on the birth of the national suffrage movement, though less on the role of local societies like this. For a brief introduction, see Smith, *The British*, and for a useful time-line of women's organisations between 1880 and 1934 Harrison, *Prudent Revolutionaries*, pp. 4–5. Also Hulme, *The National*. For recent feminist reinterpretations see Joannou and Purvis, *The Women's Suffrage*. On the different theoretical approaches to justifying the female vote – equality, equality with difference, the women's mission, maternalism – see Bolt, *Feminist Ferment*, pp. 8–48 and 90. An excellent regional study is Liddington and Norris, *One Hand*.

14 Mildred Haslam wrote to local newspapers in April 1908 to inform the public of the formation of the Society. It should be noted that there are several female poor law guardians on this committee, as well as women who had stood as candidates but failed to be elected, and women – Taylor and Hulton for instance – who were at the very forefront of philanthropic activity in the town though they did not hold office.

15 On suffrage processions, see Holton, *Feminism and Democracy*, pp. 99–102.

16 On the importance of suffrage banners, see Tickner, *Spectacle*.

17 Women's politics in provincial communities like Bolton could often be very complex. On the absence of any Conservative venues, and on wider attitudes towards suffrage in the Conservative community, see Walker, "Party political women", pp. 165–91.

18 The annual report of the Society puts the figure at 2200. See Bolton Record Office (hereafter BRO) FW 2/4, Printed Annual Reports of the Bolton Women's Suffrage Association.

19 These were exactly the sorts of tactics used by Liberal women in their campaigning and electoral canvassing work on behalf of the Liberal party and in elections for poor law guardians in the later nineteenth century. See Levine, *Feminist Lives*, pp. 107–20.

20 For more detailed work on these and other women activists, see Harrison, *Prudent Revolutionaries*; Levine, *Feminist Lives*; Balshaw, "Sharing the burden", pp. 135–57; Herstein, *A Mid-Victorian*, and Wilson, *Women*, p. 48. Also, and importantly, Caine, *Victorian Feminists*.

21 What does not come out from this text or the annual report was that Mary Haslam and her daughter divided the town into four divisions, with campaign teams rotating between the divisions on a weekly basis. The Association also took on a paid organiser. See BRO FW 2/1, Bolton Women's Suffrage Association Minute Book.

22 The campaign was supported by a series of publicity stunts on the part of Bolton Suffragists. These included a well-publicised rally that brought huge over-reaction from the town authorities (200 police mobilised, theatres and shops boarded up etc.) and thus promoted support, and a speech given by Mrs Lloyd on the Suffragist cause from inside a lion cage with five lions. See *Bolton Evening News*, 19 January 1910.

23 On the nature of male support for women's suffrage, see John and Eustance, "Introduction", pp. 1–20; Spring, "The political", pp. 158–81.

24 The Minutes for this year noted that "only 318 were indifferent or against votes for women". BRO FW 2/1, Bolton Women's Suffrage Association Minute Book.

25 Again, a familiar organizing tactic.

26 On anti-suffrage activities amongst men and women see Harrison, *Separate Spheres*; Bush, "British women's".

27 This refusal is surprising given previous steadfast Liberal support for local suffrage and poor law campaigns. As Caine, *English Feminism*, p. 103, points out, many feminists eventually had to choose between their Liberalism and feminism.

28 The text does not note that Mary Haslam gave £25 to bolster funds, nor that the Association agreed to appoint an organiser and that "Mrs and Miss Haslam would be responsible for her salary if the association would pay the general expenses". See BRO FW 2/1, Bolton Women's Suffrage Association Minute Book.

29 The annual report notes that "From the Manchester Federation Report on the newspapers in this district it appears that twenty-four are friendly, twenty not particularly friendly, but giving fair reports, while only six are unfriendly". See BRO FW 2/4, Printed Annual Reports of the Bolton Women's Suffrage Association. On newspapers and suffrage more generally, see Harrison, *Separate Spheres*.

30 BRO FW 2/4, Printed Annual Reports of the Bolton Women's Suffrage Association.

31 On the political situation just before the war, see Bolt, *Feminist Ferment*, p. 28 and Pugh, *Women's Suffrage*.

32 Socialist feminism was one of the "faces of feminism" explored by Banks, who argued that socialist activists faced a constant tension between sex and class and were often dismayed at the limited goals of the suffrage movement. Banks, *Faces*, pp. 53 and 116; Thane, "The women".

33 Helped by the fact, not acknowledged here, that such associate members had a lower subscription rate. See BRO FW 2/1, Bolton Women's Suffrage Association Minute Book.

34 On the political allegiances of the working class in Lancashire, see Griffiths, *The Lancashire*.

35 This statement reflects strongly Mary Haslam's view that considered and reasoned argument, carefully applied to situations in which there were fault lines other than gender, would eventually achieve more than radical action. See Caine, *English Feminism*, who argues that radical working class suffragists from the north of England also disliked militant tactics.

36 The committee wished that "She be informed how deeply grateful the committee feel to her for her splendid work in founding and carrying on the society". BRO FW 2/4, Printed Annual Reports of the Bolton Women's Suffrage Association.

37 Reported in the *Bolton Evening News* from the perspective of one of the marchers, on 7 July 1913.

38 For alternative views of his motivations, see Lewis, *Women in England*, p. 97 who argues that Asquith consented to receive a deputation only of working class women from Sylvia Pankhurst's East London Federation because "The separation of spheres was less rigidly prescribed" for such women.

39 There was also a more radical side to the campaign, which included pouring oil into post boxes and defacing public property. See *Bolton Evening News*, 15 March 1913.

40 BRO FW 2/2, Bolton Women's Suffrage Association Minute Book.

41 The actions of radical Suffragists increased awareness of the campaign, for instance burning down cottages and setting fire to cars. See *Bolton Evening News*, 8 July 1913.

42 Mrs Blincoe also disrupted church services by demanding the saying of prayers for suffragists. See *Bolton Evening News*, 22 June 1914.

43 The campaign was reported in, and supported by, the *Bolton Evening News*.

44 See the debate in BRO FW 2/2, Bolton Women's Suffrage Association Minute Book. On the suffrage movement in wartime, see Wiltsher, *Most Dangerous*; Pugh, *Votes for Women*.

45 This was in addition to the wider feeding programme for the poor that had been organised annually in Bolton for the previous thirty years.

46 On the resumption of suffrage activities, see Pugh, *Women* and Bolt, *Feminist Ferment*, pp. 53–62.

47 On the very different reactions of individuals and groups to limited extension of the franchise, see Alberti, *Beyond Suffrage*; Holton, *Feminism and Democracy*; Caine, *English Feminism*, p. 166.

48 While many commentators have seen suffrage as sapping the wider campaigning and philanthropic energies of women activists, in Bolton at least women like Haslam maintained a wide array of interests throughout

the campaign. On social and maternalist feminists, see Bolt, *Feminist Ferment*, p. 28.

49 There is considerable support here for Maynard's conclusion that members of the women's movement were not simply "doing" on a variety of fronts but instead constructing an overarching critique of women's position, seeking "an interrelated framework of explanation" and seeing the solution in absolute equality. See Maynard, "Privilege and patriarchy", pp. 237–42.

50 For a reflection on the Women's Citizen Association, see BRO *Pioneers! O Pioneers! A Survey of the Bolton Women Citizens' Association 1918–1950.* Of course, the formation of the society must be seen in the context of the development of a much wider concept of national and local citizenship between 1900 and 1914. See Harris, *Private Lives*, pp. 180–4.

51 For the national context on the fate of local suffrage societies, see Hannam, *Isabella Ford*, pp. 188, 196, who notes the disappointment of Ford that young post-war women did not campaign for a lowering of the voting age for women. Also Pugh, "Politicians", p. 372 and Bolt, *Feminist Ferment*, pp. 54 and 61.

52 On Fawcett, see Harrison, *Prudent Revolutionaries*; Hannam, *Isabella Ford*, p. 194; Rubinstein, *A Different World*. Other prominent activists have also been the vehicle for exploring suffrage issues. See Holton, *Suffrage Days*; Forster, *Significant Sisters*; Murray, *Strong-Minded*. Also Banks, *Becoming a Feminist*, who analyzes the biographical details of ninety-eight feminists.

53 Again, testimony to the considerable longevity and depth of women's campaigning in Bolton.

54 On the overarching theoretical framework, see Caine, *English Feminism*, p. 166.

55 On friendship and networks amongst feminists, see Levine, *Feminist Lives*, pp. 11–28; Caine, *Victorian Feminists*.

56 On the Unitarian ethic in this respect, see Holt, *The Unitarian*; Levine, *Feminist Lives*, p. 32.

57 Dyhouse has argued that a critique of the Victorian bourgeois family informed and drove feminist activity. This does not seem to have been the case for Haslam. See Dyhouse, *Feminism*.

58 As Yeo warns, the women's movement as a whole had many contradictions and such contradictions "preclude a politics of self-representation for all women". Yeo, "Introduction", pp. 16–17. For other views on the unity and close personal ties that underpinned the women's and suffrage movements, see Levine, *Feminist Lives*, pp. 11–28. On the attempt to keep public unity in the face of schisms, see Bolt, *Feminist Ferment*, p. 62.

59 A claim also made for Isabella Ford. See Hannam, *Isabella Ford*, p. 203

60 Canning and Rose, "Gender, citizenship", p. 14. There is also support for Levine, *Feminist Lives*, p. 14, who characterises feminism as "more of a life-style than merely a form of organised political activism".

Bibliography of Secondary Sources

Mary Abbott, *Family Ties: English Families 1540–1920* (London: Routledge, 1993).

Thomas Ainsworth, *An Inquiry and Consideration of the State of Charitable Resources in the Area around Bolton* (Bolton: Privately Published, 1723).

Johanna Alberti, *Beyond Suffrage: Feminists in War and Peace, 1914–1928* (Basingstoke: Macmillan, 1989).

Sally Alexander, *Becoming a Woman and Other Essays in Nineteenth and Twentieth Century Women's History* (London: Virago, 1994).

William Apfel and Peter Dunkley, "English rural society and the new poor law in Bedfordshire, 1834–1847", *Social History*, 10 (1985): 37–68.

David Ashforth, "Settlement and removal in urban areas: Bradford 1834–71", in Michael Rose (ed.), *The Poor and the City: The English Poor Law in its Urban Context 1834–1914* (Leicester: Leicester University Press, 1985).

Thomas Ashton, *Economic and Social Investigations in Manchester 1833–1933* (Manchester: Manchester University Press, 1934).

Herman Ausubel, *In Hard Times: Reformers Among the Late Victorians* (New York, Columbia University Press, 1960).

Jenny Balshaw, "Sharing the burden: the Pethick Lawrence's and women's suffrage", in Angela John and Claire Eustance (eds), *The Men's Share? Masculinities, Male Support and Women's Suffrage in Britain, 1890–1920* (London: Routledge, 1997).

Olive Banks, *Faces of Feminism: A Study of Feminism as a Social Movement* (Oxford: Martin Robertson, 1981).

——, *A Biographical Dictionary of British Feminists, Volume 1: 1800–1930* (Brighton: Wheatsheaf, 1985).

——, *Becoming a Feminist: The Social Origins of First Wave Feminism* (Brighton: Harvester, 1986).

Peter Bartlett, *The Poor Law of Lunacy: The Administration of Pauper Lunatics in Mid-Nineteenth Century England* (London: Leicester University Press, 1999).

Paula Bartley, "Preventing prostitution: The ladies' association for the care and protection of young girls in Birmingham 1887–1914", *Women's History Review*, 7 (1998): 37–60.

——, *Prostitution: Prevention and Reform in England 1860–1914* (London: Routledge, 2000).

——, *Emmeline Pankhurst* (London: Routledge, 2002).

Michelle de Larra Beiti, "Conspicuous before the world: The political rhetoric of the Chartist women", in Eileen Yeo (ed.), *Radical Femininity: Women's Self-Representation in the Public Sphere* (Manchester: Manchester University Press, 1998).

Louisa Billington and Rosamund Billington, "A burning zeal for righteousness: Women in the British anti-slavery movement, 1820–1860", in Jane Rendall (ed.), *Equal or Different? Women's politics 1800–1914* (Oxford: Blackwell, 1987).

Lucy Bland, *Banishing the Beast: English Feminism and Sexual Morality, 1885–1914* (London: Penguin, 1995).

Gisela Bock and Pat Thane, "Introduction", in Gisela Bock and Pat Thane (eds), *Women and the Rise of the European Welfare States 1880–1950* (London: Routledge, 1991).

——, "Challenging dichotomies: perspectives on women's history", in Karen Offen, Ruth Pierson and Jane Rendall (eds), *Writing Women's History: International Perspectives* (Basingstoke: Macmillan, 1991).

Gisela Bock and Susan James, "Introduction: Contextualising equality and difference", in Gisela Bock and Susan James (eds), *Beyond Equality and Difference: Citizenship, Feminist politics and Female Subjectivity* (London: Routledge, 1992).

Christine Bolt, *Feminist Ferment: The Woman Question in the USA and England 1870–1914* (London: UCL Press, 1995).

Bolton 1838–1930 (Bolton: Public Assistance Department, 1930).

Arthur Bowley and Alexander Burnett-Hurst, *Livelihood and Poverty: A Study in the Economic Conditions of Working Class Households in Northampton, Warrington, Bolton and Reading* (London: Bell, 1915).

Arthur Bowley, *Wages and Income in the UK since 1860* (Cambridge: Cambridge University Press, 1937).

Inga Brandes, "'Odious, degrading and foreign institutions': The analysis of Irish workhouses in the nineteenth and twentieth centuries', in Andreas Gestrich, Steven King and Lutz Raphael (eds), *Being Poor in Modern Europe* (Bern: Peter Lang, 2005).

Joseph O'Brien, *William O'Brien and the Course of Irish Politics 1881–1918* (Berkeley: University of California Press, 1976).

Mary Brigg, *A Lancashire Weaver's Journal 1856–1864, John O Neil of Low Moor Clitheroe* (Manchester: Record Society of Lancashire and Cheshire, 1986).

William Brown, *Robert Heywood of Bolton 1786–1816* (East Ardley: S.R. Publishing, 1970).

Anthony Brundage, *The Making of the New Poor Law: The Politics of Inquiry, Enactment and Implementation, 1832–39* (New Brunswick: Rutgers University Press, 1978).

——, *The English Poor Laws, 1700–1930* (Basingstoke: Palgrave, 2002).

John Burn, *Charitable Effort and Civic Pride in Blackburn, 1750–1914* (Blackburn: Privately Published, 1936).

John Burnett, *Destiny Obscure: Autobiographies of Childhood, Education, and Family From the 1820s to the 1920s* (London: Allen Lane, 1994).

——, *Idle Hands: The Experience of Unemployment 1790–1990* (London: Routledge, 1994).

Julia Bush, "British women's anti-suffragism and the Forward policy, 1908–14", *Women's History Review*, 11 (2002), 431–54.

Anne Butler, *Poor Relief in Bolton During the Cotton Famine, 1861–63* (Bolton: Privately Published, 1972).

James Buzard, *The Beaten Track: European Tourism, Literature and the ways to Culture 1800–1918* (Oxford: Clarendon, 1993).

Barbara Caine, *Victorian Feminists* (Oxford: Oxford University Press, 1992).

——, "Feminist biography and feminist history", *Women's History Review*, 3 (1994): 156–92.

——, *English Feminism, 1780–1980* (Oxford: Oxford University Press, 1997).

——, "Mothering feminism/mothering feminists: Ray Strachey and *The Cause*", *Women's History Review*, 8 (1999): 295–310

Kathleen Canning and Sonya Rose, "Gender, citizenship and subjectivity: Some historical and theoretical considerations", in Kathleen Canning and Sonya Rose (eds), *Gender, Citizenship and Subjectivities* (Oxford: Blackwell, 2002),

Maurice Caplan, "The new poor law and the struggle for union chargeability", *International Review of Social History*, 23 (1978): 267–300.

Carl Chinn, *Poverty Amidst Prosperity: The Urban Poor in England 1834–1914* (Manchester: Manchester University Press, 1995).

Anna Clark, *The Struggle for the Breeches: Gender and the Making of the British Working Class* (London: Rivers Oram, 1995).

——, "Gender, class and the constitution: Franchise reform in England, 1832–1928", in James Vernon (ed.), *Re-reading the Constitution: New Narratives in English Political History* (Cambridge: Cambridge University Press, 1996).

——, "The new poor law and the breadwinner wage: Contrasting assumptions", *Journal of Social History*, 34 (2000): 261–82.

Lynda Clark, *The Rise of Professional Women in France. Gender and Public Administration Since 1830* (Cambridge: Cambridge University Press, 2000).

James Clifford, "Travelling cultures", in Lawrence Grossberg, Cary Nelson and Paula Treichler (eds), *Cultural Studies* (London: Routledge, 1992).

Gloria Clifton, *Professionalism, Patronage and Public Service in Victorian London: The Staff of the Metropolitan Board of Works 1856–1889* (London: Athlone, 1992).

John Coleman, *Sussex Poor Law Records: A Catalogue* (Chichester: West Sussex County Council, 1960).

Stefan Collini, *Public Moralists: Political Thought and Intellectual Life in Britain 1860–1930* (Oxford: Clarendon, 1991).

Richard Cox, *The Development of the Dutch Welfare State. From Workers'
Insurance to Individual Entitlement* (Pittsburgh: Pittsburgh University Press,
1993).

Frank Crompton, *Workhouse Children* (Stroud: Sutton, 1997).

Virginia Crossman, *Local Government in Nineteenth Century Ireland* (Belfast:
Institute of Irish Studies, 1994).

——, "The humanization of the Irish poor law: Reassessing developments in social
welfare in post-famine Ireland", in Andreas Gestrich, Steven King and Lutz
Raphael (eds), *Being Poor in Modern Europe* (Bern: Peter Lang, 2005).

——, "Welfare and nationality: The poor laws in nineteenth century Ireland", in
Steven King and John Stewart (eds), *Welfare Peripheries in Modern Europe*
(Forthcoming, Peter Lang, 2005).

Anne Crowther, "The later years of the workhouse 1890–1929", in Pat Thane
(ed.), *The Origins of British Social Policy* (London: Croom Helm, 1978).

——, *The Workhouse System 1834–1929: The History of an English Social
Institution* (London: Batsford, 1981).

——, "The workhouse", in Christopher Smout (ed.), *Victorian Values* (Oxford:
Oxford University Press, 1992).

——, "Health care and poor relief in provincial England", in Ole Grell, Andrew
Cunningham and Robert Jutte (eds), *Health Care and poor Relief in 18th and
19th Century Northern Europe* (London: Ashgate, 2002).

Pat Cummings, *An Examination of the Treatment of Paupers by Bolton
Guardians 1837–1848* (Bolton: Privately Published, 1974).

Hugh Cunningham, "Introduction", in Hugh Cunningham and Joanna Innes
(eds), *Charity, Philanthropy and Reform: From the 1690s to 1850* (Basingstoke:
Macmillan, 1998).

Martin Daunton (ed.), *Charity, Self-Interest and Welfare in the English Past*
(London: UCL Press, 1996).

Deirdrie David, *Intellectual Women and Victorian Patriarchy: Harriet Martineau,
Elizabeth Barrett Browning, George Eliot* (Basingstoke: Macmillan, 1987).

Leonore Davidoff, *The Best Circles: Society, Etiquette and the Season* (London:
Cresset Library, 1973).

——, *World's Between: Historical Perspectives on Gender and Class* (Cambridge:
Polity Press, 1995).

Celia Davies, "The health visitor as mother's friend: A woman's place in public
health, 1900–14", *Social History of Medicine*, 1 (1988): 39–59.

Rosemary O'Day and David Englander, *Mr Charles Booth's Inquiry: Life and
Labour of the People in London Reconsidered* (London: Hambledon, 1993).

Rosemary O'Day, *The Family and Family Relationships 1500–1900: England,
France and the United States of America* (Basingstoke: Macmillan, 1994)

Teresa Deane, "Late nineteenth century philanthropy: The case of Louisa
Twining", in Anne Digby and John Stewart (eds), *Gender, Health and Welfare*
(London: Routledge, 1996).

Anne Digby, "The labour market and the continuity of social policy after 1834:
the case of the eastern counties", *Economic History Review*, 38 (1975): 69–83.

——, *Pauper Palaces* (London: Routledge and Kegan Paul, 1978).

——, "Women's biological straitjacket", in Susan Mendus and Jane Rendall (eds), *Sexuality and Subordination: Interdisciplinary Studies of Gender in the Nineteenth Century* (London: Routledge, 1989).

——, "Victorian values and women in public and private", in Christopher Smout (ed.), *Victorian Values* (Oxford: Oxford University Press, 1992).

——, "Poverty, health and the politics of gender in Britian 1870–1948", in Anne Digby and John Stewart (eds), *Gender, Health and Welfare* (London: Routledge, 1996).

Felix Driver, "The historical geography of the workhouse system in England and Wales, 1834–1883", *Journal of Historical Geography*, 15 (1989): 269–86.

——, *Power and Pauperism: The Workhouse system 1834–1884* (Cambridge: Cambridge University Press, 1993).

Robert Dryburgh, "Individual, illegal and unjust purposes: Overseers, incentives, and the Old Poor Law in Bolton, 1820–1837", *Oxford University Discussion Papers in Economic and Social History*, 50 (2003).

Peter Dunkley, "The hungry forties and the poor law: A case study", *Historical Journal*, 17 (1974): 329–46.

Carol Dyhouse, *Girls Growing up in Late Victorian and Edwardian England* (London: Routledge and Kegan Paul, 1981)

——, *Feminism and the Family in England 1880–1939* (Oxford: Blackwell, 1989).

David Eastwood, *Governing Rural England: Tradition and Transformation in Local Government 1780–1840* (Oxford: Oxford University Press, 1994).

Nicholas Edsall, *The Anti-Poor Law Movement 1833–44* (Manchester: Manchester University Press, 1971).

David Englander, *Poverty and Poor Law Reform in Britain: From Chadwick to Booth 1834–1914* (London: Longman, 1998).

David Englander and Rosemary O'Day, *Retrieved Riches: Social Investigations in Britain 1840–1914* (Aldershot: Scolar Press, 1995).

Eric Evans, *Social Policy 1830–1914: Individualism, Collectivism and the Origins of the Welfare State* (London: Routledge and Kegan Paul, 1978).

Geoffrey Finlayson, *Citizen, State and Social Welfare in Britain 1830–1990* (Oxford: Clarendon, 1994).

David Fitzpatrick, *Irish Emigration 1801–1921* (Dublin: Economic and Social History Society of Ireland, 1984).

Michael Flinn, "Medical services under the new poor law", in Derek Fraser (ed.), *The New Poor Law in the Nineteenth Century* (Basingstoke: Macmillan, 1976).

Alice Foley, *A Bolton Childhood* (Manchester: Manchester Extra-Mural Studies, 1973).

Margaret Forster, *Significant Sisters: The Grassroots of Active Feminism 1839–1939* (London: Secker and Warburg, 1986).

John Foster, *Class Struggle and the Industrial Revolution: Early English Capitalism in Three English Towns* (Basingstoke: Macmillan, 1974).

Derek Fraser, "Poor law politics in Leeds 1833–55", *Publications of the Thoresby Society*, 15 (1971): 23–49.

——, *The Evolution of the British Welfare State* (Basingstoke: Macmillan, 1973).

—— (ed.), *The New Poor Law in the Nineteenth Century* (Basingstoke: Macmillan, 1976).

——, "The poor law as a political institution", in Derek Fraser (ed.), *The New Poor Law in the Nineteenth Century* (Basingstoke: Macmillan, 1976).

——, "The English poor law and the origins of the British welfare state" in Wolfgang Mommsen and Wolfgang Mock (eds), *The Emergence of the Welfare State in Britain and Germany, 1850–1950* (London: Croom Helm, 1981).

Rachel Fuchs and Victoria Thompson, *Women in Nineteenth Century Europe* (Basingstoke, Palgrave, 2005).

Ian Gazeley, *Poverty in Britain, 1900–1965* (Basingstoke: Palgrave, 2003).

Peter Gordon (ed.), *Politics and Society: The Journals of Lady Knightley of Fawsley, 1885–1913* (Northampton: Northamptonshire Record Society, 1999).

Eleanor Gordon and Gwyneth Nair, *Public Lives: Women, Family and Society in Victorian Britain* (New Haven: Yale University Press, 2003).

Martin Gorsky, "The growth and distribution of English friendly societies in the early nineteenth century", *Economic History Review*, 51 (1998), 489–511.

——, *Patterns of Philanthropy: Charity and Society in Nineteenth Century Bristol* (Woodbridge: Boydell, 1999).

Trevor Griffiths, *The Lancashire Working Classes c.1880–1930* (Oxford: Oxford University Press, 2001).

Lesley Hall, *Sex, Gender and Social Change in Britain since 1880* (Basingstoke: Macmillan, 2000).

Stuart Hall and Bill Schwarz, "State and Society, 1880–1930", in Mary Langan and Bill Schwarz (eds), *Crises in the British State 1880–1930* (London: Hutchinson, 1985).

John Hamer, *Bolton: The Development of a Town* (Bolton: Privately Published, 1921).

Sophie Hamilton, "Images of femininity in the Royal Commissions of the 1830s and 1840s", in Eileen Yeo (ed.), *Radical Femininity: Women's Self-Representation in the Public Sphere* (Manchester: Manchester University Press, 1998).

James Hamerton, *Cruelty and Companionship: Conflict in Nineteenth Century Married Life* (London: Routledge, 1992).

June Hannam, *Isabella Ford* (Oxford: Oxford University Press, 1989).

——, "Women and politics", in June Purvis (ed.), *Women's History: Britain 1850–1945* (London: Routledge, 2000).

June Hannam and Karen Hunt, *Socialist Women: Britain 1880s to 1920s* (London: Routledge, 2002).

Bernard Harris, *The Origins of the British Welfare State: Social Welfare in England and Wales, 1800–1945* (Basingstoke: Palgrave, 2004).

Jose Harris, *Unemployment and Politics: A Study in English Social Policy 1880–1914* (Oxford: Clarendon, 1972).

——, *Private Lives, Public Spirit: Britain 1870–1914* (London: Penguin, 1994).

—— (ed.), *Civil Society in British History: Ideas, Identities, Institutions* (Oxford: Oxford University Press, 2003).

Brian Harrison, "Philanthropy and the Victorians", *Victorian Studies*, 9 (1966): 353–74.

——, *Separate Spheres: The Opposition to Women's Suffrage in Britain* (London: Croom Helm, 1978).

——, *Peaceable Kingdom: Stability and Change in Modern Britain* (Oxford: Clarendon, 1982).

——, *Prudent Revolutionaries: Portraits of British Feminists Between the Wars* (Oxford: Clarendon, 1987).

Mary Haslam, *Women's Suffrage in Bolton* (Bolton: Privately Published, 1920).

Peter Hennock, "Poverty and social theory in England: The experience of the 1880s", *Social History*, 1 (1976): 67–91.

——, *British Social Reform and German Precedent: The Case of Social Insurance 1800–1914* (Oxford: Clarendon, 1987).

Ursula Henriques, "How cruel was the Victorian poor law", *Historical Journal*, 11 (1968): 365–71.

——, "Jeremy Bentham and the machinery of social reform", in Harry Hearder and Henry Loyn (eds), *British Government and Administration: Studies Presented to S. B. Chrimes* (Cardiff: University of Wales Press, 1974).

——, *Before the Welfare State: Social Administration in Early Industrial Britain* (London: Longman, 1979).

Sheila Herstein, *A Mid-Victorian Feminist: Barbara Leigh Smith Bodichon* (New Haven: Yale University Press, 1985).

Martin Hewitt (ed.), *The Emergence of Stability in the Industrial City: Manchester 1832–67* (Aldershot: Scolar, 1996).

Robert Heywood, *A Journey to Italy in 1826* (Cambridge: Privately Published, 1919).

——, *A Journey to America in 1834* (Cambridge: Cambridge University Press, 1919).

——, *A Journey to the Levant in 1845* (Cambridge: Cambridge University Press, 1919).

——, *A Journey in Russia in 1858* (Manchester: Manchester University Press, 1919).

Janet Hill, *Nelson: Politics, Economy, Community* (Keele: Ryburn Publishing, 1998).

Tim Hitchcock, Peter King and Pamela Sharpe (eds), *Chronicling Poverty: The Voices and Strategies of the English Poor 1640–1840* (Basingstoke: Macmillan, 1997).

Ruth Hodgkinson, *The Origins of the NHS: The Medical Services of the New Poor Law 1834–1871* (London: Wellcome Trust, 1967).

Patricia Hollis (ed.), *Pressure From Without in Early Victorian England* (London: Edward Arnold, 1974).

—— (ed.), *Women in Public 1850–1900: Documents of the Victorian Women's Movement* (London: George, Allen and Unwin, 1979).

——, *Ladies Elect: Women in English Local Government 1865–1914* (Oxford: Clarendon, 1987).

——, "Women in council: Separate spheres, public space", in Jane Rendall (ed.), *Equal or Different: Women's Politics 1800–1914* (Oxford: Blackwell, 1987).

Raymond Holt, *The Unitarian Contribution to Social Progress in England* (London: George, Allen and Unwin, 1938).

Sandra Stanley Holton, *Feminism and Democracy: Women's Suffrage and Reform Politics in Britain 1900–1918* (Cambridge: Cambridge University Press, 1986).

——, "In sorrowful wrath: Suffrage militance and the romantic feminism of Emmeline Pankhurst", in Harold Smith (ed.), *British Feminism in the Twentieth Century* (Aldershot: Edward Elgar, 1990).

——, *Suffrage Days: Stories From the Women's Suffrage Movement* (London: Routledge, 1996).

Sarah Horrell and Jane Humphries, "Old questions, new data and alternative perspectives: Families' living standards in the industrial revolution", *Journal of Economic History*, 52 (1992): 849–80.

Michael Huberman, *Escape From the Market: Negotiating Work in Lancashire* (Cambridge: Cambridge University Press, 1996).

Paul Huck, "Infant mortality and living standards of English workers during the Industrial Revolution", *Journal of Economic History*, 55 (1995): 528–50.

Lesley Parker Hulme, *The National Union of Women's Suffrage Societies* (New York: Columbia University Press, 1982).

Robert Humphreys, *Sin, Organised Charity and the Poor Law in Victorian England* (Basingstoke: Macmillan, 1995).

Edward Hunt, "Industrialisation and regional inequality: Wages in Britain 1760–1914", *Journal of Economic History*, 46 (1986): 935–66.

Edward Hunt and Frank Botham, "Wages in Britain during the industrial revolution", *Economic History Review*, 40 (1987): 380–99.

Felicity Hunt (ed.), *Lessons for Life: The Schooling of Girls and Women 1850–1950* (Oxford: Blackwell, 1987).

Felicity Hunt, *Gender and Policy in English Education: Schooling for Girls 1902–1944* (Brighton: Harvester, 1991).

Elizabeth Hurren, "Labourers are revolting: Penalising the poor and a political reaction in the Brixworth union, Northamptonshire, 1875–1885", *Rural History*, 11 (2000): 37–55.

——, "Agricultural trade unionism and the crusade against outdoor relief: Poor law politics in Brixworth union, Northamptonshire, 1870–75", *Agricultural History Review*, 48 (2000): 200–22.

——, "'A pauper dead-house': The expansion of the Cambridge anatomical teaching school under the late-Victorian poor law, 1870–1914", *Medical History*, 48 (2004): 69–94.

Joanna Innes, "State, church and volunterism in European welfare 1690–1850", in Hugh Cunningham and Joanna Innes (eds), *Charity, Philanthropy and Reform From the 1690s to 1850* (Basingstoke: Macmillan, 1998).

Pat Jalland, "Victorian spinsters: Dutiful daughters, desperate rebels and the tran-

sition to the New Woman", in Patricia Crawford (ed.), *Exploring Women's Past: Essays in Social History* (London: George, Allen and Unwin, 1983).
——, *Women, Marriage and Politics* (Oxford: Clarendon, 1986).
Herbert James, *A Wigan Heritage* (Lancaster: Privately Published, 1897).
Sheila Jeffreys, *The Spinster and her Enemies: Feminism and Sexuality, 1880–1930* (London: Pandora, 1985).
Marloula Joannou and June Purvis (eds), *The Women's Suffrage Movement: New Feminist Perspectives* (Manchester: Manchester University Press, 1998).
Angela John and Claire Eustance (eds), *The Men's Share? Masculinities, Male Support and Women's Suffrage in Britain 1890–1920* (London: Routledge, 1997).
Paul Johnson, "Risk, redistribution and social welfare in Britain from the poor law to Beveridge", in Martin Daunton (ed.), *Charity, Self-Interest and Welfare in the English Past* (London: UCL Press, 1996).
Helen Jones, *Women in British Public Life, 1914–50: Gender, Power and Social Policy* (London: Longman, 2000).
Terry Jordan, *Victorian Childhood: Themes and Variations* (Albany: New York University Press, 1987).
Ludmilla Jordanova, "Natural facts: A historical perspective on science and sexuality", in Carol MacCormack and Marilyn Strathern (eds), *Nature, Culture and Gender* (Cambridge: Cambridge University Press, 1980).
Cheryl Jorgensen-Earp, " 'The transfiguring sword': The Just War of the Women's Social and Political Union* (London: University of Alabama Press, 1997).
Barbara Kanner, "The women of England in a century of social change, 1815–1914: A select bibliography part II", in Martha Vicinus (ed.), *A Widening Sphere: Changing Roles of Victorian Women* (London: Methuen, 1980).
Robert Kennedy, *The Irish: Emigration, Marriage, Fertility* (Berkeley: University of California Press, 1973).
Alan Kidd, "Charity organisation and the unemployed in Manchester *c.* 1870–1914", *Social History*, 9 (1984): 45–66.
——, "Outcast Manchester: Voluntary charity, poor relief and the casual poor, 1860–1905", in Alan Kidd and William Roberts (eds), *City, Class and culture: Studies of Cultural Production and Social Policy in Victorian Manchester* (Manchester: Manchester University Press, 1985).
——, *Manchester* (Keele: Ryburn Publishing, 1993).
——, "Philanthropy and the social history paradigm", *Social History*, 21 (1996): 180–92
——, *State, Society and the Poor in Nineteenth Century England* (Basingstoke: Macmillan, 1999).
Lynne Kiesling, "The long road to recovery: Postcrisis coordination of private charity and public relief in Victorian Lancashire", *Social Science History*, 21 (1997): 219–43.
Steven King, *Poverty and Welfare in England 1700–1850: A Regional Perspective* (Manchester: Manchester University Press, 2000).

——, *A Fylde Country Practice: Medicine and Society in Lancashire 1700–1850* (Lancaster: Centre for Northwest Regional Studies, 2001).

——, "Locating and characterising poor households in late seventeenth century Bolton: Sources and interpretations", *Local Population Studies*, 68 (2002): 11–37.

——, "We might be trusted: female poor law guardians and the development of the New Poor Law: The case of Bolton, England, 1880–1906", *International Review of Social History*, 49 (2003): 27–46.

——, "The English proto-industrial family: Old and new perspectives", *History of the Family*, 140 (2003): 1–23.

——, "'It is impossible for our Vestry to judge his case into perfection from here': Managing the distance dimensions of poor relief 1800–1840", *Rural History*, 16 (2005): 1–29.

—— and Geoffrey Timmins, *Making Sense of the Industrial Revolution* (Manchester: Manchester University Press, 2001).

—— and Alannah Tomkins (eds), *The Poor in England 1700–1850: An Economy of Makeshifts* (Manchester: Manchester University Press, 2003).

—— and John Stewart, "Death in Llantrisant: Henry Williams and the New Poor Law in Wales", *Rural History*, 15 (2004): 69–87.

Christine Kinealy, *The Great Irish Famine: Impact, Ideology and Rebellion* (Basingstoke: Macmillan, 2002).

John Knowles, *A Study in Public Service for Wigan and Southport* (Southport: Privately Published, 1968).

Seth Koven and Sonya Michel, "Womanly duties: Maternalist policies and the origins of the welfare state in France, Germany, Great Britain and the USA, 1880–1920", *American Historical Review*, 95 (1990): 379–96.

Seth Koven, "Borderlands: Women, voluntary action, and child welfare in Britain, 1840–1914", in Seth Koven and Sonya Michel (eds), *Mothers of a New World: Maternalist Politics and the Origins of Welfare States* (London: Routledge, 1993).

——, *Slumming: Sexual and Social Politics in Victorian London* (Princeton: Princeton University Press, 2005).

Joan Landes, "The public and the private sphere: A feminist reconsideration", in Joan Landes (ed.), *Feminism, the Public and the Private* (Oxford: Oxford University Press, 1998)

Penny Lane, Neil Raven and Keith Snell (eds), *Women, Work and Wages in England, 1600–1850* (Woodbridge: Boydell, 2004).

Jane Lawson, Mike Savage and Alan Warde, "Gender and local politics: Struggles over welfare policies 1918–1939", in The Lancaster Regionalism Group (eds), *Localities, Class and Gender* (London: Prion, 1985).

Richard Lawton, "Regional population trends in England and Wales, 1750–1971", in John Hobcraft and Phillip Rees (eds), *Regional Demographic Development* (London: Croom Helm, 1978).

Keith Laybourn, *Popular Politics in Early Industrial Britain: Bolton 1825–1850* (Keele: Ryburn Publishing, 1995).

Clive Lee, *British Regional Employment Statistics 1814–1871* (Cambridge: Cambridge University Press, 1979).

Lynne Hollen Lees, *Poverty and Pauperism in Nineteenth Century London* (Leicester: Leicester University Press, 1988).

——, *The Solidarities of Strangers: The English Poor Laws and the People 1700–1948* (Cambridge: Cambridge University Press, 1998).

Marco van Leeuwen, "Histories of risk and welfare in Europe during the eighteenth and nineteenth centuries", in Ole Grell, Andrew Cunningham and Robert Jutte (eds), *Health Care and Poor Relief in 18th and 18th Century Northern Europe* (London: Ashgate, 2002)

Philippa Levine, "So few prizes and so many blanks: Marriage and feminism in later nineteenth century England", *Journal of British Studies*, 28 (1989): 150–74.

——, *Feminist Lives in Victorian England: Private Roles and Public Commitment* (Oxford: Blackwell, 1990).

——, *Victorian Feminism 1850–1900* (Orlando: University of Florida Press, 1994).

Jane Lewis, *Women in England 1870–1950: Sexual Division and Social Change* (Brighton: Wheatsheaf, 1984).

——, *Before the Vote was Won: Arguments for and Against Women's Suffrage* (London: Routledge and Kegan Paul, 1987).

——, *Women and Social Action in Victorian and Edwardian England* (Cheltenham: Edward Elgar, 1991).

——, "Women and late-nineteenth century social work", in Carol Smart (ed.), *Regulating Womanhood: Historical Essays on Marriage, Motherhood and Sexuality* (London: Routledge, 1992).

——, "Gender, the family and women's agency in the building of the Welfare state: The British case', *Social History*, 19 (1994): 37–55.

——, *The Voluntary Sector, the State and Social Work in Britain: The Charity Organisation Society/Family Welfare Association Since 1869* (Aldershot: Scolar, 1995)

Jill Liddington, "Women cotton workers and the suffrage campaign: The radical suffragists in Lancashire 1893–1914", in Sandra Burman (ed.), *Fit Work for Women* (London: Croom Helm, 1979).

——, *The Life and Times of a Respectable Rebel: Selina Cooper 1864–1946* (London: Virago, 1984).

Jill Liddington and Jill Norris, *One Hand Tied Behind Us: The Rise of the Women's Suffrage Movement* (London: Virago, 1985).

William Lubenow, *The Politics of Government Growth: Early Victorian Attitudes Towards State Intervention, 1833–1848* (Newton Abbot: David and Charles, 1978).

John Lyons, "Family response to economic decline: Handloom weavers in early nineteenth century Lancashire", *Research in Economic History*, 12 (1989): 45–91.

Alison Mackinnon, "English poor law policy and the crusade against out relief", *Journal of Economic History*, 47 (1987): 603–25.

Peter Mandler, "Tories and paupers: Christian political economy and the making of the new poor law", *Historical Journal*, 33 (1990): 81–103.

——, *The Uses of Charity: The Poor on Relief in the Metropolis* (Philadelphia, University of Pennsylvania Press 1990).

Hilary Marland, *Medicine and Society in Wakefield and Huddersfield 1780–1870* (Cambridge: Cambridge University Press, 1987).

Laura Nym Marshall, "The rhetorics of slavery and citizenship: Suffragist discourse and canonical texts in Britain, 1880–1914", in Kathleen Canning and Sonya Rose (eds), *Gender, Citizenships and Subjectivities* (Oxford: Blackwell, 2002).

——, *The Militant Suffrage Movement: Citizenship and Resistance in Britain, 1860–1930* (Oxford: Oxford University Press, 2003).

Eric Martin, "From parish to union: Poor law administration 1601–1865", in Eric Martin (ed.), *Comparative Developments in Social Welfare* (London: George Allen and Unwin, 1978).

Mary Maynard, "Privilege and patriarchy: Feminist thought in the nineteenth century", in Susan Mendus and Jane Rendall (eds), *Sexuality and Subordination: Interdisciplinary Studies of Gender in the Nineteenth Century* (London: Routledge, 1989).

Norman McCord, "The implementation of the poor law amendment act on Tyneside", *International Review of Social History*, 14 (1969): 90–108.

——, "Ratepayers and social policy", in Pat Thane (ed.), *The Origins of British Social Policy*, (London: Croom Helm, 1978).

Kathleen McCrone, "Feminism and philanthropy in Victorian England: The case of Louisa Twining", *Canadian Historical Association Historical Papers* (1976): 123–39.

Mary McFeely, *Lady Inspectors: The Campaign for a Better Workplace, 1893–1921* (Oxford: Blackwell, 1988).

Simon Mencher, "Introduction to the poor law reports of 1834 and 1909", in Roy Lubove (ed.), *Social Welfare in Transition: Selected English Documents 1834–1909* (Pittsburgh: University of Pittsburgh Press, 1982).

Claire Midgley, *Women Against Slavery: The British Campaigns 1780–1870* (London: Routledge, 1992).

Eric Midwinter, "State intervention at the local level: The New Poor Law in Lancashire", *Historical Journal*, 10 (1967): 111–42.

——, *Social Administration in Lancashire 1830–1860* (Manchester: Manchester University Press, 1969).

Steven Mintz, *A Prison of Expectations: The Family in Victorian Culture* (New York: New York University Press, 1983).

Arthur Mitchell, *Labour in Irish Politics 1890–1930: The Irish Labour Movment in an Age of Revolution* (Dublin: Irish University Press, 1974).

Gordon Mitchell, *The Hard Way up: The Autobiography of Hannah Mitchell, Suffragette and Rebel* (London: Virago, 1968).

Michael Moore, "Social work and social welfare: The organisation of philanthropic resources in Britain, 1900–1914", *Journal of British Studies*, 16 (1977): 85–104.

David Morgan, *Suffragists and Liberals. The Politics of Woman Suffrage in England* (Oxford: Blackwell, 1975).

Mary Morris (ed.), *The Virago Book of Women Travellers* (London: Virago, 1994).

Frank Mort, "Purity, feminism and the state: Sexuality and moral politics 1880–1914", in Mary Langan and Bill Schwarz (eds), *Crises in the British State 1880–1930* (London: Hutchinson, 1985).

Janet Murray (ed.), *Strong Minded Women and Other Lost voices from Nineteenth Century England* (London: Penguin, 1982).

William Neild, "Comparative statement of the income and expenditure of certain families of the working class in Manchester and Dukinfield in the years 1836–1841", *Journal of the Statistical Society of London*, 4 (1841): 1–37.

David Neville, *To Make their Mark: The Women's Suffrage Movement in the North East of England 1900–1914* (Newcastle: Centre for Northern Studies, 1997).

Miles Ogborn, "Local power and state regulation in nineteenth century Britain", *Transactions of the Institute of British Geographers*, 17 (1992): 215–26.

David Ormrod, *Up Our Street* (Preston: Privately Published, 1972).

David Owen, *English Philanthropy, 1660–1960* (Cambridge MA: Harvard University Press, 1964).

Emmeline Pankhurst, *My Own Story* (London: Eveleigh Nash, 1914).

Julia Parker, *Women and Welfare: Ten Victorian Women in Public Social Service* (Basingstoke: Macmillan, 1988).

Carole Pateman, "The patriarchal welfare state", in Amy Gutman (ed.), *Democracy and the Welfare State* (Princeton: Princeton University Press, 1988).

——, "Equality, difference, subordination: The politics of motherhood and women's citizenship", in Gisela Bock and Susan James (eds), *Beyond Equality and Difference: Citizenship, Feminist Politics and Female Subjectivity* (London: Routledge, 1992).

Susan Pedersen, *Family, Dependence, and the Origins of the Welfare State: Britain and France 1914–1945* (Cambridge: Cambridge University Press, 1993).

Joan Perkin, *Victorian Women* (London: John Murray, 1994).

Anne Phillips, *Divided Loyalties: Dilemmas of Sex and Class* (London: Virago, 1987).

Colin Phillips and John Smith, *Lancashire and Cheshire From 1540AD* (London: Longman, 1993).

Mary Pooley and Colin Pooley, "Health, society and environment in nineteenth century Manchester", in Robert Woods and John Woodward (eds), *Urban Disease and Mortality in Nineteenth Century England* (Cambridge: Cambridge University Press, 1984).

Mary Poovey, *Uneven Developments: The Ideological Work of Gender in Mid-Victorian England* (Chicago: University of Chicago Press, 1988).

Belinda Corrada Pope, "Angels in the devil's workshop: Leisured and charitable women in nineteenth century England and France", in Renate Bridenthal and Claudia Koonz (eds), *Becoming Visible: Women in European History* (Boston: Houghton and Miffin, 1977).

Dorothy Porter, "Health care and the construction of citizenship in civil societies in the era of the enlightenment and industrialisation", in Ole Grell, Andrew Cunningham and Robert Jutte (eds), *Health Care and Poor Relief in 18th and 19th Century Northern Europe* (Aldershot: Ashgate, 2002).

Frank Prochaska, "Women in English philanthropy, 1790–1830", *International Review of Social History*, 19 (1974): 426–45.

——, *Women and Philanthropy in Nineteenth Century England* (Oxford: Clarendon, 1980).

——, *The Voluntary Impulse: Philanthropy in Modern Britain* (London: Faber and Faber, 1988).

Winifred Proctor, "Poor law administration in Preston union 1838–1848", *Transactions of the Historic Society of Lancashire and Cheshire*, 117 (1965): 145–66.

Martin Pugh, *Women's Suffrage in Britain 1867–1928* (London: Historical Association, 1980).

——, *Women and the Women's Movement in Britain 1914–1959* (Basingstoke: Macmillan, 1992)

——, "Politicians and the women's vote, 1914–1918", *History*, 59 (1994): 68–92.

——, *Votes for Women in Britain, 1865–1928* (London: Historical Association, 1994).

——, *The March of the Women. A Revisionist Analysis of the Campaign for Women's Suffrage 1866–1914* (Oxford: Oxford University Press, 2002).

——, "Working class experience and state social welfare, 1908–1914: Old age pensions reconsidered", *Historical Journal*, 45 (2002): 775–96.

June Purvis, *A History of Women's Education in England* (Milton Keynes: Open University Press, 1991).

——, "Reassessing representations of Emmeline and Christabel Pankhurst, militant feminists in Edwardian Britain: On the importance of a knowledge of our feminist past", in Mary Maynard and June Purvis (eds), *New Frontiers in Women's Studies: Knowledge, Identity and Nationalism* (London: Taylor and Francis, 1996).

——, "From women worthies to poststructuralism? Debate and controversy in women's history in Britain", in June Purvis (ed.), *Women's History: Britain 1850–1945: An Introduction* (London: Routledge, 2000).

——, *Emmeline Pankhurst: A Biography* (London: Routledge, 2002).

Gordon Ramsden, *A Responsible Society. The Life and Times of the congregation of Bank Street Unitarian Chapel, Bolton* (Horsham: Slinfold, 1985).

Terence Raybould, *A Survey and Appreciation of the Charitable Endeavours of the Parishes and Unions of Leigh, Southport and Croston, by a Public Servant* (Southport: Mercer, 1874).

Russell Rees, *Nationalism and Unionism in 19th Century Ireland* (Newtonards: Colourpoint Press, 2001).

Jane Rendall, *The Origins of Modern Feminism: Women in Britain, France and the United States 1780–1860* (Basingstoke: Macmillan, 1985).

——, "Introduction", in Jane Rendall (ed.), *Equal or Different? Women's Politics 1800–1914* (Oxford: Blackwell, 1987).

——, "'A moral engine?' Feminism, Liberalism and the English Woman's Journal", in Jane Rendall (ed.), *Equal of Different?: Women's Politics 1800–1914* (Oxford: Blackwell, 1987).

——, "Friendship and politics: Barbara Leigh Smith Bodichon (1827–91) and Bessie Rayner Parkes (1829–1925)", in Susan Mendus and Jane Rendall (eds), *Sexuality and Subordination: Interdisciplinary Studies of Gender in the Nineteenth Century* (London: Routledge, 1989).

——, "Citizenship, culture and civilisation: The languages of British suffragists, 1866–1874", in Caroline Daley and Melanie Nolan (eds), *Suffrage and Beyond: International Feminist Perspectives* (New York: New York University Press, 1994).

——, "Women and the public sphere", *Gender and History*, 11 (1999): 475–88.

——, "The citizenship of women and the Reform Act of 1867", in Catherine Hall, Keith McClelland and Jane Rendall (eds), *Defining the Victorian Nation: Class, Race, Gender and the British Reform Act of 1867* (Cambridge: Cambridge University Press, 2000).

George Revill and Richard Wrigley, "Introduction", in Richard Wrigley and George Revill (eds), *Pathologies of Travel* (Amsterdam: Rodopi, 2000).

Denise Riley, *'Am I That Name?' Feminism and the Category of Women in History* (Basingstoke: Macmillan, 1989).

Jean Robin, "The relief of poverty in mid-nineteenth century Colyton", *Rural History*, 1 (199): 193–218.

Christine Roberts, *The Radical Countess: The History of the Life of Rosalind, Countess of Carlisle* (Carlisle: Tandem, 1962).

David Roberts, "How cruel was the Victorian poor law?", *Historical Journal*, 6 (1963): 97–106.

——, *Victorian Origins of the British Welfare State* (New Haven: Yale University Press, 1969).

Michael Roberts, "Reshaping the gift relationship: The London mendacity society and the suppression of begging in England 1818–1869", *International Review of Social History*, 36 (1991): 201–31.

——, "Head versus heart? Voluntary associations and charity organisation in England 1700–1850", in Hugh Cunningham and Joanna Innes (eds), *Charity, Philanthropy and Reform* (Basingstoke: Macmillan, 1998).

Helen Rogers, *Women and the People: Authority, Authorship and the Radical Tradition in Nineteenth Century England* (Aldershot: Ashgate, 2000).

Michael Rose, "The anti-poor law movement in the north of England", *Northern History*, 1 (1966): 41–73.

——, *The English Poor Law 1780–1930* (Newton Abbot: David and Charles, 1971).

——, "The crisis of poor relief in England 1860–1890" in Wolfgang Mommsen and Wolfgang Mock (eds), *The Emergence of the Welfare State in Britain and Germany, 1850–1950* (London: Croom Helm, 1981).

——, "Culture, philanthropy and the Manchester middle class", in Alan Kidd and Keith Roberts, *City, Class and Culture: Studies of Social Policy and Cultural Production in Victorian Manchester* (Manchester: Manchester University Press, 1985).

Andrew Rosen, *Rise up Women! The Militant Campaign of the Women's Social and Political Union, 1903–1914* (London: Routledge and Kegan Paul, 1974)

Constance Rover, *Women's Suffrage and Party Politics in Britain 1866–1914* (London: Routledge and Kegan Paul, 1967).

David Rubinstein, *Before the Suffragettes: Women's Emancipation in the 1890s* (Brighton: Harvester, 1986).

——, *A Different World for Women: The Life of Millicent Garrett Fawcett* (London: Harvester, 1991).

Phillippa Rose, *Parallel Lives: Five Victorian Marriages* (London: Chatto and Windus, 1984).

Karl de Schweinitz, *England's Road to Social Security: From the Statute of Laborers in 1349 to the Beveridge Report of 1942* (New Brunswick: Rutgers University Press, 1943).

John Seed, "Unitarianism, political economy and the antinomies of Liberal culture in Manchester 1830–50", *Social History*, 7 (1982): 1–25.

Mary Shanley, *Feminism, Marriage and the Law in Victorian England, 1850–1895* (London: I.B.Tauris, 1989).

Peter Shapley, "Charity, status and leadership: Charitable image and the Manchester man", *Journal of Social History*, 32 (1998): 157–77.

——, *Charity and Power in Victorian Manchester* (Manchester: Chetham Society, 1999).

Margaret Simey, *Charity Rediscovered: A Study of Philanthropic Effort in Nineteenth Century Liverpool* (Liverpool: Liverpool University Press, 1992).

Paul Slack, *From Reformation to Improvement: Public Welfare in Early Modern England* (Oxford: Oxford University Press, 1999).

Brian Abel-Smith, *A History of the Nursing Profession* (London: Heinemann, 1960).

Harold Smith, *The British Women's Suffrage Campaign, 1866–1928* (London: Longman, 1998).

Richard Smith, "Ageing and well being in early modern England: Pension trends and gender preferences under the English Old Poor Law 1650–1800", in Paul Johnson and Pat Thane (eds), *Old Age From Antiquity to Postmodernity* (London: Routledge, 1998).

Keith Snell, *Annals of the Labouring Poor: Social Change and Agrarian England 1660–1900* (Cambridge: Cambridge University Press, 1985).

Byung Song, "Continuity and change in English rural society: The formation of poor law unions in Oxford", *English Historical Review*, 114 (1999): 314–38.

Carolyn Spring, "The political platform and the language of support for women's suffrage, 1890–1920", in Angela John and Claire Eustance, *The Men's Share? Masculinities, Male Support and Women's Suffrage in Britain, 1890–1920* (London: Routledge, 1997).

Barry Stapleton, "Inherited poverty and life-cycle poverty: Odiham, Hampshire, 1650–1850", *Social History*, 18 (1993): 339–55.

Jon Stobart, *The First Industrial Region: North-West England, 1700–60* (Manchester: Manchester University Press, 2004).

Anne Summers, "A home from home: women's philanthropic work in the nineteenth century", in Sandra Burman (ed.), *Fit Work for Women* (London: Croom Helm, 1979).

John Sutherland, *Mrs Humphrey Ward: Eminent Victorian, Pre-Eminent Edwardian* (Oxford: Clarendon, 1990).

Richard Symonds, *Inside the Citadel: Men and the Emancipation of Women, 1850–1920* (Basingstoke: Macmillan, 1999).

Peter Taylor, *Popular Politics in Early Industrial Britain: Bolton 1825–1850* (Keele: Ryburn Publishing, 1995).

William Cooke Taylor, *Notes on a Tour of the Manufacturing Districts of Lancashire* (New York: Augustus Kelley, 1968).

Pat Thane, "Introduction" in Pat Thane (ed.), *The Origins of British Social Policy* (London: Croom Helm, 1978).

——, "Non-contributory versus insurance pensions 1878–1908", in Pat Thane (ed), *The Origins of British Social Policy* (London: Croom Helm, 1978).

——, "Women and the poor law in Victorian and Edwardian England", *History Workshop Journal*, 6 (1978): 29–51.

——, *The Foundations of the Welfare State* (London: Longman, 1982).

——, "The women of the British Labour Party and feminism, 1906–45", in Harold Smith (ed.), *British Feminism in the Twentieth Century* (Aldershot: Ashgate, 1990).

——, "Visions of gender in the making of the British welfare state: The case of women in the British labour party and social policy, 1906–45", in Gisela Bock and Pat Thane (eds), *Maternity, and Gender Policies: Women and the Rise of the European Welfare States, 1880–1950* (London: Routledge, 1991).

—— and Gisela Bock (eds), *Maternity and Gender Policies: Women and the Rise of the European Welfare State 1880–1950* (London: Routledge, 1991).

——, "Government and society in England and Wales 1750–1914", in Michael Thompson (ed.), *The Cambridge Social History of Britain 1750–1950* (Cambridge: Cambridge University Press, 1999).

——, *Old Age in English History: Past Experiences, Present Issues* (Oxford: Oxford University Press, 2000).

David Thomson, "The welfare of the elderly in the past: a family or community responsibility?", in Margaret Pelling and Richard Smith (eds), *Life, Death and the Elderly: Historical Perspectives* (London: Routledge, 1991).

Lisa Tickner, *The Spectacle of Women: Imagery of the Suffrage Campaigns 1907–1914* (London: Chatto and Windus, 1989).

Geoffrey Timmins, *The Last Shift* (Manchester: Manchester University Press, 1993).

——, *Made in Lancashire* (Manchester: Manchester University Press, 1998).

John Tosh, "The making of masculinities: The middle class in late nineteenth century Britain", in Angela John and Claire Eustance (eds), *The Men's Share? Masculinities, Male Support and Women's Suffrage in Britain 1890–1920* (London: Routledge, 1997).

——, *A Man's Place: Masculinity and the Middle Class Home in Victorian England* (New Haven: Yale University Press, 1999).

John Treble, *Urban Poverty in Britain 1830–1914* (London: Batsford, 1979).

Louisa Twining, *Recollections of Life and Work* (London: Black, 1893).

Laura Ugolini, "'By all means let the ladies have a chance'. The Workman's Times, independent labour representation and women's suffrage 1891–94", in Angela John and Claire Eustance (eds), *The Men's Share? Masculinity, Male Support and Women's Suffrage in Britain 1890–1920* (London: Routledge, 1997).

Diane Urquhart, *Women in Ulster Politics 1890–1940: A History Not Yet Told* (Dublin: Irish Academic Press, 2000).

John Vase, *A Quaker Upbringing* (Manchester: Hurst Press, 1902).

Amanda Vickery, "Golden age to separate spheres? A review of the categories and chronology of English women's history", *Historical Journal*, 36 (1993): 383–414.

Andrew Vincent, "The poor law reports of 1909 and the social theory of the charity organisation society", *Victorian Studies*, 27 (1984): 343–63.

Martha Vicinus (ed.), *A Widening Sphere: Changing Roles of Victorian Women* (London: Methuen, 1980).

David Vincent, *Bread, Knowledge and Freedom: A Study of Nineteenth Century Working Class Autobiography* (London: Europa, 1981).

——, *Poor Citizens: The State and the Poor in Twentieth Century Britain* (London: Longman, 1991).

Rachel Vorspan, "Vagrancy and the new poor law in late Victorian and Edwardian England", *English Historical Review*, 92 (1977): 59–81.

Lex Herma van Voss (ed.), *Petitions in Social History* (Cambridge: Cambridge University Press, 2001).

Linda Walker, "Party political women: A comparative study of Liberal Women and the Primrose League, 1890–1914", in Jane Rendall (ed.), *Equal or Different? Women's Politics 1800–1914* (Oxford: Blackwell, 1987).

John Walton, *Lancashire: A Social History 1558–1939* (Manchester: Manchester University Press, 1987).

Christine Webb, *The Woman with the Basket: The History of the Women's Co-Operative Guild, 1883–1927* (Manchester: Manchester University Press, 1927).

Gordon Williams, *The New Poor Law and its Administration in the Fylde after 1832* (Preston: Privately Published, 1973).

Karel Williams, *From Pauperism to Poverty* (London: Routledge and Kegan Paul, 1981).

Elizabeth Wilson, *Women and the Welfare State* (London: Tavistock Publications, 1977).

Anne Wiltsher, *Most Dangerous Women: Feminist Peace Campaigners of the Great War* (London: Pandora, 1985).

Frank Wood and Karen Wood (eds), *A Lancashire Gentleman: The Letters and Journals of Richard Hodgkinson, 1763–1847* (Stroud: Sutton, 1992).

George Wood, "The statistics of wages in the United Kingdom during the nineteenth century", *Journal of the Royal statistical Society* (1910): 128–63.

Peter Wood, "Finance and the urban poor law: Sunderland union 1836–1914", in Michael Rose (ed.), *The Poor and the City: The English Poor Law in its Urban Context 1834–1914* (Leicester: Leicester University Press, 1985).

——, *Poverty and the Workhouse in Victorian Britain* (Stroud: Sutton, 1991).

Eileen Yeo, "Introduction", in Eileen Yeo (ed.), *Radical Femininity: Women's Self-Representation in the Public Sphere* (Manchester: Manchester University Press, 1998).

Unpublished

William Rhodes Boyson, "The history of poor law administration in north east Lancashire 1834–1871" (Unpublished MA Thesis, University of Manchester, 1960).

Robert Dryburgh, "The mixed economy of welfare: The New poor Law and charity in mid nineteenth century England" (Unpublished DPhil Thesis, University of Oxford, 2004).

David Gadian, "A comparative study of popular movements in northwest industrial towns 1830–1850" (Unpublished PhD Thesis, Lancaster University, 1976).

Elizabeth Hurren, "The 'Bury-al Board': Poverty, politics and poor relief in the Brixworth union Northamptonshire 1870–1900" (Unpublished PhD Thesis, University of Leicester, 2000).

Ellen Ross, "Women in poor law administration" (Unpublished MA Thesis, University of London, 1955).

Andrea Tanner, "The City of London poor law union 1837–1869" (Unpublished PhD Thesis, University of London, 1995).

Index

The following abbreviations are used in the index:
BU = Bolton Union; MH = Mary Haslam.